Y0-BUN-713

Lyrics and Borrowed Tunes of the American Temperance Movement

Lyrics and Borrowed Tunes of the American Temperance Movement

ML
3561
.T45
L9
2006
west

Compiled and Edited by Paul D. Sanders

University of Missouri Press / Columbia and London

Copyright © 2006 by
The Curators of the University of Missouri
University of Missouri Press, Columbia, Missouri 65201
Printed and bound in the United States of America
All rights reserved
5 4 3 2 1   10 09 08 07 06

Library of Congress Cataloging-in-Publication Data

Lyrics and borrowed tunes of the American temperance movement /
compiled and edited by Paul D. Sanders.
       p.   cm.
   Summary: "Systematically presents hundreds of lyrics set to borrowed
tunes that were used by the American temperance movement (ca. 1840–
1920) to further the cause of alcohol prohibition. Includes
introductory text and musical notations for 32 borrowed tunes, grouped
by song type"–Provided by publisher.
     Includes bibliographical references (p.   ) and index.
     ISBN-13: 978-0-8262-1645-8 (hard cover : alk. paper)
     1. Temperance–Songs and music–History and criticism. 2. Tem-
perance–United States–History. 3. Temperance–Songs and music.
I. Sanders, Paul D., 1956– comp.
     ML3561.T45L9 2006
     782.42'1592–dc22

                                                          2006000126

∞ ™ This paper meets the requirements of the
American National Standard for Permanence of Paper
for Printed Library Materials, Z39.48, 1984.

Designer: Kristie Lee
Typesetter: Crane Composition, Inc.
Printer and binder: Thomson-Shore, Inc.
Typefaces: Goudy Old Style and Poppl-Exquisit

Contents

Preface

L ittle has been written on the music of the temperance movement. George W. Ewing's *The Well-Tempered Lyre* (1977), the only major work on this topic, presents an outstanding overview of the various themes of the movement through music and verse, but it makes no effort to systematically present the music and lyrics of temperance reformers.

While many songs were composed specifically for the temperance movement, most temperance songs set new words to familiar melodies. The present volume features thirty-two of the most popular borrowed tunes, many of which are still familiar today, accompanied by dozens of sets of lyrics. Aside from providing brief commentary, this book does not attempt to put these songs in the context of nineteenth- and early twentieth-century society. Instead, the compelling story of the movement unfolds through primary sources, as the writers of the day speak for themselves. It is my hope that readers will share my fascination with both the messages and sheer volume of these lyrics.

My thanks to staff members at the Ohio Historical Society Archives, the Performing Arts Reading Room at the Library of Congress, and the Ohio State University Libraries for their assistance with this project.

Lyrics and
Borrowed Tunes
of the
American Temperance
Movement

1. Introduction

The American temperance movement spanned well over a century, beginning prior to the 1800s and continuing until the passage of national Prohibition in 1919. Modern readers often have difficulty understanding why such a movement was important and often dismiss it as a failure, citing the repeal of the Eighteenth Amendment in 1933. However, the seemingly naive attempt to prohibit the sale and consumption of alcohol is easier to grasp when one considers the role of alcohol in early America. In colonial times, alcohol was a regular part of the daily diet. Jack S. Blocker notes "virtually everyone drank virtually all the time." Workers often received part of their wages in alcohol, and soldiers were given alcohol as part of their daily ration. Farmhands, clergy, and businessmen all drank. Liquor was an indispensable part of the workday and an important part of almost every major event. According to Jed Dannenbaum, "no festival, holiday, christening, wedding, funeral, building dedication, or ordination was considered complete without plentiful toasts." This practice continued and worsened into the 1800s. By 1830, Americans age fifteen and older were drinking an average of 9.5 gallons of hard liquor each year, almost four times the amount consumed in the late twentieth century.[1]

The urbanization of America and the decline of family-centered work environments led to greater public awareness of the alcohol problem. Drinkers who were previously sheltered from the public eye became more visible to the surrounding community. Beginning in the early nineteenth century, the Second Great Awakening with its widespread religious revivals provided additional ammunition for the fight against alcohol consumption.[2]

1. Jack S. Blocker Jr., *American Temperance Movements: Cycles of Reform*, 3; Jed Dannenbaum, *Drink and Disorder: Temperance Reform in Cincinnati from the Washingtonian Revival to the WCTU*, 1; W. J. Rorabaugh, *The Alcohol Republic: An American Tradition*, 232–33.
2. Robert James Branham and Stephen J. Hartnett, *Sweet Freedom's Song: "My Country 'Tis of Thee" and Democracy in America*, 72–73; Dannenbaum, *Drink and Disorder*, 1–4, 7; Norman Harding Dohn,

By 1826, it was apparent that some sort of social action was required to control the alcohol problem, and the first of many American temperance organizations, the American Temperance Society (later renamed the American Society for the Promotion of Temperance), was formed in Boston. From the beginning, the organization had strong church connections. In fact, almost all the successful temperance organizations of the nineteenth and early twentieth centuries had church ties. By 1834, there were approximately five thousand temperance societies with a combined membership of over one million.[3]

In spite of the stereotypical view of temperance reformers, cultivated during the years of national Prohibition (1920–1933), as controlling, single-minded, puritanical people, the diversity of views represented by temperance reformers leads Blocker to think in terms of several separate temperance *movements* with a common goal, instead of a single movement. Temperance reform began as a grassroots effort in the Northeast, and by the late nineteenth century, the Midwest became the center for prohibition. The final front against alcohol consumption, prior to national Prohibition, was in the South and West. While men led early temperance reform efforts, women were involved from the beginning and began to play a dominant role in 1873. Although many of the upper class supported temperance reform—in part because they believed alcohol consumption would lead to decreased production and profits in industrial America—the temperance movement found its strongest support among the working and middle classes. Since it is impossible to provide a single viewpoint that serves the entire movement, it may be helpful to briefly explore the perspectives of some of the dominant temperance organizations. Four of these groups were particularly important: the Washingtonians, the Independent Order of Good Templars, the Woman's Christian Temperance Union, and the Anti-Saloon League.[4]

The Washingtonians were unique among the temperance organizations of the nineteenth century, in part because they intentionally avoided connections with the church. Established at a Baltimore tavern in April 1840, the Washingtonian founders were six working-class men who saw the devastation alcohol had caused in their lives and vowed to abstain from all intoxicating substances. The Washingtonians named themselves after the first U.S. president, and they had an uncommon view of religion and politics; they agreed

---

"The History of the Anti-Saloon League," 4–9; Joseph R. Gusfield, *Symbolic Crusade: Status Politics and the American Temperance Movement*, 5.

3. Branham and Hartnett, *Sweet Freedom's Song*, 73; Jane Anne Peterson, "Rum, Ruin, and Revival: Protestant Hymns and the Temperance Movement," 48–49; Dohn, "History of the Anti-Saloon League," 9.

4. Blocker, *American Temperance*, xi–xiv, 30, 80, 106; Branham and Hartnett, *Sweet Freedom's Song*, 71, 73; Ernest H. Cherrington, *The Evolution of Prohibition in the United States of America*, 145.

"to recognize no creed of religion, nor party in politics; and that neither political nor religious action of any kind, should ever be introduced into the society's operations. Personal abstinence from all intoxicating drinks was to be the basis and only requisite of membership. Moral suasion was to be the only means by which they as a body, were to induce others to adopt their principles." "Moral suasion," also known as "assimilative reform" or simply "suasion," assumes equality between the reformer and his or her listener and appeals to the emotions and intellect when arguing the case for abstaining from the consumption of alcohol. The Washingtonians favored this approach over efforts to enact laws controlling or prohibiting the sale of alcohol.[5]

From the original six members, the Washingtonians increased to three hundred by the Christmas of 1840, and as Washingtonian speakers traveled to other cities, the organization spread like wildfire. Thirty-six hundred people signed the Washingtonian pledge in Pittsburgh during a two-week period in July 1841. Thousands of recruits in the South and hundreds of thousands in the North joined the society. Unlike the American Temperance Society and other earlier groups, the Washingtonians met at least weekly. One feature of these meetings was the "experience speech," in which one of the members would recount how sobriety had improved his life. Music also played a prominent role in their meetings. Group singing and concerts by professional singers, including the famous Hutchinson family, provided entertainment for these gatherings, and bands accompanied temperance parades at Washingtonian conventions. Charles Dickens provides a stirring account of a Washingtonian Convention in Cincinnati during his American tour in 1842:

> There happened to be a great Temperance Convention held here on the day after our arrival. . . . It comprised several thousand men; the members of various "Washington Auxiliary Temperance Societies"; and was marshaled by officers on horseback, who cantered briskly up and down the line, with scarves and ribbons of bright colors fluttering out behind them gaily. There were bands of music too, and banners out of number; and it was a fresh, holiday-looking concourse altogether. . . . After going round the town, the procession repaired to a certain appointed place, where as the printed programme set forth, it would be received by the children of the different free schools, "singing Temperance Songs."[6]

While Washingtonians objected to the sale of liquor, they attempted to retain many of the more positive social elements of the tavern experience including

5. John Zug, *The Foundation, Progress, and Principles of the Washington Temperance Society of Baltimore*, 6; Blocker, *American Temperance*, xiv–xv; Gusfield, *Symbolic Crusade*, 6–7.

6. Charles Hamm, *Yesterdays: Popular Song in America*, 147–48; Charles Hamm, *Putting Popular Music in Its Place*, 100–101; Charles Dickens, *American Notes; and The Uncommerical Traveler*, 196–97.

songs and fellowship.[7] Their suasionist songs often encouraged listeners to take the pledge to give up alcohol or extolled the virtues of drinking cold water, as in the following verse set to "Yankee Doodle":

Cold Water Is the Drink

1. Cold water is the drink for me,
   Of all the drinks the best, sir;
Your grog, of whate'er name it be,
   I dare not for to taste, sir.
Give me dame nature's only drink,
   And I can make it do, sir;
Then what care I what others think,
   The best that ever grew, sir.[8]

Unfortunately, it was the entertainment aspect, along with their secular and suasionist views, that eventually led to the demise of the Washingtonian movement. Washingtonians were accused of being irreligious, of programming "disgusting recitals" with men belting out humorous songs, and of naively believing that moral suasion without the aid of legal suasion could bring an end to the alcohol problem. Although Washingtonian groups continued in Boston until 1860 and Worcester, Massachusetts, into the 1870s, the organization's influence began to wane in early 1845.[9]

The Independent Order of Good Templars was founded in Saratoga, New York, in 1851. The Good Templars had a membership of almost half a million by 1867, and by 1886 there were chapters in every state and more than twenty other countries. Music played a prominent role in the over ten thousand meetings each week held by the chapters. Thirty-nine songs were used for the various rituals of these chapters, and all of these songs borrowed their tunes from other well-known songs, including eight settings to "America," five each to "Hold the Fort" and "Battle Hymn of the Republic," four each to "Battle Cry of Freedom" and "Auld Lang Syne," and three each to "Sweet By and By" and "Home, Sweet Home." These "odes" and other songs were printed in numerous temperance songbooks, including George Root's *Musical Fountain* and J. H. Leslie's *Good Templar Songster*. The Good Templars began to explore the question of political activity in 1867, leading to the establishment of the Prohibition party in 1869 and moving further away from moral suasion toward

---

7. Blocker, *American Temperance*, 39–45.

8. *Washington Temperance Songbook*, 45–46; A. D. Fillmore, *Temperance Musician*, 176; *The Union Temperance Song Book*, 20–21; *The Women's Temperance Songster*, 9–10.

9. Blocker, *American Temperance*, 46–47; Leonard U. Blumberg, "The Institutional Phase of the Washingtonian Total Abstinence Movement," 1591–92.

legal suasion or coercion.[10] Coercive reform proposed not only the enacting of laws but also the use of force in some cases to prohibit the sale of alcohol, as in another setting of "Yankee Doodle":

'Tis Time to Swing Our Axes

> 1. We've had enough of license laws,
>   Enough of liquor's taxes
> We've turned the grindstone long enough,
>   'Tis time to swing our axes.
> This deadly upas tree must fall—
>   Let strokes be strong and steady,
> Pull out the stumps! grub out the roots!
>   O brothers! are you ready?[11]

Five years after the establishment of the Prohibition party, the Woman's Christian Temperance Union (WCTU) was formed. Following a successful crusade by a group of women in Hillsboro, Ohio, in December 1873, a convention in Cleveland in 1874 marked the official beginning of this important women's organization. The dominant theme of the WCTU was the danger liquor posed to the home, as articulated in their slogan "For God and Home and Native Land." Their concern was not only for women and children, but also for the spiritual welfare of the drunkards, and this led them to use a combined approach of moral and legal suasion. This view is reflected in the singing of hymns during temperance crusades. As Michelle Stecker notes, "crusaders carefully selected music to convert saloonkeepers and saloon patrons. They were trying to save souls." By 1887, the WCTU claimed two hundred thousand members, and the organization continues its work to the present day.[12]

The Prohibition party failed to meet its goals in part because voters were unwilling to break their traditional party loyalties. While many favored Prohibition, they continued to vote for Democrats or Republicans. In addition, the Prohibition party took on other issues beyond the essential party plank, including woman suffrage, which detracted from its primary purpose. Although

10. G. F. Root, *The Musical Fountain*, 106–24; J. H. Leslie, *Good Templar Songster* (1886 and 1888), 62f; Cherrington, *Evolution of Prohibition*, 145 and 163; Branham and Hartnett, *Sweet Freedom's Song*, 166.

11. J. N. Stearns and H. P. Main, *Trumpet Notes for the Temperance Battle-Field*, 57. The upas tree is a tropical plant with poisonous milky sap. It became a common metaphor for the alcohol problem in America after the publication of Lydia Sigorney's song "The Upas Tree" in the 1830s. See George W. Ewing, *The Well-Tempered Lyre: Songs and Verse of the Temperance Movement*, 228–30.

12. Michelle J. Stecker, "A Respectable Revolution: The Dynamics of Religion and Gender in the Ohio Woman's Temperance Crusade, 1873–74," 37; Blocker, *American Temperance*, 76; Branham and Hartnett, *Sweet Freedom's Song*, 165.

both the Prohibition party and the WCTU continued as organizations, in most states they also cooperated with a new organization, the Anti-Saloon League, which would finally achieve national Prohibition in 1919. Delegates from the Ohio and Washington Anti-Saloon Leagues and representatives from forty-nine state temperance groups founded the Anti-Saloon League on December 18, 1895. Less than a decade later, the Anti-Saloon League had chapters in thirty-eight states with two hundred full-time employees, twenty-two state newspapers, and annual revenues of $250,000. The success of the Anti-Saloon League may be attributed to its organizational structure and its focus on a single issue. As Blocker notes, "by wooing the churches, keeping to its single issue, and reassuring the major parties of its peaceful intentions, the League demonstrated its willingness to accept American society as it was except for the existence of the liquor business."[13]

Each of the four organizations mentioned above published temperance songsters and included music in their meetings. Numerous publishers contributed additional songbooks to the temperance cause, and from the 1830s until 1919, hundreds of temperance songbooks were compiled. Some of these songbooks contained original music, but the lion's share of temperance songs set new lyrics to borrowed tunes of the day, a common practice among nineteenth-century writers of hymns and popular songs. In fact, many of the tunes borrowed by temperance reformers had previously been borrowed from elsewhere. For example, "The Star-Spangled Banner" used the tune "To Anacreon in Heaven," "America" borrowed its tune from "God Save the King," and "The Battle Hymn of the Republic" used the tune from "John Brown's Body," which in turn borrowed its tune from "Glory Hallelujah."[14]

In spite of the temperance movement's tremendous influence on American society and the prominent place of music within that movement, very little has been written about the large volume of new lyrics it produced. Most of the temperance songsters exist only in archives and research libraries and are in increasingly fragile condition. George Ewing's *Well-Tempered Lyre* (1977), the only extensive work on the music and verse of the temperance movement, presents an outstanding overview of the various themes of the movement, and more recently Robert James Branham and Stephen J. Hartnett devote two sections to the temperance movement in *Sweet Freedom's Song* (2002), which traces the appropriation of the melody of "God Save the King" for "America" and numer-

---

13. Dohn, "History of the Anti-Saloon League," 32–34; Blocker, *American Temperance*, 75, 103–6.
14. Ewing, *Well-Tempered Lyre*, 201; David Ewen, *All the Years of American Popular Music*, 73; Irwin Silber, *Songs of the Civil War*, 10–11; Sigmund G. Spaeth, *A History of Popular Music in America*, 36–46, 147–50. For a detailed discussion of the practice of borrowing music, see J. Peter Burkholder, "Borrowing."

ous other settings. While these are significant contributions to temperance music research, neither systematically presents the lyrics and tunes of the movement.[15]

The present volume allows readers to examine hundreds of sets of temperance lyrics, collected in one place and presented with the thirty-two tunes that were most often borrowed by the movement. Numerous other tunes, both borrowed and original, were employed for temperance reform, but exhaustive research at the Library of Congress, the Ohio Historical Society, and other institutions reveals that the tunes included in this volume were the most popular with the movement, based on the number of temperance settings and the frequency of publication. Not surprisingly, many of the tunes, including "The Star-Spangled Banner," "America," "Auld Lang Syne," and "The Battle Hymn of the Republic," are still familiar to modern readers. However, because the versions of the original music included in this book were published during the temperance movement, many are slightly different than their modern versions.[16]

The tunes and their lyrics are arranged into chapters by category—patriotic songs, hymns and hymn tunes, traditional Scottish songs, popular songs, and Civil War songs. Each chapter begins with a brief introduction followed by the original tunes that served as the basis for temperance songs. The first verse of each original song is included to help readers recall the tune, and select temperance lyrics and commentary follow. The tunes are arranged chronologically within each chapter according to their first-known date of publication, as are the sets of additional lyrics included at the end of each chapter. Lyricists' names, if known, are listed below the song titles.

Jane Anne Peterson notes that temperance music contributes "a unique record and insights not readily apparent from more conventional sources." While many of these songs may seem naive or even comical to twenty-first-century readers, the lyrics reflect a sincere effort on the part of temperance writers to eliminate the alcohol problem in nineteenth- and early-twentieth-century America, so they provide a clearer picture of that history. Thus, this song collection provides a lens through which the evolution of the American temperance movement comes into sharper focus.[17]

---

15. Ewing, *Well-Tempered Lyre*; Branham and Hartnett, *Sweet Freedom's Song*.

16. These variations may be seen, for example, in the penultimate measure of "America" and in the anacrusis of "The Star-Spangled Banner."

17. Peterson, "Rum, Ruin, and Revival," 60.

2. Patriotic Songs

Judging from the sheer volume of temperance texts, patriotic songs, and what we call Civil War songs (which would have also been considered patriotic by many people of the day), were the two most important sources for temperance lyricists. Branham and Hartnett note that "national songs were produced in response to social exigencies and/or perceived threats from without or within, including the threat of invasion ('La Marseillaise'), insurrection ('America'), or loss of independence ('The Star-Spangled Banner')." Temperance reformers saw alcohol as a serious internal threat to the nation and freely borrowed patriotic tunes to promote their antialcohol message.[1]

America

"America," the patriotic song most frequently borrowed by the temperance movement, takes its tune from the British national anthem, "God Save the King." Both the text and tune of "God Save the King" have often been attributed to Henry Carey, who sang them at a dinner in 1740 celebrating the capture of Portobello by Admiral Edward Vernon. However, the tune is similar to several earlier ones, including one composed by John Bull in 1619. The first published version of "God Save the King" appeared in the 1744 edition of the annual collection *Thesaurus Musicus*.

Samuel Francis Smith wrote the lyrics for "America" in 1831. Lowell Mason, an early American music educator and composer, had asked Smith, who was a student at Andover Theological Seminary, to translate songs from various German music collections or to write his own lyrics to the German tunes. When Smith came upon the tune for "God Save the King" in a German music book, it had been adapted for use as a German anthem, and he didn't recog-

---

1. Branham and Hartnett, *Sweet Freedom's Song*, 18.

America

Samuel Francis Smith

Attr. Henry Carey

My coun - try! 'tis of thee, Sweet land of lib - er - ty Of thee I

sing: Land where my fath - ers died; Land of the pil - grim's pride;

From ev - 'ry moun - tain - side, Let free - dom ring.

One Hundred and One Best Songs, no. 20.

nize it as the British national anthem. Smith wrote new lyrics on a scrap of paper in about half an hour, drawing on lyrics from an earlier song, "The Children's Independence Day," which he had written the previous year.

"America" was first performed on July 4, 1831, at Park Street Church in Boston. This church was a significant center for social reform; in 1826, the American Temperance Society was founded at Park Street Church, and exactly two years prior to the introduction of "America," abolitionist William Lloyd Garrison made his first public speech against slavery there. The July 4 celebration in 1831 was advertised as an alternative to the drunken Independence Day celebrations that were so common in the day, so even at its first performance, "America" already had a strong connection to the temperance movement.[2]

Among the thirty-eight sets of temperance lyrics to this tune, many liken the shame of slavery to alcohol in this "sweet land of liberty." Also, the "Fourth of July Ode" makes an important connection to the origins of America by referring to the date it was first performed and draws comparisons between the founding fathers' struggle with Britain and the drunkard's struggle with alcohol.

2. Ibid., 19, 55–60, 71; Leon Dallin and Lynn Dallin, *Heritage Songster: 332 Folk and Familiar Songs,* 67; Ewen, *All the Years,* 55; Homer A. Rodeheaver, *Hymnal Handbook for Standard Hymns and Gospel Hymns,* 140; Spaeth, *History of Popular Music,* 28–30, 69.

Fourth of July Ode

1. With patriotic glee,
   Columbia's jubilee
   Once more we hail:
Let nothing damp our joys—
   The Temp'rance pledge destroys
The last foe that annoys—
   Quail, monster, quail!

2. To aid us in the fray
   A new and bold array
   Push to the field:
Men who for years have quaff'd
   The devil's fiery draught,
Have grappled with the Craft,
   Thundering "YIELD!"

3. Through this most blessed breach
   The drunkard we can reach!
   Oh! joyful sound!
The wife's crushed hopes revive—
   The drunkard's children thrive—
The dead return alive—
   The lost are found!

4. The captive to unbind—
   To save from wreck the mind,
   Torn, tempest-tossed—
May Heaven this labor speed
   Till from the foe we're freed,
And not one heart shall bleed
   For loved ones lost.

5. Our fathers, when they broke
   Proud Britain's galling yoke,
   Fought one good fight!
A better one fight they
   Who "cast the bowl away,"
And toast this glorious day
   In water bright.

6. Reformers, go ahead!
   No more let it be said
   By freedom's foe,
That this, our fair domain,
   Wears worse than British chain,

Under the tyrant reign
Of "Death & Co."[3]

"Come Sign the Vow" presents one of the significant themes of the temperance movement. Encouraging listeners to take the pledge to give up alcohol was one of the primary suasionist tactics of the early temperance movement.

Come Sign the Vow!

1. Come, sign the Temperance pledge,
   Thou on life's tottering edge,
   Come sign the vow!
What though thy hair be gray,
   Languid thy pulses play,
Give us thy parting day,
   Quick sign the vow.

2. Manhood, with sinewy form,
   Breasting the hard world's storm,
   Come sign the vow!
Here, dry thy partner's tears,
   Here, hush thy children's fears,
Here, bless thy coming years,
   Now sign the vow.

3. Childhood, with earnest glance,
   Hither thy steps advance,
   Come, sign the vow!
Haste, thy young promise bring,
   Pure, simple offering,
Fresh, from th'Eternal Spring,
   Now sign the vow.

4. Sinner of many cares,
   Wilder'd with doubts and snares,
   Come sign the vow!
Give us thy trembling hand,
   Soon shall foul habit's band,
Break like an osier wand.
   Come sign the vow.

5. Maiden, untouched by care,
   Lovely, and fresh and fair,
   Come sign the vow!

3. John Pierpont, *Cold Water Melodies and Washingtonian Songster*, 58.

Turn here thy sparkling eye,
    Lend us thy check's soft dye,
In all thy charms stand by,
    And sign the vow.

6. Youth, with thy upward look,
    Which not a stain can brook,
Come sign the vow!
On, for thy country's weal,
    On, at dear home's appeal,
Take, for thy soul this seal—
    Come sign the vow.[4]

Yankee Doodle

"Yankee Doodle" is unique among the songs in this chapter because of its blending of patriotic and humorous elements. The origins of the song are not fully known, but it is mentioned in the libretto of the first American opera, Andrew Barton's *The Disappointment, or The Force of Credulity*, published in 1767. British army surgeon Dr. Richard Shuckburgh may have introduced the tune to continental soldiers in 1755, but there is no evidence he actually wrote the song. The familiar lyrics, attributed to Edward Bangs, probably date from 1775, during George Washington's time at Provincial Camp in Cambridge, Massachusetts. There were printed broadsides (handbills with lyrics but no music) of the song as early as 1776, and G. Willig of Philadelphia published the first American edition containing both words and music in 1798. "Yankee Doodle" has often been used as a tune for political campaign songs and was often set by temperance authors. Of the twenty-three versions in this collection, several share the comic character of the original song, including "A Lanky Dude" and "Fol-De-Rol."[5]

A Lanky Dude
(C. M. Fillmore)

1. A lanky dude once came to town,
    A lanky dude, a dandy,
He filled himself with lager beer,
    And wine and gin and brandy.

4. Ibid., 11.
5. Ewen, *All the Years*, 5–7; Spaeth, *History of Popular Music*, 15–21; Dallin and Dallin, *Heritage Songster*, 92.

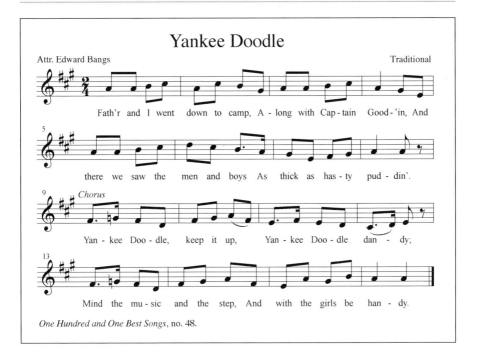

Yankee Doodle

Attr. Edward Bangs

Traditional

Fath'r and I went down to camp, A - long with Cap - tain Good - 'in, And
there we saw the men and boys As thick as has - ty pud - din'.

Chorus

Yan - kee Doo - dle, keep it up, Yan - kee Doo - dle dan - dy;

Mind the mu - sic and the step, And with the girls be han - dy.

One Hundred and One Best Songs, no. 48.

Chorus
Lanky dudy, dudy dude,
    Wasn't he a dandy,
Lanky dudy, dudy dude,
    Lanky dudy dandy.

2. But when his money was all gone,
    His cronies did forsake him,
He then was kicked from the saloon,
    And the police did take him. *To Chorus*

3. Next day the Justice of the Peace
    Unto his tale did listen,
He fined him for his drunkenness,
    And sent him off to prison. *To Chorus*

4. In prison he worked out his fine,
    Because he had no money,
And then went home a wiser man,
    Upon his little pony. *To Chorus*[6]

6. Charles M. Fillmore and J. H. Fillmore, *Fillmores' Prohibition Songs*, no. 103.

Although sharing the comic character of "A Lanky Dude," "Fol-De-Rol" uses humor to point to the hypocrisy of those who gave "lip service" to the temperance movement but whose actions on election day supported liquor licensing.

Fol-De-Rol
(C. M. Fillmore)

1. There was a farmer had a cow,
    He fed her on rich clover,
She gave a bucket full of milk,
    And then she kicked it over.

Chorus
Fol-de-rol-, de-rol, de-rol,
    Fol-de-rol, de-rolly,
Fol-de-rol, de-rol, de-rol,
    What a piece of folly.

2. There was a woman had a hen,
    The breed called Cochin China,
Although she never laid nor set,
    The woman called her "Fine," ah! *To Chorus*

3. There was a father had a son
    "Be sober," he would tell him,
Then vote to license the saloon,
    That they might liquor sell him. *To Chorus*

4. There was a parson in the town,
    For temperance he exhorted,
But when election day came round,
    With brewers he consorted. *To Chorus*[7]

Others settings of "Yankee Doodle" take a more serious tone. "Temperance Folks, Wake Up" addresses the failure of temperance reformers' suasionist tactics to eliminate the alcohol problem.

Temperance Folks, Wake Up

1. The temp'rance folks are waking up
    Throughout this Yankee nation,
To put the liquor traffic down,
    And drive it from creation.

7. Ibid., no. 104.

Chorus
That's the way to win the day;
    Wait a little longer;
Rum shall fall, with tyrants all,
    When Temp'rance votes are stronger.

2. The drinking dens are surely doomed,
    For God will come with vengeance,
Since all good men are going in
    United for No license. *To Chorus*

3. Too long King Alcohol has reigned,
    All moral suasion scorning;
Too long his murd'rous savages
    Have filled the land with mourning. *To Chorus*

4. Rumsellers care not for our prayers
    Or tears of admonition;
But there's a power can make them quake,
    'Tis well-enforced No license. *To Chorus*

5. Rum's hindered many a noble plan,
    And scattered death and ruin;
But soon we'll show the best we can,
    What Temp'rance votes are doing. *To Chorus*[8]

La Marseillaise

Claude-Joseph Rouget de L'isle (1760–1836) wrote both the words and music to "La Marseillaise" on April 24, 1792, intending it as a marching song. It was adopted as the French National Anthem on July 15, 1795. Although Rouget de L'isle was a royalist, his march became the battle song of French revolutionaries. Both the Communards and the opposing troops sang "La Marseillaise" in 1848. In the southern United States it was an extremely well-known song during the Civil War. Confederates identified with the French Revolution and the spirit of rebellion that "La Marseillaise" conveyed. A. E. Blackmar's new lyrics for "Southern Marseillaise" also contributed to the wartime popularity of the tune, but the number of temperance songs based on this tune during the antebellum period suggest that "La Marseillaise" was already well known as early as the 1840s. Many of the temperance settings of this

---

8. W. O. Miller, ed. *Patriotic No-License Songster*, no. 7. See the additional lyrics at the end of this chapter. Most of this song is borrowed from "Hurrah for Prohibition" and "Bands of Hope Are Growing Stronger."

La Marseillaise

Claude-Josef Rouget de L'isle
English trans., Percy Bysshe Shelley

Claude-Josef Rouget de L'isle

Ye sons of France, a - wake to glo - ry! Hark! hark! what my - riads bid you rise! Your chil - dren, wives, and grand - sires - hoar - y, Be - hold their tears and hear their cries! Be - hold their tears and hear their cries! Shall hate - ful ty - rants, mis - chief breed - ing, With hire - ling hosts, a ruf - fian band, Af - fright and des - o - late the land, While peace and lib - er - ty lie bleed - ing? To arms, to arms, ye brave! Th'a - veng - ing sword un - sheathed! March on, march on! All hearts re - solved on vic - to - ry or death.

One Hundred and One Best Songs, no. 35.

tune conveyed the activists' own sense of rebellion, in this case, individual rebellion against the unhealthy influence of "tyrant alcohol," not only for the drinker, but for his family.[9]

Ye Sons of Freedom

1. Ye sons of Freedom, burst asunder
     The chains that now your souls enthrall;
Come forth, no longer slumber under
     The sway of tyrant alcohol!
The sway of tyrant alcohol!
     Your wives and children, deeply wailing,
With tears of anguish in their eyes,
     Are calling on you to arise;
And shall their tears be unavailing?
     Arise! be free, be free! Assert your liberty!

Chorus
Arise, arise, Be brave, firm and true!
     For God and Temperance.
Arise, arise, Be brave, firm and true!
     For God and Temperance.

2. Hark, hark, the trump of temp'rance ringing,
     Triumphantly from shore to shore,
Hark, hark, the myriad voices singing,
     King Alcohol shall rule no more!
King Alcohol shall rule no more!
     Too long, too long his reign has lasted,
His reign of terror and despair;
     Our blooming hopes and prospects fair,
Too long has fell intemp'rance blasted,
     But now we're free, we're free! We've gained our liberty! *To Chorus*[10]

Realizing the failure of purely suasionist efforts, Priscilla Owens and other later authors chose to direct their efforts to legal reform:

9. Branham and Harnett, *Sweet Freedom's Song,* 27; Silber, *Songs of the Civil War,* 49.

10. *Collection of Hymns and Songs for Temperance Meetings and Festivals,* 12–13; Fillmore, *Temperance Musician,* 142. Asa Hull, *Hull's Temperance Glee Book,* 46–48, entitles this song "Temperance Marseilles."

To Christian Patriots
(Priscilla J. Owens)

1. Ye Christian Patriots, wake to danger;
   Unnumbered voices bid you rise;
A ruthless foe, to peace a stranger,
   Assails each home, and gladness dies.
Shall drinking hordes, wild mischief breeding,
   Affright and desolate the land,
Cast down your rights with cruel hand,
   While hope and happiness lie bleeding?

Chorus
Arise! Arise with might,
   Break down the tyrant's sway;
For Prohibition all unite,
   And God will lead the way. March on!

2. Far spreads the storm of rum and riot,
   Our children weep, our grandsires mourn;
Rapine and murder break law's quiet,
   While wives and widows droop forlorn.
And shall we tamely view the ruin,
   That treats our homes on every side,
From poison cups o'erflowing wide?
   Up, Sons of Freedom, and be doing! *To Chorus*

3. O noble cause, free voters waken,
   Against rum traffic boldly stand;
Nor be your faith by faction shaken,
   Join valiant heart and gallant hand.
Spread out Truth's banner fair and glorious,
   Be worthy of your sires of old;
Each vile saloon, each robber bold,
   Shall fall before your aim victorious. *To Chorus*[11]

The Star-Spangled Banner

The melody for "The Star-Spangled Banner" was taken from "To Anacreon in Heaven," the constitutional song of the Anacreontic Society of London, founded in honor of Anacreon, a Greek poet. It is generally believed that John Stafford Smith, an English composer, wrote the music for this song. "To

---

11. *Prohibition Campaign Songster*, 1.

The Star-Spangled Banner

Francis Scott Key

John Stafford Smith

Oh, say can you see, by the dawn's ear-ly light, What so proud-ly we hailed at the twi-light's last gleam-ing, Whose broad stripes and bright stars, through the per-il-ous fight, O'er the ram-parts we watched were so gal-lant-ly stream-ing? And the rock-ets' red glare, the bombs burst-ing in air, Gave proof through the night that our flag was still there. Oh, say, does that star-span-gled ban-ner yet wave O'er the land of the free and the home of the brave?

One Hundred and One Best Songs, no. 12.

Anacreon in Heaven" was a familiar tune in America long before Francis Scott Key penned the "Star-Spangled Banner." One well-known song to the tune, "Adams and Liberty" by Robert Treat Paine, dates from 1798. There were numerous other uses of this tune in America; Sigmund Spaeth lists more than twenty, including an earlier setting by Francis Scott Key entitled "The Warrior's Return."[12]

Key wrote the lyrics to "The Star-Spangled Banner" in September 1814. He had successfully negotiated the release of his friend Dr. William Beanes from the British admiral Cochrane. However, because the British were preparing to attack Fort McHenry in Baltimore, they would not allow Key, Beanes, or Mr.

12. Spaeth, *History of Popular Music,* 36.

Skinner, a government official who accompanied Key, to return to Baltimore until after the bombardment. Key and Skinner remained on deck watching the bombardment through the night, and after the dawn, they were elated to see that the Stars and Stripes still flew over the fort.

Key began writing "The Star-Spangled Banner" that very night and finished it as his boat returned to shore. The attack on Fort McHenry took place September 14–15, 1814, and Key's lyrics appeared in the *Baltimore Patriot* on September 20 and the *Baltimore American* on September 21, although they may have been printed as a broadside prior to its publication in the newspapers. It has long been considered the national anthem, but "The Star-Spangled Banner" was not officially adopted as such until March 3, 1931. Numerous temperance versions of this song begin with Key's opening phrase, "Oh say, can you see," including "Defence of Fort Temperance."[13]

Defence of Fort Temperance

1. Oh, say, can you see, on this bright dawning day,
    What so proudly we hail, all these efforts so cheering?
The demon Intemp'rance we're driving away,
    And a happier dawn to mankind is appearing;
The vict'ry we'll gain o'er the foe that has slain
    Its millions who now in the grave low are lain;
Then success to our cause! May it spread far and wide,
    With an impulse as endless as Time's rolling tide.

2. Already recede from the force of our arms,
    The savage, the ruthless, the death-dealing foe;
Confusion, defeat, and a host of alarms,
    Attend and pursue them wherever they go.
Then *on to the fight!* Ere the sun sets to-night,
    We all shall have cause to exult in our might;
    Then success to our cause, *etc.*

3. Pursue them with sword, and pursue them with fire,
    Lay upon the foul fiends and show them no quarter;
We will make of their remnants a vast funeral pyre
    That shall light the whole earth, from the field of their slaughter.
No trace will we leave for mankind to receive
    Of what has caused thousands of thousands to grieve.
    Then success to our cause, *etc.*

4. The victory won, a new era will dawn,
    And earth will be proud of her emancipation;

13. Dallin and Dallin, *Heritage Songster*, 155; Spaeth, *History of Popular Music*, 36–46.

No more then shall myriads of wretches, forlorn,
 So lowly be laid by foul contamination.
Then up and away, we'll pursue while we may,
 The advantage we've gained in this *glorious* affray;
 Then success to our cause, *etc.*[14]

Other versions exploit the symbol of the banner with themes such as "The Temperance Banner," "The Washington Banner," "The Spotless White Banner," and "Prohibition's Banner," including the following setting by Fanny Crosby, a well-known lyricist of gospel hymns.

The Banner of Temperance
(Fanny Crosby)

1. Oh, say did you see on the brow of the night,
 That star like a watch-fire so tranquilly burning;
'Tis the day-beam of hope and the promise of light,
 And joy to the hearts of the wretched returning.
Then away to the fields with our standard and shield,
 Our course is progressing. The tyrant must yield:
And the banner of temp'rance in triumph shall wave,
 O'er the land of the free and the home of the brave.

2. Though strong is our foe, let us work with our might,
 The arrows of death from his quiver descending;
We'll haste to the ground, while we boldly unite,
 Our cause with the vigor of heroes defending;
Our colors unfold for we still do behold
 The day-beam of hope in its beauty untold,
And the banner of temp'rance, *etc.*

3. The time is not far when the tear of despair
 Shall be changed to a smile like the sunshine of gladness;
When the drunkard reclaimed to his children shall bear
 The soul cheering news that will banish their sadness.
Be strong, O, be strong, we shall conquer e'er long.
 Cold water, bright water, our motto and song:
And the banner of temp'rance, *etc.*[15]

After its introduction in Bradbury and Stearns's *Temperance Chimes* (1867), other temperance songbooks borrowed Crosby's lyrics, and as was typical of

14. Bigelow and Grosh, *Washingtonian Pocket*, 94–96; W. F. Gould and A. B. Grosh, *Washingtonian Pocket Companion*, 64–65; Fillmore, *Temperance Musician*, 108.

15. Wm. B. Bradbury and J. N. Stearns, *Temperance Chimes* (1867, 1878), 52; J. N. Stearns, *National Temperance Hymn and Song Book*, 39.

the time, some chose to make minor adjustments. *Prohibition Campaign Song Book* and Stearns's *Prohibition Songster* replace the third verse with verse 4 from Miller's "The Temperance Banner" (included among the additional lyrics at the end of this chapter). "The Banner of Temperance" also appears in Miller but is renamed "The No-License Banner." The words "banner of temp'rance" in verses 1 and 2 are replaced with "no-license banner." Verse 3 is replaced, and a fourth verse is added:

> 3. Then where'll be the band who so vauntingly boast
>   That the price of men's souls is their lawful possession?
> They will join in the ranks of the temperance host,
>   Ashamed of the traffic and glad of repression.
> Even now we can see what most surely will be—
>   With No-license the watchword from sea unto sea.
> For the No-license banner in triumph shall wave
>   O'er the land of the free and the home of the brave!

> 4. Oh, thus be it e'er when true freemen shall stand
>   With their votes to repel the rum fiend's desolation;
> Then shall women and children with uplifted hand
>   Praise the Power that has made us a Temperance nation!
> Then conquer we must, for our cause is most just;
>   And this is our motto: "In God we will trust."
> And the No-license banner, O, long may it wave
>   O'er the land of the free and the home of the brave![16]

Hail to the Chief

The tune for "Hail to the Chief" was first introduced by the New York publisher John Paff around 1812, with words from Sir Walter Scott's *The Lady of the Lake* and music by James Sanderson. How the song came to be performed in honor of the president of the United States at ceremonial occasions is unknown, but after its performance at the inauguration of President Polk on March 4, 1845, "Hail to the Chief" gradually assumed this role. Albert Gamse contributed the presidential lyrics, but "Hail to the Chief" has always been better known as an instrumental piece than as a song. Its martial spirit provided inspiration to the temperance cause throughout the entire movement, with the first temperance version appearing in the *Washingtonian Pocket Companion* (1842) and the last being printed in *Best Temperance Songs* (ca. 1913). Perhaps

---

16. *Prohibition Campaign Song Book*, 8; J. N. Stearns, *Prohibition Songster*, no. 45; Miller, *Patriotic No-License*, no. 20.

Hail to the Chief

N. H. Aitch, *The Golden Book of Favorite Songs*, 28.

because of their connection to America's first president, the Washingtonians seemed to favor this tune. The following "pledge song" was one of many settings included in songbooks of this early temperance organization.[17]

Pledge for the Chieftain

1. Pledge for the chieftain immortal in story,
    Honored and blest be our Washington's name;
Sons of the sires whom his sword led to glory,
    The longer we flourish the broader his fame.
Pledge for the chieftain immortal in story,
    Honored and blest be our Washington's name;
Sons of the sires whom his sword led to glory,
    The longer we flourish the broader his fame.
Pledge ev'ry hand and heart,
    Pledge never more to part,
True to the bond that unites us in one;
        Let ev'ry mother's son shout for our Washington,
        "On, brothers, on, till the battle is done."

2. Ours is no summer-pledge, gone with the fountains,
    That gush from the heart, while the tide-feeling flows.
Firm it shall stand, as the rock-seated mountains,
    Stainless our faith as their ever-white snows.
Ours is no summer-pledge, *etc.*
    Widow and orphan child,
Wailing in accents wild,
    Beckon us onward, and point to their woe;
Let every western glen
    Ring to our shout again,
    "On, brothers, on, till their tears cease to flow."

3. Vainly our tyrants and tempters would chain us,
    Toiling like slaves, while they gather our gains;
Vainly they'll seek by their poison to tame us,
    Pledge-bound to freedom, we scorn their vile pains.
Vainly our tyrants and tempters, *etc.*
    Grogshop, or groghotel,
Where'er the bane they sell,
    In hovel or palace, the pest is the same;
Vainly the sordid crew
    Long for our gold anew,
    Cursing our pledge as the cause of their shame.

17. Ewen, *All the Years*, 19; Spaeth, *History of Popular Music*, 66.

4. Warm glows the hearth, and the wife smiles beside it;
   Night lacks her gloom, and the winter his cold;
O, the sweet, prattling babe—let the miser deride it;
   Mine be the hearth-stone, and his be the gold.
Warm glows the hearth, *etc.*
   O! that our noble cause,
Health of our land and laws,
   Wide may prevail, till the curse is no more,
Till prairie, land, and glen
   Send us their loud AMEN.
   God bless our country from centre to shore.

5. Come, brothers, come, now's the time to be writing
   The bond that will make every heavy heart light.
Of all in the world here's the pledge we delight in,
   It keeps out of wrong, and it binds to the right.
Come brothers, come, *etc.*
   Pledge, then, each hand and heart,
Pledge never more to part,
   True to the tie that unites us in one:
Shout, every mother's son—
   Shout, till the work is done—
   "God for the poor, and the victory won!"[18]

Columbia, the Gem of the Ocean

British sources claim that "Columbia, the Gem of the Ocean" was originally composed by an Englishman, Thomas E. Williams, set to lyrics by an Irish journalist, Stephen J. Meany, in 1842, and entitled "Britannia, the Pride of the Ocean." However, in America, a singer named David T. Shaw was identified as the lyricist, composer, and performer of "Columbia, the Land of the Brave" when it was first published here in 1843. It is now generally accepted that Shaw commissioned an actor named Thomas a'Becket to write the music and lyrics, and subsequent printings credit a'Becket with this composition, changing the title to "Columbia, the Gem of the Ocean." Borrowing from the chorus of the original song, patriotic references to the "red, white, and blue" abound in the temperance versions, including "The Red, White, and Blue" and "For Home and the Red, White, and Blue."[19]

18. *Washington Temperance,* 24–26. Also in *The Washingtonian Tee-Totalers' Minstrel,* 46–48.
19. Dallin and Dallin, *Heritage Songster,* 65; Ewen, *All the Years,* 55–56; Spaeth, *History of Popular Music,* 98–99.

Columbia, the Gem of the Ocean

Thomas a'Becket

Thomas a'Becket

O Co-lum-bia, the gem of the o-cean, The home of the brave and the free, The shrine of each pa-triot's de-vo-tion, A world of-fers hom-age to thee. Thy man-dates make he-roes as-sem-ble, When Lib-er-ty's form stands in view; Thy ban-ners make tyr-an-ny trem-ble, When borne by the red, white, and blue! When borne by the red, white, and blue! When borne by the red, white, and blue! Thy ban-ners make tyr-an-ny trem-ble, When borne by the red, white, and blue!

One Hundred and One Best Songs, no. 4.

The Red, White, and Blue
(E. E. Hewitt)

1. "O, Columbia the gem of the ocean,"
   The land we most honor and love,
We tender our deepest devotion,
   While proudly our flag floats above;
No stain on thy "star spangled banner,"
   No blot on thy shield would we view;
Away with the wine-cup forever,
   Three cheers for the red, white, and blue!
Three cheers for the red, white, and blue,
   Three cheers for the red, white, and blue,
Away with the wine-cup forever,
   Three cheers for the red, white, and blue!

2. Though rum "winged its wide desolation,
   And threatened the land to deform,"
True patriots for its salvation,
   The strongholds of vice take by storm;
Then down with the treacherous destroyer,
   There's death in the cup he will brew;
Away with King Alcohol's slaughter!
   Three cheers for the red, white, and blue! *etc.*

3. The banner of temperance bring hither.
   By freedom's bright flag let it wave;
May ev'ry saloon close its portals
   And liquor no longer enslave;
Remember, O men, your Creator;
   To country and firesides be true;
Away with the wine-cup for-ever!
   Three cheers for the red, white, and blue! *etc.*[20]

For Home and the Red, White, and Blue

1. Oh, come, let your manhood be plighted,
   To help us again to restore
The Freedom with Virtue united
   Our forefathers brought to the shore;
When law never licensed temptation,
   And Conscience to Right was so true;
Oh, bring back those days to the nation
   That gave us the Red, White and Blue.

20. *Ohio State Prohibition Campaign Songs,* 3.

Chorus
That gave us the Red, White and Blue,
 That gave us the Red, White and Blue—
Oh, bring back those days to the nation
 That gave us the Red, White and Blue.

2. Our motto is "Home and our Children,"
 Our platform a great moral one,
Our party to strengthen each other,
 We've hatred or malice for none:
Our mission, redeeming the nation,
 And raising old landmarks anew;
The end is a true reformation
 For Home, and the Red, White and Blue.

Chorus
For Home, and the Red, White and Blue,
 For Home, and the Red, White and Blue,
The end is a true reformation
 For Home, and the Red, White and Blue.[21]

21. L. B. Cake, *Popular Campaign Songs*, n.p.

America

Hymn

1. My country! 'tis of thee,
   Sweet land of liberty—
   Of thee I sing;
Land where my fathers died;
   Land of the Pilgrims' pride;
From every mountain side
   Let Temp'rance ring.

2. My native country! thee—
   Land of the noble free—
   Thy name I love;
I love thy rocks and rills,
   Thy woods and templed hills;
My heart with rapture thrills,
   Like that above.

3. Let music swell the breeze,
   And ring from all the trees,
   Sweet freedom's song;
Let infant tongues awake;
   Let all that breathe partake;
Let rocks their silence break;
   The sound prolong.

4. Our fathers' God! to thee,
   Author of liberty,
   To thee we sing;
Long may our land be bright
   With temperance's holy light;
Protect us by thy might,
   Great God, our King![22]

Juvenile Temperance Ode

1. We sing the praise of Water;
   . Come, every son and daughter
   Of Freedom's land!
With such a theme before us,
   With God's great shield held o'er us,
Who will not join the chorus
   Of our young band?

2. You silver fountain's basin,
   'Tis sweet to see thy face in,
Fair harvest moon!
And, when the sun has shone in,
   On the white pebbles thrown in,
'Tis sweet to see our own in,
   At sultry noon.

3. Sweet is the light that quivers
   On water brooks and rivers;
   Fresh are the trees,
Whose feet the wave caresses,
   And fresh the bloom that dresses
Their loose and fragrant tresses
   For evening's breeze.

4. Grateful the cloud, that over
   Wide fields of blooming clover
   Swims, charged with rain;
Grateful the fill, that gushes
   From heights where day first blushes,
And down the hill-side rushes
   To bless the plain.

5. Streams of the wood-crowned mountain,
   Children of cloud and fountain,
   Who dance and sing
O'er snow-beds iced and glossy,
   O'er rocks with green tufts bossy,
Down paths all clean and mossy!
   Your tribute bring.

6. To all earth's sons and daughters
   "The circuit of the waters"
   Gives joy and health;
Floats the gay barge of pleasure,
   And, without stint or measure,
Wafts on that heavenly treasure,
   TRUE WISDOM'S WEALTH.[23]

Temperance Call

1. Come ye who love our cause,
   Whose hearts for freedom's laws,
   With rapture glow.
Come join our noble band,
   Be with us heart and hand,
To save our happy land
   From sin and woe.

---

22. *Collection of Temperance Songs*, n.p.; Pierpont, *Cold Water Melodies*, 30–31; R. K. Potter, *The Boston Temperance Songster*, 1:8.

23. Pierpont, *Cold Water Melodies*, 78.

2. Come ye who quaff the bowl,
   Death's billows near you roll,
   Come ere you're lost.
Burst from the tyrant's reign
   Break now the tempter's chain,
Be freemen once again,
   Join with our host.

3. Come ye, who drink but wine,
   Round you it soon will twine
   Its fetters strong:
Leave now the tempting cup,
   Touch not a single drop,
Leave while there yet is hope,
   Join in our song.

4. Come young and old, come all,
   Come fight at freedom's call,
   For liberty.
Loud let our songs arise,
   Till heaven, with glad surprise,
Join in our joyous cries,
   Till all are free.[24]

Hymn 77

1. Let the still air rejoice,
   Be every youthful voice
   Blended in one;
While we renew our strain,
   To Him with joy again,
Who sends the evening rain,
   And morning sun.

2. His hand in beauty gives
   Each flower and plant that lives,
   Each sunny rill.
Springs! which our footsteps meet—
   Fountains! our lips to greet—
Waters! whose taste is sweet,
   On rock and hill.

3. So let each thoughtful child
   Drink of this fountain mild,
   From early youth;
Then shall the song we raise,

Be heard in future days,
   Ours be the pleasant ways
   Of peace and truth.

4. Now let each heart and hand
   Of all this youthful band,
   United, move!
Till on the mountain's brow,
   And in the vale below,
Our land may ever glow
   With peace and love.[25]

Overthrow of Alcohol

1. It comes, the joyful day,
   When alcohol's proud sway,
   A curse to man—
Shall to the ground be hurled;
   The Temp'rance flag unfurled
Shall wave through the world
   In ev'ry land.

2. Then let the drunkards hear,
   And every one draw near,
   And sign the pledge.
Alone you shall not stand,
   For ever all the land
Is found a noble band,
   By vow engaged.

3. And moderate drinkers too,
   The voice addresses you,
   Come, go along.
You surely are to blame
   While in the drinking train,
For alcohol has slain
   His thousand strong.

4. This work may soon be done,
   If all unite as one,
   To push it on.
Then shall the *truth* and *right*
   O'er all prevail in fight,
And all the world unite
   In one glad song.

---

24. Ibid., 136.

25. G. Bigelow and A. B. Grosh, *Washingtonian Pocket Companion*, 77. T. D. Bonner, *The Mountain Minstrel*, 110, and James M. Guthrie, *The Manual for the Teetotal Army*, 9–10, omit verse 4. W. F. McCauley, *Anti-Saloon Songs*, 56, adds a new verse 3 and replaces verse 4 with a slightly modified version of verse 3.

5. For since Goliath's dead,
   The Philistines are fled
   In wild dismay.
Then let us gladly bring
   Our thanks, and loudly sing,
Through David's God and sling
   We've won the day.[26]

The Land Our Fathers Trod
(P. H. Sweetser)

1. The land our fathers trod,
   The favored land of God,
   Light of the age!
Intemp'rance doth defame,
   And with its lurid flame,
Becloud thy glorious name,
   Thy hist'ry's page.

2. Arise, ye sons of light,
   And stay this withering blight,
   Our country's shame!
Wipe out its cursed stains,
   And break the galling chains;
Where'er the tyrant reigns,
   His guilt proclaim!

3. The truth in love declare,
   But ne'er to speak forbear,
   Hence, evermore!
Oh! let the watchwords be
   Temperance and Liberty,
And Death or Victory,
   Till time is o'er!

4. Heaven will your efforts bless,
   And crown them with success,
   And keep you free!
The temperance flag shall wave
   High o'er the monster's grave!
Then chant His praise who gave
   The victory![27]

Great Patriarch Above

1. Great Patriarch above,
   Spirit of Truth and Love,
   Whom all adore;

Let peace our steps attend,
   Prove each a faithful friend,
And may this cause extend
   From shore to shore.[28]

Temperance Hymn

1. Once more we meet again,
   True friends of God and men
   Hither we come,
From dome and lofty tower,
   From cot and lowly bower,
With all our might and power,
   Stern foes of rum.

2. Let now our prayers arise
   To Him, who in the skies,
   Reigns over all,
In him we put our trust,
   Through Him we conquer must
Our foes shall to the dust
   Forever fall.

3. O God to us give ear,
   O come be with us here,
   Grant us Success;
Thy Spirit from above,
   Send down on wings of love,
Our plans and acts approve,
   Do thou them bless.

4. Saviour, who whilst on earth,
   Sought'st those of humble birth,
   To thee we pray.
Thou, then, the outcasts' friend,
   Do now on us attend,
Our hallowed Cause defend,
   And be our Stay.

5. Let Temperance o'er our land,
   Stretch forth her mighty hand
   Thousands to save;
Haste, Lord that happy time,
   When Rum vice, want and Crime
Shall cease from every Clime,
   No being have.

---

26. *Collection of Hymns and Songs*, 23–24; *Union Temperance*, 32–33.
27. Job Plimpton, *The Washingtonian Choir*, 68.
28. Sons of Temperance, *Music and Odes of the Order*, 10–11.

6. Bring in our holy band
   All those within our land
   Thy name that Love;
So, shall thy kingdom Come
   So, shall thy will be done
By all beneath the Sun
   As 'tis above.29

Welcoming Ode

1. Welcome to join our band,
   Welcome with us to stand,
   In this pure cause.
Welcome the pledge to take,
   Welcome these vows to make,
And for sweet Temperance' sake
   To keep her laws.

2. As pledged in truth you stand,
   Angels, a heavenly band,
   Take up the song:
"Welcome, young souls, to be
   In vows of purity,
From dark temptation free,
   In virtue strong.

3. "Welcome! we bend in love
   From the bright heaven above,
   And bid you come.
Our love, with tireless wing,
   Shall strength and blessing bring,
Until in heaven we sing
   Your welcome home."

4. Then welcome to our band,
   And with us, hand in hand,
   Welcome to go;
To give our cause success,
   And with the pledge to bless,
Bring health and happiness,
   And banish woe.

5. Welcome to joy and peace,
   To virtue's sure increase,
   And wisdom's ways;
And may we ever be
   From the destroyer free,

To sing our victory
   In love and praise.30

The Pledge

1. Come ye whose bosoms swell,
   While we our story tell,
   Come take the pledge;
Then health and happiness
   Your homes and hearts will bless,
O come with cheerfulness,
   And take the pledge.

2. Brothers, why will ye die?
   From the destroyer fly,
   And take the pledge;
Why should ye longer be
   Slaves to your enemy?
O, 'tis no slavery
   To take the pledge.

3. May he who reigns above,
   Each friend and brother move
   To take the pledge.
Then hand in hand we'll go,
   Cheering each house of woe,
Come, then, both high and low,
   Come take the pledge.31

[In Honor's Name We Meet]

1. In Honor's name we meet,
   With Love's fond smiles we greet
   Friends of our cause.
Our hearts by Hope made strong,
   We'll press our work along.
And teach the erring throng
   God's holy laws.

2. Firm let each brother stand
   United heart and hand,
   To Love and Truth;
Here let poor drunkards come,
   We'll burst their chains from rum,
And give life's hope and bloom
   To age and youth.

29. Hugh S. Dunn, *Temperance Hymns*, n.p.

30. Edwin Thompson, comp., *Thompson's Band of Hope Melodies*, 34–35. Guthrie, *Teetotal Army*, 6, omits verse 5. Sidney Herbert, *Young Volunteer Campaign Melodist*, 41, includes verses 1 and 4, with some changes.

31. Guthrie, *Teetotal Army*, 13.

3. Come, sign the pledge, and live!
    'Twill brighter blessings give
    Than dazzling gold.
Then temp'rance, with pure light,
    Shall make your path more bright,
And cheer your life's last night
    With joys untold.[32]

[Thou God of Earth and Sky]

1. Thou God of earth and sky,
    To Thee we humbly cry,
    hear from Thy throne;
Thou art our Father still,
    Teach us Thy perfect will,
Guard us from every ill
    and lead us on.

2. The drunkard's family
    Behold in misery
    from day to day;
Spread truth and holiness,
    Drunkards restore and bless,
Removing all distress
    from earth away.

3. Fill every heart with love,
    Our nation's woe remove
    forevermore,
And not our land alone,
    but where strong drink has gone
Be love and temperance known
    from shore to shore.[33]

Teetotal Anthem

1. Great God of earth and skies,
    Open the drinker's eyes
    To see his state;
Show him that gin and ale
    Make men to weep and wail;
Orphans and widows pale,
    Throng the work-house gate.

2. God save the drunkard's wife,
    Bowed down with care and strife,
    Day after day;
Doomed to foul kicks and blows,
    In lieu of meat and clothes,
Thinking to end her woes—
    Makes life away.

3. God save the landlord too,
    May he in earnest view
    His ill-got gain.
Blighting all germs of good,
    His hand defiled with blood,
Grieved for by great and good,
    May he abstain.

4. God bless the Temperance band,
    May they spread o'er the land,
    And still increase.
Till woe and misery
    Shall to oblivion flee,
And all men happy be,
    And live in peace.[34]

[God of the Temp'rance Cause]

God of the Temp'rance cause,
    Bless those who seek Thy laws,
    Owning their power;
Be Thou to them a shield,
    Teach them Thy sword to wield,
Upon temptation's field
    In sin's dark hour.[35]

Ode to Temperance

1. Sweet Temp'rance 'tis of thee,
    Replete with blessings, free,
    Of thee we sing:
Our hearts with hopes are bright;
    Lead by the beacon light,
Onward to do the right
    And succor bring.

---

32. Nathaniel Saunders, *The Temperance Songster*, 43.

33. Ibid., 5.

34. *The Crusaders' Temperance Songster*, 22.

35. Hull, *Hull's Temperance*, 121; Bradbury and Stearns, *Temperance Chimes* (1867 and 1878), 109; W. F. Sherwin and J. N. Stearns, eds., *Bugle Notes for the Temperance Army*, 119; J. C. Macy, *Temperance Song-Herald*, 89.

2. Sweet Temp'rance! thou, our song!
    We will thy notes prolong
    Through all the land,
In accents loud and clear,
    Pervading every sphere,
Obeying, without fear,
    Thy high command.

3. Sweet Temp'rance! thou, our pride!
    We will by thee abide,
    O guiding star!
Move on, we follow thee;
    Move on, eternally,
Till all redeemed shall be,
    Near and afar.

4. Shine on, O star of Love!
    While we in concourse move,
    Beam full around;
Come, all, fear no dismay;
    Our Father leads the way,
Where tears are wiped away,
    And peace is found.[36]

Our Land Redeemed

1. My country! broad and fine,
    Cursed by both beer and wine,
    Of thee I sing;
Land where my fathers died,
    Land which King George defied
And slavery set aside,
    Thy deeds shall ring.

2. My native country, thee,
    From center to the sea,
    All know thy fame;
We love thy hills and dales,
    Thy mounts and pleasant vales,
But hate thy whiskey sales,
    Thy blackest shame.

3. Let wailing swell the breeze,
    And ring from all the trees,
    And creatures dumb;
Let women brave awake,
    Let men their honor stake,

The churches strive to break
    The curse of rum.

4. Our fathers' God, to Thee,
    Author of purity,
    To Thee we sing;
Redeemed from rum and wine,
    O, may our country shine,
And we be wholly Thine,
    Great God, our King.[37]

Come with Us to the Spring

1. Why to the wine-cup's brim
    Where mirth and folly swim
    Press thy young lip?
Veiled from the careless eye
    Madness and murder lie
Low in its depths. Then why
    The poison sip?

2. Come join us at the spring!
    Come join us while we sing
    Cold water's praise!
Drink with us and be strong!
    And independence long
Shall bless the temperance throng,
    And length of days.[38]

God Save Each Noble State

1. Ye sons of Temperance, wake!
    See the bright morning break!
    The dawn is near!
Rum's dragons of the night,
    They whip their wings in flight,
O'er the fair mountain height,
    They disappear!

2. Welcome the glorious day,
    When Temperance shall display
    Her banner fair,
From Maine, the Pine-tree State,
    To the far "Golden Gate,"
Where Temperance doth await
    Her triumphs there!

36. William Oscar Perkins, *The Crystal Fountain*, 106-7.
37. W. O. Moffitt, *The National Temperance Songster*, 15; Leslie, *Good Templar* (1886 and 1888), 7.
38. Stearns, *National Temperance*, 49.

3. Welcome all hearts to thee,
    Whose love of Liberty
    Enchants—Inspires!
The coming Temperance day
    Shall flood all gloriously
The hills with light, and they
    Be beacon fires.

4. God save each noble State—
    The truly grand and great—
    The drunkard's shame!
How burns true souls to see
    Rum's craven shadow flee,
And manhood's liberty
    Uprise again![39]

Let Prohibition Come
(Wm. B. Marsh)

1. God bless our temperance band,
    May it spread o'er our land,
    Its numbers grow;
May Prohibition come,
    And gladden every home,
Where once the tyrant rum
    Brought deepest woe.

2. God hear our earnest prayer.
    Do thou our country spare,
    And set us free:
May Church and State unite
    In this great 'natal fight,
To guard us from this blight
    And misery.[40]

New America

1. Our Country, Land we love!
    We lift our hearts above,
    For thee we pray—
Pray that thy light may shine,
    Pray for Peace and Truth divine
Where waves the Palm and Pine,
    Or Flag holds sway.

2. Our hills and plains are dear,
    Our lakes and rivers clear,
    And all we see;
Oh, may we love thee more,
    Thy heroes all adore,
And every sin deplore,
    'Till all are free!

3. Oh, Land by Jesus crowned!
    Oh, Land our fathers found,
    And died to free!
May we, as sons of thine,
    Eternal Right enshrine,
Nor cease our ware on Wine
    'Till Wrong shall flee!

4. Old wrongs around us lie,
    Grog-shops our Flag defy
    In numbers vast;
But God is God to-day!
    Our foes we soon shall slay,
Our prayers the evil stay,
    And win at last!

5. Our Land no foe will spare,
    Nor rum-shops long ensnare
    On soil so free;
Our homes we yet shall save,
    For heroes true and brave
Will cause our Flag to wave
    In Jubilee![41]

Freedom from Rum

1. Our native land must be
    From bondage truly free—
    The curse of rum!
Our homes have suffered long,
    From license party's wrong,
But now our hearts grow strong—
    Its doom has come.

2. We have appealed in vain
    To party, to restrain
    The liquor trade;

---

39. Ione G. Daniels, *Temperance Songster*, 8–9.

40. Oscar A. Perine and William E. Mash, *The National Prohibition Hymnal and Gospel Temperance Songbook*, 40.

41. H. C. Munson, *The Gospel and Maine Law Temperance Hymn Book*, 28–29.

But it cried "revenue,"
    And held up to our view
Its crime-stained millions, through
    Rum license made.

3. Alas! the priceless cost,
    The dear ones all have lost,
    For rum-made gold!
Alas! the blighted years,
    The hopeless sighs and tears,
The crime and strife and fears,
    Can not be told!

4. The freedom that we boast,
    While drink-enslaved, at most,
    Is but a name;
A greater slav'ry reigns,
    Than erst, on Southern plains,
And blots with fouler stains,
    Our flag with shame.

5. Down with the licensed still,
    Whose deadly fountains fill
    The land with woe;
Hail, Prohibition, Hail!
    And over rum prevail;
Thy ballot shall not fail
    To smite the foe.

6. Thy banner proudly floats,
    And leads a million votes,
    On to the light,
To bury rum so deep
    That it accursed shall sleep,
And few its loss shall weep—
    God speed the Right![42]

Blest Temperance! 'Tis of Thee

1. Blest Temp'rance 'tis of thee,
    In fav'rite melody,
    Of thee we sing!
Thy banners proudly wave,
    Thy hand is strong to save;
Thou art the boon we crave,
    Thy praises ring!

2. Blest Temp'rance! 'tis for thee,
    In this broad land so free,
    For thee we pray!
Let ev'ry statesman's name
    Be on thy role of fame!
Let all our laws proclaim,
    Thy truth today.[43]

God Bless Our Temperance Band

1. God, bless our temp'rance band;
    Firm may we ever stand
    For truth and right;
Help us to work and pray;
    Teach us in wisdom's way,
Our nation's curse to stay
    By thine own light.

2. Help us the chains to break
    That greed and av'rice make
    By licensed laws;
Help us that we may be
    Champions of liberty;
Help set the bondmen free
    Through our dear cause.[44]

For God and Home and Native Land

1. Our father's God! of thee
    Thou who hast made us free,
    Of thee we sing;
Roll on this Temperance wave,
    Help us our land to save,
Help us our foes to brave,
    Great God, our King.

2. For home our prayers arise,
    To God above the skies,
    To him we pray;
Thou who art ever nigh,
    Guarding with watchful eye,
Wilt hear our humble cry,
    Save thou this day.

3. God bless our native land,
    Firm may she ever stand,

---

42. Horace B. Durant, *Prohibition Home Protection Army Campaign Songs*, 7–8.

43. Macy, *Temperance Song-Herald*, 85.

44. J. N. Stearns, comp., *Band of Hope Songster*, 42; Leslie, *Good Templar* (1886 and 1888), 6; Flora Hamilton Cassel, *White Ribbon Vibrations*, no. 106.

Through storm and night;
And when fierce foes assail,
   O, may they not prevail,
Thou who can'st all avail,
   Help by thy might.[45]

My Country, 'Tis to Thee

1. My country! 'Tis to thee,
   From ocean unto sea,
   I'd raise my song;
Enlist thy brave and true
   'Neath the Red, White, and Blue,
All soldiers, old and new,
   In one great throng!

2. Great God! our country save
   From the dishonored grave
   Which Rum must bring;
Shorten misfortune's hour,
   In this thy day of power,
From heaven's lofty tower,
   Let Freedom ring.

3. Let temp'rance flags be waved
   O'er homes thy sons once saved
   From slavish power.
Protect this Nation, bright,
   From Rum's long reign of night,
Give freedom's holy light
   In this dark hour.[46]

God Bless Our Cause

1. God bless our sacred cause!
   We plead for righteous laws,
   Our homes to shield.
Our land has suffered long,
   From an accursed wrong,
Whose roots are deep and strong,
   Nor do they yield.

2. We plead! but all in vain;
   The people's deep felt pain,
   Finds no redress.
This deadly Upas tree

Spreads out, despite our plea,
And plants its rootlets free;
   To our distress.

3. The men we've placed in trust,
   Who should be true and just,
   Our laws to make.
Do, at their party's word,
   Deny our plea, unheard;
Nor by our prayers are stirred,
   Its power to break.

4. Now let the people come,
   And vote for God and home,
   And temperance laws!
We'll be no more deceived;
   Our land must be retrieved,
And from this curse relieved!
   God bless our cause![47]

Freedom's Day
(George W. Bungay)

1. God bless our rock-bound coast,
   The land we love the most,
   Our native land;
Land where our noble sires
   Lit freedom's beacon fires
And shook with bells the spires,
   A patriot band.

2. And when they died 'twas well
   Their starry mantle fell
   On heroes free;
And be their colors true,
   The red, the white, the blue,
The white light shining through,
   On Liberty.

3. 'Tis here our fathers sought
   The boon their valor bought
   With bleeding scars.
Firm as the granite hills
   Were their unbending wills,
And now sweet freedom fills
   Our flag with stars.

---

45. Leslie, *Good Templar* (1886 and 1888), 7.
46. Ibid.
47. Stearns, *Prohibition Songster*, no. 43. C. H. Mead and G. E. Chambers, *The Clarion Call*, 57, omits verse 3.

4. When the saloon is sealed,
   And broken hears are healed,
   And speech is dumb–
That would, if uttered, be
   Filth and profanity,
Then our glad eyes shall see
   God's kingdom come.[48]

Anniversary Hymn

1. Father, our heavenly King,
   Accept our offering
   Of life and youth;
Now, while our hymns we raise,
   Help us thy name to praise,
For thou hast crowned our days
   With peace and truth.

2. For mercies of the year
   Gladly we gather here,
   Thy name to bless;
Seed which our hands have sown,
   To ripening fruit has grown;
Do thou the future crown
   With true success.

3. Father, our souls inspire,
   Fill us with one desire,
   Banish our fears,
Send us a gracious shower
   Of blessing at this hour,
Then shall we own thy power
   In coming years.

4. May every heart and hand
   Of this our Temp'rance Band
   United move.
Strengthened with holy might,
   Stand valiant for the right,
Till in thy glorious sight,
   We meet above.[49]

Temperance, Thy Noble Name

1. Temperance, thy noble name
   We will to all proclaim
   With trumpet blast,

Thy glorious deeds to show,
   That each thy truth may know,
And in thy pathway go
   While life shall last.

2. The fame of thy good deeds
   In all our land precedes,
   Our guide to be.
For truth and right are thine,
   Wisdom in thee doth shine,
Oh, may we all resign
   Ourselves to thee.

3. And when thy victory's won,
   And all our duty's done,
   We'll sing thy praise;
Honor and peace be there,
   Freedom for all to share,
And joy beyond compare,
   To endless days.[50]

America's New Tyrant
(Harriet D. Castle)

1. Our father's God to Thee,
   Author of liberty,
   To Thee we pray;
Once more a tyrant reigns
   Over our hills and plains;
Loved ones are in his chains;
   Break them away.

2. Rum is the tyrant's name;
   At Satan's call he came
   our land to spoil.
Oh, tell us what to do!
   People, and rulers too,
Swell his vast retinue,
   Fast in his toil.

3. Evil, the seed he sows,
   Only too fast it grows,
   Nothing by tares.
Almshouses overflow,
   Many the prisoners grow,
Downward the drunkards go;
   Sad fruit it bears.

48. Stearns and Main, *Trumpet Notes*, 7.
49. Anna A. Gordon, *Songs of the Young Woman's Christian Temperance Union*, 61.
50. Walter K. Fobes, *Temperance Songs and Hymns*, 19.

4. Great God of liberty,
    Oh, set thy people free
    From Rum's foul blight.
Make them a nation pure,
    None other can endure,
Once more to rest secure,
    Saved by thy might.[51]

Our Country

1. Our country, 'tis for thee,
    That thou mightst rescued be
    From power of rum;
That those who've suffered long
    From cruelty and wrong,
May free be made and strong,
    For this we come.

2. Our native country, thee,
    Who has been twice made free
    To thee we call;
Once more exert thy might,
    Maintain the cause of right,
The liquor traffic smite,
    Once and for all.

3. Oh voters, true and brave,
    Shall the rum king enslave
    This land so bright?
Shall crime and want increase,
    O, shall this traffic cease?
Shall strife give way to peace,
    And wrong to right?[52]

We'll Dare and Do

1. Come, raise your banners high,
    And join our battle cry;
    "No license here."
Come, swell the valiant throng
    Who fight against the wrong,
And shout the rallying song;
    "We'll dare and do."

2. The foe is fierce and strong;
    The conflict may be long;
    But we'll be true,

We've 'listed for the fight,
    Our cause is just and right,
Strong is our Captain's might,
    We'll dare and do.

3. Ye gallant temp'rance host,
    Stand firm at duty's post,
    The fight renew;
We'll ne'er give up the strife,
    E'en though with danger rife;
While God shall give us life
    We'll dare and do.[53]

National Temperance Hymn

1. Our native country, thee,
    Blest land of liberty,
    The freeman's home;
Oh! may thy people stand,
    In one great temp'rance band,
And drive from out our land,
    The curse of rum.

2. Let children march along,
    With women, brave and strong,
    Against the foe;
Let Christians work and pray,
    And by their ballots say,
That from the land today,
    Saloons must go.

3. We love our banner bright,
    Emblem of truth and right,
    Red, White and Blue;
Long may she proudly wave
    In triumph o'er the brave,
Till earth's without a slave,
    And all men true.

4. Great God of liberty,
    Hasten the victory,
    Of truth and love;
Justice and peace shall reign,
    O'er mountain, hill and plain,
All earth will be the same
    As heav'n above.[54]

51. E. S. Lorenz, *New Anti-Saloon Songs*, 103.
52. Miller, *Patriotic No-License*, no. 9.
53. Ibid., no. 27.
54. Frank E. Roush, *Temperance Rally and Campaign Songs*, 1.

National W.C.T.U. Hymn

1. Our nation, grand and free,
   Earth's pow'r on land and sea,
   'Gainst sin and shame;
Oh! may our union grow;
   Rum's forces overthrow,
Conquering as we go,
   In thy great name.

2. Let children work and pray
   And help to bring the day,
   Of peace and joy;
Let Christians join our band,
   To help us firmly stand,
And in this rum-cursed land,
   Saloons destroy.

3. Great God of liberty,
   We humbly pray to thee,
   True source of light.
Help us to ever be,
   Striving continually,
To win the victory,
   Of truth and right.[55]

National L.T.L. Hymn

1. Columbia, brave and free,
   Pride of the great blue sea,
   Our nation grand;
Oh! may our temp'rance throng
   March as a legion strong,
And conquer sin and wrong,
   Throughout the land.

2. Great God of liberty,
   Help us to ever see,
   That truth is might;
Help us as soldiers true,
   Our courage to renew,
And lead us safely through
   The Temp'rance fight.

3. May we in Christ's great name,
   hasten the glorious reign,
   Of peace and love;
Then earth will praise her King,
   As joy bells gaily ring;

Bright angel bands will sing
   in heav'n above.[56]

New America
(G. W. Dungan)

1. How glad will be the day,
   With license put away,
   In all our land!
When drink shall not dismay
   And Prohibition's sway,
Shall have the right of way,
   On ev'ry hand.

2. Now thanks to God for light,
   Our map is turning white!
   Near ev'ry State!
In Local Option's track,
   Is throwing off the black,
And hurling License back,
   Which seals its fate.

3. God hasten, then, the sight
   When it shall all be white,
   No black remain!
When rum and ruin's sway,
   Shall us no more dismay;
God, hasten the glad day!
   We pray again.[57]

Liquor Has Had Its Day

1. Liquor has had its day!
   Out from beneath its sway,
   Ohio brave!
Now rises in her might,
   Throws off its deadening blight
Rejoices in the right
   Her homes to save!

2. Liquor has had its day!
   Out from beneath its sway,
   Fair Buckeye State!
From lake to river shore
   Open saloons no more
Shall curse us, as of yore,
   They're out of date.

---

55. Ibid., 16.
56. Ibid., 22. "L.T.L." stands for the Loyal Temperance Legion.
57. George W. Dungan, Ernest A. Boom, and H. L. Gilmour, eds., *Acorn Temperance Songs*, no. 44.

3. Who can defend the ways,
   What man can sing the praise
   Of the saloon?
It lives for selfish ends!
   Loves man for what he spends,
It has no real friends!
   Down with it soon!

4. Lovers of Liberty
   Help us our state to free
   From curse of rum,
Vote old Ohio dry,
   Stop starving children's cry,
Wipe tears from women's eye,
   Help save the home.[58]

Yankee Doodle

Dedicated to Victory Hose Company, No. XV

1. See Fifteen comes with heart and hand,
   To join the Temp'rance band, sir,
They drag along a Temp'rance cart
   And fearless take their stand, sir.

Chorus
Then dash ahead my hearts of oak,
   Fear not the Tyrant's frown boys,
The Demon's galling chain we've broke,
   And now we'll keep him down boys.

2. We've suffered more than tongue can tell
   By Rum and Brandy tippling,
But now we'll seek the stone-curbed well
   Where water sweet is rippling. *To Chorus*

3. The monster's pow'r with us is past,
   No more his reign is o'er us,
We've broken off his chains at last,
   Like those who've gone before us.
      To Chorus

4. We'll taste no more the damning cup,
   The course of sin and sorrow;
We give the fatal bev'rage up,
   And Temp'rance pleasures borrow.
      To Chorus

5. Henceforth we strike in Freedom's name,
   We heed not scoffs or jeers now,
We light no more Rum's lurid flame;
   Nor shed pale sorrow's tears now.
      To Chorus

6. Our wives, our children, bless the day
   We signed the "Declaration,"
And hail the glorious Temp'rance ray,
   That banished dissipation. *To Chorus*[59]

Cold Water Is the Drink

1. Cold water is the drink for me,
   Of all the drinks the best, sir;
Your grog, of whate'er name it be,
   I dare not for to taste, sir.
Give me dame nature's only drink,
   And I can make it do, sir;
Then what care I what others think,
   The best that ever grew, sir.

2. Your artificial drinks are made
   The appetite to please, sir,
And help along the honest trade
   Of those who live at ease, sir.
But they who buy, most dearly pay
   For all such drinks as these, sir;
For what they take to "wet their clay,"
   Is sure to bring disease, sir.

3. Your logwood wine is very fine,
   I think they call it "Port," sir;
You'll know it by this certain sign,
   Its roughness in the throat, sir.
'Tis true that Yankees are most shrewd,
   And wooden nutmegs make, sir;
But who'd have thought Port wine was brewed
   This side the big salt lake, sir.

4. We need not to send to Portugal,
   Nor go to old Spain, sir;
The best of wine is at our call,
   Port, Lisbon, or Champagne, sir.
They'll make us any kind we choose,
   Without the aid of grape, sir;
And when 'tis done, will not refuse
   A price to make it take, sir.

---

58. *Ohio State Prohibition*, 15.
59. A. Bensel, *The Temperance Harp*, 23–24.

5. Some love to swig New England rum,
    And some do Cider choose, sir;
But so they only make "drunk come,"
    No matter what they use, sir.
But I'll not touch the poisonous stuff,
    Since all the brooks are free, sir:
Give me cold water, 'tis enough,
    That cannot injure me, sir.[60]

Temperance Yankee Doodle

1. There was a time—that time has passed—
    When whisky, rum, and brandy—
Were drunk by men of every caste,
    And most folks kept it handy

Chorus
Yankee noodles are no more,
    Temperance is the dandy:
Enter not the groggery door
    For whisky, rum, or brandy.

2. The parson gave it to his flock,
    And sugared some for ma'am, too;
The judge his 'leven and four o'clock
    Would take, and think no harm, too.
      To Chorus

3. The doctor, in each doubtful case,
    Would make his patients dozy,
And even lovely woman's face
    With rum was painted rosy. *To Chorus*

4. The sailor could not sing "Ye-ho,"
    Until he first got frisky;
The soldier could not face a foe,
    Except he had his whisky. *To Chorus*

5. The farmer could not make his hay
    Until his punch was ready;
And some mechanics, every day,
    Would drink, their nerves to steady.
      To Chorus

6. The lawyer, merchant, trader, too,
    Would pass the bowl, and joke it,
And all, except a precious few,
    In "auld lang syne" would soak it.
      To Chorus

7. At length the fashion changed, and wine
    Became the genteel fancy;
'Twas great to meet at Bacchus' shrine,
    While toasting Kate or Nancy. *To Chorus*

8. But soon the sparkling *wine* was found,
    E'en as of old, a mocker;
Besides, when reckoning-day came round,
    It left an empty locker. *To Chorus*

9. Again the fashion took a jog,
    And *cider* was the dandy:
But burn the stuff, 'tis worse than grog
    Of whisky, rum, or brandy. *To Chorus*

10. I've tried most liquors, cold and hot,
    And here's the way I view it,
"O touch not, taste not, handle not,"
    For if you do, you'll rue it. *To Chorus*[61]

Jonathan's Declaration of Independence

1. Says Jonathan, says he, "To-day
    I *will* be independent,
And so my grog I'll throw away,
    And that shall be the end on't.
Clear the house! the 'tarnal stuff
    Shan't be here so handy;
Wife has giv'n the winds her snuff;
    So now here goes my brandy!

2. Our fathers, though a sturdy folk,
    Were sometimes rather skittish;
And so they wouldn't wear the yoke
    Brought over by the British.
Yonder, on old Bunker's head,
    From their necks they shook it;
There they fired off all their lead,
    And then they had to hook it.

3. The tyrant that our fathers smoked
    Lay skulkin' in a tea-pot;
There's now 'a worser' to be choked,
    In bottle, jug, or wee pot;
Often in a glass he shows
    What he calls his 'body';
And often wades, up to his nose,
    In a bowl of toddy.

60. *Washington Temperance*, 45–46; Fillmore, *Temperance Musician*, 176. *Union Temperance*, 20–21, and *Women's Temperance*, 9–10, list this song as "Song for Independence Day."
  61. *Washington Temperance*, 46–47; *Collection of Hymns and Songs*, 15–16.

4. Sometimes he creeps up, through the slim
   Stem of a very fine pipe;
And sometimes plunges, for a swim,
   All over in a wine-pipe;
But, he's tickled, most of all,
   When he hears the summons
Down his favorite pipes to crawl—
   The wind-pipes of the rum-uns.

5. And when he gets the upper hand,—
   This tyrant, base and scurvy—
He strips a man of house and land,
   And turns him topsy-turvy.
Neck and heels he binds him fast,
   And says that he is his'n;
But lets him have, rent-free, at last,
   A poor-house or a prison."

6. "And now," says Jonathan, "Tow'rds Rum
   I'm desp'rate unforgivin';
The tyrant, never more, shall come
   Into 'The house I live in.'
Kindred spirits, too, shall in-
   to outer darkness go forth;
Whiskey, Toddy, Julep, Gin,
   Brandy, Beer, and so forth.

7. While this COLD WATER fills my cup,
   Duns dare not assail me;
Sheriffs shall not lock me up,
   Nor my neighbors bail me;
Lawyers will I never let
   'Choose me as defendant';
Till to death I pay my debt,
   I WILL BE INDEPENDENT."[62]

Come, All Ye Young Teetotalers

1. Come, all ye young teetotalers,
   Come with us while we go
To fight with old King Alcohol—
   A brave and mortal foe.

Chorus
Then rouse, my lads, then rouse ye up;
   Come forward, every one;

We'll banish far the poison cup,
   Nor stop till vict'ry's won.

2. A hard old enemy is he,
   And brave and bold in fight;
But labor hard—we'll soon be free,
   For God defends the right. *To Chorus*

3. But though he may be brave and bold,
   We'll show what we can do;
We're not the temp'rance men of old—
   We go for something new. *To Chorus*

4. "We touch not, taste not, handle not,"
   What can intoxicate;
We'll live and die without a blot,
   And shun the drunkard's fate. *To Chorus*

5. Grog men may laugh, and joke, and sneer;
   They laugh and tremble too;
For when the boys take hold, they fear
   There's something then to do. *To Chorus*

6. And now, my boys, since we've begun,
   The cause must never fall;
Let each man bring some other one,
   And soon we'll have them all. *To Chorus*[63]

The Frog

1. Of all the funny things that live
   In woodland, Marsh, or bog,
That creep the ground, or fly the air,
   The funniest is the frog.
The frog—the scientificest
   Of nature's handy work—
The frog that never walks nor runs,
   But goes it with a jerk.

2. With pants and coat of bottle green,
   And yellow fancy vest,
He plunges into mud and mire,
   All in his Sunday best;
When he sits down, he's standing up,
   As Paddy O'Kinn once said;
And, for convenience sake, he wears
   His eyes on the top of his head.

---

62. *Collection of Temperance Songs*, n.p. Fillmore, *Temperance Musician*, 53, omits the final two verses. Pierpont, *Cold Water Melodies*, 46–48, and *Washingtonian Tee-Totalers' Minstrel*, 45–46, add a new verse 3.
   63. Pierpont, *Cold Water Melodies*, 28–29; *Washingtonian Tee-Totalers' Minstrel*, 10; Thompson, *Thompson's Band*, 35–36.

3. You see him sitting on a log,
　　Above the "vasty deep,"
You feel inclined to say, old chap—
　　"Just look before you leap!"
You raise your cane to hit him on
　　His ugly looking mug;
But ere you get it half way up,
　　A-down he goes kerchug.

4. He keeps about his native pond,
　　And ne'er goes on a spree,
Nor gets "how-come-you-so" for a
　　Cold water chap is he;
For earthly cares he ne'er gets drunk,
　　He's not the silly fool;
But when they come he gives a jump,
　　And drowns 'em in the pool.[64]

Maine Law

1. The friends of truth are rising up,
　　Throughout our mighty nation,
To put the liquor traffic down,
　　And drive it from creation.
King Alcohol's black flag too long
　　Have we been marching under.
Now let us raise our battle-cry
　　In tones as loud as thunder.

2. We've tried PERSUASION long enough,
　　We'll try it now no longer,
It will not stop the traffic, and
　　We now want something STRONGER,
We'll brand each villain with disgrace
　　Who manufactures hog-slop,
We'll pour their poison on the ground,
　　And close up every grog-shop.

3. Though some oppose our noble cause,
　　We've arguments invincible,
Which never can be overthrown
　　By men who have no principle;
From East to West, from North to South,
　　Our banner's waving proudly,
And Freedom's sons, and DAUGHTERS, too,
　　Are shouting bravely, loudly.

4. Arise, ye noble friends of truth,
　　In every rank and station,
And let us put the traffic down,
　　And drive it from creation;
Our banner's waving to the breeze,
　　Come, freemen, and march under,
And let us raise our battle cry
　　In tones of loudest thunder.[65]

We'll Stand by Water Pure

1. Come, let us stand by water pure;
　　Come, shun both beer and brandy;
And if we're true, we'll free our land
　　From all their curses one day.

Chorus
Then old and young, come join the song,
　　Come, link both heart and hand too,
For Temperance must win the day
　　And rule our Yankee land through.

2. The cheerless home will then grow gay,
　　The cold ones will grow warm, too;
And poverty will slink away
　　With all his ugly swarm, too. *To Chorus*

3. The little hearts will dance with glee,
　　The old ones smile with mirth then,
And love will cast her summer looks
　　Around the humblest hearth, then.
　　　　To Chorus

4. Crime, grog-shops, whiskey-dens and bars,
　　With gin, the fiend that serves them,
Must yield before young Yankee hearts,
　　For Yankee freedom nerves them.
　　　　To Chorus[66]

Bands of Hope Are Growing Stronger

1. Now don't you know the reason why
　　The Temperance cause is winning?
Our Bands of Hope resolve to try
　　The pledge when life's beginning.

---

64. Fillmore, *Temperance Musician*, 242.
65. Ibid., 124.
66. Lucius Hart, ed., *The Juvenile Temperance Harp*, 35. Guthrie, *Teetotal Army*, 11, entitles this selection "We'll Stand by Water Pure" and omits verse 4.

Chorus
That's the way to win the day,
    Wait a little longer;
Drink shall fall with tyrants all,
    When Bands of Hope are stronger.

2. King Alcohol, a giant great,
    Will find that he's not wanted,
For Bands of Hope shall fill the state,
    In every quarter planted. *To Chorus*

3. He's blundered many a noble plan,
    And scattered death and ruin;
But soon we'll show him, every man,
    What Bands of Hope are doing.
        To Chorus

4. We'll give him such a mighty blow
    He never will recover,
And then, we'll set to work, you know,
    And turn his kingdom over. *To Chorus*

5. The gin shop built in rich design
    Shall wear a lofty steeple,
And serve for school and college, fine,
    To educate the people. *To Chorus*[67]

Love at Home

1. There is beauty all around,
    When there's love at home,
There is joy in every sound,
    When there's love at home.
Peace and plenty here abide,
    Smiling sweet on every side;
Time doth softly, sweetly glide,
    When there's love at home.

2. In the cottage there is joy—
    When there's love at home;
Hate and envy ne'er annoy,
    When there's love at home.
Roses blossom at our feet,
    All the earth's a garden sweet,
Making life a bliss complete,
    When there's love at home.

3. Kindly heaven smiles above,
    When there's love at home,
All the earth is full of love,
    When there's love at home.
Sweeter sings the brooklet by,
    Brighter beams the azure sky;
O, there's One who smiles on high,
    When there's love at home.[68]

Conscientious Young Man

1. Now Frankie, sir, you said one day
    You would do what I bid you,
So if you're frank then don't delay,
    But take the pledge, it's good, sir,

Chorus
O, yes I know, but hold a bit,
    For that was all between us,
I cannot from my socials quit,
    I am very conscientious.

2. Ah, so dear friend, your ear now lend,
    I have been at the meetings,
Where good folks say, O do not bend
    To all the young men's reasonings.
        To Chorus

3. I think you mean just what you say,
    That you'll not in a gin-shop go,
But then I heard the other day,
    You'd take it when a mind to. *To Chorus*

4. Ah, yes I see your scruples hinge
    Upon your social gatherings,
But they say your nose will tinge,
    All from these frequent treatings.
        To Chorus

5. Now if your conscience troubles so,
    And you must keep up drinking,
I am now resolved to let you know,
    On me no more be thinking. *To Chorus*

6. I'll now repeat that no young man
    So scrupulously drinking,
Shall be allowed to take my hand,
    So you go elsewhere seeking. *To Chorus*[69]

---

67. Saunders, *Temperance Songster*, 20; Bradbury and Stearns, *Temperance Chimes* (1867 and 1878), 99. Stearns, *Band of Hope*, 37, replaces "blundered" with "hindered" in verse 3 and omits verse 5.
68. James Alexander Mowatt, ed., *Mowatt's Temperance Glee Book, No. 1*, 13.
69. A. G. Nichols, *The Iron Door and Other Temperance Songs*, 18–19.

Rum-Sellers' Convention
(Samuel Jarden)

1. Come listen to me, gentlemen,
    Whilst I rehearse a ditty,
Not long ago, rum-sellers met
    In this, your favorite city;
One stalwart rum-seller got up,
    And danced around quite frisky,
Said he, my friends, I've much to say,
    In the interest of whiskey.
Of course he had, ha! ha! ha! ha!
    He was one of our law-makers;
But while *he* made the laws for *us*,
    Himself was a law-breaker.

2. Mr. President, I move you, sir,
    That *we*, as whiskey-sellers,
For the old Judges cast our votes,
    And not those untried fellows;
Well, had they not a right to meet,
    And make their own selection,
And cast their votes for whom they pleased,
    At the Judicial election?
Of course they had, ha! ha! ha! ha!
    But, sirs, this is the query;
Did not their zeal help to defeat,
    Pinkney, Gilmore and Garey?

3. Now have *we* not a right to meet,
    In mutual consultation;
To mature a plan, by which we can,
    From rum redeem our nation?
And have *we* not a right to pass
    A freeman's resolution,
That to this end, we will amend
    Our own State Constitution!
Of course we have, hail! hail! all hail!
    The dawn of our salvation;
Our God is raising up good men,
    To save, and rule our nation.[70]

Hurrah for Prohibition

1. The Temp'rance folks are waking up
    Throughout the Yankee nation,

To put the liquor traffic down,
    And drive it from creation.
The stills and drinking dens are doomed
    To lawful demolition;
For all good men are going in
    For legal Prohibition.

Chorus
Prohibition is the song,
    We'll shout it through the nation;
Prohibition to the wrong
    Is right through all creation.

2. Too long King Alcohol has reigned,
    All moral suasion scorning;
Too long his murd'rous savages
    Have filled the land with mourning,
Rumsellers care not for our prayers,
    Or tears, or admonition;
But there's a pow'r can make them quake—
    'Tis legal Prohibition. *To Chorus*

3. No scoffs or foes or doubts of friends
    Shall weaken our endeavor
To brand the traffic with disgrace,
    And wipe it out forever!
Right on shall go the noble work
    Until its full completion;
We'll "fight it out upon the line"
    Of total Prohibition! *To Chorus*[71]

Prohibition Is the Song

1. Prohibition is the theme
    The Temp'rance folks delight in;
We'll write it down to fit the tune
    Our fathers made for fighting.
If you want to stop a man
    From drinking rum and brandy,
Don't give a license to the shop
    That always keeps it handy.

Chorus
Prohibition is the song
    We'll shout it through the nation;
Prohibition to the wrong
    Is right through all creation.

---

70. Samuel Jarden, *The Prohibition Banner*, 25–26. This song has a different chorus for each verse.

71. Stearns, *National Temperance*, 51; Leslie, *Good Templar* (1886 and 1888), 47; R. E. Hudson, *Temperance Songster*, no. 63; Stearns, *Prohibition Songster*, 27. This song requires that the verse be repeated before going to the chorus.

2. Prohibition is the law
   To stop the crime of murder;
Don't you think it would be well
   To go a little further—
Stop the cause, and then the crime
   Will never have beginning;
The surest way to stop a sin
   Is just to stop the sinning. *To Chorus*[72]

When Old Enough to Vote

1. When we are old enough to vote
   We'll make a great commotion;
We'll sweep the land of whisky clean,
   From ocean unto ocean.

Chorus
"Old Alcohol" will have to fall
   From his exalted station;
We'll smite him right, we'll smite him left
   And drive him from the nation.

2. Some day the world will bless the men
   Who now are only boys, sir,
For we are learning lessons true,
   With all fun and noise, sir. *To Chorus*

3. So, when we're old enough to vote,
   There'll be a mighty rattle
Of falling forts and castles gray
   For right will win the battle. *To Chorus*

4. We will not fear to speak the words
   That God would have us speak, sir,
With Him for our right hand, you know
   We never can be weak, sir. *To Chorus*[73]

'Tis Time to Swing Our Axes

1. We've had enough of license laws,
   Enough of liquor's taxes
We've turned the grindstone long enough,
   'Tis time to swing our axes.
This deadly upas tree must fall—
   Let strokes be strong and steady,
Pull out the stumps! grub out the roots!
   O brothers! are you ready?

2. No longer will we shield this foe
   To manhood, love and beauty;
We've had enough of compromise—
   The right alone is duty,
Enough of weak men and distrust;
   The burden grows by shifting;
Let's put our shoulder to the wheel!
   And do our share of lifting.

3. We've had enough of forging chains
   This demon drink to fetter,
Good bullets from the ballot box
   Well sped, will fix him better!
Will ye not hunt him to the death!
   Speak out! speak out, O brothers!
Will ye not sound the bugle call,
   O sisters, wives and mothers!

4. We've had enough of shame and woe;
   Of cruel spoilation,
Who fears to say it out enough
   To thrill our land and nation?
God help us all to work like men,
   In earnest agitation,
Till we have crushed the power of rum
   By righteous legislation.[74]

No License, High or Low

1. We want no license, high or low,
   We want no local option;
'Tis prohibition that we want,
   Of Uncle Sam's adoption.
For Uncle Sam's a giant bold,
   'Tis he that rules the nation,
And he'll enforce the laws he makes
   If he moves all creation.

2. For license high or license low
   Is but a foolish notion,
Now law can make a license right
   Though wealth flows in like ocean.
And local option in a town
   Will always cause commotion;
It's yearly voted up or down
   As people take a notion.

72. Stearns, *National Temperance*, 54; Stearns, *Prohibition Songster*, 60. The verse must be repeated before going to the chorus. Note that this chorus is the same as in "Hurrah for Prohibition," above.
   73. Leslie, *Good Templar* (1886), 47.
   74. Stearns and Main, *Trumpet Notes*, 57.

3. Prohibition stops the thing
    And hinders all confusion.
Ask Uncle Sam to put it in-
    To his old Constitution.
For Uncle Sam's a giant bold,
    'Tis he that rules the nation,
And he'll enforce the laws he makes
    If he moves all creation.[75]

No License Is Our Theme

1. Friends, No license is the theme,
    We Temp'rance folks delight in;
We'll write it down to fit the tune
    Our fathers made for fightin'

Chorus
Yes, No license is the song
    We'll shout it through the nation;
Strict No license to the wrong,
    Is right through all creation.

2. If you want to stop a man
    From drinking rum and brandy,
Don't give a license to the shop
    That keeps it always handy. *To Chorus*

3. No scoffs of foes or doubts of friends
    Shall weaken our endeavor
To brand the traffic with disgrace,
    And wipe it out forever. *To Chorus*[76]

Say, Voters, Are You Ready?

1. Come friends and listen to a song,
    About our mighty nation;
On ev'ry hand where'er there's rum,
    You'll find sad dissipation.

Chorus
Temperance voters, keep it up,
    Give our homes protection;
Knock the rummies out of sight
    At every town election.

2. Now listen, friends, for we propose,
    To give some common sense,

And that is, "stop this curse of rum
    By voting for No license!" *To Chorus*

3. We've had enough of license laws,
    Enough of liquor taxes,
We've turned the grind-stone long enough,
    'Tis time to swing our axes. *To Chorus*

4. This deadly Upas tree must fall—
    Let strokes be strong and steady;
Pull up the stumps! grub out the roots!
    Say, voters, are you ready? *To Chorus*[77]

Free Your Town
(E. A. Hoffman)

1. We'll vote the curse of liquor down,
    The people's ruination;
We'll vote the evil from our town,
    And from our noble nation;
We to the polls will early go,
    The friends of Prohibition,
Assured we have the people's votes
    To carry out our mission.

Chorus
We've resolved to free the town,
    And to free our nation,
From the curse that causes only
    Crime and ruination.

2. 'Tis not the man of the saloon
    We temp'rance folks are after;
It is the traffic we condemn,
    A robber and a grafter.
For men who like ourselves, have souls
    We have a kindly feeling,
But we are tired of the saloon,
    The trade in which they're dealing.
        To Chorus

3. Too long we have submitted to
    The traffic's domination;
At last we hurl at the saloon
    Our wrath and condemnation;
The money that for harmful drink
    So long has been expended

---

75. Fobes, *Temperance Songs*, 15.

76. Miller, *Patriotic No-License*, no. 12. This song borrows material from "Prohibition Is Our Song" and "Hurrah for Prohibition."

77. Ibid., no. 6. This song borrows verse 1 from "'Tis Time to Swing Our Axes" for verses 3 and 4.

Shall to the honest business man
    From henceforth be extended.
        To Chorus[78]

W.C.T.U. Rally Song

1. We are the W.C.T.U.,
    We have a glorious mission,
Our Leader is the Lord of Hosts,
    Our goal is Prohibition.

Chorus
Prohibition's on the way,
    Let the drums be drumming;
God is with us and we'll win,
    For Prohibition's coming.

2. Without the ballot we have left
    But little ammunition.
But we will sing and work and pray
    To hasten Prohibition. *To Chorus*

3. A crucial hour has come at last,
    And all must make decision
To rally with the liquor force
    Or stand for Prohibition. *To Chorus*

4. O, men who love your country well,
    Her weal your high ambition,
Give heart and hand to aid the cause
    And vote for Prohibition. *To Chorus*[79]

Get Prohibition
(Anna A. Gordon)

1. Prohibition's sure to come
    In our beloved state, sir;
That's what boys and girls believe,
    The only thing that's straight, sir.

Chorus
State-wide prohibition law,
    Voters, please remember!
That's what we are bound to have
    Early next November!

2. Prohibition is the law
    The liquor dealers fight, sir;

That's the reason we should say
    It's just exactly right, sir. *To Chorus*

3. All the world is looking on
    To see what we will do, sir;
If we win this splendid law
    They'll know that we are true, sir.
        To Chorus

4. Voters love the girls and boys
    Far better than the beer, sir;
Please protect us with the law
    For which we children cheer, sir.
        To Chorus[80]

La Marseillaise

Ye Sons of Bacchus
(J. S. Fowler)

1. Ye sons of Bacchus, wake from sleeping,
    See, see what mis'ry bids you rise;
Your children wives and mothers weeping,
    Behold their tears and hear their cries!
Their faithful bosoms anxious feeling,
    The pallid cheek, the blighted youth,
They tell with melancholy truth,
    Their woes and misery revealing;
Arise, arise, awake,
    Your drunken slumbers cease.

Chorus
Come on, come on, your hearts resolved
    On Abstinence and peace.

2. For now the rays of morn are dawning,
    And temp'rance sheds her hallowed light,
The glorious sun breaks on the morning,
    The radiant star illumes the night;
And shall we basely waste in dreaming
    Our senses and our lives away!
Debased slaves to Alcohol's sway
    When Liberty's bright light is beaming;
Arise, arise, awake,
    Your drunken slumbers cease. *To Chorus*

---

78. *Anti-Saloon Campaign Songs*, no. 14; Elisha A. Hoffman, *Woman's Christian Temperance Union Campaign Songs*, no. 14. The verse should be repeated before going to the chorus.

79. Hoffman, *Woman's Christian Temperance*, no. 50.

80. Anna A. Gordon, *Popular Campaign Songs*, 26.

3. Hark! hark the temp'rance call is
    sounding,
    Awake and stay your children's tears,
Destroy the curse in wine abounding,
    Your wives' distress, their anxious fears,
Behold our standard proudly waving,
    Come join our Washingtonian band;
The pledge gives freedom to our land,
    Our glorious cause, a world is saving,
Arise, arise, awake,
    Your drunken slumbers cease. *To Chorus*[81]

Ye Sons of Temperance

Ye sons of Temp'rance wake to glory,
    Hark! hark, what myriads bid you rise,
Your children, wives, and grand-sires hoary,
    Behold their tears, and hear their cries,
Behold their tears and hear their cries,
    Shall Alcohol, foul mischief breeding,
With hireling host, a ruffian band,
    Spread crime and mis'ry o'er the land,
While peace and liberty lie bleeding!
    To arms! to arms! ye brave;
Your wives and children save.
    March on, march on,
All hearts resolved,
    On vict'ry with the brave.[82]

Ye Friends of Temperance
(W. Sugden)

1. Ye friends of temp'rance self denying,
    Hark! hark! what myriads bid you rise;
See wretched drunkards round you dying,
    Behold their tears and hear their cries,
Behold their tears and hear their cries.
    Shall hateful customs mischief breeding,
With woes and cries, a direful band,
    Afflicted and desolate the land
While peace and happiness lie bleeding?
    Arise! arise to save; Your standard wide
    unfold.

Chorus
March on, march on, All hearts resolved
    On victory or death.
March on, march on, All hearts resolved
    On victory or death.

2. No joy of heart or hope resigning,
    Our bosoms glow with gen'rous flame;
No narrow bounds the soul confining,
    Shall e'er our noble ardor tame.
Shall e'er our noble ardor tame.
    Too long our land has been bewailing,
The giant ills which far and wide,
    Stalk through its bounds with guilty
    stride,
O'er prostrate virtue's powers prevailing.
    Arise! arise to save; Your standard wide
    unfold. *To Chorus*[83]

Awake! Arise!

1. Awake! Arise! all ye who sleeping,
    Who hear not yet the echo loud
Of virtue's voice, her high watch keeping,
    Proclaiming to that victim crowd
How misery and madness lending
    The poisoned arrows Bacchus gave
The free-born heart to enslave.
    Gay youth and hoary age are sending
Offerings to sorrow's grave.
    Press on! Press on! with heart and soul
    To free the fettered slave.

2. Long has the patriot been grieving
    O'er gen'rous aspirations spurned—
Vain dreams of glory—hope relieving
    The fire which in his bosom burned.
The shrieks of suicide's sad fate—
    The groans which rend a father's heart—
The swoon of mothers thus to part—
    The tears of sisters, shed too late.
Unbind! unbind the slaves!
    Press on! Press on! with heart and soul,
    Fill not the tyrant's graves.

81. Plimpton, *Washingtonian Choir*, 40–41.
82. Fillmore, *Temperance Musician*, 79.
83. Hart, *Juvenile Temperance*, 32. Bradbury and Stearns, *Temperance Chimes* (1867 and 1878), 70, Sherwin and Stearns, *Bugle Notes*, 109–11, and Stearns, *National Temperance*, 38, all name this selection "Arise! Arise to Save."

3. The cypress sad—her dark hair waving—
　　With grief has shaded virtue's path.
The genii of the vine enslaving,
　　Absorbing nations in her wrath.
Man cannot tell the ensanguined story
　　Receding vision leaves behind,
The tainted leprosy of mind,
　　The race of devastation gory.
Asunder rend the chain.
　　Press on! Press on! with heart and soul
　　The freeman's right maintain.

4. But, hark! 'Tis Temperance thus speaking,
　　Her lamp of knowledge now on high
With meteor glare the darkness breaking
　　In lambent streams lights every eye.
One song of joy earth's sons are singing,
　　Triumph of virtue, lowly born,
Charming the dawn of reason's morn.
　　Beauty's daughters true hearts bringing
To free, to free the slave.
　　Press on! Press on! with heart and soul.
　　True glory courts the brave.[84]

Arise! The Work Begin!
(Mrs. C. L. Shacklock)

1. Rise to the work of reformation,
　　Press nobly onward to the goal,
Enslaved is our beloved nation,
　　Strike for the freedom of the soul!
Strike for the freedom of the soul!
　　Our battle cry is "Prohibition,"
Aye, let it ring throughout the land.
　　United let us ever stand,
Fulfilling our divine commission.
　　Arise! the work begin, o'ercome the
　　　host of sin;

Chorus
Arise, arise, press bravely on
　　Till victory is won!
Arise, arise, press bravely on
　　Till victory is won!

2. A mighty contest is before us,
　　A foeman who will never yield,

But with the God of battles o'er us,
　　We'll win the day, we'll sweep the field,
We'll win the day, we'll sweep the field.
　　The prayers of brokenhearted mothers
To ev'ry heart for aid appeal,
　　Renew our strength, inspire our zeal,
To save our weak and erring brothers.
　　Arise! the work begin, o'ercome the host
　　　of sin, *To Chorus*

3. We'll seek the outcast and the sinning,
　　We'll build again the wrecks of home,
Save all the downward path beginning—
　　The year of jubilee has come!
The year of jubilee has come!
　　Once more shall our beloved nation
As in her day of triumph stand,
　　While like a tide throughout the land
Shall sweep a glorious reformation!
　　Arise! the work begin, o'ercome the host
　　　of sin, *To Chorus*[85]

Win and Hold the Field
(Samuel Jarden)

1. Ye sons of Howard, wake to glory,
　　Hark! hark! what myriads bid you rise,
Your sisters, wives and grand dames hoary,
　　Behold their fears, and hear their cries;
Too long has moral suasion failed you,
　　And half your labors spent for naught,
Whilst license laws have still assailed you,
　　And back to rum, your converts brought.

Chorus
To arms, to arms ye brave,
　　The freeman's ballot wield;
March on, march on, all hearts resolved,
　　To win, and hold the field.

2. Look! see you not the day is breaking?
　　The glorious sun will soon arise,
All o'er this land, are freemen waking;
　　To fill the world with glad surprise
They see the crime and desolation
　　That rum has caused throughout our
　　　land;

84. John M'Kechnie, *The Lyre of Temperance*, 9–11.
85. T. M. Towne, *Temperance Anthems*, 26–28.

They are coming now, a mighty nation,
  In one united, patriot band. *To Chorus*

3. Unite, Republicans and Democrats,
  Take a firm decided stand,
Let the North, South, East and West
    combine,
  To drive the monster from our land;
Then will come the great millennium,
  All o'er this free and happy land,
And across the bloody chasm
  We'll grasp and clasp each other's hand;
Oh, yes, it will be joy, when our toils and
    labor's o'er,
  We'll grasp and clasp each other's hand,
  Forever, evermore. *To Chorus*[86]

Prohibition Marsellaise

1. Behold the cruel tyrant reigning,
  Where boasted Freedom's banner waves;
Hark to the millions loud complaining,
  That lash and chain enslaves,
And yearly sends to lonely graves!
  Full sixty thousand born as freemen,
With manly heart and priceless soul,
  Enthralled by rum's enticing bowl,
  Are slain by this accursed demon!

Chorus
From rum we must be free;
  From rum we shall be free!
Arm! Arm to meet the liquor foe!
  On! on, to victory!

2. Upheld by servile license party,
  The crime and woe-producing still,
And sends forth streams of death at will,
  That both the soul and body kill,
And fill unnumbered homes with weeping;
  That crowd the almshouse, prison, jail,
While eyes grow dim, and cheeks grow pale,
  And broken hearts are lowly sleeping!
    To Chorus

3. Six hundred thousand drunkards yearly,
  On the sure road to ruin sent;

One hundred million dollars, dearly
  Reaped from two thousand millions
    spent,
With ruin, crime and sorrow blent,
  Not speaking of the loss eternal,
Not speaking of the yearly dead!
  Such is the trade to party wed;
  Such is the cost of rum infernal! *To Chorus*

4. How long shall drink continue slaying,
  And, with its crime-cursed, blood-stained
    gold,
Boast that our revenue 'tis paying,
  While license party to its use is sold?
Aye, it would wrap its serpent fold
  Around all sacred rights; 'twould marry
Rum with the church, dramshop to school;
  And, armed with legislative rule,
  Its trade of hell to Heaven would carry!
    To Chorus[87]

The Marseilles
(Palmer Hartsough)

1. Columbia's Sons, the world is calling,
  In chains of drink the nations be,
While tears of dark despair are falling,
  With hope they look, fair land, to thee,
With hope they look, fair land, to thee;
  And shall we still in slumber lying,
The growing pow'r of rum disdain,
  Till, helpless in its dreadful chain,
E'en we ourselves its slaves be dying?
  Arise, arise, ye brave,
The world, the world to save.

Chorus
O, break; O, break Rum's mighty pow'r,
  The world, the world to save.
O, break; O, break Rum's mighty pow'r,
  The world, the world to save.

2. Columbia's Sons, the coils are tight'ning,
  And we at ease unmindful still;
The nation's blood the monster bright'ning,
  The nation's heart numb with his chill,
The nation's heart numb with his chill;
  And we before this king of evils,

86. Jarden, *Prohibition Banner*, 4–5.
87. Durant, *Prohibition Home*, 17–18.

Refuse, in fear or base dislike,
    The prohibition blow to strike,
And end the hellish work of devils.
    Arise, arise, ye brave,
The world, the world to save. *To Chorus*

3. Columbia's Sons, the angels o'er thee
    Would lead thee on with beck'ning hand;
And in His might thy God before thee,
    Would sweep the demons from the land,
Would sweep the demons from the land;
    Then fear not Satan's opposition,
But in the name of Jesus go,
    And for your loved ones strike the blow,
That wins the fight for Prohibition.
    Arise, arise, ye brave,
The world, the world to save. *To Chorus*[88]

Star-Spangled Banner

The Washington Banner

1. Rejoice, for the day of deliverance is come,
    O'er the land and the sea waves the
        Washington Banner;
And voices that wailed in the drunkard's sad
    home,
    Now are cheering us on with a joyful
        Hosanna!
Let us swell the glad sound, send the chorus
    around!
    Oh shout, for the pledge of our safety is
        found!
'Tis the Washington Banner; oh, long may it
    wave,
    O'er the land of the free and the home of
        the brave.

2. Rejoice, for the homes that are once more
    made glad,
    For the eyes that are bright where the big
        tears were streaming;
Rejoice for the hearts that no longer are sad,
    For the sweet tears of joy, and the smiles
        that are beaming;

Let the rich and the poor touch the poison
    no more,
    Oh, let the red wine cup be banished each
        door!
Till the Washington Banner in triumph shall
    wave,
    O'er the land of the free and the home of
        the brave!

3. Rejoice, for the names we can now call our
    own,
    For the brothers we claim who are
        holding high places;
Rejoice for the fair, they would conquer
    alone!
    It is well they have joined us, God bless
        their bright faces!
Through the length of the land, oh let none
    coldly stand,
    And proudly refuse us the warm helping
        hand!
For the Washington Banner in triumph must
    wave,
    O'er the land of the free and the home of
        the brave![89]

Come, Sons of Columbia

1. Come, sons of Columbia, while proudly
    and high,
    Every heart with the love of our freedom
        is swelling,
While our star-blazoned bird has his home in
    the sky,
    And tyranny's death-song is heard in each
        dwelling,
Come, the bright chalice drain—and again
    and again,
    Let our pledge, and our toast, in a far
        sounding strain,
Be water—pure water, bright sparkling with
    glee,
    That flows, like our life's blood,
        unfettered and free.

88. Fillmore and Fillmore, *Fillmores' Prohibition*, no. 142.
89. Mary S. B. Dana, *The Temperance Lyre*, 48–49; Bonner, *Mountain Minstrel*, 46. Mowatt, *Mowatt's Temperance Glee*, 45, replaces the title "Washington Banner" with "Temperance Banner" and also changes these words in each verse.

2. Oh! the wine-cup may sparkle in ruby drops bright,
   And o'er its glad brim, in gay phalanx advancing,
Fair gossamer spirits, in rainbow-like light,
   May to Bacchanal music be gracefully dancing:
While they dazzle our eyes with the hues of the skies,
   Soft and silvery tones on the breeze seem to rise,
'Tis the gush of pure water, bright sparkling with glee,
   That flows, like our life's blood, unfettered and free.

3. Oh! then hail to thee, water—the Bacchanal's toast
   May be drunk in red wine, that in ruddy light flashes
But Columbia's freemen still proudly shall boast,
   Of the free gift of God, that o'er hill and vale dashes:
The diamond's bright ray seems forever to play
   On the full glancing cup—and the soul-breathing lay,
Shall be praise of pure water, bright sparkling with glee,
   The gift of our God—and the drink of the free.[90]

The Temperance Banner #1

1. O say, can you see, by the "signs of the time,"
   That men are reforming, themselves setting free
From all that destroys their bodies and minds,
   Resolving to plant a new liberty tree.
Their condition no more they lament and deplore,
   Their bondage is broken, their thraldom is o'er;
For the Temperance Banner in triumph doth wave,
   O'er the heads of the rescued, free sons of the brave.

2. In the past plainly seen, through the midst of their tears,
   Is the sorrow, and anguish, and pain they have suffered,
The sad loss of all that to manhood is dear—
   The time when none kindness and sympathy offered.
But the trial has past, though long did it last,
   And their chains and their bondage far from them they've cast;
And the Temperance Banner in triumph doth wave, *etc.*

3. Oh, where is the promise that *Alcohol* gave,
   To place the poor victim 'bove sorrow and anguish,
Of all his false hopes, not one now remains,
   And his many fair dreams, all, all are now banished.
His promise was air and false was as fair,
   And again them to offer, he never will dare;
While the Temperance Banner in triumph doth wave, *etc.*

4. Thus be it ever, while the reformed shall stand,
   Between his dread foe, and his heart's desolation,
Thus happy and free may the now rescued band,
   Bless the power that brought them again to their station.
And conquer we must for our cause is most just,
   And this be our motto—in God let us trust;
And the Temperance Banner forever will wave,
   O'er the heads of the rescued, Free sons of the brave.[91]

90. Pierpont, *Cold Water Melodies*, 106–7; Bonner, *Mountain Minstrel*, 91.
91. Bigelow and Grosh, *Washingtonian Pocket*, 79. Bradbury and Stearns, *Temperance Chimes* (1867 and 1878), 53, omits verse 3. Gould and Grosh, *Washingtonian Pocket*, 62–63, and Bonner, *Mountain Minstrel*, 101, make changes at the beginning of verse 1.

Star of Temperance

1. O, say, can you see, through the dark
mental night,
   That star in our pathway, so faintly now
gleaming?
Soon will it enlarge, like the bright orb of
night,
   Awaking the soul that in darkness lies
dreaming;
Now it catches the eye, as it darts from the
sky,
   Bringing blessings and peace from the
regions on high.
'Tis the bright Star of Temperance, long may
it shine,
   Enlightening the soul with its radiance
divine.

2. And where is that host by Intemperance
led,
   To virtues and truth breathing death and
destruction?
Like chaff on the wings of the wind they have
fled,
   Or listened to Temp'rance's hallowed
instruction.
There's a refuge can save the intemperate
slave,
   From the horror of death and the
criminal's grave;
'Tis the bright Star of Temperance, *etc.*

3. Thus, be it ever, when mankind shall
come,
   No longer base slaves in the drunkard's
dominion.
They shall rise, like the Phoenix, from ashes
and gloom,
   And rejoice as they float on glad Hope's
airy pinion;
Then prosper they must, for their cause is
most just,
   And will aid them in splendor to rise
from the dust;
And the bright Star of Temperance, *etc.*[92]

Temperance Anthem

1. Oh! say can you tell why those glad sounds
arise,
   Which so loudly are heard through this
world's vast creation,
Whose joyful notes spread, where'er sunlight
is shed,
   And give back the echo of human
salvation,
And the dark shades of night rendered joyous
and bright
   Wear the semblance of day in its proud
robes of light.
'Tis the Temperance Anthem whose glad
sounds arise
   And mingle their tones with the choir of
the skies.

2. Is the demon subdued, whose temptations
we know,
   And whose shackles have bound us in
deep degradation;
Who oft led us to sin, when his power we
were in,
   And wrought our soul's and heart's
desolation.
Oh yes, he's subdued, our lives are renewed,
   And these shouts are thanksgivings from
where he once stood.
For the Temperance Anthem whose glad
sounds arise,
   Is hallowed by heaven, and reaches the
skies.

3. Hark! the widow's deep grief has at length
found relief,
   And the orphan no more sheds the tear
of starvation,
For in Temperance they trust, and conquer
they must,
   'Tis Heaven's appeal and 'tis God's own
creation.
Then with joy let us raise our loud voices in
praise,

---

92. Bensel, *Temperance Harp*, 24-25; Plimpton, *Washingtonian Choir*, 48; Fillmore, *Temperance Musician*, 133.

And sing our proud triumph in
temperance lays.
For the Temperance Anthem, whose glad
sounds arise
Is hallowed by Heaven and reaches the
skies.[93]

The Clarion

1. The clarion, the clarion of freedom now
sounds,
From the east to the west independence
resounds;
From the hills and the streams and the far
distant skies
Let the shout "Independence from
Alcohol" rise.
From the hills and the streams,
And the far distant skies,
Let the shout "Independence from
Alcohol" rise.

2. The army, the army have taken the field,
The hosts of cold water no never will
yield;
From fountains refreshed animation now
glows,
With ardor immortal they rush on their
foes.
From the hills and the streams, *etc.*

3. The armor, the armor that gilds every
breast,
Is the hope of deliverance for thousands
distressed;
With words of persuasion we call on the
throng,
Desert the black banner and join in our
song.
From the hills and the streams, *etc.*

4. The banners, the banners of freedom now
wave,
Lo the eagle now covers the ranks of the
brave;
With the shout "Independence" creation
shall sing

From the cruel taxation of alcohol king.
From the hills and the streams, *etc.*

5. The conflict, the conflict will shortly be
o'er,
And the Demon Intemperance triumph
no more
O'er the tears and the sighs and premature
graves—
See the flag of our freedom eternally
waves.
From the hills and the streams, *etc.*

6. The empire, the empire of freedom divine,
Like the gray vault of heaven forever shall
shine;
Then as wide as creation her blessings shall
roll,
And a star of new glory illumine each
pole.
From the hills and the streams, *etc.*

7. The laurel, the laurel unfading shall wave,
On the brows that have rescued their
friends from the grave,
And the thanks of a nation forever be given
To the heroes immortal, co-workers with
heaven.
From the hills and the streams, *etc.*[94]

Wild Is the Path

1. O, wild is the path of the son of the sea,
Who launches his bark on the perilous
tide;
But wilder by far is the reef-studded lee,
Where drunkards, 'mid billows of
drunkenness ride.
O, fierce is the storm that the mariner braves,
'Mid thunder and lightnings, afar on the
foam;
But the storm of the land has more
dangerous waves,
Where drunkards 'mid billows of
drunkenness roam.

2. O, hungry as death are the monsters that
prey

---

93. *Collection of Hymns and Songs*, 3.
94. *Union Temperance*, 54–55.

On the corpse of the sailor, far down in
the deep;
But hungrier still are the monsters who prey,
Where drunkards, 'mid billows of
drunkenness creep.
O, God save the sailor with heavenly force,
From drunkards and drunkenness keep
him afar;
O, steer him safe on in a temperance course,
By the mild cheering light of this bright
morning star.[95]

The Foe of Church and Freedom

1. Old rum license parties, are taking their
leave
Of the country long cursed with their
traffic in liquor;
To gloom they are sinking, and no one
should grieve,
May the shadows around them fall darker
and thicker!
Prohibition grows bright, they are taking
their flight,
With rum still and rum tax, fit comrades
of night;
We'll chase the vile brood from hill, valley
and plain;
Then, Hurrah! Prohibition triumphant
shall reign!

2. The foes of American liberty seek
Through the traffic in liquor to hasten its
ending;
On Bible, Free-school and the Sabbath they
wreak
All their hate, while their dark dens of
vice still extending;
The most sensible way all their danger to stay,
Is to pray Prohibition, and vote as we
pray:
We'll chase the vile brood from hill, valley
and plain;
Then, Hurrah! Prohibition triumphant
shall reign!

3. Our churches are sleeping, their precepts
are vain,
Their regard for old party their practice
controlling,
Each vote for a license, rum-party most plain,
For the church and religion, a death-knell
is tolling!
Oh, then, cease to be dumb, in your pulpit,
on rum,
Ye ministers, held under rum-party
thumb,
And chase the vile brood from hill, valley and
plain;
Then, Hurrah! Prohibition triumphant
shall reign!

4. Both parties, upholding the traffic in
drink,
In the church pews are sitting, and
list'ning devoutly;
That this they are doing, few ever once think
Yet oppose Prohibition in *"politics,"*
stoutly!
We believe most will see, how un-Christian
this be,
And presently, out of old rum-parties flee,
And chase the vile brood from hill, valley and
plain;
Then, Hurrah! Prohibition triumphant
shall reign!

5. Arouse, all ye millions! shall liquor
enslave?
Shall this Government perish by rum and
its minions?
No, no! Still the star-spangled banner shall
wave,
From this slavery free, o'er our boundless
dominions;
Not an eye shall behold on a star, stripe or
fold,
One stain from this curse, blood-revenue
gold,
As proudly it floats o'er hill, valley and plain:
Then, Hurrah! Prohibition triumphant
shall reign![96]

95. Fillmore, *Temperance Musician*, 143.
96. Durant, *Prohibition Home*, 28–29.

The Spotless White Banner

1. The spotless white banner of Temp'rance
       for me,
    That proudly waves over the happy and
       free,
'Twill guide me to virtue, contentment and
    health,
    The emblem of peace, the precursor of
       wealth.
Its battles are bloodless, it conquers to raise,
    And those it subdues sing aloud in its
       praise.
Then the spotless white banner of
       Temp'rance for me,
    That floats in the breeze o'er the sober
       and free!

2. The drunkard may boast of his full flowing
       bowl,
    The serpent coiled there may dart death
       through his soul;
Moderation may simper, and sip off his wine,
    His ale, or his porter, and call it divine;
Till feeling is blunted, and habit is formed—
    He falls, silly man, to a drunkard
       transformed.
But the spotless white banner of Temp'rance
       for me,
    That flutters aloft o'er the fair and the
       free.

3. Its conquests o'er poverty, mis'ry, and
       crime,
    Are felt and acknowledged in every clime;
And thousands proclaim to a wondering
    world,
    The triumphs achieved since it first was
       unfurled
By our own great Matthew 'twas raised in a
       day,
    The sons of "old Erin" submit to its sway.
Then the spotless white banner of
       Temp'rance for me.
    And long may it wave o'er the happy and
       free.[97]

Prohibition Will Triumph
(Wm. B. Marsh)

1. Hark! the war-dogs are howling, and the
       tempest rolls high;
    The lightning's bright flashes shed a glare
       'neath the sky;
While the foam-crested waves lash in fury our
       shore,
    As though, roused to madness, they
       predicted the battle.
And the young screaming eaglets, their broad
       pinions shake,
    Are screeching our war cry, wide-awake,
       wide-awake.
The day of deliverance is fast drawing nigh,
    Prohibition will triumph and the tempter
       must die.

2. Hark! the call of the bugle, ringing clear
       on the blast,
    Prohibition's bright ensign flutters out
       from the mast;
While gathering around it, all defiantly stand
    A grand temperance army, prohibitionist
       soldiers.
They swear to defend it, a band true and
       brave,
    Will conquer or perish, Columbia to save.
Our sisters, God bless them, have showed us
       the way,
    Prohibition will triumph, and rum must
       obey.

3. Then fall back dishonored, relinquish thy
       stand,
    No monster so hellish can rule our fair
       land;
Our forefathers fell on the land, on the sea,
    And left us this country, undivided
       forever.
In peace we are gentle, but, as in times
       before,
    We can shake hands in friendship, or
       fight you in war.
We're proud of our country, its triumphs and
       gain,

97. Mowatt, *Mowatt's Temperance Glee*, 6.

It can't be dishonored by rum's filthy stain.[98]

Prohibition's Banner
(Samuel Jarden)

1. Oh can you not see, by the signs all
    around!
    That a great reformation o'er our
    Country is dawning;
Maine struck the first chord, Kansas catches
    the sound,
    Iowa joins in the chorus and sends forth
    this warning,
The engine's fired up, get off the track,
    The cars are in motion, and we'll never
    turn back,
Till Prohibition's Banner in triumph shall
    wave
    O'er the land of the free, and the home
    of the brave.

2. Stop! stop! cries the Croaker, it would suit
    best the occasion,
    To leave license alone, and to use moral
    suasion;
The answer comes back, we have tried that
    and failed,
    For rum, with its license, all our converts
    assailed,
So jump on the train, or get out of the way,
    For rum, and its votaries, have too long
    held sway,
For Prohibition's Banner, we're determined
    shall wave,
    O'er the land of the free, and the home
    of the brave.

3. Here, good men of all parties, can gladly
    combine,
    And unite, heart and hand, to fight it out
    on this line,
To all such, we say, come, jump on our train,
    We will bear you in triumph from Texas
    to Maine;
But to Bosses, and Henchmen, and to
    trimmers we say,

You have failed us too long, so get out of
    the way,
Your machine is broke down, you must get
    off the track,
    Be ye Republican, Green backer, or
    Democrat;
For Prohibition's Banner, we proclaim it
    again,
    Shall be carried in triumph from Texas to
    Maine.[99]

The Temperance Banner #2
Mary E. Parker

1. Oh, say, can you see by the dawn's early
    light
    What so long we have hoped for with
    hearts sorely aching
The swift flash of the sword that will fall in
    its might,
    The power of King Alcohol evermore
    breaking?
Nay, the Wine-god's red glare and the
    drunkard's wild prayer
    Give proof through the night that the
    curse is still there.
Oh, say, does the Star Spangled Banner now
    wave
    O'er a land of the free and the home of
    the brave!

2. Now the Truth's dimly seen through the
    smoke of the fray,
    Advancing unharmed where the dread foe
    reposes,
With a sling and a stone the huge giant she'll
    slay,
    Though a demon-forged armor his body
    encloses.
Oh the people will shout when his life-blood
    ebbs out,
    And a million rum slaves will join in the
    rout;
When the Star Spangled Banner in triumph
    doth wave,
    O'er the land of the free and the home of
    the brave?

98. Perine and Mash, *National Prohibition Hymnal*, 49.
99. Jarden, *Prohibition Banner*, 3–4.

3. Then where'll be that band who so
    vauntingly swore,
    'Mid the havoc of rum and the traffic's
    confusion,
The homes and the country they'd curse
    evermore?
    Our votes shall wash out their foul
    footsteps' pollution;
No refuge will save Rumsellers who gave
    So much anguish to hearts they have sent
    to the grave;
Oh, the Star Spangled Banner, long may it wave
    O'er the land of the free and the home of
    the brave!

4. Oh, thus be it ever when freemen shall
    stand
    Between their loved homes and foul
    rum's desolation.
Blest with Temp'rance and peace, may our
    heav'n rescued
    Praise the Power that made and preserved
    us a nation.
And conquer we must, for our cause it is just
    And this be our motto: "In God is our
    trust."
And the Star Spangled Banner in triumph
    shall wave
    While the land of the free is the home of
    the brave.[100]

Prohibition Banner
(T. J. Merryman)

1. Oh, say! can you see, there ariseth a light,
    To banish the darkness and gloom of the
    night,
That has curtained with shrouds all this land
    of the brave,
    And consigned our fair sons to the
    drunkard's dark grave?
And the heart-broken mothers, from sorrow
    and grief
    Have in vain sought for comfort, or asked
    for relief.
Oh, say! shall the Star Spangled Banner soon
    wave

O'er the sober and free, where no drink
    can enslave.

2. The demon of drink has encompassed all
    lands.
    And captured its victims, and bound
    them with bands,
Till its slaves without number are chained to
    its wheels
    And are pleading for rescue with pitiful
    peals;
For no bondsman nor surf has a service so
    low,
    As the slave to his cups, who no pleasure
    can know.
Oh, say! shall the Star Spangled Banner, *etc.*

3. The prayer of the fallen ascendeth on high,
    And the hosts of God's people are now
    drawing nigh,
To o'erthrow this vile monster, and loose all
    the chains,
    Of the victims he curses, till not one
    remains;
For these victims are husbands and brothers
    and sons,
    And are highly esteemed by their own
    loving ones.
Oh, say! shall the Star Spangled Banner, *etc.*

4. From hamlet and mansion the edict has
    come,
    That the use of strong drink is destructive
    to home;
And this curse of all nations and foe of
    mankind,
    Shall no longer continue our loved ones
    to bind;
For "the land of the free and the home of the
    brave,"
    Will no longer give license its sons to
    enslave.
And then shall the Star Spangled Banner e'er
    wave,
    O'er the sober and free, where no drink
    can enslave.[101]

100. Silver Lake Quartette, *Prohibition Bells and Songs of the New Crusade*, 85. Miller, *Patriotic No-License*, no. 19, makes some minor changes in the final lines of each verse.
    101. T. J. Merryman, *Amendment Songs Set to Familiar Tunes*, no. 1.

The White Ribbon Star-Spangled Banner
(Kate Lunden Sunderlin)

1. Fling it out to the breeze; let it tell to the
world,
   That the faith which has raised it will
never surrender;
Let it tell that the love which our banner
unfurled,
   Is the guard of the home, and the nation's
defender.
Let it gleam as a star, for the shipwrecked
afar,
   Like a beacon that warns of the
treacherous bar;
Let the banner of freedom and purity wave
   Like a signal of hope 'midst the perils we
brave.

2. Hold that banner aloft, let our colors be
seen
   From Siberian snowfields to African
valleys;
Lift it up for the truth; let the rays of its
sheen
   Drive the shadow of night from the
byways and alleys.
Let it tell to the lost that we count not the
cost,
   That our bridges are burned and our
Rubicon crossed;
That the banner of mother-love ever shall
wave
   Till the paths are made straight for the
sin-burdened slave.

3. Let it fly at the front; it is washed in our
tears,
   And the smoke of the battle increases its
whiteness;
Though our hearts may be pierced by the
enemy's spears,
   Yet the flow from our wounds shall but
add to its brightness.
And this ensign of light, it shall float o'er the
fight,
   Till our wrongs are avenged by the
triumph of right;

And in radiant victory at last it shall wave
   O'er the ramparts we've stormed, o'er
King Alcohol's grave.

4. Swing it out from the staff, let it shadow
the ground
   Where the fathers of liberty sleep 'neath
the mosses;
Run it up o'er the homes where the mothers
are found,
   Who through watches of anguish are
counting their losses.
In the tear-moistened sod that our martyrs
have trod,
   We are planting it deep for our Land and
our God,
And this banner of world-circling love e'er
shall wave
In the name of our Christ who is mighty to
save.[102]

Hail to the Chief

[Hail to the Day]

1. Hail to the day that arises in splendor,
   Let freemen rejoice for that day is at
hand,
The foul demon is banished, and has no
defender,
   And Temperance reigns all over our land.
Heaven bless our noble cause, protected by
our nation's laws,
   We will rear a fair temple of fame to thy
sky;
And write on its base that time can't deface:
   This is Liberty's altar, and for it we'll die.

2. Ours is no cause that sprang up from
scission,
   Its truth is as plain as a fountain of light,
And so just that the base dare not offer
derision,
   As onward it moves and takes its bold
flight.
Then let us rejoice with a thundering voice,
   And spread the glad tidings of liberty far,

---

102. Anna A. Gordon, *The Temperance Songster*, no. 15; Gordon, *Popular Campaign*, 30; *Red White and Blue Songster*, 25; Anna A. Gordon, *Jubilee Songs*, 15.

Our banners unfurled, we'll conquer the
world,
    And place in the Heavens our temperance
    star.[103]

Hail to the Cause

1. Hail to the cause that in triumph
advances,
    Pledged from our country Intemperance
    to drive;
Long may the joy that in thousand eyes
glances,
    Cheer all its triumphs and keep it alive!
Heaven send it happy dew, men lend it aide
anew,
    Suasion and kindness, its motto, still
    wave,—
Till ev'ry mount side, ev'ry plain and valley
wide,
    (*shout*) "Washingtonians, onward and
    save!"

2. Plead, brethren, plead for the drunkard in
blindness,
    Leaves yet his family to woe, shame and
    pain;
Redouble your labors of love and of
kindness—
    Give them their husband and father
    again!
Swift be your efforts now, gently stoop and
raise the low—
    Clothe them and feed them and snatch
    from the grave!
Press again the warm appeal, cause their
long-numbed hearts to feel;
    On, Washingtonians, rescue and save!

3. Rouse thee—Oh, rouse thee! too long hast
thou slumbered;
    Slave to your beer, ale, cider, or wine—
Rouse thee! or soon all your hopes will be
numbered,
    Mis'ry, and ruin, and shame will be thine!
Hear your father's fervent prayer, see your
mother's wild despair—

Wake from delusions, be no longer a
slave!
Friends and brothers all unite. Wife and
sisters both invite.
    Turn "Washingtonian," and rescue and
    save!

4. Ours is a cause that will never deceive you,
    All it doth promise is certain and true;
Pledged to cold water, it soon will relieve you,
    Health is in waiting and happiness too!
Join, then, heart and hand, In the total
abst'nence band—
    Freely dispense what as freely it gave;
And be your battle-cry, Of onset and victory,
    "On, Washingtonians, rescue and
    save!"[104]

The Temperance Tree

1. Hail to our cause which in triumph
advances,
    Honoured and blest be the Washington
    band;
They planted a tree, in you banner it glances,
    O! long may it flourish, the pride of our
    land!
Honoured and blest be the Washington
band;
    They planted a tree, in you banner it
    glances,
O! long may it flourish, the pride of our land!
    Heaven send it happy dew,
Earth lend it sap anew,
    Gaily to branch out, and broadly to grow,
While every hill and glen,
    Sends the shout back again
    Our temperance tree, then, *dhu ho ieroe.*

2. Ours was a sapling, reared by a full
fountain,
    Not blooming in summer, in winter to
    fade.
When the whirlwind has stripped every leaf
from the mountain,
    The more shall our brave band exult in its
    shade:
Ours was a sapling, *etc.*

---

103. Bigelow and Grosh, *Washingtonian Pocket*, 71. This version uses only the tune's verse.
104. Ibid., 81. This version uses only the tune's verse.

Moored in the rifted rock,
Proof to the tempest's shock
  Intemperance gales in tornadoes may
  blow,
Washington men, then,
  Echo its praise again,
  Our temperance tree, then, *dhu ho ieroe.*

3. In Baltimore nobly our *monument* rises,
  The noise of an army, hark, hark, from
  the west,
New York too, and Boston, are stopping
  before us,
  In Pittsburgh we number her bravest and
  best.
In Baltimore nobly, *etc.*
  Widow and blooming maid,
Long, long shall bless our aid,
  Smile away tears shed in fear and in woe,
Soon shall each western glen,
  Send the shout back again,
  Our temperance tree, then, *dhu ho ieroe.*

4. Come, come, sign our pledge, and march
  under our banners,
  Join heart and hand with the Washington
  band;
O, that each man were a thousand in
  number,
  How soon would we take, for we must
  take, the land.
Come, come, sign our pledge, *etc.*
  Auxiliary *branches*, then,
Worthy such noble stem,
  Thousands and strong in its shadow
  might grow,
While every hill and glen,
  Sent our shout back again,
  Our temperance tree, then, *dhu
  ho ieroe.* 105

Hail to the Men!

1. Hail to the men who are proudly
  advancing,
  Cheered by the sound of our
  Washington's name.

Joy sparkles bright from the eyes on them
  glancing,
  Glows in each bosom a patriot flame.
Hail to the men who are proudly advancing,
  Cheered by the sound of our
  Washington's name,
Joy sparkles bright from the eyes on them
  glancing,
  Glows in each bosom a patriot flame.
See! how their banners wave,
  Borne by the young and brave!
Holy and just is the war that we wage;
  Hark! from the distant hills
How the sweet music thrills!
  Surely they'll conquer when thus they
  engage.

2. Come, brothers come, let us marshal our
  forces,
  Gaily our banners we spread to the
  breeze;
Proudly the blood through our veins quickly
  courses,
  Why should we falter with feelings like
  these?
Come, brothers come, let us, *etc.*
  When 'tis to save the lost,
Why should we fear the cost?
  Spurning all danger, we'll boldly march
  on;
Come to the conflict then,
  Strangers and countrymen!
  Join in our watchword, and shout
  WASHINGTON! 106

To General T. D. Bonner
(O. Whittlesey)

1. Hail! to the cause we unite in supporting,
  Shoulder to shoulder, be ready and firm;
Honor and fame are yours, for promoting
  The watch-fire of freedom, that dimly did
  burn.
Stand by your banner, men,
  Let the shout ring again,
The tyrant is conquered, Columbia is free.
  Stand by your banner, men,

105. *Washington Temperance*, 26–27.
106. Dana, *Temperance Lyre*, 20–24.

Let the shout ring again,
> The tyrant is conquered, Columbia is
> free.

2. Hail! to the HERO who makes the press
> thunder—
Hurling defiance at alcohol's king;
His subjects deserting—he shaking with
> wonder,
> O'er mountain and valley our tocsin doth
> ring.
Charge! charge! ye gallant men,
> Drive from his dismal den,
The monster, King Alki', who would you
> enslave,
> Charge! charge! ye gallant men, *etc.*

3. On! champion, on! the victory's before
> you,
> The struggle will weave you bright laurels
> of fame,
The God of our army will ever watch o'er
> you,
> Go! conquer and save, in great
> Washington's name.
Mothers and orphans save,
> See! see! our banners wave;
Beyond this dark world, is the Champion's
> reward.
> Mothers and orphans save, *etc.* 107

Come to the Meeting

1. Hark—hark! the shout of the working-man
> Rings in the welkin, swells on the breeze;
Haste, haste, wait not till the work's began,
> Which shall send freedom the slave to
> release.
Ardor is growing—friendship is glowing,
> Spreading the welcome of joy all around,
Gen'rous mirth fills the air, banishing grief
> and care
> Gladdening drooping hearts with its gay
> sound.

2. Long, long has the foulest oppression been
> Crushing the masses, filching their toil;
Long, long has the fury of passion seen

Myriads of victims involved in its coil.
Give but the rum around, misery will soon
> abound,
> Virtue defacing, laughing to scorn
Kind-hearted father's sighs, fond mother's
> weeping eyes,
> Dark'ning the hour when her dearest was
> born.

3. Come, come to the greatest of meetings,
> Held by brave men whose hearts have
> been rung,
Come, come, list their fond greetings,
> Soon shall the dirge of the rum fiend be
> sung.
Stern independence there shall sterling truth
> declare
> Reckless of aught but the good it can do;
Hear the brave working-man tell of the better
> plan,
> How you may vice disarm—virtue renew.

4. Come from the shed where the furnace is
> glowing,
> Where labor and fire are scorching the
> brow;
Come from the anvils where anchors are
> growing,
> Extending their limbs 'neath the teetotal
> vow.
Show them your brawny arms free from the
> drunkard's charms,
> Tell them how healthy, how happy they'll
> be;
Dash down the poison cup, raise the pure
> water up,
> That is the grog for all nature and me.

5. Come from the shop where the wan child
> is toiling,
> Come from the home of the shuttle and
> loom;
Come from the graves where the chemist is
> boiling,
> Poisonous vapors from earth's hidden
> gloom.
Come from the miner's cave, many a true
> heart's grave,

107. Bonner, *Mountain Minstrel,* 79–80.

Come from the giant steam factory's
chain;
Tell your poor countrymen, echo the shout
again,
Ye are teetotalers, and still will remain.

6. Long were we taught that drinking was
food for us,
Folly and passion led us astray;
Now we have found out a charm which is
good for us,
Strewing with blessings our path every
day.
Melting soft hearts which were hardened by
grief and care,
Giving fresh hope to the weary and faint,
Swelling again the stream of past love's happy
dream,
Waking soft mem'ries to banish
complaint.108

Rally, Men Rally!

(Anthony B. McKeenan, adapted by
J. G. Lawson)

1. Rally, men rally! the morning is breaking,
Slowly the long night of terror has passed;
Millions in bondage from slumber awak'ning
Hail the bright dawn of our freedom at
last.
Rally, men, rally! the morning is breaking.
Slowly the long night of terror has passed;
Millions in bondage from slumber awak'ning,
Hail the bright dawn of our freedom at
last.

Chorus
Young men and old men, strong men and
bold men,
Prepare ye for temp'rance good services to
do;
In danger or war's alarm guard her from ev'ry
harm,
Hurrah! for our country, the home of the
true.

2. Bright shine the hopes we for centuries
cherished

To free our country from alcohol's stain;
Discord, once rife in our ranks, now has
perished—
All are united our rights to maintain.
Bright shine the hopes, *etc. To Chorus*

3. Bravely our forefathers struggled to sever
Chains forged to bind them—the
manacles vile,
We, their true children, renew the endeavor,
With hope wafting to us her kindliest
smile.
Bravely our forefathers, *etc. To Chorus*109

Columbia, the Gem of the Ocean

Love, Purity, and Fidelity

1. O, Temp'rance! bright star of Life's ocean,
Thou art setting thy glad thousands free,
From Alcohol's raging commotion,
And true hearts give homage to thee.
Thy mandates make warriors assemble
When Rum's fearful curse stands in view,
Thy banners make Alcohol tremble,
When borne by the Red, White, and
Blue.
When borne by the Red, White, and Blue,
When borne by the Red, White, and
Blue,
Thy banners make Alcohol tremble,
When borne by the Red, White and Blue.

2. Where Rum sends its fierce desolation
Brave hearts, and sweet homes to deform,
Our Orders, the drunkard's salvation,
In triumph opposes the storm;
With garlands of victory streaming
She presses to conquer anew,
While hearts throb, and bright eyes are
beaming,
The pride of the Red White, and Blue.
etc.

3. Then our flag, sisters, brothers, bring
hither,

108. M'Kechnie, *Lyre of Temperance*, 34–36.
109. W. E. Biederwolf and J. Gilchrist Lawson, *Best Temperance Songs*, no. 6.

Its proud motto gives to the sun;
May our faith in the cause never wither,
    Nor faint till the vict'ry is won.
May Purity, Fidelity, Love ever
    Inspire us our pledge to renew,—
Our glorious order forever,
    Three cheers for the Red, White, and
        Blue. *etc.*[110]

Our Ribbon of Blue

(Frank C. Filley)

1. Oh the Gospel Temperance Cause is in
        motion,
    And spreading o'er land and the sea,
'Tis a work full of love and devotion,
    Each slave of the cup we'll set free.
No more shall the tempter ensnare them,
    His vile stuff from our land we'll pursue,
Oh, God bless this grand temperance
        movement,
    Three cheers for our Ribbon of Blue.
Three cheers for our Ribbon of Blue.
    Three cheers for our Ribbon of Blue.
Oh, God bless this grand temperance
        movement,
    Three cheers for our Ribbon of Blue.

2. While Rum spreads its wide desolation,
    It threatens our land to deform,
But the Ark of our Organization
    Will safely ride over the storm.
With the garlands of Temperance above her,
    To victory she'll carry her brave crew,
Alcohol we will drive from our country,
    By the help of our Ribbon of Blue.
Three cheers for our Ribbon of Blue, *etc.*

3. Oh, a cup of cold water bring hither,
    And fill ye the glass to the brim,
May the Gospel Temperance movement ne'er
        wither,
    Or the star of our cause e'er grow dim.
May our Ribbon Brigade ne'er sever,
    But stand to our colors so true.

Oh, the Gospel Temperance movement
        forever,
    Three cheers for our Ribbon of Blue.
Three cheers for our Ribbon of Blue, *etc.*[111]

The Ribbon of Blue

1. The Temp'rance wave is far-spreading,
    And rolling all over the land;
The people in might are uprising
    To help us with heart and with hand.
We're seeking to raise the down-trodden,
    To make them both sober and true;
Then rally around our fair banner,
    And wear the bright ribbon of blue.

Chorus
Three cheers for the ribbon of blue,
    Hurrah for the ribbon of blue;
We'll ever be singing and praying
    God bless the bright ribbon of blue.

2. Oh, Temp'rance! bright star of life's ocean.
    Thou'rt setting thy glad thousands free
From Alcohol's raging commotion,
    And true hearts give homage to thee.
Thy mandates make warriors assemble,
    When Rum's fearful curse stands in view;
Thy banners make Alcohol tremble,
    Three cheers for the ribbon of blue.
        To Chorus

3. Oh, think of the homes that are happy,
    Of hearts that are gladdened today;
Of mothers and sisters rejoicing,
    Of friends that we love, far away,
Because that our young men and women,
    With purpose so high and so true,
Are pledged to stop drinking forever,
    And wear the bright ribbon of blue.
        To Chorus[112]

The Hope of the Nation

1. O Temperance! the hope of the nation,
    The ark of our safety and power,

---

110. Bradbury and Stearns, *Temperance Chimes* (1867 and 1878), 126. Stearns, *National Temperance*, 42, omits verse 3.

111. Frank C. Filley, *Red, White, and Blue Ribbon Gospel Temperance Songster*, 5–6.

112. Stearns, *National Temperance*, 46.

The anchor of manhood's salvation,
　　The issue supreme at this hour.
At thy summons true heroes assemble,
　　The brave ones who dare for the right,
While the foes of humanity tremble,
　　When thy squadrons are set for the fight.
When thy squadrons are set for the fight,
　　When thy squadrons are set for the fight,
While the foes of humanity tremble,
　　When thy squadrons are set for the fight.

2. Then banish the wine cup forever,
　　The serpent of death lurks within,
The hand of a woman shall never
　　Again tempt a brother to sin.
The conquering heroes are coming,
　　They are coming from near and afar,
And a glorious future is dawning
　　From the light of our Temperance star.
From the light of our Temperance star,
　　From the light of our Temperance star,
And a glorious future is dawning
　　From the light of our Temperance star.

3. Our cause spreads from ocean to ocean,
　　The hope of the brave and the free,
Thy shrine woos each true man's devotion
　　And woman waits, praying for thee.
Cold water, cold water, bring hither
　　And fill every cup to the brim,
For the laurels we've won shall ne'er wither
　　Nor the star of our legion grow dim.
Nor the star of our legion grow dim,
　　Nor the star of our legion grow dim,
For the laurels we've won shall ne'er wither
　　Nor the stars of our legion grow dim.

[Repeat Chorus] Three cheers for the cold
　　water Boys!
　　Three cheers for the cold water Boys!
Pure water, pure water for ever!
　　Three cheers for the cold water Boys![113]

We Will Amend Our State Constitution
(Samuel Jarden)

1. Up! up! with the Prohibition Banner,
　　To the breeze let it gaily now float;

We will rally around it till victory
　　O'er license, is determined by vote,
All around us the hosts are advancing,
　　How anxious and eager are they;
Their noble steeds dancing and prancing,
　　Impatient to join in the fray.
Three cheers for our glorious cause,
　　Three cheers for our glorious cause;
We'll amend our own State Constitution,
　　And abolish all rum license laws.

2. Alcohol shall no longer reign o'er us,
　　Though his minions like demons may
　　　fight;
Press on then the victory's before us,
　　God will help those who battle for right.
The ballot is Prohibition's sword,
　　A weapon all freemen can wield;
We will vote, work and trust in the Lord,
　　And we will not retire from the field.
But will fight in the glorious cause,
　　We will fight in this glorious cause;
We'll amend our State Constitution,
　　And abolish all rum license laws.[114]

Vote Down the Vile Traffic

1. Rum-license, thou curse of the nation!
　　Destroyer of body and soul!
Down, down with thy cursed vocation,
　　The ballot thy death-knell shall toll!
The vile dens of liquor are scattered
　　By law, from the home to the grave;
And life-hopes the fairest are shattered,
　　A crime-license party to save.

Chorus

Three cheers for the downfall of rum!
　　Three cheers for the downfall of rum!
We'll vote down its traffic forever!
　　Three cheers for the downfall of rum!

2. Our homes are demanding protection,
　　From drink and its numberless woes,
That shock us in ev'ry direction,
　　Where liquor with demon-step goes!
Our children a price we are paying,
　　For blood-money coined from the still;

113. Daniels, *Temperance Songster*, 16–18.
114. Jarden, *Prohibition Banner*, 24–25.

While license with pitiless slaying,
    Drops gold in the rum-seller's till!
      To Chorus

3. Alas! for our hollow professions—
    With revenue gathered from drink!
Upholding its monstrous oppressions—
    'Tis horrible even to think!
On liquor-bound party still doting,
    Yet praying—"Thy kingdom to come!"
It will not agree with your voting
    For party that licenses rum. *To Chorus*

4. Columbia, shall the foul demon,
    Of rum, blight thy mighty domain?
Shall millions who boast themselves freemen,
    Be slaves that such tyrant may reign?
Lead on, Prohibition, to battle!
    Our ballots in face of the foe,
More deadly than bullets shall rattle,
    'Till down the rum slav'ry shall go.
      To Chorus [115]

A Band of Hope Pledge Song

1. Away with your beer and your whiskey,
    Away with your cider and ale;
God gives us a drink that is better
    Than any you offer for sale.
It strengthens the ox in his labor,
    The horse as he speeds in the race;
The bird as he heavenward flieth
    Remembers the bright water's place.

Chorus
Three cheers for the water so pure!
    Three cheers for the water so pure!
No drink is so good as cold water,
    Three cheers for the water so pure!

2. Then give me the clear-flowing water
    That bursts from our own rocky hills,
That sweeps to the sea in the river,
    And laughs in the bright little rills.
'Tis the drink that never makes drunkards;
    'Tis the cup that never makes sad;
The friend and the help of the toiler—

It makes ev'ry humble home glad.
    To Chorus [116]

In This Land of the Red, White, and Blue

1. O Columbia! the gem of the ocean,
    The home of the brave and the free,
The shrine of each patriot's devotion,
    A world offers homage to thee.
Thy mandates make heroes assemble,
    When Liberty's form stands in view,
But never let Rum be the victor
    In this land of the red, white, and blue!
In this land of the red, white, and blue,
    In this land of the red, white, and blue,
But never let Rum be the victor
    In this land of the red, white, and blue!

2. While rum spreads its wide desolation,
    And threatens the land to deform,
We'll stand on a Temp'rance foundation,
    Unshaken we'll stand through the storm;
With garlands of vict'ry around her,
    While she smiles on the loyal and true,
Brave Temp'rance will yet be the victor
    In this land of the red, white, and blue!
      etc.

3. The clear crystal water bring hither,
    And fill your glass to the brim!
May the wreaths we have won never wither,
    Nor the star of our glory grow dim!
May our service united ne'er sever,
    But we to our pledges prove true!
Cold water and Temp'rance forever
    In this land of the red, white, and blue!
      etc. [117]

The Home Guard
(Kate Lunden Sunderlin)

1. Who will stand for the homes of our
    nation,
    The homes that were built by the brave?
Who will save them from Rum's desolation,
    And dig for the tyrant a grave?
Who will sweep from the folds of Old Glory

115. Durant, *Prohibition Home*, 31–32.
116. Stearns, *Band of Hope*, 63.
117. Macy, *Temperance Song-Herald*, 32–34.

The clouds which are dark'ning its stars?
Who will blot from our world-honored story
    The word which its pages now mar?
Who will stand for the red, white, and blue,—
    Our star-spangled red, white, and blue?
Who will sweep from the folds of Old Glory
    The clouds which now hang o'er its blue?

2. We are coming, the scions of heroes,
    To prove that they died not in vain;
And we challenge the sin-hardened Neros
    Who play o'er the graves of the slain.
Away with the laws of protection
    Which shelter their infamous trade!
We are coming to show by our action
    The strength of the vows we have made.
We will stand for the red, white, and blue,—
    Our star-spangled red, white, and blue;
We will sweep from the folds of Old Glory
    The clouds which now hang o'er its blue.

3. We're the Home Guard that never
        surrenders,
    The Legions of honor and truth;
We're Columbia's Loyal Defenders
    Who have pledged her our unspotted
        youth.
For God, who is marching before us,
    For Home, whose protectors we are,
For the glorious Country that bore us,
    We've enlisted for life in this war.
We'll unfurl the red, white, and blue,—
    Our star-spangled red, white, and blue—
And we'll sweep from the folds of Old Glory
    The clouds which now hang o'er its
        blue.[118]

Anti-Saloon Battle Hymn

(G. W. Dungan)

1. The mighty are gath'ring for conflict;
    The right is arrayed against wrong;
The hosts of the righteous are singing,
    And this is the voice of their song:

Chorus
The Saloon, it must go! Do you hear us?
    Repeat it again and again.
They strive to make millions of money;
    We strive to save millions of men!
We strive to save millions of men,
    We strive to save millions of men.
They strive to make millions of money;
    We strive to save millions of men!

2. The curse of the traffic, how awful!
    No language can tell it; and then,
It makes millions of widows and orphans,
    And drunkards of millions of men.
        To Chorus

3. The prison it crowds with its victims;
    Asylums are filled with its woes;
It curses and blights ev'ry being
    As far as its influence goes. *To Chorus*

4. This awful, unspeakable monster,
    Must be banished from out our bright
        land.
From its shackles, O God, do Thou free us!
    And for Freedom we ever will stand.
        To Chorus[119]

118. Gordon, *Temperance Songster*, no. 25.
119. Dungan et al., *Acorn Temperance*, no. 4.

3. Hymns

Temperance reformers borrowed a number of hymn tunes in the nineteenth and early twentieth centuries. Even the Washingtonians, a largely secular temperance organization, included hymns in their songbooks. During the women's movement of the 1860s and 1870s, crusaders sang secular temperance songs at social gatherings and in their homes, but they particularly favored hymns, gospel tunes, and camp meeting songs along with prayers to inspire them during their crusades. They also believed that hymns would help to convert the saloonkeepers and their patrons to abstinence and Christianity. Gospel hymns were particularly empowering to women. Although they couldn't vote and were not allowed to preach in most churches, women could employ gospel hymns as a public voice for their beliefs without the aid of men.[1]

Since hymns were such a critical part of the temperance movement, it isn't surprising that temperance poets also wrote new verses to some of the best-known sacred songs. Traditional hymn tunes borrowed from Europe, such as "Old Hundred" and "Coronation," were first used beginning in the 1830s and 1840s along with tunes by American composers Lowell Mason, George Webb, and others. After the Civil War, gospel hymns began to appear on the scene as a reaction to the staid hymns of mainline churches. Although criticized by some as overly sentimental, gospel hymns such as "Bringing in the Sheaves," "Hold the Fort," and "Sweet By and By" were enthusiastically received as songs for revivals and social use.[2]

1. Stecker, "Respectable Revolution," 36–38.
2. Henry Wilder Foote, *Three Centuries of American Hymnody*, 263–71.

Doxology

The tune for the "Doxology," "Old Hundred," first appeared in Louis Bourgeois's *Genevan Psalter* of 1551, and the tune is often attributed to him. Many texts have been set to this familiar hymn tune, but the tune is named because of its use of a setting of Psalm 100 in the *Ainsworth Psalter* of 1612, which the Pilgrims brought to the New World in 1620. It was a preferred tune among the colonists and was included along with eleven other tunes in the 1698 edition of the *Bay Psalm Book*. The most familiar text for this tune is Thomas Ken's "Doxology." Like Henry's "Temperance Doxology" and the selection of the same name from Biederwolf's collection, many temperance writers borrowed this text with only minor alterations.[3]

Temperance Doxology
(S. M. I. Henry)

> Praise God from whom all blessings flow;
> Praise Him who heals the drunkard's woe;
> Praise Him who leads the temp'rance host;
> Praise Father, Son and Holy Ghost.[4]

Temperance Doxology

> Praise God, from whom all blessings flow,
> Praise Him who saves from sin and woe,
> The King who leads the temp'rance host;
> Praise Father, Son and Holy Ghost.[5]

Like the previous examples (and most other settings of this tune), the earliest known temperance setting, located at the Library of Congress, also carries strong religious overtones. Mrs. L. H. Sigourney's lyrics first appeared in a broadside, dated 1836.

3. Gilbert Chase, *America's Music: From the Pilgrims to the Present*, 7; Dallin and Dallin, *Heritage Songster*, 249; Maurice Frost, ed., *Historical Companion to Hymns Ancient and Modern*, 233; Spaeth, *History of Popular Music*, 21–22.

4. Anna A. Gordon, *Marching Songs for Young Crusaders*, 61. See also Silver Lake Quartette, *Prohibition Bells*, 87; Merryman, *Amendment Songs*, no. 19; Gordon, *Songs of the Young Woman's*, 93; and Cassel, *White Ribbon*, no. 115. Gordon, *Temperance Songster*, no. 88, and *Anti-Saloon Campaign*, no. 58, change the second line to "Praise him who saves from deepest woe."

5. Biederwolf and Lawson, *Best Temperance Songs*, no. 36.

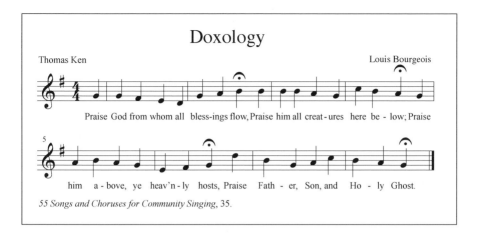

Doxology

Thomas Ken

Louis Bourgeois

Praise God from whom all bless-ings flow, Praise him all creat-ures here be - low; Praise

him a - bove, ye heav'n - ly hosts, Praise Fath - er, Son, and Ho - ly Ghost.

55 Songs and Choruses for Community Singing, 35.

[We Praise Thee]
(Mrs. L. H. Sigourney)

 1. We praise thee,—if one rescued soul,
  While the past year prolonged its flight,
 Turned shuddering from the poisonous bowl,
  To health, and liberty, and light.

 2. We praise thee,—if one clouded home,
  Where broken hearts despairing pined,
 Beheld the Sire and Husband come,
  Erect, and in his perfect mind.

 3. No more a weeping wife to mock,
  Till all her hopes in anguish end—
 No more the trembling child to shock,
  And sink the father in the fiend.

 4. Still give us grace, Almighty King!
  Unwavering at our posts to stand;
 Till grateful at thy shrine we bring
  The tribute of a ransomed land.

 5. Which from the pestilential chain
  Of foul intemperance, gladly free,
 Shall spread an annal, free from stain,
  To all the nations, and to Thee.[6]

6. *Collection of Temperance Songs,* front side.

All Hail the Power of Jesus' Name

"All Hail the Power of Jesus' Name" was one of the most beloved early hymns among temperance reformers. Oliver Holden composed the tune, "Coronation," which was first published with Edward Perronet's lyrics in *The Union Harmony or Universal Collection of Sacred Music* in 1793. According to Henry Wilder Foote, this tune is the earliest American hymn still in general use. Among the suasionist settings of this tune, many refer to the benefits of abstinence. "All Hail the Power of Abstinence" was by far the most popular of these settings, appearing in five collections in the 1840s with only minor alterations.[7]

All Hail the Power of Abstinence

1. All hail the power of Abstinence!
   Let drunkards prostrate fall!
Bring forth the Washingtonian Pledge,
   And let us sign it all.
Bring forth the Washingtonian Pledge,
   And let us sign it all.

2. Ye brandy drinkers ne'er forget
   There's poison in the cup;
'Twill taint your sweetest springs of life,
   And on your vitals sup, *etc.*

3. Save, you who love the temperance cause,
   The tippler from his fate;
Now is the time to stop his course,
   Before it is too late, *etc.*

4. O, save them from so dread an end;
   'Tis duty to your God!
And in the rescued drunkard's thanks
   You'll find a sure reward, *etc.*

5. Strive on! our power at last will part
   The drunkard from his bane;
'Twill overcome the hydra's strength,
   Till all his heads are slain, *etc.*

6. Then for the monster's ruthless foot
   No resting-place is found;
His magic spell no more shall slay,
   But be forever bound, *etc.*

7. Foote, *Three Centuries*, 122; Rodeheaver, *Hymnal Handbook*, 44–45.

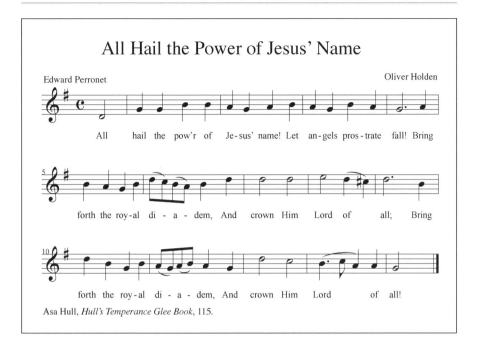

All Hail the Power of Jesus' Name

Edward Perronet

Oliver Holden

All hail the pow'r of Je-sus' name! Let an-gels pros-trate fall! Bring

forth the roy-al di - a - dem, And crown Him Lord of all; Bring

forth the roy-al di - a - dem, And crown Him Lord of all!

Asa Hull, *Hull's Temperance Glee Book*, 115.

7. Yes! when we join the Temperance Pledge,
   The tyrant then must fall;
We'll shout with joy at his demise,
   And this shall be his pall, *etc.*[8]

Two settings present a popular personification of the alcohol problem. "King Alcohol," referring to the power of alcohol to rule people's lives, may have first been used by the famous singing Hutchison family when they contributed new temperance lyrics to the well-known song "King Oliver" in 1843.[9]

Dethrone King Alcohol!

1. Come friends of temperance, let us join
   Our efforts, one and all,
And our united powers combine
   To banish alcohol.
And our united powers combine
   To banish alcohol.

8. *Collection of Hymns and Songs*, 30–31. Plimpton, *Washingtonian Choir*, 55, makes changes in verses 6 and 7. Potter, *Boston Temperance*, 1:7, Bonner, *Mountain Minstrel*, 44, and Macy, *Temperance Song-Herald*, 82, make changes in verse 1 and omit verses 2 and 7.

9. Ewing, *Well-Tempered Lyre*, 100–101; Hamm, *Yesterdays*, 147.

2. Ye lovers of Humanity,
   Heed and obey the call—
Work on, until the world shall be
   Uncursed by alcohol. *etc.*

3. The sad and broken-hearted wives
   Whose tears of anguish fall,
Will give their efforts, prayers, and lives,
   To banish alcohol. *etc.*

4. The little children too, although
   They may be young and small,
Are not too weak to strike a blow
   Against King Alcohol. *etc.*

5. The victims who, in years gone by,
   Have groaned beneath his thrall,
Will join their strength with ours, and try
   To banish alcohol. *etc.*

6. A mighty multitude we stand,
   Determined, one and all,
To sweep forever from our land
   The curse of alcohol. *etc.*

7. O God of Love, who reigns on high,
   To Thee for help we call,
Dethrone and utterly destroy
   The tyrant Alcohol. *etc.* [10]

Gospel Temperance Rally Song
(Frank C. Filley)

1. God bless our Gospel Temperance band,
   Down with King Alcohol.
Come sign our pledge and pin our badge
   Upon the breast of all.
Come sign our pledge, and pin our badge
   Upon the breast of all.

2. God bless our good and glorious cause,
   That's going o'er our land.
God bless those noble ladies too,
   The Temperance praying band, *etc.*

3. Oh, prayer is mighty safe and sure,
   And never fails to save,

10. J. L. McCreery, *A Collection of Temperance Songs for Common Tunes*, 32–33.

'Twill save you from a life impure,
　　And from a drunkard's grave, *etc.*

4. Come everyone and sign our pledge,
　　Your life it will renew,
Pray God for help to keep it too
　　With our bright badge of Blue, *etc.*[11]

Watchman, Tell Us of the Night

"Watchman, Tell Us of the Night," with lyrics by Sir John Bowring and tune by the American music educator Lowell Mason, was also well known by temperance writers.[12] One early setting of "Watchman" serves as a welcome song for temperance meetings. It is assumed that two verses of text are combined to fit with the tune, and that verse 7 either repeats the music for the last four lines or stops at the midpoint of the song.

[Welcome, Brothers]

1. Welcome, brothers, welcome here!
　　Cheerful are our hearts today,
Tell us, we would gladly hear,
　　How our cause speeds on its way.

2. Brothers, we are glad to know
　　That your zeal doth not grow cold.
We no truce have given the foe,
　　Yet his step is firm and bold.

3. Brothers, have you then a doubt
　　How the contest is to end?
Though the Law has let him out
　　Still on God we may depend;

4. He will hear the sufferer's cry,
　　He will speed our cause along:
He will rescue those that die,
　　He will stay the drunkard's throng.

5. Brothers, then the foe shall fall
　　When we take our father's seats,
Here we pledge us one and all
　　We will drive him from our streets;

11. Filley, *Red, White, and Blue*, 15–16.
12. Frank J. Metcalf, *American Writers and Compilers of Sacred Music*, 211; Rodeheaver, *Hymnal Handbook*, 126.

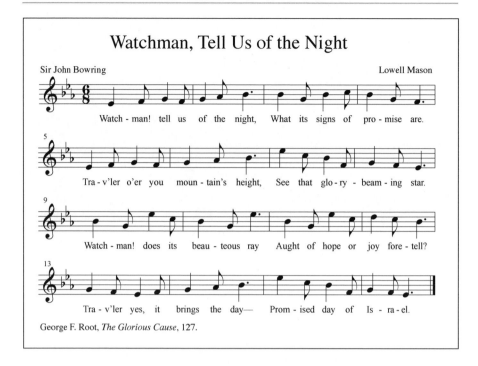

Watchman, Tell Us of the Night

Sir John Bowring

Lowell Mason

Watch - man! tell us of the night, What its signs of pro - mise are.

Tra - v'ler o'er you moun - tain's height, See that glo - ry - beam - ing star.

Watch - man! does its beau - teous ray Aught of hope or joy fore - tell?

Tra - v'ler yes, it brings the day— Prom - ised day of Is - ra - el.

George F. Root, *The Glorious Cause*, 127.

6. 'Tis on us the work depends,
   On the young and rising race;
   And we'll try to make amends
   For our country's deep disgrace.

7. Here we pledge ourselves anew,
   Not to touch the drunkard's drink;
   Proving faithful, proving true,
   We will make the demon shrink.[13]

"Welcome, Brothers" is another excellent example of shared lyrics among temperance writers. Later sources borrowed verses 1 and 7 of the previous welcome song to create the following verse.

[Friends of Temp'rance]

Friends of Temp'rance, welcome here,
   Cheerful are our hearts today;

13. *Collection of Temperance Songs*, front side. *Collection of Temperance Songs*, n.p. Bigelow and Grosh, *Washingtonian Pocket*, 75, is very similar, but the verses are sung alternately by girls or boys—sections sung by boys replace the word "Brothers" with "Sisters," and all sing verse 7. Pierpont, *Cold Water Melodies*, 53–54, presents verses 1, 2, 6, and 7 only.

Tell us—we would gladly hear—
  How our cause speeds on its way.
Here we pledge ourselves anew,
  Not to touch the drunkard's drink;
Proving faithful, proving true,
  We will from no duty shrink.[14]

Perkins and Stearns add the following second verse:

Come and aid us in the fight,
  Make our growing armies strong;
Joyfully with us unite,
  Swelling the triumphal song
Then the foe will swiftly fail,
  When we take our fathers' seats.
Here we pledge us one and all
  We will drive him from the streets.[15]

Stand Up, Stand Up for Jesus

After the Civil War, the most preferred hymn of temperance workers was "Stand Up, Stand Up for Jesus." George James Webb's tune and many of Rev. George Duffield's lyrics were adapted to at least fifteen temperance songs that appeared in more than thirty temperance collections. The original lyrics by Duffield were inspired by the dying words of Rev. Dudley Tyng of Philadelphia in 1858. Tyng, speaking about another important social cause—the abolition of slavery—reportedly encouraged listeners to "Stand up for Jesus." Webb's familiar tune, dating from 1830, first accompanied Duffield's lyrics in William B. Bradbury's *The Golden Chain* in 1861. Foote points out that "Its stirring quality and excellence as a hymn of the Christian warfare made it popular among the soldiers of the Union army during the Civil War." Based on the many settings that encouraged temperance soldiers in their battle against alcohol, these same qualities appealed to temperance reformers.[16]

Unlike the many warlike settings of this tune, the following suasive lyrics emphasize the benefits of drinking cold water, conveying a joyous tone. Odd as this may seem to modern readers who know Webb's tune only with Duffield's

14. Bradbury and Stearns, *Temperance Chimes* (1867 and 1878), 107.
15. Perkins, *Crystal Fountain,* 107; Stearns, *Band of Hope,* 11.
16. Frost, *Historical Companion,* 308; J. Ithel Jones, E. A. Payne, A. Ewart Rusbudge, and E. P. Sharpe, *The Baptist Hymn Book Companion,* 340; Metcalf, *American Writers,* 241; Rodeheaver, *Hymnal Handbook,* 79–80; Foote, *Three Centuries,* 213.

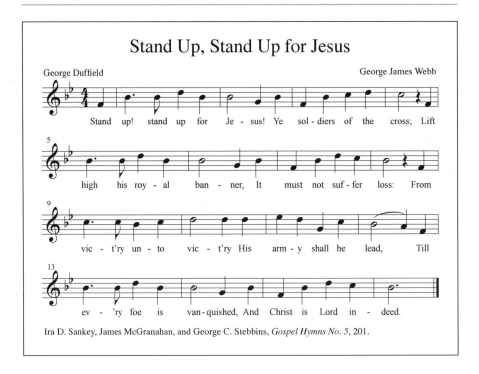

Stand Up, Stand Up for Jesus

George Duffield

George James Webb

Stand up! stand up for Je - sus! Ye sol - diers of the cross; Lift

high his roy - al ban - ner, It must not suf - fer loss: From

vic - t'ry un - to vic - t'ry His arm - y shall he lead, Till

ev - 'ry foe is van-quished, And Christ is Lord in - deed.

Ira D. Sankey, James McGranahan, and George C. Stebbins, *Gospel Hymns No. 5*, 201.

lyrics, this example predates that association, and thus the lyricist had no particular reason to make the connection to Christian warfare that would later become so common.

Cold Water

> 1. The sun is brightly beaming
>   O'er hill and over dale,
> The sweet May-buds are blooming
>   Down in the winding vale,
> The crystal drops are falling
>   On every leaf and flower,
> To life and beauty calling
>   The shady woodland bower,
> Cold water, ever flowing,
>   Thy diamond drops are free,
> Cold water, sparkling, glowing—
>   We love to drink of thee.
>
> 2. The wild deer on the mountain,
>   The eagle on the steep,
> Drink of the gushing fountain,

So limpid and so deep;
It's heaven's own distilling,
    For the sparkling waters glide
O'er earth's broad bosom, filling
    The ocean with its tide.
    Cold water, *etc.*

3. The amber wine-cup gleaming
    With sweet grapes' crimson glow,
Its wizard drops are teeming
    With bitterness and woe.
Dark goblet! O how cheating,
    Tho' thy brim may jewel'd be,
The pleasures, O how fleeting
    To those who drink of thee.
    Cold water, *etc.*[17]

After Webb's tune was set to Duffield's lyrics in 1861, themes of coercive reform dominated future settings, including the following example, first published in Root's *Musical Fountain* in 1867.

[Stand Up, Stand Up for Temperance]

1. Stand up, stand up for Temperance,
    Ye soldiers of our cause;
Lift high our royal banner,
    Nor let it suffer loss.
From victory to victory
    Our army shall be led,
Till every foe is vanquished,
    And all are free indeed.

2. Stand up, stand up for Temperance,
    Against unnumbered foes;
Your courage rise with danger,
    And strength to strength oppose;
Forth to this mighty conflict—
    Go in this glorious hour—
Where duty calls, or danger
    Be never wanting there.[18]

---

17. Fillmore, *Temperance Musician*, 207.

18. Root, *Musical Fountain*, 112; Hull, *Hull's Temperance*, 123; Bradbury and Stearns, *Temperance Chimes* (1867 and 1878), 113; Sherwin and Stearns, *Bugle Notes*, 122; Macy, *Temperance Song-Herald*, 95; Stearns and Main, *Trumpet Notes*, 73; *Songs of the Temperance Reform*, 42.

In an even stronger example of coercive reform, C. M. Fillmore's setting calls temperance workers to stand up and be counted at the voting booth:

Stand Up for Prohibition
(C. M. Fillmore)

1. Stand up for prohibition,
    Ye patriots of the land;
All ye who love your country,
    Against saloons should stand.
Behold against this traffic,
    Your country's greatest foe;
Let word and deed and ballot
    Proclaim, "saloons must go."

2. Stand up for prohibition,
    Ye soldiers of the Lord,
Put on the gospel armor,
    And wield the spirit's sword,
"From vict'ry unto vict'ry,
    His army shall he lead,"
Until the foe is vanquished
    "And Christ is Lord indeed."

3. Stand up for prohibition,
    The trumpet call obey,
Forth to the mighty conflict,
    In this His glorious day;
Ye that are men now serve Him,
    Against unnumbered foes;
Let courage rise and danger,
    And strength to strength oppose.[19]

Sweet By and By

The chorus of "Sweet By and By" provided another opportunity for borrowing by temperance writers. This hymn, with words by Sanford F. Bennett and music by Joseph P. Webster, was composed in 1868 and first appeared in their songbook *The Signet Ring*. The most frequently used temperance setting refers to the "sweet by-and-by, when Christians will vote as they pray," pointing

---

19. Fillmore and Fillmore, *Fillmores' Prohibition*, no. 145; Gordon, *Temperance Songster*, no. 90; *Prohibition Campaign Song Book*, 26.

Sweet By and By

Sanford F. Bennett

Joseph P. Webster

There's a land that is fair-er than day, And by faith we can see it a-far. For the Fath-er waits o-ver the way, To pre-pare us a dwell-ing-place there. *Chorus* In the sweet by and by, We shall meet on that beau-ti-ful shore; In the sweet by and by, We shall meet on that beau-ti-ful shore.

Asa Hull, *Hull's Temperance Glee Book*, 102.

to the supposed inconsistency of many Christians who refused to vote against the legal sale of alcohol.[20]

When Christians Will Vote as They Pray

1. There's a time that is coming at last—
    Oh! hasten the long looked for day,
When the rum fiend no shackles can cast,
    For all Christians will vote as they pray.

Chorus
In the sweet by-and-by,
    We shall welcome the beautiful day;
In the sweet by-and-by,
    When all Christians will vote as they pray.

2. When the fire shall go out at the still,
    And the worm shall be taken away;
And its ruins give place to the mill,
    Making bread that doth hunger allay. *To Chorus*

20. Ira D. Sankey, *My Life and the Story of the Gospel Hymns*, 285; Ewing, *Well-Tempered Lyre*, 32–37.

3. And the prisons shall close, every door,
    And the poor-houses tenantless stand,
When the dram-shop shall darken no more
    The dear homes of our beautiful land. *To Chorus*

4. When the church and the state shall arise,
    In the strength of their virtue and might;
And improve every moment that flies,
    In their daring to vote for the right. *To Chorus*[21]

Even in settings where the "Sweet By and By" text wasn't borrowed, temperance lyricists looked forward to the prohibition of alcohol much as the original text by Bennett anticipated eternal life.

In a Few Fleeting Years

1. There's an hour far more precious than gold,
    'Tis the hour at sweet daylight's decline,
When we muse on the mercies untold
    And the love of our Father divine.

Chorus
In a few fleeting years
    We'll be free from the deep curse of wine;
In a few fleeting years,
    If we trust in a Father divine.

2. We shall sing in our beautiful land
    The sweet songs of rejoicing and mirth,
When by virtue of God's high command,
    Rum shall flee from the face of the earth. *To Chorus*

3. Then the poor helpless children of men,
    Who now quail at the beast in his lair,
Like young Daniels shall step from the den,
    The rich blessings of freedom to share. *To Chorus*

4. From the lips of the heart-broken wives
    Shall loud anthems of thankfulness roll,
As they gaze on the beautiful lives
    That like sunbeams illumine the soul. *To Chorus*

5. Soon the chains of this demon will break,
    And the earth be relieved of its rod;

21. *Prohibition Campaign Song Book*, 4; Stearns, *Prohibition Songster*, no. 17; Leslie, *Good Templar* (1888), 37; E. Norine Law, *Temperance Bells, No. 1*, no. 37; J. G. Dailey and C. H. Mead, *Prohibition Chimes and What's the News?* no. 48. Miller, *Patriotic No-License*, no. 23, entitles this selection "The Good Time Coming." *Anti-Saloon Campaign*, no. 40, "The Looked For Day," strongly resembles this song.

And the sooner the masses awake,
    Shall we dwell in the sunlight of God. *To Chorus*[22]

Finally, a rather unusual setting, "We'll Treat When We're Dry," seems to be a song supporting the licensing of alcohol. However, a line from the chorus, "For we'll lie-cense so high that we'll never get drunk any more," reveals the true intent of the song. Because of the duration of the first syllable and the spelling of "lie-cense," in conjunction with the absurd degree of support for licensing alcohol in each verse, the lyricist is clearly using sarcasm to make the case that those who advocate licensing of alcohol as a means of controlling the problem are liars.

We'll Treat When We're Dry

1. Let us build a saloon on each hill,
    And a still in the valley below,
And up there about half-way between,
    Have the school where our children must go.

Chorus
Oh, we'll treat when we're dry,
    But we'll never get drunk any more,
For we'll lie-cense so high
    That we'll never get drunk any more.

2. Put saloons in each town's public square,
    By the court houses let them appear;
Then the license will keep in repair
    All the laws that we break with the beer. *To Chorus*

3. On each street corner license a bar,
    Where our boys may drop in when they pass;
And their fathers need not go so far
    From their wives when they're weak for a glass. *To Chorus*

4. By the home let a beer saloon rise,
    So the children to play will go there;
For the scenes will be good for their eyes,
    And they'll learn how to drink and to swear. *To Chorus*

5. By the church place a brewery near,
    And the tax for the preacher will pay;
And the sinners we make with the beer,
    We can save at the church cross the way. *To Chorus*[23]

---

22. Moffitt, *National Temperance*, 24.
23. Cake, *Popular Campaign*, n.p.

Hold the Fort

Philip Paul Bliss wrote the words and music to "Hold the Fort" in May 1870, following an inspiring address by Major D. W. Whittle at a Sunday school meeting in Rockford, Illinois. Whittle told of General Sherman's advance to relieve the fort at Altoona Pass during the Civil War. While under attack from the Confederate army, the Union troops in the fort saw a signal from a mountaintop twenty miles away: "Hold the fort, for I am coming. W. T. Sherman." Whittle's speech inspired Bliss to write "Hold the Fort," which was first performed in Chicago the following day. Temperance reformers retained the reference to the fort from Bliss's chorus in defense of those who suffered the abuses of alcohol. Four of the choruses begin "hold the fort," including the following, which also freely borrows other lyrics from Bliss's chorus.[24]

The Temperance Standard

1. Round the Temperance Standard rally
   Friends of humankind,
Snatch the devotees of folly,
   Wretched, poor, and blind.

Chorus
Hold the fort, for I am coming,
   Jesus signals still;
Hark! we hear their answer echo,
   By God's help we will.

2. Bear the blissful tidings onward
   All the world around;
Let the millions thronging downward
   Hear the joyful sound. *To Chorus*

3. Plant the Temperance Standard firmly,
   Round it live and die;
Young and old, defend it sternly,
   Yours the victory. *To Chorus*[25]

In contrast, "Battle for the Right" changes the tone from defensive to offensive by encouraging listeners to "storm the fort" of demon rum.

---

24. Rodeheaver, *Hymnal Handbook*, 150; Silber, *Songs of the Civil War*, 351.
25. Stearns, *National Temperance*, 6; Stearns, *Band of Hope*, 62.

Hold the Fort

Philip P. Bliss   Philip P. Bliss

Ho! my com-rades, see the sig-nal Wav-ing in the sky!

Re - in-force-ments now ap-pear-ing, Vic-to-ry is nigh!

Chorus

"Hold the fort, for I am com-ing," Je - sus sig-nals still,

Wave the an-swer back to heav-en, "By thy grace, we will."

P. P. Bliss, "Hold the Fort!" sheet music from "Music for the Nation: American Sheet Music,"
Library of Congress.

Battle for the Right

1. Storm the fort, ye gallant soldiers,
   With your army strong.
We are ready now for battle,
   Gird your armor on.

Chorus
Storm the fort! No longer falter.
   Work with nerve and will.
Prohibition and cold water
   Shout o'er vale and hill.

2. Storm the fort! and plant your banner
   O'er the traitor foe;
Put to flight Rum's hosts forever,
   Lay the demon low. *To Chorus*

3. Storm the fort! and give no quarter,
   Battle for the right;
Soon the foe shall fall before us—
   Onward to the fight! *To Chorus*[26]

26. Stearns, *National Temperance*, 53; Leslie, *Good Templar* (1888), 13.

Onward, Christian Soldiers

Another war hymn used by temperance writers was Sullivan and Baring-Gould's "Onward, Christian Soldiers." Originally written for a children's festival in Yorkshire, England, in 1864, S. Baring-Gould's text was set to Sir Arthur S. Sullivan's tune "St. Gertrude" in 1871. Temperance authors appropriated the tune and the sentiments of the text to spur the "temperance army" forward in their duty. Like Baring-Gould's original text, the following setting by Anna A. Gordon, who long served as the secretary of the Woman's Christian Temperance Union, was written for children's voices. It first appeared in *Marching Songs for Young Crusaders* and again later, with some minor modifications, in the *Red White and Blue Songster*.[27]

Onward, We Are Marching
(Anna A. Gordon)

1. Onward we are marching, alcohol to fight;
   With the pledge of honor ever in our sight.
We are little soldiers and the foe is strong.
   But with God to help us, this shall be our song:

Chorus
Onward we are marching, alcohol to fight,
   Valiant little soldiers, battling for the right.

2. See the mighty monster ruling in our land,
   Shall we be his subjects? 'neath his banner stand?
No, we will not serve him, since he's in the wrong,
   But with God to help us, this shall be our song: *To Chorus*

3. We shall soon be voters, strong in heart and brain;
   Then we'll fight with ballots, that shall fall like rain.
Won't you come and join us, to our Band belong,
   Help us fight our battle, help us sing our song? *To Chorus*[28]

Bringing in the Sheaves

No other hymn borrowed by the temperance movement conveyed the evangelical spirit and the desire to save souls like "Bringing in the Sheaves." Knowles Shaw wrote the lyrics and a tune to accompany them in 1874, but a tune composed by Civil War veteran George A. Minor in 1880 later replaced Shaw's

27. Frost, *Historical Companion*, 474; Jones et al., *Baptist Hymn Book*, 327.
28. Gordon, *Marching Songs*, 38–39. *Red White and Blue Songster*, 24, modifies the text in verse 1, the second line of the chorus, and verse 3.

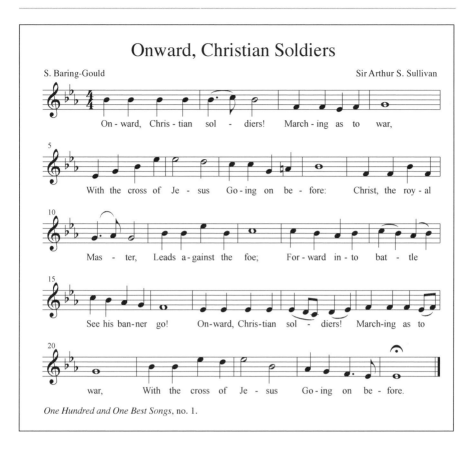

Onward, Christian Soldiers

S. Baring-Gould

Sir Arthur S. Sullivan

On - ward, Chris - tian sol - diers! March - ing as to war,

With the cross of Je - sus Go - ing on be - fore: Christ, the roy - al

Mas - ter, Leads a - gainst the foe; For - ward in - to bat - tle

See his ban - ner go! On - ward, Chris - tian sol - diers! March - ing as to

war, With the cross of Je - sus Go - ing on be - fore.

One Hundred and One Best Songs, no. 1.

tune. "Bringing in the Sheaves" was often used in its original form by the women's temperance crusade, but temperance lyricists chose not to emphasize the evangelical aspect of the song. Most of the parodies of "Bringing in the Sheaves" focus on voting for prohibition, including "When the Victory Is Won."[29]

When the Victory Is Won

1. Vote for reformation, vote for prohibition,
   Vote against the foe of church and school and home;
   Looking unto Jesus for His help and guidance;
   We will gain our freedom, when the vict'ry's won.

Chorus
When the vict'ry's won, when the vict'ry's won,
   Earth will be like heaven, when the vict'ry's won,

29. Stecker, "Respectable Revolution," 36–38.

Bringing in the Sheaves

Knowles Shaw

George A. Minor

Sow-ing in the morn-ing, sow-ing seeds of kind-ness, Sow-ing in the noon-tide

and the dew-'y eve: Wait-ing for the har-vest, and the time of reap-ing,

We shall come, re-joic-ing, bring-ing in the sheaves.

Chorus

Bring-ing in the sheaves.

Bring-ing in the sheaves, We shall come, re-joic-ing, Bring-ing in the sheaves.

Bring - ing in the sheaves, Bring - ing in the sheaves,

We shall come, re - joic - ing, Bring - ing in the sheaves.

J. N. Stearns, *Prohibition Songster*, no. 19.

When the vict'ry's won, when the vict'ry's won,
   We'll wear crowns of glory, when the vict'ry's won.

2. Drive the liquor traffic from the plains and mountains,
   So saloons and license will never rule again,
And the voice of angels chanting in the heavens,
   Will proclaim the tidings, "Peace, good will to men." *To Chorus*

3. Help to save Columbia from the wiles of Satan;
   Fight with honest hearts for truth and purity;
Smite forevermore the evils of intemp'rance;
   Hasten final vict'ry—glorious jubilee. *To Chorus*[30]

30. Roush, *Temperance Rally*, 32.

Other settings of "Bringing in the Sheaves" proclaimed that particular states, the nation, and even the world are "going dry." The following setting by Elisha A. Hoffman allows singers to insert the name of their own city, county, or state.

Going Dry
(Elisha A. Hoffman)

> 1. Hearken, brave crusaders, to the message cheering,
>   Temp'rance waves are rising round us, mounting high;
> Over all the land saloons are disappearing,
>   Cities, towns and hamlets all are going dry.
>
> *Chorus*
> _____ going dry, _____ going dry,
>   Pass along the watchword, _____ going dry.
> _____ going dry, _____ going dry,
>   Pass along the watchword, _____ going dry.
>
> 2. To the front, crusaders, where the fight is waging,
>   For the liquor traffic has been doomed to die;
> Gird you on the armor, and the foe engaging,
>   Pass along the watchword, _____ going dry. *To Chorus*
>
> 3. God's strong arm of justice is reached forth to save us,
>   And unto the fight he summons from on high;
> Banish the saloon from the good land he gave us,
>   And be this our watchword, _____ going dry. *To Chorus*
>
> 4. Forth, O men of faith! and be ye full of courage,
>   And the hosts of evil in His strength defy,
> For the Lord Jehovah pledges glorious vict'ry;
>   Rally for the watchword, _____ going dry. *To Chorus*[31]

"The Advancing Host" blends the suffrage and temperance issues. This song presents one of the great frustrations of many women who worked diligently for the temperance cause but who were not allowed to vote for prohibition.

The Advancing Host
(Deborah Knox Livingston)

> 1. See the host advancing! from the west they're marching,
>   Thousands of the women, armed with voting strength;

31. *Anti-Saloon Campaign*, no. 15.

See a bow of promise! O'er the skies 'tis arching,
    Read its glowing message, "Power has come at length."

Chorus
Women want the vote, women want the vote,
    To bring in prohibition, women want the vote.
Women want the vote, women want the vote,
    To make a sober nation, women want the vote.

2. Long have they been praying to the God of Heaven
    For the weapon needed to aid them in their fight;
Now the answer cometh, and the boon is given,
    They will have the ballot, to gird them for the right. *To Chorus*[32]

32. Gordon, *Popular Campaign*, 29.

THE DRUNKARD'S FAMILY.

Doxology ("Old Hundred")

Before Thy Throne, We Boast the Name

1. Before thy throne, we boast the name
    Of freemen; God thy frown is just;
Immortals break your bonds of shame!
    Arise, inebriates, from the dust.

2. Slavery and death the cup contains;
    Dash to the earth the poisoned bowl!
Softer than silk are iron chains,
    Compared with those that chafe the soul.

3. Hosannas, Lord, to thee we sing,
    Whose power the giant fiend obeys.
What countless thousands tribute bring,
    For happier homes and brighter days!

4. Thou wilt not break the bruised reed,
    Nor leave the broken heart unbound;
The wife regains a husband freed!
    The orphan clasps a father found!

5. Spare, Lord, the thoughtless, guide the
        blind;
    Till man no more shall deem it just
To live, by forging chains to bind
    His weaker brother in the dust.

6. With nature's draught the goblet fill,
    And pledge the world that ye are free!
God of eternal truth, WE WILL!
    Our cause is thine, our trust in thee![33]

Evening Hymn

1. This day, O God, thy blessed hand
    Hath thrown wide open all thy stores,
And filled with bounty every land,
    The sea, and all its sounding shores.

2. Beast, bird, fish, insect, thou hast fed
    With fish or flesh, with grass or grain;
For man a table hast thou spread
    From field, flood, air, or roaring main.

3. But, for all things o'er earth that move,
    In air or ocean soar or sink,
One thing hath thine unbounded love,
    And only one, prepared for drink.

4. 'Tis water! In the living spring
    It gusheth up to meet our lip;
In brooks we hear it murmuring,
    From mossy rocks we see it drip.

5. It filleth Health and Beauty's cup,
    And wrath and sorrow doth it drown,
As from our wells it cometh up,
    As from thy clouds it cometh down.

6. For the cool water we have quaffed,
    Source of all good! we owe thee much;
Our lips have touched no burning draught
    This day, nor shall they ever touch.

7. When we retire to our repose,
    And Night's dark curtains round us draw,
O guard us, as thou guardest those
    Who trust thy care, and keep thy law![34]

[Hail Temperance, Fair Celestial Ray]

1. Hail Temperance, fair celestial ray!
    Bright herald of a new born day!
Long did we need thy cheering light
    To chase away our darksome night.

2. Deep and appalling was the gloom,
    'Twas like the darkness of the tomb,
When first our much delighted eyes
    Beheld thy beauteous beams arise.

3. 'Twas God in mercy bade thee shine;
    We hail thee as a boon divine.
And now in grateful strains would raise
    Our voices in his matchless praise.

4. Eternal Lord! we own thy grace,
    In all that aids our guilty race.
Now send thy Spirit from above,
    And fill our hearts with joy and love.[35]

---

33. Pierpont, *Cold Water Melodies*, 43. Plimpton, *Washingtonian Choir*, 50, has only verses 1, 2, and 6. *Collection of Temperance Songs*, front side, has verses 3–5 and titles the song "Hosannas, Lord, to Thee We Sing."

34. Pierpont, *Cold Water Melodies*, 82; Bonner, *Mountain Minstrel*, 109–10.

35. Bonner, *Mountain Minstrel*, 63.

Temperance Hymn

(Geo. Lansing Taylor)

1. Great God, whose hand outpours the rills
     And springs that burst from all the hills,
  At whose command the rock was riven,
     Who send'st on all thy rain from heaven.

2. We bless thee for the crystal draught
     By sinless man in Eden quaffed;
  Type of that fount whose streams, above
     Flood endless worlds with life and love!

3. If there the drunkard may not dwell,
     But woes crowd thick his path to hell,
  Oh! wake, assist us, Lord, to save
     Their souls from thirst beyond the grave!

4. Help us to heed thy word divine,
     And look not on the crimson wine,
  To fear and flee th'accursed thing
     As serpent's bite or adder's sting.

5. Stay thou, O Lord! the tide of death!
     Rebuke the demon's blasting breath!
  And speed, Oh! speed, on every shore,
     The day when strong drink slays no
       more![36]

Temperance Hymn

1. O Lord, to thee we humbly pray,
     In mercy help us to the end,
  And lead us in the narrow way,
     Thou art our Father and our Friend.

2. For temperance and for truth divine,
     To thee shall grateful songs ascend;
  For ever be the glory thine,
     Thou art our Father and our Friend.

3. Still round our path thy blessings shed,
     On Thee, O Lord, we now depend,
  The temperance cause in mercy spread,
     Thou art our Father and our Friend.[37]

Temperance Hymn

1. O Lord, Thy waiting servants bless,
     And crown our labors with success;
  Strong drink from every home remove,
     And send the time of joy and love.

2. The time when our dear land shall be,
     The home of purer liberty;
  And drunkards all Thy laws obey,
     And love to walk in wisdom's way.[38]

Temperance Hymn #4

1. Each effort to redeem our race,
     That by intemp'rance are made slaves,
  And lead them back to paths of peace,
     The blessing of our God receives.

2. Assured that He will still approve,
     And bless our labors to the end,
  Let us in this employ of love,
     Look unto God our Guide and Friend.[39]

Parting Hymn

1. Come, friends of temperance, ere we part,
     Join every voice and every heart;
  One solemn hymn to God we raise—
     One final song of grateful praise.

2. Together we may meet no more;
     But there is yet a happier shore,
  And there, released from toil and pain,
     May we forever meet again.[40]

[Lord, Let Our Minds]

1. Lord, let our minds be filled with light;
     Direct our footsteps in the right;
  Imbue our hearts with saving grace;
     Thy holy image on us trace.

2. O may we crush the monster sin,
     The work of "Volunteers" begin,
  And bring the drunkard from his woe,
     To joys that true abstainers know.[41]

---

36. Bradbury and Stearns, *Temperance Chimes* (1867 and 1878), 104.
37. Ibid.
38. Ibid.
39. Ibid.
40. Stearns, *National Temperance*, 60.
41. Herbert, *Young Volunteer*, 46.

All Hail the Power of Jesus' Name ("Coronation")

To Teetotalers

1. Press on ye band who nobly brave
   A world's unpitying scorn;
Ye stand erect in virtue's cause
   By virtue's strength upborne.
Ye stand erect in virtue's cause
   By virtue's strength upborne.

2. Can scorn unfix creation's base,
   Or shake the throne of God?
Can taunts, however fierce, disarm
   Stern justice of her rod? *etc.*

3. No! nor shall they daunt your zeal,
   Nor bend your souls to yield;
But ye shall wave, exultingly,
   Your banners o'er the field, *etc.*

4. No dying groans, no mother's shriek,
   Shall mar your triumph hymn,
No blood shall stain your battle flag,
   No cloud your glories dim! *etc.*

5. But there shall follow in your train
   A holy, happy throng,
The wise and good will soon abstain,
   And join the conq'rer's song, *etc.*[42]

All Hail the Cause
(J. F. Coles)

1. All hail the cause of Temperance!
   The cause of all mankind!
The old, the young, the rich, the poor,
   May here rich blessings find.
The old, the young, the rich, the poor,
   May here rich blessings find.

2. The soul whom Alcohol has bound,
   With all his magic powers,
May free itself, and henceforth walk
   A pathway strewn with flowers! *etc.*

3. God gave to us the gushing spring,
   The brook and murmuring rill;

From these we all can quench our thirst,
   And be His children still, *etc.*

4. Not so the slave of Alcohol,
   Who sips from fashion's bowl;
Each draught is poison, and pollutes
   The body and the soul, *etc.*

5. Then hail, all hail bright Temperance!
   Friend of the true and brave!
Long o'er Columbia's happy homes,
   May thy broad banner wave, *etc.*[43]

The Rally

1. Come, freemen rally once again—
   Come, rally in your might,
From mountain side, and hill and plain,
   To strike for Truth and Right!
From mountain side, and hill and plain,
   To strike for Truth and Right!

2. Fling out that gallant flag once more,
   And nail it to the mast;
A meteor-light from shore to shore
   To glance upon the blast! *etc.*

3. From North to South the anthem swells—
   From East to Western wave;
A better day for man it tells—
   The drunkard shall be saved! *etc.*

4. From shop, and field and warm hearthside
   Come, swell the patriot band;
With flag, and shout, we'll on with pride,
   For God and native land! *etc.*[44]

Banish Alcohol

1. All hail the power of abstinence!
   Let tipplers heed the call;
Arise in manhood's moral might,
   And banish alcohol!
Arise in manhood's moral might,
   And banish alcohol!

2. Let every youth and maiden shun
   Its wormwood and its gall;
Arise in moral might sublime,
   And banish alcohol! *etc.*

42. Pierpont, *Cold Water Melodies*, 27–28.
43. Potter, *Boston Temperance*, 2:7.
44. Perkins, *Crystal Fountain*, 108.

3. Let childhood's tender grace beware!
  Lest it in ruin fall;
Avoid the road that leads to death,
  And banish alcohol! *etc.*

4. Let ev'ry poor deluded soul
  On this terrestrial ball,
Arise in moral strength sublime,
  And banish alcohol! *etc.*

5. O Lord! we seek thy sovereign might,
  For help, upon Thee call;
Direct our honest efforts, Lord,
  To banish alcohol! *etc.*

6. Earth's suff'ring sons will shout for joy
  When broken is its thrall;
And hell's foundations heave and shake,
  O'er dying Alcohol! *etc.*[45]

The Power of Christ

1. All hail the power of Jesus' name!
  For this will conquer Rum,
And men will sing with one acclaim,
  "Oh Lord, thy Kingdom come!"
And men will sing with one acclaim,
  "Oh Lord, thy Kingdom come!"

2. All hail the Truth Judea heard!
  New England hears it now;
Our hearts within are deeply stirred,
  And all our foes shall bow, *etc.*

3. All hail the Love on Calv'ry seen!
  That Love can never die;
The world shall bloom as Eden green
  Beneath a Heavenly Sky, *etc.*

4. All hail the Grace which Jesus brought
  To mortals here below!
By this within apostles wrought
  To banish human woe, *etc.*

5. All hail the Lord, the King of kings!
  He leads our army strong,
And on our ears his order rings
  As now we fight the wrong, *etc.*

6. All hail the power of Jesus' name!
  Resistless is his might;
It is within a Holy Flame,
  Without a Glowing Light, *etc.*[46]

Soon o'er the Earth

1. Soon o'er the earth shall Temperance reign
  And Rum's foul rule destroy,
Release all homes from woe and pain
  And fill all hearts with joy.
Release all homes from woe and pain
  And fill all hearts with joy.

2. Oh, then to bring that glorious time
  We'll arm with courage now,
To fight for home and native land
  We take a solemn vow. *etc.*

3. That glorious time will soon be here,
  If we fight manfully,
And hand in hand, and heart to heart,
  Strive for the mastery. *etc.*[47]

Watchman, Tell Us of the Night ("Watchman")

The Temperance Star #1

1. Long and gloomy was the night
  Hanging on our mental sight,
While intemp'rance, dark and drear,
  Filled the lowering atmosphere.
But behold a star arise,
  Brilliant in these western skies,
Coming like redeeming power,
  In the last despairing hour.

2. Onward speed thy radiant way,
  Harbinger of dawning day!
Let the nations from afar—
  Hail New England's morning star.
Sun of righteousness appear,
  Fill the moral hemisphere—
On the scattering shades of night
  Pour a flood of heavenly light.[48]

45. Moffitt, *National Temperance*, 7.
46. Munson, *Gospel and Maine*, 9.
47. Fobes, *Temperance Songs*, 13.
48. Pierpont, *Cold Water Melodies*, 158.

The Temperance Star #2

1. Watchman, tell us of the night,
   What its signs of promise are;
Traveler! o'er yon mountain's height,
   See that glorious Temperance star.
Watchman, does its beauteous ray
   Aught of hope or joy foretell?
Traveler! yes, it brings the day
   When shall end the tyrant's spell.

2. Watchman, tell us of the night,
   Higher yet that star ascends;
Traveler! blessedness and light,
   Peace and truth its course portends.
Watchman, will its beams alone
   Gild the spot that gave them birth?
Traveler! ages are its own;
   See! it bursts o'er all the earth![49]

The Latest News

1. Watchman, tell the latest news,
   Are the nations all awake?
Brother, few the pledge refuse,
   All the world will soon partake!
Watchman, does its golden band
   Hold the signers to the test?
Brother, trust His mighty hand,
   He'll sustain the trusting breast.

2. Watchman, tell the latest news,
   For the churches seem to shine;
Brother, yes, some now refuse
   At the altar, foaming wine.
Watchman, do the nations hope,
   Earth from rum and wine to save?
Brother, look in rapture up,
   Rum is hastening to its grave.

3. Watchman, tell the latest news,
   For the saints seem blest with joy.
Brother, 'twill thy breast amuse,
   Praise will soon all tongues employ.

Watchman, will this temp'rance flame
   Sweep with rapture all the earth?
Brother, in Jehovah's name
   For this purpose it had birth.[50]

When the Triumph

1. Statesman wise, of thee we ask,
   When our land in peace shall rest,
When shall end our weary task,
   And the earth with joy be blest?
Workman bold, that day will be
   When our land now cursed by Rum
From the sin of drink is free,
   And the Right to earth shall come.

2. Preacher, tell us of the Day—
   When the Lord on earth shall reign,
When the Cross the world shall sway,
   And our Land true glory gain?
Christians, not till mocking wine
   From the earth is banished far,
And your land shall own divine
   The long-look'd-for Risen Star.

3. Pet, tell us when the time
   That the world shall clearly see
Beauty found in every clime,
   And rejoice in vision free?
Raptured hearts, when souls are pure,
   Rightly use the grains and fruits,
Never yield where wines allure,
   Live above the senseless brutes.

4. Angels, tell us when the hour
   That our world shall be as yours,
And we all shall feel the Power
   Felt upon the Unseen Shores!
Friends we left, when men shall own
   Christ should reign instead of Sin,
And the world shall seek the Throne
   Found in joy by faith within.[51]

49. Guthrie, *Teetotal Army*, 10; Stearns and Main, *Trumpet Notes*, 63; Dailey and Mead, *Prohibition Chimes*, n.p.

50. Moffitt, *National Temperance*, 25.

51. Munson, *Gospel and Maine*, 26–27.

Stand Up, Stand Up for Jesus ("Webb")

The Temperance Battle

1. Lift high the temperance banner!
      Ay, proudly let it wave,
To save the poor inebriate
      From a degraded grave.
Then, children, at your station,
      To quell the raging storm;
Let hearts and hands united
      Strive for a glad reform.

2. Come, join the noble army,
      Enlist now for the fight;
Maintain our nation's honor,
      Firm stand ye for the right.
Promote the cause of temp'rance,
      T'assist poor, fallen man;
Put on the glorious armor;
      Be foremost in the van.

3. Then rally round the standard,
      And let the work go on,
Until the last dim vestige
      Of intemp'rance is gone.
Be earnest in the battle,
      Your weapons boldly wield;
You'll surely gain the victory,
   And make the monster yield.[52]

Oh! Patiently We've Waited
(W. C. Baker)

1. Oh! patiently we've waited,
      To see the happy day,
When man shall tempt his brother
      No more to go astray;
And all shall strive together,
      To lift the fallen up,
And teach the weak and wretched,
      To leave the cruel cup.

2. With words and deeds of kindness,
      With words of love and cheer,
O treat thy fellow being,

Through all his trials here;
There's poverty and sorrow,
      Wherever we may go—
Then let us, like the angels
      Be kind to all below.

3. Be true to all the living,
      For but a transient hour,
And love and comfort giving,
      Will be beyond our power,
Give misery our pity,
      And treat our fellow man,
As though he were our brother
      And help him while we can.[53]

The Hosts Are Waking

1. Earth's mighty hosts are waking,
      From their calm sleep of years;
The voice of Truth is breaking,
      With music, on their ears;
Each to the other crying,
      "The hour at length is come,
When each—his prowess trying—
      Shall smite the brow of Rum!"

2. From distant State and nation,
      We hear this glad refrain,
"We rise with indignation,
      And Rum shall cease to reign!"
The winds catch up the story,
      And chant it o'er and o'er
"True manhood in its glory,
      Shall feel its curse no more!"

3. With hearts and hands united,
      Our efforts will not fail;
Our might and honor plighted,
      They cannot but prevail!
We swell the praise to heaven,
      And let the tidings roll;
"The power of Rum is riven
      And freedom crowns the soul."[54]

Oh! Rouse Ye, Christian Women

1. Oh, rouse ye, Christian women,
      Come, sisters, one and all;

52. Guthrie, *Teetotal Army*, 7; Bradbury and Stearns, *Temperance Chimes* (1867 and 1878), 50.
53. Bradbury and Stearns, *Temperance Chimes* (1867 and 1878), 50.
54. Moffitt, *National Temperance*, 6.

Why longer do you tarry?
Oh! hear ye not the call?
Then sound it loud and louder,
Swell high the clarion notes,
Till from each Christian household
An answering echo floats.

2. Oh! will you longer tarry
Just at the outer gate,
While sorrowing hearts in silence
For their deliverance wait?
Come, sisters, to the rescue;
Come, brothers, close the ranks;
In God's own time we'll conquer,
And at His feet give thanks.55

The Pledge

1. The pledge, the pledge, we hail it,
The symbol of the free;
The sign of coming ages
Of truth and liberty.
The good and true will own it,
The proud and false may scoff,
But 'tis the friend of drunkards,
And strikes their fetters off.

2. The pledge, with power and blessing,
Like a smiling angel comes,
And pours the light of gladness
On long-benighted homes.
It is a sword of triumph,
'Tis armor 'gainst the foe,
A sure and trusty anchor
When tempests fiercely blow.56

A Better Day

1. A better day is nearing,
The dawn we now can see,
Its gleams of light appearing,
We are from doubting free;
The cause of God is gaining
In every isle and land,
No longer lips complaining
We follow Christ's command.

2. The drunkard's drink forsaking,
The thousands swell the song,
And thousands more are waking
To join the mighty throng;
Each day to us is bringing
The news of men redeemed,
And plains and isles are ringing
With hymns the prophets dreamed.

3. Oh, come, ye idlers, dreaming!
Your lips and hands engage,
Go seek the souls blaspheming,
For God the battle wage;
Go to the weak and blinded,
The slaves of Beer and Gin,
Go speak as one reminded
Of trophies all should win.

4. Our cause is onward speeding,
Resistance is in vain;
The tide of sin receding,
The right o'er wrong shall reign!
Then aid, oh aid, the dawning,
With word, and deed, and prayer,
Come save from graves now yawning,
And bid the world "Beware!"57

The Temperance Banner

1. Unfurl the Temperance banner,
And fling it to the breeze,
And let the glad hosanna
Sweep over land and seas:
To God be all the glory
For what we now behold—
Oh! let the cheering story
In every ear be told.

2. Fight on! fight on for Temperance,
Nor let your courage fail,
The Lord is just and mighty,
The Right shall e'er prevail.
Though fierce may be the conflict,
Though noisy be the fray,
Yet ours shall be the triumph,
Success shall crown the day.58

---

55. McCauley, Anti-Saloon Songs, 56; Stearns, National Temperance, 7.

56. Stearns, National Temperance, 56.

57. Munson, Gospel and Maine, 22–23.

58. Stearns, Band of Hope, 42. Stearns, Prohibition Songster, no. 14, uses this verse 1 then borrows verses 2 and 3 from "The Temperance Battle" above. Stearns and Main, Trumpet Notes, 107, uses the

Glorious Day

1. A glorious day is breaking
   Upon the sinful earth,
Our land to life is waking,
   With shouts of joyous mirth;
Our army is preparing
   To meet the rising sun,
On all its banners bearing
   The name of Washington.

2. We meet today in gladness,
   To sing of conquests won,
No note of painful sadness
   Is mingled with our song;
This day renowned in story—
   The day of freedom's birth,
We hail in all its glory,
   We highly prize its worth.

3. The temp'rance flag is waving
   O'er valley, hill, and plain,
Where ocean's sons are braving
   The dangers of the main;
The pledge, the pledge is given
   To float on every breeze,
Waft it, propitious heaven,
   O'er all the earth and seas.

4. Our cause, our cause is gaining
   New laurels every day;
The youthful mind we're training
   To walk in virtue's way;
Old age and sturdy manhood
   Are with us heart and hand,
Then let us all united
   In one firm phalanx stand.[59]

The Dawning Light

1. A glorious day is dawning,
   Upon our sinful earth;
We hail the happy morning,
   With shouts of joy and mirth.

The Temp'rance cause in triumph
   Is marching through the land;
The men are true that lead it—
   A firm and dauntless band.

2. We meet to-day in gladness,
   And sing of conquests won,
No note of painful sadness
   Is mingled with our song.
The Temp'rance flag is waving
   O'er valley, hill and plain;
Where Ocean's sons are braving
   The dangers of the main.

3. Our holy cause is gaining
   New laurels ev'ry day;
The youthful mind we're training
   To walk in Virtue's way;
Old age and sturdy manhood
   Are with us, heart and hand;
Then let us all united
   In one firm phalanx stand![60]

The Two Ships

1. The good ship "Prohibition,"
   With every sail unfurled,
Now moves with expedition
   On her way 'round the world;
And at her mast-head flying
   The flag of "Abstinence"
Streams wide, its foe defying,
   Foul, black "Intemperance."

2. That pirate craft, "Intemperance,"
   Is also cruising 'round,
On human freedom preying
   Wherever it is found.
The good ship "Prohibition"
   Will shortly scuttle her,
And mankind sail with safety
   From shore to farthest shore.[61]

---

same text as Stearns, *Prohibition Songster*, no. 14, but entitles it "Unfurl the Temperance Banner."
Hoffman, *Woman's Christian Temperance*, no. 42, also uses this title but adds new verses 2 and 3.

  59. Fillmore, *Temperance Musician*, 173; Macy, *Temperance Song-Herald*, 57. Fillmore, *Temperance Musician*, 39, and Perkins, *Crystal Fountain*, 104, omit verse 1.

  60. Leslie, *Good Templar* (1886), 29; Stearns, *National Temperance*, 28. Note similarities to verses 1, 2, and 4 of "A Glorious Day Is Breaking."

  61. Fobes, *Temperance Songs*, 14.

Stand Up for Prohibition
(E. T. Cassel)

1. Stand up for Prohibition,
 Ye soldiers true and brave,
Lift high the temp'rance banner;
 From rum your country save.
From vict'ry unto vict'ry
 Press forward in the fray,
Till all rum's hosts are vanquished,
 And dawns a brighter day.

2. Stand up for Prohibition,
 Stand in God's strength alone,
The arm of flesh will fail you,
 Ye dare not trust your own;
Put on the gospel armor,
 And, watching unto prayer,
Where duty calls, or danger,
 Be never wanting there.

3. Stand up for Prohibition,
 The strife will not be long,
If every one is loyal
 Against the giant wrong:
Let every heart be faithful,
 Let every hand be strong,
And soon the battle finish
 And then the victor's song.[62]

The Coming Day

1. The day of hope is dawning,
 Along the Eastern sky;
The day for which we're longing,
 The day of peace and joy.
The darkness disappearing
 Our new glad hearts beat high,
At last our prayers are answered,
 And victory is nigh.

2. The midnight darkness holding
 Its sad and dismal sway;
The night of death and terror
 Is breaking into day;
For see! In light unfolding,
 Our Temp'rance banner gleams;
With hope and peace and gladness
 Abounding in its beams.

3. The heart, once bowed in sadness,
 Is filled with mirth and cheer;
The mind, once filled with madness,
 Is lifted bright and clear.
The license to do evil
 Has vanished with the past,
Praise God! praise God! we're singing,
 We're saved from drink at last.[63]

Stand Up for Temperance
(Stella Connelly Masters)

1. Stand up, stand up for Temp'rance,
 Ye soldier of the cross;
Unfurl the blood-stained banner,
 We must not suffer loss.
Come bravely don the armor
 With Jesus in the lead,
Until the foe is vanquished,
 And Christ is Lord indeed.

2. Stand up, stand up for Temp'rance,
 Christ came to save from sin;
Lift high His royal banner,
 And bring the lost ones in.
From vict'ry unto vict'ry
 We'll shout it as we go,
Till homes of gloom and darkness,
 With Gospel light shall glow.

3. Stand up, stand up for Temp'rance
 In answer to Christ's call;
Unsheathe the Spirit's weapon,
 And slay King Alcohol.
Put on the Gospel armor,
 Nor to the world give heed
Let us then unite our forces,
 Then Christ shall reign indeed.

4. Stand up, stand up for Temp'rance
 God's loving call obey,
Ye host of loyal women,
 We'll surely win the day.
Come, let us press the battle,
 And look to God in prayer,
Till "Victory through Jesus"
 Shall echo every where![64]

62. Cassel, *White Ribbon*, no. 104.
63. Dungan et al., *Acorn Temperance*, no. 43.
64. Law, *Temperance Bells*, no. 8.

Sweet By and By

Dawn of the Millennium

1. When the right over wrong shall prevail,
    When the woes of wine-drinking shall
        cease,
Then all nations and people shall hail
    With a shout the grand triumph of peace.

Chorus
It will come by-and-by,
    When the race out of childhood has grown;
It will come by-and-by,
    Then the age of true manhood shall
        dawn.

2. Right ordains that the old wrongs shall
        cease,
    And make way for the growth of reform;
Truth and wisdom proclaim from on high
    That the triumph of virtue must come.
        To Chorus

3. To the fountain of unfailing love
    We will pray that the time soon may
        come,
When the truth, as revealed from above,
    Stops the sale and the making of rum.
        To Chorus[65]

The Glad By-and-By

1. What a glorious world this will be,
    When the Angel of Temp'rance shall
        reign,
And the nations are evermore free
    From the bondage of Alcohol's chain.

Chorus
In the glad By-and-By,
    What a glorious world this will be,
    In the glad By-and-By[66]

2. When the doors of the dramshop shall
        close,
    As they will in that bright coming time,
Then farewell to the worst of our woes,
    And the widespread dominion of crime.
        To Chorus

3. Then the murderer's hand shall be stayed:
    Then contentions and hatred shall cease:
Then the homes now a hell shall be made
    Into Edens of love and of peace. *To Chorus*

4. Then the heart-broken wives, from whose
        eyes
    The hot tear-drops of anguish have
        streamed,
With renewed hope and courage shall rise,
    And rejoice over husbands redeemed.
        To Chorus

5. And the children, who often have fled
    From their own father's footsteps in
        fright,
Then shall watch for the sound of his tread,
    And shall welcome him home with
        delight. *To Chorus*

6. Friends of Temp'rance, unite all your powers,
    And unceasingly work, heart and hand,
To abolish this curse, until ours
    Is a happy and prosperous land.
        To Chorus[67]

Victory

1. The Lord is our refuge and strength,
    His promises never can fail;
We've learned the sweet lesson at length,
    His grace over sin can prevail.

Chorus
In the sweet by-and-by
    We'll conquer the demons of rum;

65. Hull, *Hull's Temperance*, 103. Perkins, *Crystal Fountain*, 108, Stearns, *National Temperance*, 9, Stearns, *Band of Hope*, 11, and Stearns and Main, *Trumpet Notes*, 145, omit verse 3. Perkins, Stearns, and Stearns and Main name this song "The Right Shall Prevail." Leslie, *Good Templar* (1886), 35, and Leslie, *Good Templar* (1888), 37, also entitle this song "The Right Shall Prevail" and make several minor changes. Dungan et al., *Acorn Temperance*, no. 38, presents another version of "The Right Shall Prevail," using the original three verses from "Dawn of the Millennium" with a new chorus.

66. No final line is given for the chorus. The author may have intended that singers should repeat the last line of the previous verse.

67. McCreery, *Collection of Temperance Songs*, 10–11.

In the sweet by-and-by
    The kingdom of Heaven will come.

2. Oh, the wonderful power of His love,
    Bending low to humanity's need!
Every soul may His faithfulness prove,
    Every slave by His mercy be freed.
        To Chorus

3. With God and with Truth on our side,
    No foe can our efforts withstand;
In vain they resist and deride;
    We are an invincible band. *To Chorus*

4. We follow our Heavenly King,
    His cross is our banner and shield;
Our all to the conflict we bring,
    To conquer or die on the field.
        *To Chorus*68

We Will Rise over Sin
(Wm. B. Marsh)

1. Here is health without pain, you can try,
    Here is happiness, too, for your gain,
A relief from your pain if you try
    From the demon of drink to abstain.

Chorus
It will give, while we live,
    Hope and comfort if we are but brave;
And at last, when life's past,
    We may rise over sin and the grave.

2. God the nectar of life has bestowed
    On us mortals, when we are athirst;
Silvery streams down the mountain have
        flowed,
    Since the sunlight of nature first burst.
        To Chorus

3. Come and drink from the clear glassy rill,
    It is pleasant and sweet to the taste,
If ye thirst ye may come drink your fill,
    For your substance it never will waste.
        To Chorus

4. Pure and sparkling 'tis offered to you,
    In the raindrops that fall from the sky;
Drink but this, 'twill expose to your view
    That sweet home in the sweet by-and-by.
        *To Chorus*69

Prohibition Is Coming

1. Prohibition is coming at last.
    We have battled and prayed for it long;
Soon the thralldom of drink shall be past,
    And we'll pour forth a jubilant song.

Chorus
We shall be glad and free
    From the woes and the sorrows of rum;
We shall be glad and free,
    From the crime and ruin of rum.

2. Hail the day, when both body and soul,
    Now a price to the rum traffic paid,
Shall be free from its slavish control,
    And in reason and manhood arrayed.
        To Chorus

3. Then no longer shall party be sold
    To a rum-trade for sake of its vote;
Nor be bought by its revenue gold,
    With its clutch on the national throat.
        To Chorus

4. Then no tears shall despairingly fall,
    And no hearts shall be broken by rum;
But contentment and gladness to all,
    With the downfall of liquor shall come.
        *To Chorus*70

The Coming Day and the Promised Land
(G. N. Davidson)

1. There's a great shining day drawing near,
    And its glory is coming to stay;
See the light of its dawning appear,
    Driving darkness and sorrow away;
'Tis the great temperance day;
    And its glory is now drawing near;

68. Stearns, *National Temperance*, 18. Stearns, *Band of Hope*, 63, and Leslie, *Good Templar* (1886), 35, and (1888), 37, replace verse 3.

69. Perine and Mash, *National Prohibition Hymnal*, 21.

70. Durant, *Prohibition Home*, 12–13.

'Tis the sweet coming day;
  See the light of its dawning appear.

2. O! the beautiful light of that day,
    Shining forth o'er the land and the sea,
Will the voice of all gladness obey;
    And the captives of rum will set free.
Let us hail the true light,
    Shining forth o'er the land and the sea,
It will banish the night,
    And the captives of rum will set free.

3. Then a beautiful land will arise,
    Where no rum fiend can ever destroy;
Where a bounteous love will devise,
    All the blessings of comfort and joy.
'Tis the sweet promised land,
    Where no rum fiend can ever destroy;
'Tis a bright happy land,
    With the blessings of comfort and joy.

4. In that wonderful land of delight,
    Happy friendship and love will abound;
And the beauties of virtue and right,
    Ev'ry house in that land will surround.
'Tis our own temp'rance land,
    Shall we labor to raise it on high?
'Tis the sweet promised land;
    O! that all to its refuge may fly.[71]

Prohibition By and By
(T. J. Merryman)

1. There ariseth a long looked for day,
    And its dawning is glorious and grand;
For the rule of the rum-fiend shall cease,
    Prohibition will sweep o'er the land.

Chorus
In the sweet by and by
    Prohibition will sweep o'er the land.
In the near by and by,
    Prohibition will bless all our land.

2. Then the merchant and butcher shall
        thrive,
    And all classes of business increase,
When no money is wasted for beer,

And the drain of the drink-curse shall
    cease. *To Chorus*

3. Oh what joy in the home there will be!
    When the father no longer is slave
To the habit which ruins his life,
    And leads down to the drunkard's dark
        grave. *To Chorus*

4. When the husband is loving and true,
    To his wife, long neglected and sad.
When the larder no longer runs low;
    And the children are all neatly clad.
        To Chorus

5. When saloons shall no longer entice,
    And ensnare many young men and boys;
But in homes of refinement and peace,
    They shall drink from the fountain of
        joys. *To Chorus*

6. Let us each labor on with our might,
    Till the demon of drink is o'erthrown,
Then shall peace and prosperity reign,
    And the blessings of temp'rance be
        known. *To Chorus*[72]

We'll Take Part in the Fight

1. 'Tis a duty we proudly should do,
    To take part in the conflict today,
Strive to vanquish the foe of the home,
    And the tide of intemperance stay.

Chorus
We'll take part in the fight
    'Gainst the foe whose foul crimes are
        untold.
With our might for the right,
    We will conquer the demon so bold.

2. Come and join in the contest so grand,
    'Gainst intemp'rance, the worst of all
        crimes.
Strive with head and with heart and with
        hand
    'Gainst an evil that covers all climes.
        To Chorus[73]

71. Leslie, *Good Templar* (1886), 49.
72. Merryman, *Amendment Songs*, no. 3.
73. Fobes, *Temperance Songs*, 28.

Christian Voting

1. We will vote out saloons from our land,
   With an army so true and so brave,
And for temp'rance, we boldly will stand,
   While old glory so grandly doth wave.

Chorus
We will vote out saloons,
   From Columbia the land of the free;
We will vote out saloons,
   And we'll then have complete victory.

2. For the faith of our Captain, the Lord,
   Every Christian should stand for the right,
With a ballot of truth as his sword,
   Ever marching to win in the fight.
      To Chorus

3. From the blue arch of heaven above,
   Comes a cry to the Christians today;
'Tis the voice of the angel of love,
   Pleading for them to vote as they pray.
      To Chorus[74]

The Looked for Day

1. O, an hour will be coming at last,
   A glorious, long-looked-for day,
When the traffic in drink will be past,
   For the people will vote it away.

Chorus
O the sweet by and by!
   We shall welcome the beautiful day;
O the sweet by and by,
   When the traffic is voted away!

2. Then the prisons will close every door,
   And the poor-houses tenantless stand.
When the dram-shops shall darken no more
   The dear homes of our beautiful land.
      To Chorus

3. When the church and the state shall arise
   In the strength of their virtue and might,
Then will praises ascend to the skies
   For the triumph of Justice and Right.
      To Chorus[75]

Hold the Fort

Prohibition Advancing

1. Prohibition is advancing
   All along our lines
Liquor parties give of failure
   Unmistaken signs.

Chorus
We will break the galling fetters
   Of the tyrant rum
Hear the trample of our legions
   See! They come! They come!

2. Politicians now are quaking,
   Filled with sore dismay;
License capital will fail them,
   Almost any day. *To Chorus*

3. Revenue a hundred millions,
   Party proudly boasts
Premium for crime and ruin
   Price of slaughtered hosts! *To Chorus*

4. Crime-stained, tear-stained, blood-stained
      money!
   Who can count its cost?
Honor, fortune, earth and Heaven,
   Soul and body—lost! *To Chorus*

5. In mere sense, financial, ev'ry
   Dollar loses ten;
Would a business be thus managed,
   By sane business men? *To Chorus*

6. Yet, this government is doing
   Just that very thing;
And its boasted rum investments,
   Boundless losses bring! *To Chorus*

7. Rally, voters, to the rescue;
   Women give us aid!
Prohibition is our war-cry
   Down with liquor trade! *To Chorus*[76]

---

74. Roush, *Temperance Rally*, 13.

75. *Anti-Saloon Campaign*, no. 40; Hoffman, *Woman's Christian Temperance*, no. 40; Biederwolf and Lawson, *Best Temperance Songs*, no. 41.

76. Durant, *Prohibition Home*, 15–16.

Storm the Fort for Prohibition

1. Hark! ye voters, hear the bugle
   Calling to the fray;
"Prohibition" is our watchword,
   Right shall win the day.

Chorus
Storm the fort for Prohibition,
   Captives signal still,
Answer back to their petition,
   "By our votes we will."

2. See the haughty rum-shops' banner
   On the fortress walls;
Hurl the temp'rance ballots 'gainst it
   Till the rampart falls. *To Chorus*

3. Face the grog-shops' bold defiance,

Never fear or quail.
Coward foes will soon surrender;
   Voters, do not fail! *To Chorus*

4. By the God who freedom gave us,
   With immortal souls!
Crush the foes who dare enslave us—
   Forward to the polls! *To Chorus*[77]

The Badge of Blue
(Arthur W. French)

1. Hail! my brothers, with the signal
   Of the ribbon blue,
Emblem that you have enlisted
   In a cause so true.

Chorus
Sign the pledge and keep it brothers,
   This is the song for you;
Join the glorious temp'rance army
   Wear the badge of blue.

2. Onward moves this mighty army
   With a song of thanks
For the thousands that are proudly
   Filling up the ranks. *To Chorus*

3. Underneath the temp'rance banner
   Labor while you can;
Always ready, up and doing,
   Save a fellow man. *To Chorus*

4. Never falter or grow weary
   When there's hope to win,
Where you find a falling brother,
   Lift him out of sin. *To Chorus*

5. Hail! my brothers, with the signal
   Of the ribbon blue,
In the noble cause of temp'rance
   Proudly dare and do. *To Chorus*[78]

Hold the Fort for Prohibition #1
(C. W. Dennison)

1. Ho! my comrades, see our banner,
   Waving in the sky!
Hear our rallying hosannas,
   Echoing on high!

Chorus
"Hold the fort for prohibition!"
   Freedom signals still;
Answer back to her petition,
   "By our votes we will!"

2. All our land the foe engages!
   Let no freeman lag!
See! the battle fiercely rages!
   Rally round the flag! *To Chorus*

3. Hear the groans of thousands dying
   On the slaughter field!
By the ensign o'er us flying
   We will never yield! *To Chorus*

4. Hear the shrieks of woe appalling
   Pierce through all the air!
Hear the wretched victims calling;
   Save us from despair. *To Chorus*

5. By the land our fathers bought us,
   With their precious blood!

---

77. *Prohibition Campaign Song Book*, 13. Stearns, *Prohibition Songster*, no. 55, and Mead and Chambers, *Clarion Call*, 61, omit verse 4. Leslie, *Good Templar* (1888), 12, identifies the author as Frank J. Sibley but makes several modifications in the above verses, replaces verse 4, and adds a verse 5. Miller, *Patriotic No-License*, no. 26, entitles this song "Storm the Fort for No License" and replaces the word "Prohibition" with "No license" in verse 1 and the chorus. Miller also substitutes new lyrics for verse 4.

78. Perkins, *Crystal Fountain*, 103.

By the birth-rights they have brought us
    Stem the battle's flood! *To Chorus*

6. By the God who freedom gave us,
    With immortal souls!
Crush the foe who dares enslave us—
    Forward to the polls! *To Chorus*[79]

Be a Sober Man
(Dr. M. D. Merrick)

1. Ho! my brother, see the danger
    Lurking in your way;
See, the foe of peace is waiting,
    Watching for his prey.

Chorus
Sign the pledge and God will help you—
    Break off while you can—
Break the bonds of social custom—
    Be a sober man.

2. In your path a gulf is yawning,
    Heed our warning cry;
Stand erect in princely manhood,
    Strong drink to defy. *To Chorus*

3. Noble men are round you falling;
    Will you help to save—
Help to rescue friends and brothers
    From a drunkard's grave. *To Chorus*

4. Let the weight of your example
    Speak for truth and right,
And your words, like angel voices,
    Leading to the light. *To Chorus*[80]

Come, Sign the Pledge
(Frank C. Filley)

1. See, the mighty throng approaching,
    Led by leaders brave,
'Tis the Gospel Temperance legions,
    Coming, all to save.

Chorus
Come, sign the pledge, for it will save you,
    Sign the pledge tonight,
Pray to God and he will keep you
    By his gracious might.

2. On each breast the azure Ribbon,
    Shows each heart is true.
And King Alcohol we'll conquer,
    By our badge of Blue. *To Chorus*

3. Blessings on our glorious Order,
    Bless each comrade true,
Bless the Gospel Temperance Union,
    God will help us through. *To Chorus*

4. See our glorious banner streaming,
    Hear the trumpet blow,
In Our Leader's name we'll triumph
    Over every foe. *To Chorus*[81]

Victory in the Air

1. See our mighty host assemble,
    For the fight prepare,
Temperance thunder makes them tremble;
    Victory's in the air!

Chorus
Hold the fort for we are coming,
    Millions of us strong,
And we'll keep the battle "humming"
    As we march along.

2. Hold the fort, the day spring deepens
    And the dawn is near,
See how rum's grim column weakens,
    How it quakes with fear. *To Chorus*

3. For the glorious contest rally,
    For the fight prepare,
Send the shout o'er hill and valley,
    Victory's in the air! *To Chorus*[82]

---

79. McCreery, *Collection of Temperance Songs*, 33–34; Leslie, *Good Templar* (1888), 13. Stearns, *National Temperance*, 53, omits verse 4 and reverses verses 5 and 6. Stearns, *Prohibition Songster*, no. 28, and Law, *Temperance Bells*, no. 25, are the same as Stearns, *National Temperance*, 53, but also omit verse 3. Miller, *Patriotic No-License*, no. 14, entitles the song "Hold the Fort for No License," and makes minor changes.

80. Filley, *Red, White, and Blue*, 22.

81. Ibid., 8–9.

82. Daniels, *Temperance Songster*, 15.

[Brothers! Rally for the Conflict]

1. Brothers! rally for the conflict,
    See the banner wave;
Temperance bands are pressing onward
    Fallen men to save.

Chorus
Hear a mighty host of freemen
    Songs of triumph raise;
Love hath conquered, chains are broken;
    Give to God the praise.

2. Swift the day of life is passing,
    Soon will fall the night;
Urge we then the glorious conflict,
    Battling for the right. *To Chorus*

3. Burst the tyrant's bands asunder,
    Set the captives fee;
Let rejoicing wives and mothers
    Shout the jubilee. *To Chorus*[83]

Temperance Rallying Ode
(J. B. Gibbs)

1. Ho! my Brethren, true and faithful,
    See our banner wave!
And around the sacred standard,
    Gather all the brave.

Chorus
Come and join our noble army,
    Raise the banner high!
Keep the pledge and never falter,
    Dare to do or die!

2. Satan and his host surround us,
    With his legions strong!
But with truth and God to aid us,
    We'll triumph over wrong! *To Chorus*

3. See the gentle, brave Crusaders,
    Earnest, firm and bold—
Strong in faith, they're nobly fighting
    Satan's strongest hold! *To Chorus*

4. Let our prayers ascend to heaven,
    Asking help divine!

Stay the hand that desolates,
    And fills our land with crime. *To Chorus*

5. Sons of Temp'rance and Good Templars,
    Do your duty well!
Sound your grand victorious chorus—
    Ring the Temp'rance Bell! *To Chorus*[84]

The Temperance Banner

1. Fling aloft the temperance banner,
    Float its folds on high;
Rapidly the ranks are filling,
    "Victory is nigh."

Chorus
Sign the pledge, 'twill prove a blessing,
    Fruitful unto thee;
'Tis a record made in heaven—
    Sign it and be free.

2. Many a brother, tried and tempted,
    Needs our help once more;
Fling aloft the temperance signal,
    Wave him toward the shore. *To Chorus*

3. Reach the hand to save the fallen—
    Thousands need our aid;
Speak a word the weak to strengthen;
    Urge, constrain, persuade. *To Chorus*

4. Wave aloft the temperance banner,
    Wave it high and higher;
Keep the signal brightly flashing
    Like a beacon-fire. *To Chorus*

5. Then unto our Lord Christ Jesus
    Point the erring one;
God protect us from the demon
    Through His only Son! *To Chorus*[85]

Hold the Fort for Prohibition #2
(Mrs. S. H. Hunter)

1. Hold the fort for prohibition,
    In our noble state;
Satan ruled it long with whisky;
    Now he yields to fate.

83. Hudson, *Temperance Songster*, no. 72.
84. Leslie, *Good Templar* (1888), 13.
85. Ibid.

Chorus
Hold the fort for prohibition,
　　Save our noble boys,
Overthrow the liquor traffic,
　　Ere it them destroys.

2. Liquor men are now advancing,
　　Crying as they come,
Give us whisky, beer and brandy,
　　And our much loved rum. *To Chorus*

3. But our ranks stand firm and steady,
　　For our cause is just,
Right shall triumph is our watchword,
　　And in God we trust. *To Chorus*

4. Day by day come reinforcements,
　　Temperance is near,
Prohibition eighteen ninety,
　　Cheer, my workers, cheer. *To Chorus*[86]

Temperance Reformation

1. Hail! the temperance reformation,
　　See it march along.
Hail! redeemer of our nation.
　　Worthy of our song!

Chorus
Hold the fort for I am coming,
　　Jesus signals still.
Hark! we hear their answer echo,
　　By God's help we will.

2. Though we triumph, gracious Heaven,
　　Still thy help we need,
Let thy helping hand be given,
　　More the cause to speed. *To Chorus*

3. Bless each Temperance celebration,
　　Our flag's now unfurled,
Bless the march of reformation,
　　All around the world. *To Chorus*[87]

The Salvation Army

1. Freemen, to the standard rally,
　　Of the true and just,

"Save our homes" shall be our motto,
　　And "In God our trust."

Chorus
Hip, hurrah for Gov'nor Sherman,
　　And for Manning true;
Once again for Reed and Akers,
　　And our (Representative) too.

2. More than twenty years of glory,
　　Crown our party's name;
And its leaders are the grandest,
　　On the roll of fame. *To Chorus*

3. When the Union was in peril,
　　First among the brave;
Now when every home is threatened
　　We'll be first to save. *To Chorus*

4. When the battle waxed the warmest,
　　We were foremost then;
Now when Right with Wrong is struggling
　　"Go to th' front again." *To Chorus*

5. Freedom from her throne of glory,
　　Spurns the Bourbon guise;
Those who barter Home for Office
　　Fail to win the prize. *To Chorus*

6. Here's the grand Salvation Army
　　That once wore the Blue;
Rally, boys, let's win the victory,
　　As we used to do. *To Chorus*[88]

Onward, Christian Soldiers ("St. Gertrude")

Join the Temperance Army
(Belle P. Mappin)

1. See the temp'rance army! gath'ring near
　　and far,
　　Sober, strong, and valiant, mighty men of
　　war!
Forth they go to battle, battle for the right,
　　Steadfast in their purpose, 'tis a noble
　　sight.

86. Merryman, *Amendment Songs*, no. 15.
87. Dailey and Mead, *Prohibition Chimes*, n.p.
88. Cake, *Popular Campaign*, n.p. Singers were to insert their representative's name into the first verse.

Chorus
Come and join this army, in the struggle be;
  Join the temp'rance army, help to make
    men free.

2. Do these warriors battle only with the foe?
  No, they seek for brothers held in chains
    of woe.
Hear from wives and mothers cries for succor
  come,
  For their loved ones captured by the
    demon rum. *To Chorus*

3. Let us then in pity for each ruined home,
  Forth unto the rescue of these brothers
    come.
Never cease the struggle, stand as do the brave,
  'Til the temp'rance banners o'er rum's
    dungeons wave. *To Chorus*[89]

Onward, Christian Voters

1. Onward, Christian voters! marching to the
    polls,
  In the cause of freedom, dear to freemen's
    souls.
Like a mighty army, move against the foe,
  Vote for God and country, with your
    legions go.

Chorus
Onward, Christian voters! marching to the
    polls,
  In the cause of freedom, dear to freemen's
    souls.

2. To your knees ye Christians! do not doubt
    nor fear,
  God our blessed Savior, every prayer will
    hear.
Forward then ye voters, waver not or fail,
  Trusting to our Captain, will the right
    prevail. *To Chorus*

3. Upward then and onward! ever for the fight,
  Gird you on your armor, ready for the
    fight,

Haste ye to the battle, right against the
  wrong,
  God will give the vict'ry, sing the triumph
    song. *To Chorus*[90]

Onward, Temperance Soldiers!
(James Rowe)

1. Onward, temp'rance soldiers, bravely
    onward go;
  We must free our country from this awful
    foe;
Let there be no quarter given, but, in joy,
  This destroying demon utterly destroy.

Chorus
Onward temp'rance soldiers, to the holy war;
  Jesus Christ your Captain, trod the way
    before.

2. Onward, temp'rance soldiers; children
    starve and die,
  Mothers, loving mothers, bruised and
    bleeding lie;
"Double quick" the order, onward, then,
    with speed;
  Souls in sorrow call us, souls despairing
    plead. *To Chorus*

3. Onward, temp'rance soldiers; true and
    fearless be,
  Till our dear Columbia from this curse is
    free,
Surely God will shield us, and no harm shall
    come;
  We must free our country from this
    monster Rum. *To Chorus*[91]

Temperance Soldiers
(James Rowe)

1. We are temp'rance soldiers, standing for
    the right;
  And till rum is banished, we will bravely
    fight.

89. Towne, *Temperance Anthems*, 16–17.
90. Law, *Temperance Bells*, no. 1.
91. *Anti-Saloon Campaign*, no. 1; Elisha A. Hoffman, *Local Option Campaign Songs*, no. 1; Hoffman, *Woman's Christian Temperance*, no. 1.

Drink is causing sorrow, death, and pain, and shame;
  So we mean to crush it, in our Master's name.

Chorus
Onward, Christian soldiers! marching as to war,
  With the cross of Jesus going on before.

2. We can do but little, being small, you know,
  But we'll show our colors, ev'rywhere we go;
And, with Jesus watching, ready us to shield,
  Though our lines be tempted, we shall never yield. *To Chorus*

3. We are growing stronger, ev'ry day and hour,
  And the foe will find us soon a mighty power;
Oh, we pray that quickly, may the glad day come,
  When our blessed country shall be free from rum. *To Chorus*[92]

Rally to Our Standard
(John R. Clements)

1. Rally to our standard in this fight today,
  With a hearty purpose help drive rum away;
This the day for action, this the battle hour;
  God is in the conflict, God will gird with power.

Chorus
Rally to our standard; voting as we pray;
  An unbroken phalanx, driving rum away.

2. Rally to our standard, this the crisis hour;
  Hosts of evil tremble at Jehovah's power.
God has long been patient, now His arm is bare;
  Once and twice He's spoken, Barleycorn, beware! *To Chorus*

3. Rally to our standard. Ours is freedom's land;
  Drink must face its downfall, righteousness must stand.

Right exalts the nation, sin is its disgrace.
  Rum must be forever cast from every place. *To Chorus*[93]

Bringing in the Sheaves ("Harvest")

Prohibition Law
(Wm. B. Marsh)

1. Hark, the proclamation, ringing through the nation,
  Bearing welcome tidings from Iowa's shore;
Scorning opposition, we've carried Prohibition,
  Alcohol the tyrant governs here no more.

Chorus
Welcome tidings these, welcome tidings these,
  We are all rejoicing at the tyrant's fate;
May this tidal wave, soon come here and save,
  With its Prohibition, our entire State.

2. Sweetest voices blending, welcome news are sending,
  Prohibition's spreading in the South and West;
Into line they're falling, for recruits are calling,
  There will be rejoicing if we go with the rest. *To Chorus*

3. Brave Ohio's sighing, for salvation crying,
  She would break her shackles, wear the yoke no more;
Kentucky's ranks are filling, proclaiming they are willing
  In future to be governed by Prohibition law. *To Chorus*

4. A brighter aspect viewing, let's be up and doing,
  Putting on this armor, battle with the rest;
Reformation trying, to its standard flying
  Grasp the great inducement sent us from the West. *To Chorus*[94]

---

92. R. H. Cornelius, *Cornelius' Prohibition Songs*, no. 10.
93. John R. Clements, *Shaw's Campaign Songs*, 9.
94. Perine and Mash, *National Prohibition Hymnal*, 28.

The Nation's Going Dry

(E. Norine Law)

1. Come ye loyal workers, join the
      temperance army.
    Shout for Prohibition, now our battle
      cry;
Forward be our watchword in the mighty
      conflict.
    See the cause advancing, our country's
      going dry.

Chorus
Our country's going dry, our country's going
      dry;
    See the host advancing, our country's
      going dry;
Our country's going dry, our country's going
      dry,
    See the host advancing, our country's
      going dry.

2. Saloons will soon be banished from our
      land forever;
    Hear the children singing, banners lifted
      high;
Joyous are their voices, happy are their faces;
    Glory Hallelujah! our country's going dry.
      To Chorus

3. Voting in the morning, votes for
      Prohibition.
    Voting out the darkness and the vile
      saloon,
Standing like a Daniel for a glorious purpose,
    Hear the shouts of victory! our country's
      going dry. *To Chorus*

4. Rally all ye faithful, rally to the conquest.
    Shout the glorious message, Victory is
      nigh;
Prayers will soon be answered, God is leading
      onward,
    We are sure to triumph, our country's
      going dry. *To Chorus*[95]

The State Is Going Dry

1. The liquor camp is routed, the righteous
      are pursuing,
    Praise the God of battles, shout the joyful
      cry;
Volunteer for service, forward in the conflict
    Pass along the watchword—the State is
      going dry.

Chorus
The State is going dry, the State is going dry,
    Pass along the watchword—the State is
      going dry.
The State is going dry, the State is going dry,
    Pass along the watchword—the State is
      going dry.

2. Prohibition's coming, a mighty tide is
      rising,
    Forty million voices echo back the cry;
Crush the liquor tyrant, down with rum
      forever,
    Pass along the watchword—the State is
      going dry. *To Chorus*[96]

We'll Make the Nation Dry

1. Come, ye loyal workers, join the
      temp'rance army,
    Shout for prohibition, now our battle cry;
Onward be our watchword in the mighty
      conflict,
    Hear the shouts of vict'ry, we'll make the
      nation dry.

Chorus
We'll make the nation dry, we'll make the
      nation dry!
    Hear the shouts of vict'ry, we'll make the
      nation dry!
We'll make the nation dry, we'll make the
      nation dry!
    Hear the shouts of vict'ry, we'll make the
      nation dry!

2. The liquor traffic's going from our land
      forever,

---

95. Law, *Temperance Bells*, no. 42. Gordon, *Popular Campaign*, 30, entitles this song "Montana's Going Dry" and substitutes "Montana's" for "Our country's" in all verses.

96. Hoffman, *Woman's Christian Temperance*, no. 48; Biederwolf and Lawson, *Best Temperance Songs*, no. 39.

Hear the children singing, banners lifted
   high;
Joyous are their voices, happy are their
   faces,
   Hear the shouts of vict'ry, we'll make the
     nation dry. *To Chorus*

3. Rally, all ye faithful, rally to the conquest,
   Shout the glorious message, victory is
    nigh;
Prayers will soon be answered, God is leading
   onward,
   Hear the shouts of vict'ry, we'll make the
    nation dry. *To Chorus*[97]

97. Gordon, *Popular Campaign*, 23. Note similarities to "The Nation's Going Dry." Gordon, *Jubilee Songs*, 17, "The World Is Going Dry," uses the same text with slight changes.

4. Scottish Songs

While it may seem odd to find Scottish music so well represented in the repertoire of the temperance movement, there were a number of factors that led to that occurrence. Scots were present in most of the American colonies from the beginning; however, during the period from approximately 1720 until 1776, large numbers of Scots migrated to America to escape religious persecution and other restrictions imposed on Highland society, bringing their music, philosophy, and religion with them. Lehman estimates that by the beginning of the War of Independence, Scottish immigrants and their descendants made up one-sixth or one-seventh of the entire population in the colonies. In addition, among the religious groups active in the temperance movement, the largely Scottish Presbyterian Church played a major role. The Presbyterian Church, along with the New England Congregationalists, who were also involved with the temperance movement, were the two largest and most influential churches in America by the end of the eighteenth century.[1]

Although many would consider the Scottish songs in this chapter "folksongs," we know that Robert Burns wrote or modified the lyrics for at least three of the four. Thus, the broader term "traditional song" seems more appropriate. Burns provided texts for over three hundred songs and is credited with collecting or composing tunes for forty-five of them. He was an avid collector of old Scottish songs, and many of his lyrics were based on fragments of old songs. According to Peter Cunningham, "Burns of all poets that ever breathed, possessed the most happy tact of pouring his genius through all the meanderings of music, was unrivalled in the skill of brooding over the ruder conceptions of our old poets, and in warming them into grace and life. He could glide like dew into the fading bloom of departing song, and refresh it

---

1. Alexander Leslie Klieforth and Robert John Munro, *The Scottish Invention of America, Democracy, and Human Rights*, 230–35; William C. Lehmann, *Scottish and Scotch-Irish Contributions to Early American Life and Culture*, 5–7.

into beauty and fragrance." Sadly, because Burns chose to publish his songs anonymously, and because only a few of his original manuscripts still exist, it is impossible to determine his exact contribution in many cases.[2]

According to Hamm, Burns's songs first appeared on the American scene in the early nineteenth century, and no doubt many were well known by the 1830s when temperance songs first began to appear in great number. The variety of subjects in Burns's songs must have been particularly appealing. His subject matter included patriotic songs, love songs, sentimental songs, and songs celebrating battles. These songs struck a chord with temperance writers of the nineteenth century. Many even chose to imitate Burns's dialect to maintain the Scottish flavor of the original song. Burns is an ironic source of inspiration for temperance writers for other reasons. Although his letters sometimes expressed regret about it, he drank heavily. He also wrote drinking songs, and he defended whiskey distillers.[3]

Auld Lang Syne

The best known of traditional Scottish songs, "Auld Lang Syne" was adapted by Robert Burns for George Thomson's *Scottish Airs* (1799). He wrote two of its five verses with the other three coming from an older source. Because he felt its original tune was mediocre, Burns chose instead to set it to another air, either called "The Miller's Wedding" or "I Fee'd a Lad at Michaelmas." "Auld Lang Syne" was first introduced in America in the late eighteenth or early nineteenth century. This song, so widely used to toast the New Year with "a cup of kindness," became a great favorite of temperance writers.[4]

A number of temperance settings proclaim the benefits of water over more traditional New Year's libations, including one of the best-known settings, "Virtues of Cold Water," which appears in at least ten temperance songbooks. "Virtues of Cold Water," by the composer of "Jingle Bells," J. P. Pierpont, is loaded with puns, referring first to water as *pale* in verse 2 and later mentioning the water *pail*. In verse 4 he first writes about the *bells of tulips*, meaning the blossoms of the tulips, later turning this image into the *two lips of a belle*. Finally, he notes in verse 5 that an oak tree catches rain and *gets high* (grows taller because of the rainfall) and poses the question "Then why not you and I?" suggesting water is a better drink for "getting high" than alcoholic beverages.

2. Peter Cunningham, *The Songs of England and Scotland*, 2:166.

3. Hamm, *Yesterdays*, 60–61; Francis Collinson, *Traditional and National Music of Scotland*, 191.

4. Collinson, *Traditional and National Music*, 1; Dallin and Dallin, *Heritage Songster*, 57; Ewen, *All the Years*, 4; T. S. Gleadhill, ed., *Songs of the British Isles*, 347–48; Spaeth, *History of Popular Music*, 53–54.

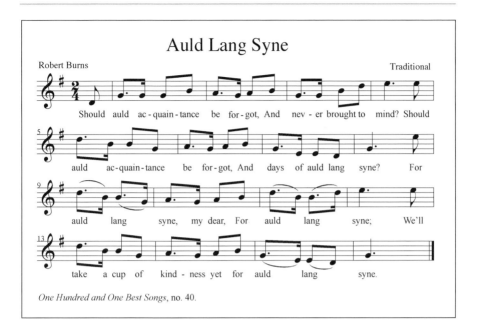

Auld Lang Syne

Robert Burns

Traditional

Should auld ac-quain-tance be for-got, And nev-er brought to mind? Should

auld ac-quain-tance be for-got, And days of auld lang syne? For

auld lang syne, my dear, For auld lang syne; We'll

take a cup of kind-ness yet for auld lang syne.

One Hundred and One Best Songs, no. 40.

Virtues of Cold Water
(Pierpont)

1. Shall e'er cold water be forgot,
 When we sit down to dine?
O no, my friends, for is it not
 Poured out by hands divine?
Poured out by hands divine, my friends,
 Poured out by hands divine:
From springs and wells it gushes forth,
 Poured out by hands divine.

2. To Beauty's cheek, though strange it seems,
 'Tis not more strange than true,
Cold water, though itself so *pale,*
 Imparts the rosiest hue:—
Imparts the rosiest hue, my friends,
 Imparts the rosiest hue:
Yes, Beauty, in a water-*pail*
 Doth find her rosiest hue.

3. Cold water too—though wonderful,
 'Tis not less true again—
The weakest of all earthly drinks,
 Doth make the strongest men:

Doth make the strongest men, my friends,
    Doth make the strongest men:
Then let us drink this weakest drink,
    And grow the strongest men.

4. I've seen the bells of tulips turn,
    To drink the drops that fell
From summer clouds;—then why should not
    The two lips of a belle?
The two lips of a belle, my friends,
    The two lips of a belle—
What sweetens more than water pure
    The two lips of a belle?

5. The sturdy oak full many a cup
    Doth hold up to the sky,
To catch the rain, and drinks it up,
    And thus the oak *gets high*;
'Tis thus the oak gets high, my friends,
    'Tis thus the oak gets high,
By having water in their cups,
    Then why not you and I?

6. Then let cold water armies give
    Their banners to the air!
So shall the boys, like oaks, be strong,
    The girls, like tulips, fair:
The girls, like tulips, fair, my friends,
    The girls, like tulips, fair:
The boys shall grow like sturdy oaks,
    The girls, like tulips, fair.[5]

Others settings of "Auld Lang Syne" focus on alcohol's detriment to the family or encourage the listener to take the pledge. "Come Friends," a setting that appeared in at least eleven songbooks beginning in the 1860s, combines these themes.

5. Pierpont, *Cold Water Melodies*, 9; Bigelow and Grosh, *Washingtonian Pocket*, 102–3; Gould and Grosh, *Washingtonian Pocket*, 34–36; *Union Temperance*, 58–59. Hart, *Juvenile Temperance*, 27, uses only verses 1, 2, and 6; and Mowatt, *Mowatt's Temperance Glee*, 7–8, omits verse 4 and slightly modifies verse 6. Another version, on page 35 in Mowatt, includes verses 1, 3, and 4. Saunders, *Temperance Songster*, 34–35, omits verses 4 and 6 and modifies the beginning of verse 3. Bradbury and Stearns, *Temperance Chimes* (1867 and 1878), 21, omits verses 2, 4, and 6, and modifies verse 3. *Crusaders' Temperance*, 29, includes only two verses: verse 3, as modified by Bradbury, and verse 5.

Come Friends

1. Come, friends and brethren, all unite
 In songs of hearty cheer;
Our cause speeds onward in its might;
 Away with doubt and fear.
We give the pledge, we join the hand,
 Resolved on Victory;
We are a bold, determined band;
 We strike for Liberty.

2. Our wives, our children, we'll defend;
 Their groans and tears no more
Shall with the maddening liquor blend:
 Down with the tyrant's power.
We give the pledge, we join the hand,
 Resolved on Victory;
We are a bold, determined band;
 We strike for Liberty.

3. Base avarice may tempt in vain!
 We will not enter where
Dwell *Rum,* and *Misery,* and *Pain,*
 And *Death* and deep *Despair.*
We give the pledge, we join the hand,
 Resolved on Victory;
We are a bold, determined band;
 We strike for Liberty.

4. The cup of death no more we take;
 That cup no more we give;
It makes the head, the bosom ache:
 Ah, who can drink and live?
We give the pledge, we join the hand,
 Resolved on Victory;
We are a bold, determined band;
 We strike for Liberty.

5. Henceforth we one and all proclaim
 Eternal war with Rum;
This is our pledge, "We drink no more."
 Come, join us, Brothers, come.
We give the pledge, we join the hand,
 Resolved on Victory;
We are a bold, determined band;
 We strike for Liberty.[6]

---

6. Potter, *Boston Temperance,* 2:56. Verses 1 and 4 are reprinted in Root, *Musical Fountain,* 109; Hull, *Hull's Temperance,* 121; Bradbury and Stearns, *Temperance Chimes* (1867 and 1878), 110; Sherwin and

Bruce's Address

Like "Auld Lang Syne," "Bruce's Address" or "Scots Wha Haé" was included in Thomson's *Scottish Airs* (1799). Its tune, "Hey, Tuttie Tattie," was believed to be the march used by Robert the Bruce at the Battle of Bannockburn in 1314. Burns wrote lyrics incorporating themes of liberty and independence that reflect what the Bruce might have said to his followers before that historic battle. Although no longer a familiar song to most Americans, the tune to "Bruce's Address" provided the sort of martial spirit needed to call listeners to action. It was borrowed, not only by temperance writers, but also for songs of the Mexican War and the Civil War. Temperance writers used the tune to encourage listeners to take the pledge, to vote for prohibition, and to join the temperance army, as, for example, in "Appeal to Freedom's Friends."[7]

Appeal to Freedom's Friends

1. Friends of Freedom, swell the song,
    Young and old, the strain prolong,
Make the Temperance army strong,
    And on to victory.
Lift your banners, let them wave,
    Onward march, a world to save,
Who would fill a drunkard's grave,
    And bear his infamy?

2. Shrink not when the foe appears;
    Spurn the coward's guilty fears,
Hear the shrieks, behold the tears
    Of ruined families.
Raise the cry in every spot,
    "Touch not, taste not, handle not,"
Who would be a drunken sot,
    The worst of miseries?

3. Give the aching bosom rest,
    Carry joy to every breast;
Make the wretched drunkard blest,
    By living soberly.

Stearns, *Bugle Notes*, 120; Perkins, *Crystal Fountain*, 107; Stearns, *National Temperance*, 5; Macy, *Temperance Song-Herald*, 90; and Stearns, *Prohibition Songster*, no. 5. Stearns and Main, *Trumpet Notes*, 75; and Miller, *Patriotic No-License*, no. 24, include verses 1 and 4 only.

7. Collinson, *Traditional and National Music*, 130; Ewen, *All the Years*, 56; Gleadhill, *Songs of the British*, 368; Willard A. Heaps and Porter W. Heaps, *The Singing Sixties*, 33; Spaeth, *History of Popular Music*, 53.

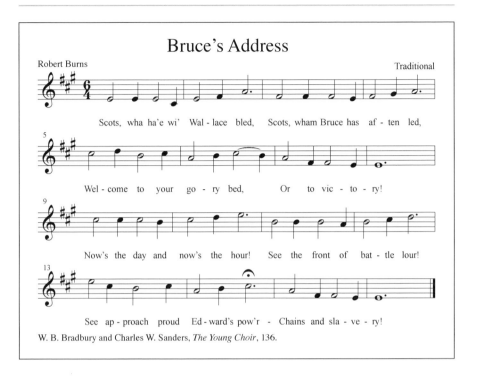

Bruce's Address

Robert Burns

Traditional

Scots, wha ha'e wi' Wal - lace bled, Scots, wham Bruce has af - ten led,

Wel - come to your go - ry bed, Or to vic - to - ry!

Now's the day and now's the hour! See the front of bat - tle lour!

See ap - proach proud Ed - ward's pow'r - Chains and sla - ve - ry!

W. B. Bradbury and Charles W. Sanders, *The Young Choir*, 136.

Raise the glorious watchword high—
   "Touch not—Taste not till you die!"
Let the echo reach the sky,
   And earth keep jubilee.

4. God of mercy! hear us plead:
   For thy help we intercede!
See how many bosoms bleed;
   And heal them speedily.
Hasten, Lord, the happy day,
   When, beneath thy gentle ray,
TEMPERANCE all the world shall sway,
   And reign triumphantly.[8]

8. Pierpont, *Cold Water Melodies*, 66–67; *Washington Temperance*, 36–37; W. B. Bradbury and C. W. Sanders, *The Young Choir*, 136–37; Plimpton, *Washingtonian Choir*, 74; *Union Temperance*, 30–31. Bigelow and Grosh, *Washingtonian Pocket*, 45, includes only verses 1 and 2 and the first half of verse 3.

The Campbells Are Coming

"The Campbells Are Coming" employs the traditional Scottish pipe tune, "Baile Inneraora," which accompanied the Campbell Clan as they marched into battle. Some sources credit Burns with the lyrics, but others consider it a true Scottish folksong. Like "Bruce's Address," this tune was also borrowed during the Mexican War.[9] Several temperance reformers utilized "The Campbells Are Coming" to recognize groups that joined the movement, as with "The Firemen's Gathering."

The Firemen's Gathering
(Dedicated to "Chatham Fire Company, No. II")

Chorus
The Firemen are coming, make room, make room,
    The Firemen are coming, make room, make room,
To Temp'rance they're swarming, their ways reforming;
    Make room for the Firemen, make room, make room.

1. Union Eighteen led on the Van,
    They signed the total pledge to a man;
And there they stand, each noble name
    Forever inscribed on the Roll of Fame. *To Chorus*

2. Thirteen and Two came hand in hand
    To join the Temperate Firemen's band,
Determined to live forever free:
    And were followed by glorious Thirty-three. *To Chorus*

3. Brave Forty-eight came next on the list,
    Resolved the enemy's neck to twist;
While the lads of the Clinton, deserting the bowl
    Dashed on to the rescue, heart and soul. *To Chorus*

4. But why enumerate all that come
    To avoid the Drunkard's terrible doom?
They're coming in bodies, Hoses, Engines and all;
    Intemp'rance is tottering and soon must fall. *To Chorus*

5. The Fireman flies when duty calls,
    No sense of danger e'er appalls;
He strives to save, and he dauntless goes
    Through tempests or flames: no fear he knows. *To Chorus*

---

9. Ewen, *All the Years*, 56; Collinson, *Traditional and National Music*, 19–20.

The Campbells Are Coming

Traditional

The Camp-bells are com-in', O ho, O ho! The

Camp-bells are com-in', O ho, O ho! The Camp-bells are com-in' to

Fine

bon - nie Loch-lev-en, The Camp-bells are com-in', O ho, O ho!

Up - on the Lo - monds I lay, I lay, Up -

on the Lo-monds I lay, I lay; I look - ed down to

D.C. al Fine

bon - nie Loch-lev-en, And heard three bon - nie pi - pers play.

M. L. Bartlett, *Bartlett's Music Reader for Day Schools*, 102.

6. With a proud, firm heart, and a flashing eye,
    The Fireman will conquer the foe or die;
  With a good stream of water, the pipe he will wield,
    He may die in the battle, but never will yield. *To Chorus*

7. Then Ladies, smile on the Fireman's task;
    Your smiles are the only rewards he'll ask;
  For you he will peril his life night and day,
    And if need be, for you he'll throw life away! *To Chorus*[10]

The most interesting of the five temperance settings for this tune, "A Slave to the Bottle Will Never Wed Me," presents the persuasive argument of a lass (with heavy Scottish dialect) who refuses to marry any man who's a drinker.

10. Bensel, *Temperance Harp*, 8; *Washingtonian Tee-Totalers' Minstrel*, 52–53.

A Slave to the Bottle Will Never Wed Me

1. Contented I live in my auld minny's cot,
    And peace is a flower that I nurse near the spot;
Of fond true love offers I've had twa or three—
    But a slave to the bottle will never wed me.
He may rouse up my cheeks, and the glance o' my een;
    And rave till he tires 'bout my shape and my mien;
But a maiden I'll live, and an auld maid I'll dee,
    Ere a slave to the bottle will ever wed me.

2. He may say he adores me, wae's me and alas!
    What love can he gie, when its a' in the glass;
For house, wife, or wee anes, he'll care na' a flea—
    O, a slave to the bottle will never get me!
O, he thinks it no sin to sit drinking a' night,
    To come staggering hame in the face o' daylight;
A' tattered and battered, no worth a baubee—
    O, a slave to the bottle will never get me!

3. What a contrast is he to the douce sober man
    Wha lives in accordance wi' nature's first plan!
Wi' health on his cheek, and true love in his e'e—
    O! a slave to the bottle will never wed me!
Like a lion to labor, he loups wi' the lark,
    And when he comes hame, 'tween the light and the dark,
Owre the fields and flowers ring his whistle o' glee—
    O, a slave to the bottle will never get me!

4. When he finds his bit biggin' baith canty and clean,
    Then he makes his fair wifie as proud as a queen;
Cracks his thumbs to the wee laughin' tot on his knee,
    O, a slave to the bottle will never wed me!
Now ilk lassie wha langs to be ca'd a gude wife,
    Let a douce sober chiel be your partner through life;
E'n take my advice, 'tis the best I can gie—
    For a slave to the bottle will never wed me![11]

Comin' thro' the Rye

Burns either wrote or adapted the lyrics for the Scottish song "Comin' thro' the Rye," which was first published in America in 1828. Two of the temper-

---

11. Mowatt, *Mowatt's Temperance Glee*, 37–38.

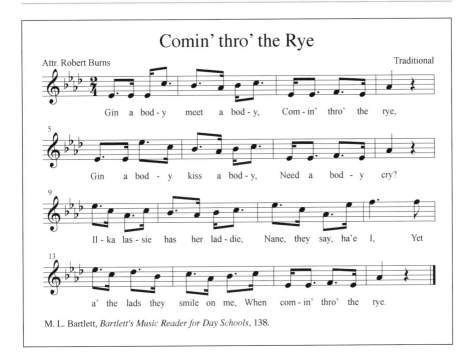

Comin' thro' the Rye

Attr. Robert Burns   Traditional

Gin   a bod-y   meet   a bod-y,   Com-in'   thro'   the   rye,

Gin   a bod - y   kiss   a bod-y,   Need   a   bod - y   cry?

Il - ka las-sie   has   her lad - die,   Nane, they say, ha'e   I,   Yet

a' the lads   they   smile on me,   When   com - in' thro'   the   rye.

M. L. Bartlett, *Bartlett's Music Reader for Day Schools*, 138.

ance settings of "Comin' thro' the Rye," "Drinking on a Sly" and "If a Body Takes His Toddy," deal with those who try to sneak a drink without others knowing.[12]

Drinking on a Sly

1. Some there are who donned the ribbon, rum to shun did try,
But have fallen and we see them drinking on a sly;
O, the danger of this habit, sipping now and then,
Nursing, feeding and creating appetite for gin.

Chorus [repeats music from last half of verse]
Come and help us, mighty Spirit, in the way that's right,
Save our nation, all the people, from the cures and blight.

2. O this custom, social tippling, how it mars the soul,
Think a moment of the thousands quaffing at the bowl;
Think again of myriad others, ruined, wretched made,
All around it so entwines us we fell to quake and dread. *To Chorus*

3. That poor man who thus addicted little knows the sin;
O, my friends, let's try and save him and keep him from the inn.

12. Gleadhill, *Songs of the British*, 56; Spaeth, *History of Popular Music*, 66.

Will not statesmen, clergy, laymen, all unite as one,
    To destroy this monster evil and abolish rum?[13]

If a Body Takes His Toddy
(J. C. Macy)

1. If a body takes his toddy, Very, very sly,
    Then some other meddling body asks a body "why?"
If a body can't drink toddy when there's no one by (hic),
    Then it's 'cause them temp'rance folks are getting through the Rye.

2. If a body buys some toddy, Very, very sly,
    Then some other busy body winks his knowing eye!
How does he my trick discover—How do you suppose (hic)?
    I'm somewhat inclined to think it's owin' to my nose!

3. If a body, full of toddy, Kiss his fav'rite girl,
    She gets sassy, very sassy, whips off with a whirl!
Cloves and lemon, spice and coffee—'taint no use to try (hic)!
    Ev'ry gal will smell my breath when I've been drinkin' Rye![14]

As with many of the other tunes, we find both suasive and coercive lyrics for "Comin' thro' the Rye." The earliest known song, "Gin a Body Meet a Body," encourages listeners to help persuade drinkers to change their ways, but the final example, "Voting Out the Rye," clearly calls for legal action to save drinkers from "liquor's blight."

Gin a Body Meet a Body

1. Gin a body meet a body coming from the inn,
    Full of stout or full of toddy, or the worse of gin.
There talk to him of Temperance, and tell him 'tis a sin,
    To hurt his health, and waste his wealth, and injure all his kin.

2. Gin a body meet a body badly clad and poor,
    Be sure that laziness and drink have brought this to his door.
Then preach to him sobriety, and tell him you are sure
    He yet may mend, and have a friend, if drink he will abjure.

3. Gin a body change this body, think what good he's done,
    All of you I see in view might thus convert your one;
And so the life of man and wife, would be a different thing,
    And soon he'd find in purse and mind, he'll be wealthy as a king.[15]

13. Nichols, *Iron Door*, 3.
14. Macy, *Temperance Song-Herald*, 80.
15. Mowatt, *Mowatt's Temperance Glee*, 31–32.

Voting Out the Rye
(Maud Russell)

1. If a body in Ohio votes against the rye,
   He will have a conscience clear from many a weary sigh.
Every voter in Ohio can help to save the state—
   Every man for Prohibition, November sixth's the date.

2. If a body loves his neighbor, which is surely right,
   He will help the Christian people make Ohio white.
   Every voter in Ohio, *etc.*

3. If a body loves his country, he'll help in this fight
   To save the laddies and the lassies from the liquor's blight.
   Every voter in Ohio, *etc.*

4. When the votes have all been counted, and our state is dry,
   Many hearts will be rejoicing, as will you and I.
   Every voter in Ohio, *etc.*[16]

16. *Ohio State Prohibition*, 13.

"Come, father! Won't you come home?"

Auld Lang Syne

The Pledge

1. I've signed the pledge! It is the bond
    Between my God and me—
'Tis done!—I've broke th'enchanted wand;
    I breathe—I live—I'm free!
Darkness, which was my world, is past,
    And sounds of discord cease;
And what was once a chaos vast,
    Is harmony and peace!

2. And as I turn me to the home,
    Once cheerless to my sight,
Seraphic voices seem to come,
    With welcome of delight.
The very faces round my hearth
    Are sweetly new to see,
And woman's love, and childhood's mirth,
    Are paradise to me.

3. O! glorious change! a beauteous world
    Appeareth now around,
The evening clouds seem flags unfurled,
    With gold and crimson bound;
The wood, the harvest field and hill,
    With living splendor glow,
While ocean, river, stream and rill,
    Give music as they flow!

4. O! that the veil were rent before,
    That I might see these things,
And glad with gratitude adore
    The power whence wisdom springs.
But mercy o'er life's pathway yet
    Her lustre will display,
As suns in cloudless light will set,
    Which led a stormy day.[17]

Teetotaller's Auld Lang Syne

1. Be days of drinking wine forgot,
    Let water goblets shine;
And from your memory ever blot
    The days of drinking wine.
Those days of drinking wine, my friend,
    Those days of drinking wine—

A temperance hour is worth a power
    Of days of drinking wine.

2. We all have quaffed to days long past
    Bright juices of the vine;
But let us from our memories cast
    Those customs of "lang syne."
Bad customs of lang syne, my friend,
    Bad customs of lang syne,
Our temperance age must blot the page
    Of customs of lang syne.

3. We twa can meet as friends should meet,
    We twa together dine,
Our bev'rage quaff from fountains sweet,
    And never think of wine.
A temperance shrine, we're pledg'd, my friend,
    We're pledged at her fair shrine
And hold her cause above all laws
    And customs of lang syne.[18]

'Tis but a Drop

1. "'Tis but a drop," the father said,
    And gave it to his son;
But little did he think a work
    Of death was then begun;
The "drop" that lured him when the babe
    Scarce lisped his father's name,
Planted a fatal appetite
    Deep in his infant frame.

2. "'Tis but a drop," the comrades cried,
    In truant school-boy tone;
"It did not hurt us in our robes,
    It will not now we're grown."
And so they drank the mixture up,
    That reeling, youthful band;
For each had learned to love the taste
    From his own father's hand.

3. "'Tis but a drop—I need it now,"
    The staggering drunkard said;
"It was my food in infancy—
    My meat, and drink, and bread,
A drop—a drop—oh, let me have,
    'Twill so refresh my soul!"

17. Pierpont, *Cold Water Melodies*, 29–30.
18. Ibid., 65–66; *Women's Temperance*, 37.

He took it—trembled—drank and died,
  Grasping the fatal bowl.[19]

Past Grief and Present Joy
(E. F. Hatfield)

1. Can we forget the gloomy time,
  When Bacchus ruled the day,
When dissipation, sloth, and crime,
  Bore undisputed sway?
The time—the time—the gloomy time,
  The time has passed away,
When dissipation, sloth, and crime,
  Bore undisputed sway.

2. Can we forget the gray haired sires,
  Who sunk by anguish riven,
To see their sons by liquid fires,
  To shame and ruin driven?
The sires, the sires, the gray haired sires,
  No more shall thus be riven,
Nor see their sons, by liquid fires,
  To shame and ruin driven.

3. Can we forget the tender wives,
  Who found an early tomb?
For ah! the partners of their lives
  Had met the drunkard's doom!
The wives, the wives, the tender wives,
  May bid adieu to gloom,
For now the partners of their lives,
  Abhor the drunkard's doom.

4. We'll ne'er forget that noble band
  Who feared no creature's frown,
And boldly pledged both heart and hand
  To put intemperance down;
The band, the band, the noble band,
  The band of best renown,
Who boldly pledged both heart and hand,
  To put intemperance down.

5. We'll praise and bless the God of love
  To whom this grace we owe,
That living waters flow above,
  And streams of health below;

The God, the God, the God of love,
  To Him our praise we owe,
That living waters flow above,
  And streams of health below.

6. Nor shall the PLEDGE be e'er forgot,
  That so much bliss creates,
We'll touch not, taste not, handle not,
  Whate'er intoxicates:
The pledge, the pledge is not forgot,
  The pledge that Satan hates,
We'll touch not, taste not, handle not,
  Whate'er intoxicates.[20]

Call to Inebriates and Their Families
(*Maine Washingtonian*)

1. Oh! would'st thou find a safe retreat,
  On earth a peaceful home,
Where friends with smiles thy presence greet,
  And turmoils never come?
Then join our Washingtonian band,
  Help fight our common foe,
We'll march together, heart and hand,
  King Alcohol lay low.

2. Long, long we worshipped at his shrine,
  Long felt his cruel reign,
Our peace and comfort did resign,
  For infamy and pain;
But Jehovah's now our King,
  His banner we've unfurled,
'Gainst Alcohol our force we'll bring,
  And arrows shall be hurled.

3. Wives, mothers, sisters, with us meet,
  Their grief has passed away,
Their presence to our hearts is sweet,
  They cheer us on our way;
Then join our Washingtonian band,
  Help fight our common foe;
We'll march together, heart and hand,
  King Alcohol lay low.[21]

---

19. *Collection of Temperance Songs,* n.p.; Bigelow and Grosh, *Washingtonian Pocket,* 113–14; Potter, *Boston Temperance,* 1:12–13; Hart, *Juvenile Temperance,* 33–34; Pierpont, *Cold Water Melodies,* 75–76.
  20. Bigelow and Grosh, *Washingtonian Pocket,* 32–33. Pierpont, *Cold Water Melodies,* 79–80, omits verses 2 and 5.
  21. Pierpont, *Cold Water Melodies,* 116; Bigelow and Grosh, *Washingtonian Pocket,* 47.

Cold Water Army

1. With banner and with badge we come,
   An *Army* true and strong,
To fight against the hosts of Rum,
   And this shall be our song:
We love the clear cold water springs,
   Supplied by gentle showers,
We feel the strength cold water brings,
   "The victory is ours."

2. *Cold Water Army* is our name,
   O faithful may we be,
And so in truth and justice, claim
   The blessings of the free.
We love the clear cold water springs, *etc.*

3. Though others love their rum and wine,
   And drink till they are mad,
To water we will still incline,
   To make us strong and glad.
We love the clear cold water springs, *etc.*

4. I pledge to thee this hand of mine,
   In faith and friendship strong,
And, fellow soldiers, we will join
   The chorus of our song.
We love the clear cold water springs, *etc.*[22]

Auld Lang Syne

1. Come, girls and boys, come young and old,
   And let us now combine
Against the tyrant who has reigned,
   In days of auld lang syne.
In days of auld lang syne, my boys,
   In days of auld lang syne,
Against the tyrant who has reigned,
   In days of auld lang syne.

2. A noble band has tried full long
   His throne to undermine,
But still he holds his iron sway,
   By right of auld lang syne.
By right of auld lang syne, my boys, *etc.*

3. But now an army we have raised,
   And 'tis our bold design
To drive the monster from the land
   Where he has reigned lang syne.
Where he has reigned lang syne, my boys, *etc.*

4. The land of Washington shall ne'er
   Beneath his power decline,
We'll wage a war, and fight it through,
   Like him in auld lang syne.
Like him in auld lang syne, my boys, *etc.*

5. Old alcohol must surely fall
   When we together join
All through the land to nullify
   The tyrant of lang syne.
The tyrant of lang syne, my boys, *etc.*

6. And warmly in this holy cause
   Dear woman too can join,
For she has suffered most of all,
   In days of auld lang syne.
In days of auld lang syne, my boys, *etc.*

7. She knows that when her bosom friend
   The temp'rance pledge shall sign,
She'll weep no more the burning tears
   She wept in days lang syne.
She wept in days lang syne, my boys, *etc.*

8. Farewell to rum, farewell to gin,
   Farewell to sparkling wine,
We'll never taste the poison more,
   Remember auld lang syne!
Remember auld lang syne, my boys, *etc.*

9. Come girls and boys, come young and old,
   And let us now combine
To drive the monster from the land
   Remember auld lang syne!
Remember auld lang syne, my boys, *etc.*[23]

The Gathering of the Redeemed

1. We come! we come, that have been held
   In burning chains so long;

22. Pierpont, *Cold Water Melodies*, 68–69; Bigelow and Grosh, *Washingtonian Pocket*, 66; *Washington Temperance*, 15–16; Bradbury and Sanders, *Young Choir*, 135; Gould and Grosh, *Washingtonian Pocket*, 53; Hart, *Juvenile Temperance*, 16; Thompson, *Thompson's Band*, 22–23; *Women's Temperance*, 4; Stearns, *National Temperance*, 27. Stearns, *Band of Hope*, 62, omits verse 2. Herbert, *Young Volunteer*, 11, uses verse 1 and replaces verse 2.
   23. Dana, *Temperance Lyre*, 14–15.

We're up! and on we come, a host
    Full fifty thousand strong.
The chains we've snapped that held us round
    The wine vat and the still;
Snapped by a blow—nay, by a word,
    That mighty word, I will!

2. We come from Belial's palaces,
    The tippling shops and bar;
And, as we march, those gates of death,
    Feel their foundations jar.
The very ground, that oft has held,
    All night our throbbing head,
Knows that we're up—no more to fall,
    And trembles at our tread.

3. From dirty den, from gutter foul,
    From watch-house and from prison,
Where they, who gave the poisonous glass,
    Had thrown us, have we risen;
From garret high have hurried down,
    From cellar stived and damp
Come up; till alley, lane and street
    Echo our earthquake tramp.

4. And on—and on—a swelling host
    Of temperance men we come,
Condemning and defying all
    The powers and priests of rum;
A host redeemed, who've drawn the sword,
    And sharpened up its edge,
And hewn our way through hostile ranks
    To the tee-total pledge.

5. To God be thanks, who pours us out
    Cold water from his hills,
In crystal springs and bubbling brooks,
    In lakes and sparkling rills.
To these to quench our thirst, we come
    With freemen's shout and song,
A host already numbering more than
    fifty thousand strong.[24]

The Wife's Appeal

1. Should auld affection be forgot,
    All drowned in Rum and Wine—
The love that blessed our happy lot
    In days of auld lang syne?

For auld lang syne, my dear,
    For auld lang syne,
Come take the *Pledge Teetotal*, now,
    For auld lang syne.

2. How happy in our early love!
    How bright each scene did shine!
But, O, what darkening clouds and storms
    Have rose from Rum and Wine!
For auld lang syne, my dear,
    For auld lang syne,
Come take the *Pledge Teetotal*, now,
    For auld lang syne.

3. In wedlock's sacred union joined,
    What blessings crowned our board!
But, O, what floods of want and woe
    In Rum and Wine have poured!
For auld lang syne, my dear,
    For auld lang syne,
Come take the *Pledge Teetotal*, now,
    For auld lang syne.

4. Still here's my hand, my husband dear
    My heart, too, still is thine:
O, give to me your own again,
    Forsaking Rum and Wine.
For auld lang syne, my dear,
    For auld lang syne,
Come take the *Pledge Teetotal*, now,
    For auld lang syne.

5. Then auld affection shall revive,
    As 'twas in auld lang syne;
Our early, wedded love shall live,
    Restored from Rum and Wine.
For auld lang syne, my dear,
    For auld lang syne,
Come take the *Pledge Teetotal*, now,
    For auld lang syne.[25]

Washingtonian Song
(Mrs. E. C. Gavitt)

1. Oh no, we cannot touch the bowl,
    There's death in every sip;
It sinks the mind—destroys the soul,
    It ne'er shall press our lip.
Cold water is the drink we love,

24. Pierpont, *Cold Water Melodies*, 54–55; Gould and Grosh, *Washingtonian Pocket*, 20–21.
25. Potter, *Boston Temperance*, 1:17.

Pure from the sparkling stream;
This cooling draught revives our strength,
    While homes with comforts gleam.

2. Let others boast the praise of wine,
    And Alcohol so bold;
We sing in notes almost divine,
    The praise of water cold.
Cold water is the drink we love,
    Pure from the sparkling stream;
This precious gift unites our hearts
    To home—where treasures gleam.

3. A band united now we stand,
    Of fearless hearts and true;
To drive the poison from our land,
    And all rum-sellers too.
Yes, all rum-sellers no must give,
    Their barb'rous traffic o'er;
We pledge to chase this demon foe,
    Far from our native shore.

4. Come join our ranks, all ye who love
    Your friends', and virtue's call;
Now with the Washingtonians move,
    And banish Alcohol.
Cold water is the drink we love,
    Pure from the sparkling stream;
This precious gift unites our hearts
    To home—where pleasures gleam.[26]

May Day Hymn
(George Russell)

1. The wint'ry cold has passed away;
    The smiling spring appears:
The lovely birds, with carols gay,
    Delight our listening ears.
Trees, plants, and flowers revive again;
    Their fragrance fills the air;
Refreshed with gentle showers of rain,
    The earth looks green and fair.

2. The clouds "cold water" do distill;
    Sweet water—Oh how fine!
"The thirsty ridges drink their fill";
    But clouds distill no Wine.
The bleating flocks in meadows green,
    Delight to skip and play;

But nothing stronger drink, I ween,
    Than what the brooks convey.

3. So we resolve, *we'll never* drink
    Rum, Brandy, Wine, or Gin:
We the "Cold Water Army" think,
    The victory, too, to win;
Since we have learned their deadly power,
    And know what they have done;
We'll grasp the pledge, and never cower;
    The serpent's wiles we'll shun.

4. We, drunkards never can become,
    If we but let alone
The all-devouring monster, Rum,
    Whose *virtues* now are known.
Like little lambs we'll "skip and play,"
    And chant in cheerful lays,
As here we do on this "May-day,"
    "Cold Water" melodies.[27]

Auld Lang Syne

1. We're soldiers of the Water King,
    His laws we still obey;
Virtue and health are his reward,
    We want no better way.
Our banner to the breeze we'll fling,
    And down with alcohol.
Then let us sing the Water King,
    Good soldiers one and all.

2. We boast no sword or glittering spear;
    Ours is a bloodless crown—
A purer, brighter, fairer thing
    Than conquerors ever won.
Then let us sing, *etc.*

3. Our strength is in the living spring,
    And long as waters run,
Or grass grows green, we'll pledge to keep
    Our Temp'rance armor on.
Then let us sing, *etc.*

4. What tho' the Fire King mocks our hosts,
    As great Goliath did,
We've temp'rance Davids in our ranks,
    Who'll bring away his head.
Then let us sing, *etc.*[28]

26. Ibid., 2:14.
27. *Collection of Temperance Songs*, n.p.
28. Fillmore, *Temperance Musician*, 96.

A Drunkard's Doom

1. I saw him, 'twas at dawn of day,
   Before a grog-shop door;
His eyes were sunk, his lips were parched
   I viewed him o'er and o'er:
His infant boy clung to his side,
   And lisping to him said,
"Come, father—mother's sick at home,
   And sister cries for bread."

2. He trembling rose, and staggered in,
   As oft he'd done before.
And to the landlord faltering said,
   "Come, give us one glass more."
The host complies: his purple lips
   Now press the venomed bowl;
He drinks, though wife and children starve,
   And ruins his own soul.

3. A year elapsed, I passed that way,
   A crowd stood at the door:
I asked the cause, when one replied,
   "Ned Burnit is no more!"
I saw his funeral move along,
   No wife, no child was there—
They too had joined their mother earth,
   And left this world of care.

4. Reflect, ye votaries of the bowl,
   And know 'tis heaven's decree:
Ye ne'er shall taste eternal life,
   Till from the bowl you flee.
Reflect, ere wife and children mourn—
   Fly from the grog-shops, fly:
Or you, like Ned, shall wretched live,
   Like him, neglected die.[29]

The Slaves of Ruby Wine

1. "Should auld acquaintance be forgot,
   And never brought to mind?"
Yes, every sot should be forgot,
   Who won't give up his wine—
Who won't give up his wine or beer,
   Who won't give up his wine;

Though thousands by it die each year,
   He won't give up his wine.

2. Can those be worthy of a place,
   Among our friends to shine,
Who will not for their dying race,
   Give up their ruby wine—
Give up their ruby wine and beer,
   Give up their ruby wine;
How can we love in friendship dear
   The slaves of ruby wine?

3. Let those upon our memory dwell,
   And round our hearts entwine,
Who strive to make their age excel
   The days of Auld Lang Syne—
The days of Auld Lang Syne, my friends,
   The days of Auld Lang Syne;
Who strive to make their age excel
   The days of Auld Lang Syne.[30]

[When Rechab's Sons]

1. When Rechab's sons, in days of old,
   Abjured the ruby wine,
And filled their cups of flashing gold
   With nectar more divine:
They quaffed their liquid diamonds, then
   And o'er life's journey trod—
A nobler race of spotless men—
   The chosen sons of God.

2. Brave men of old, the world shall own
   The greatness of your fame,
And o'er Intemperance' prostrate throne
   Shall blazon Rechab's name.
Our men your words shall ne'er forget,
   As custom's chains they break;
And all our race will echo yet—
   "The wine we ne'er will take."[31]

[A Goodly Thing]

A goodly thing it is to meet,
   In Friendship's circle bright,
Where nothing stains the pleasure sweet,

---

29. Ibid., 179.

30. *Crusaders' Temperance*, 24. Stearns, *National Temperance*, 56, omits verse 3.

31. Bradbury and Stearns, *Temperance Chimes* (1867 and 1878), 114; Macy, *Temperance Song-Herald*, 97.

Nor dims the radiant light;
No happier meeting earth can see,
    Than where the joy we prove
Of Temperance and Purity
    Fidelity and Love.[32]

[Good Night]

Good night, good night, to every one,
    Be each heart free from care,
Let every brother seek his home,
    And find contentment there.
May joy beam with tomorrow's sun
    And every prospect shine,
While wife and friends laugh merrily,
    Without the aid of wine.[33]

A Little, 'Tis a Little Word

1. A little, 'tis a little word,
    But much may in it dwell,
Then let the warning truth be heard,
    And learn the lesson well.
A little drink seems safe at first,
    Exerting little power,
But soon begets a raging thirst,
    Which cries for more and more.

2. The appetite once formed, thus feeds,
    Till the strong man is bound,
And thus the way of ruin leads
    Down, down, like slippery ground.
Just as the largest rivers run
    From small and distant springs;
The greatest crimes which men have done
    Have grown from little things.[34]

The Temperance Ship
(Frank C. Filley—dedicated
to Mrs. E. Pitt Stevens)

1. God bless our noble Temperance ship,
    God bless her gallant crew,
For everyone who walks her deck,

A ribbon wears of Blue,
There's health in every sparkling eye,
    A smile on every lip,
And every heart responsive cries,
    "God bless our Temperance ship."

2. Her sails are white, her decks are clean,
    Her riggings are secure,
For level heads have set it up;
    Forever 'twill endure,
'Tis all well rove, and firm and taut,
    And not a block can slip,
She rides the waters like a swan,
    God bless our Temperance ship.

3. No smell of whisky taints the air;
    No horrid oaths resound,
There's mutual kindness reigning there,
    And love and peace abound,
For God he watches o'er that crew,
    No winds her sails shall strip,
For pleasant breezes round her blow,
    God bless our Temperance ship.

4. And Mrs. Stevens, "Bless her soul,"
    Commands that gallant crew,
She too, upon her bosom wears
    The Ribbon of dark blue.
And when she walks the quarter-deck,
    Each hat will quickly tip,
"God bless that lady," cries each tar,
    God bless our Temperance ship.[35]

Our Kindly Greeting
(Wm. B. Marsh)

1. Again our brother's hand we shake,
    In kindly Christian cheer.
And trust our temperance friends will make
    Your visit pleasant here.
Friends from afar, friends here at home
    We cordially invite,
As workers in God's vineyard, come
    And join with us tonight.

---

32. Bradbury and Stearns, *Temperance Chimes* (1867 and 1878), 121; Sherwin and Stearns, *Bugle Notes,* 124.

33. Bradbury and Stearns, *Temperance Chimes* (1867 and 1878), 121; Sherwin and Stearns, *Bugle Notes,* 124; Leslie, *Good Templar* (1888), 87.

34. Bradbury and Stearns, *Temperance Chimes* (1867 and 1878), 21.

35. Filley, *Red, White, and Blue,* 7–8.

2. Together let us pledge renew,
    Our hearts and hands tonight,
In future still more work to do,
    Upholding what is right,
Christ is our Captain, Heaven our prize,
    And, though all earth may frown,
We'll push on boldly, upward rise
    To win the promised crown.

3. Then fill your glasses to the brim,
    With water sparkling bright,
Give undivided praise to Him
    Directs us in this fight.
Spread out your banners far and near,
    Your Gospel colors show,
Until we hear the deafening cheer—
    He dies! the drunkard's foe.[36]

The Plan of Hope
(Wm. B. Marsh)

1. Dear hearts united join this fight
    Determined you will do
In future what you know is right,
    This plan of hope pursue.
Accept the Savior's outstretched hand,
    And promise, one and all,
No more the abject slave to stand
    You were to alcohol.

2. You who have felt the serpent's sting,
    Have been racked with its pain
Are fitted best, perhaps, to bring
    You back to hope again.
From sad experience many speak,
    To them it is not new,
They sought the wine-cup that *you* seek,
    Once drank the same as *you.*

3. But there are lessons all may learn,
    Will bring you certain good,
Be sober, honest, try to earn
    Your needful share of food.
Like us you too may do the same,
    The cost all can afford,
Live sober, you can win a name
    If you will trust in God.[37]

Gird Your Armor On
(Samuel Jarden)

1. Awake! awake! put on your strength,
    And gird your armor on,
For Prohibition must at length,
    O'er this whole Nation dawn,
But first of all, dear Maryland,
    We must, we will restore;
Yes, every County in the State,
    And then old Baltimore.

2. Montgomery, Cecil, Caroline,
    Prince George's, Calvert, Kent,
Have won the fight on this same line,
    And think you they repent?
No, no, they all with one accord,
    Proclaim with joy and pride,
That Prohibition's magic word
    Is cherished far and wide.

3. Ye men of Howard, form in line,
    And emulate their deeds;
Let every district now combine,
    To heal the hearts that bleed.[38]

Our Call

1. The years now gone like prophets speak,
    Their lessons oft proclaim,
Exhorting men the lost to seek
    With kind unselfish aim;
They move our hearts with mem'ries sweet,
    And bid us live for Christ,
That earth may be a fair retreat,
    With none to drink entice.

2. Our work it is to do the will
    Of one who came to save,
Compassion feel as we would still
    The lake or ocean wave;
From hill to hill, and city street,
    We too in faith must go,
Till Christ shall come our world to greet
    A Paradise below.

3. We live in thought of good we do,
    And not in wealth possessed,

36. Perine and Mash, *National Prohibition Hymnal*, 38.
37. Ibid., 27.
38. Jarden, *Prohibition Banner*, 8. Verse 3 is incomplete.

Nor in the fame that men pursue
  With fear and wild unrest;
A drunkard's cot made Paradise
  Our Paradise will be,
And souls we save the sacrifice
  Our Father deigns to see.

4. The sins of earth, the hearts that bleed,
  The sighs that pain the ear,
The sad laments of souls in need,
  all call for love sincere;
The Master bids us feel the woes
  Of men in wine and tears,
That we may go as he still goes
  Through all the passing years.[39]

Anniversary Hymn

1. A year hath gone in mem'ries blest,
  A year of toil and tears,
But Christ hath come to manifest
  The Love that sweetly cheers;
And in his name our strength was found
  To war with evils great,
Though foes upon our labor frowned,
  The foes of God and State.

2. The changing scenes of human life
  Were varied good and ill,
But in the world with sin and strife
  We sought the Father's will;
And, as we look a-down the year,
  We gather strength and trust,
We see our work with vision clear,
  Will toil as workers must.

3. On us pour out, oh God of all,
  The Love and Truth of Christ,
That we may go where brethren fall
  And save where drink enticed;
We'll sing again in earth or skies
  Of souls we saved from sin,
The new year blest to weeping eyes,
  As we from drink shall win.[40]

With Hearts Enlisted in the Cause

1. With hearts enlisted in the cause,
  With duty for our guide,
With banners lifted high above,
  We'll brave temptation's tide!
Then give a hand to help along
  The cause we love so well,
And to the glowing temp'rance song
  Let worldwide echoes swell.

2. Oh, here's a hand, my trusted friend,
  Now give a hand of thine,
And pledge thy word along with me,
  That thou'll give up the wine;
For ev'ry evil may be found
  Within its treach'rous gleam!
So, advocate the gift of God—
  Cold water's crystal stream![41]

[We've Had Enough]

1. We've had enough of license laws,
  Enough of liquor taxes;
We've turned the grind-stone long enough,
  'Tis time to swing our axes;
This deadly Upas tree must fall—
  Let strokes be strong and steady;
Pull up the stumps! grub out the roots!
  O brothers, are you ready?

Chorus [repeats the last half of the tune]
For "Regulative" Laws, "No, No!"
  For Prohibition—"Yes!"
We'll vote for right and win the fight,
  For God the right will bless.

2. No longer will we shield this foe
  To manhood, love and beauty;
We've had enough of compromise—
  The right alone is duty;
Enough of weak men and distrust—
  The burden grows by shifting;
Let's put our shoulder to the wheel
  And do our share of lifting. *To Chorus*[42]

39. Munson, *Gospel and Maine*, 12–13.
40. Munson, *Gospel and Maine*, 43.
41. Macy, *Temperance Song-Herald*, 81.
42. Hudson, *Temperance Songster*, no. 20.

Cold Water Clear and Friendship Dear

1. Cold water clear and friendship dear
    Bring purest joys to mind,
The hope of earth was sober worth
    In auld lang syne.
For auld lang syne, my dear,
    For auld lang syne,
Our love and friendship we'll renew,
    In auld lang syne.

2. No heart that's pure can long endure
    The curse of rum and wine;
Drink made hearts sore the wide world o'er
    In auld lang syne.
For auld lang syne, my dear,
    For auld lang syne,
Our love and friendship we'll renew,
    In auld lang syne.

3. By sunny bowers and bonny flowers
    Young hearts were glad and kind;
Now down life's stream they sing serene,
    Of auld lang syne.
For auld lang syne, my dear,
    For auld lang syne,
Our love and friendship we'll renew,
    In auld lang syne.

4. The song we sung when we were young,
    Aye round our hearts will twine;
The temperate ways and sunny days
    Of auld lang syne.
For auld lang syne, my dear,
    For auld lang syne,
Our love and friendship we'll renew,
    In auld lang syne.

5. There's hope before, aye, more and more,
    When evening days are fine,
And memories dear, our hearts to cheer,
    Like auld lang syne.
For auld lang syne, my dear,
    For auld lang syne,
Our love and friendship we'll renew,
    In auld lang syne.[43]

King Alcohol

1. King Alcohol, a tyrant bold,
    Now rules o'er our great land.
On school and pulpit, bench and bar,
    He lays his heavy hand—
On workshop and on counting-house,
    On factory, farm, and ship.
On land and sea, there's naught that's free
    From his hard-handed grip.

2. Our fathers fought 'gainst Britain's king,
    But we've a despot worse.
And shall we not resist his rule,
    Resist with all our force?
For God, for home, for native land,
    For all that we hold dear,
Let us against his hellish reign
    Fight hard, without a fear.[44]

Woman's Cause Shall Win
(Horace B. Durant)

1. The conflict deepens o'er the land;
    'Tis one of woman's might,
And she is firmly moving on
    To battle for the right;
Once more her voice rings clearly out,
    To lift the race from sin,
And who can fail to plainly see,
    That woman's cause shall win.

2. The demon, drink, has long withstood
    The arguments of men;
But when the women take the field,
    Its weapons fail it then;
For it is conscious of its guilt,
    'Tis foul without, within;
'Tis self-condemned, one reason why
    This woman's cause shall win.

3. The clans of liquor ne'er have met
    Such wondrous foe before:
And they are busy canvassing
    The prospect o'er and o'er.
Yet, view the question as they may,
    Through whiskey, beer or gin,
They must confess the truth at last,
    That woman's cause shall win.

43. Stearns and Main, *Trumpet Notes*, 17.
44. Fobes, *Temperance Songs*, 12.

4. Those so-called laws, that fill the land
   With sorrow, crime and death,
Shall soon be swept away, as chaff
   Before the tempest's breath;
And though the politicians croak,
   And raise their usual din
Of danger to the revenues,
   This woman's cause shall win.

5. Man boasts that he controls the world
   With mighty hand and brain;
But woman's heart is mightier far—
   'Tis heart at last shall reign.
The one is selfish at the best;
   The other is akin
To heaven itself and that is why
   This woman's cause shall win.[45]

The Pledge
(G. W. Dungan)

1. Come let us all, with one accord,
   Our hearts and voices join,
And pledge against the use of rum,
   And beer, and gin, and wine.
We now with one accord agree,
   That this we all will do,
Forever from strong drink abstain,
   And to the cause be true.

2. We know that sorrow always flows
   From out the drunkard's bowl;
While water brings sweet happiness
   To every thirsty soul.
We now with one accord agree,
   That this we all will do,
Forever from strong drink abstain,
   And to the cause be true.

3. Then let us help each other keep
   The pledge we have in mind;
And we may each the blessing share,
   The good of all mankind.
We now with one accord agree,
   That this we all will do,

Forever from strong drink abstain,
   And to the cause be true.[46]

Drive the Saloon Away
(Elisha A. Hoffman)

1. What stir is this throughout the land?
   What does the tumult mean?
What men of earnest face are these
   Who ev'rywhere are seen?
These are the hosts of Temperance,
   Contending in the fray
To close forever the saloon,
   And drive the drink away.

2. Each face is resolute and firm,
   Each heart is brave and true;
They look like men of purpose strong,
   Like men of courage, too.
These are the hosts of Temperance,
   Contending in the fray
To close forever the saloon,
   And drive the drink away.

3. All have grown weary of the curse
   That ruled this land so long,
And have resolved to put away
   This great and cruel wrong.
These are the hosts of Temperance,
   Contending in the fray
To close forever the saloon,
   And drive the drink away.[47]

Closing Hour
(Palmer Hartsough)

1. The closing hour has come at last,
   And severs this glad throng;
But ere we go let heart and voice
   Join in a parting song;
Join in a parting song, dear friends,
   Join in a parting song,
But ere we go let heart and voice
   Join in a parting song.

---

45. Durant, *Prohibition Home*, 16–17. Anna A. Gordon, *The White Ribbon Hymnal*, 101, and Gordon, *Temperance Songster*, no. 117, omit verses 3 and 5.

46. Dungan et al., *Acorn Temperance*, no. 21.

47. *Anti-Saloon Campaign*, no. 22; Hoffman, *Local Option*, no. 23; Hoffman, *Woman's Christian Temperance*, no. 22.

2. We go to meet our ancient foe,
   United let us stand;
King Alcohol must be dethroned
   In our beloved land;
In our beloved land, dear friends,
   In our beloved land,
King Alcohol must be dethroned
   In our beloved land.

3. Then bravely forward let us go,
   And falter not nor fail;
The Lord of all is over us,
   And will at last prevail;
And will at last prevail, dear friends,
   And will at last prevail,
The Lord of all is over us,
   And will at last prevail.[48]

Bruce's Address

Address to Washingtonians

1. Ye who have from Brandy fled!
   Ye whom Gin has often led!
Welcome are ye, from the dead!
   Glorious victory!
Now's the day, and now's the hour;
   Lo! the tyrant's waning power,
Darkly o'er us still doth lower;
   Chains and slavery!

2. Who will be a traitor knave?
   Who will fill a drunkard's grave?
Who so base as be a slave?
   Do not turn and flee!
Who to virtue's king and law,
   Would not every drunkard draw?
And from sin's devouring maw
   Set them nobly free!

3. By the drunkard's woes and pains:
   By our brethren still in chains;
While the life-blood fills their veins,
   Say they shall be free!
Lay the proud usurper low;
   See, he reels at every blow!

Ends his reign of sin and woe!
   Shout for victory.[49]

[Children Who Have Rallied Now]

1. Children who have rallied now
   Where Immanuel's soldiers bow,
Who will take the Temperance vow,
   As a volunteer?
Children! hear the battle-cry,
   Sounding loud and sounding nigh
From the throne of God on high,
   Who will volunteer?

2. See! the foe is gathering fast,
   Hark! his clanging trumpet blast;
Who will fight him to the last,
   As a volunteer?
Lo! o'er all the tented field
   God will be our sun and shield,
Alcohol, the foe, shall yield,
   To the volunteer.[50]

Sign, for Freedom

1. Child, who wouldst not be a sot,
   Youth, who yet hast tasted not
Of the death that's in the pot,
   Sign, and you'll be free.
Youths and maidens blithe and gay,
   Sign the pledge and keep away
From the tyrant's awful sway,
   Sign, and you'll be free.

2. Drunkards now throughout the land,
   Join to form a noble band,
Join in heart and join in hand,
   Sign, and you are free.
Touch not, taste not, handle not,
   Is the cure for every sot,
May it never be forgot,
   Till they all are free.

3. Many sots are in the grave,
   Many lie beneath the wave,
Many live to drink and rave,
   Sign, and you'll be free.

---

48. Gordon, *Temperance Songster*, no. 119.
49. Pierpont, *Cold Water Melodies*, 36.
50. Ibid., 105–6.

Think upon the bloated face,
    Think of ruin and disgrace,
Stand not in the drunkard's place,
    Sign, and you'll be free.[51]

Sons of Liberty

1. Sons of Liberty, arise!
    Who your country's glory prize,
Spread your banner to the skies!
    Wake from apathy!
Join the Washingtonian Band,
    Firmly to your pledges stand,
Drive intemp'rance from the land,
    Crime and misery.

2. Who would not a brother save,
    Who would be himself a slave,
Who would fill a drunkard's grave,
    Let him spurn our laws—
Who his country loves and owns,
    Who would free and bless her sons,
Who would stay her tears and groans,
    Let him aid our cause.

3. Now's the time our foe to press,
    See his foll'wers less and less!
See they falter and confess!
    Haste the joyful time,
When the tyrant shall be slain,
    Universal Temp'rance reign,
And our flag without a stain,
    Wave from clime to clime.

4. While we swell our grateful lays—
    While our voices high we raise,
Loudest we will ever praise
    God who makes us free.[52]

Temp'rate Drinkers, All Beware

1. Temp'rate drinkers, all beware,
    Listen while we now declare
That alcohol will you ensnare,
    And work your ruin soon;
Safety only can be found
    Here, upon teetotal ground,

Listen to the warning sound,
    Or you will be undone.

2. To your danger now awake,
    E'en the "little drop" forsake,
For O, it is a sad mistake
    That it can do no harm;
On your path what sorrows wait
    We can well anticipate;
Now before it is too late
    We sound the loud alarm.

3. Temp'rate drinkers, drink no more,
    Sign the pledge, we do implore,
You'll never know the tyrant's power
    Till you are his slave;
If you will not hear our cry
    Listen to our prophecy—
You a mournful death must die
    And fill the drunkard's grave.[53]

Come Join
(J. P. Gage)

1. Come sisters join in songs of praise,
    With heart and hand we'll strive to raise
The inebriate from his fallen ways,
    For temp'rance must prevail.
God's laws are laws of perfect peace,
    In him we'll trust and never cease,
With hearts united, he'll increase,
    The "Washingtonians."

2. We're not ashamed to seek in cell,
    And the dark abodes where misery
        dwell,
For there we see the bosom swell,
    O who would not engage.
With pledge in hand we go to save,
    Although the poisonous cup they crave,
While we portray the drunkard's grave,
    They sign the "saving pledge."

3. We call on those who have in store
    Of this world's goods a share or more,
For something to relieve the poor,
    Nor do we call in vain.

---

51. Ibid., 110–11.
52. Ibid., 18–19. Verse 4 is incomplete.
53. Dana, *Temperance Lyre*, 10–11.

We then invite the temperate poor,
    Who signed the pledge to drink no more,
To call on us while we've a store,
    To mitigate their pain.

4. To feed the poor is one command,
    And when restored they join our band,
As living witnesses they stand,
    The many truths to tell.
Then why should we not persevere,
    For in eternity and here
Reward is ours, we need not fear,
    This is our festival.[54]

Now's the Day

1. Sots, whose health and wealth have fled,
    Sots, who groan on sleepless bed,
With fiery thirst, distracted head,
    And horror stricken brain!
See the clouds of ruin lower!
    Now's the day and now's the hour
To break the fell Destroyer's power,
    O, never taste again!

2. On the brink of ruin pause;
    Join our noble temperance cause;
Bind yourselves by wholesome laws,
    And never taste again.
By the most endearing ties,
    By your famished children's cries,
By your wives' heart-rending sighs,
    We charge you to abstain.[55]

Oh, Leave the Damning Bowl

1. Ho! ye toiling slaves of drink,
    'Tis high time that you should think!
Pause! nor down to ruin sink;
    Oh, leave the damning bowl!
Will you let vile rum destroy
    Earthly peace and Heavenly joy?
Stop! Reform! For this employ
    Your hands, your heart, your soul!

2. Be not longer under ban;
    By the grace of God, you can
Break your chains and be a man,
    Not be a sottish slave!
Ah! what bliss can earth bestow,
    When remorse fills life with woe?
Gloom above, despair below,
    And earth a hopeless grave!

3. Is it wisdom thus to lose
    Both worlds for this foe you choose,
While your path with thorns it strews,
    Piercing you with pain?
Look upon that picture there!
    Scan its horror and despair!
Say you that you do not care?
    Such reply is vain.

4. Yes, you care, and you do feel
    Anguish you cannot conceal;
Though with drunken step you reel,
    Yet you would be free!
Free for those on earth you prize,
    Free from some within the skies,
Watching you with pity'ng eyes—
    Free—yes, you may be.

5. Do you see that license den?
    'Tis a dramshop trapping men
Soul and body; pass it then—
    Yes, pass it firmly by;
Think that there you would be sold,
    Like a slave, for party gold—
To pay revenue, we're told—
    For this to toil and die!

6. Christ will aid you! Break your chains,
    Swell not license party's gains,
Banish rum and all its pains,
    And be a man once more;
Step from darkness into light,
    Life and hope will then grow bright,
And you'll feel a new delight,
    You ne'er have felt before.[56]

54. Potter, *Boston Temperance*, 2:20.
55. Bonner, *Mountain Minstrel*, 82.
56. Durant, *Prohibition Home*, 43–44.

Now's the Time for You
(Frances E. Willard)

1. Men who vote, your time has come,
   Wave the flag, and sound the drum,
Save the cause of God and Home
   And your Native land.
Now's the day and now's the hour,
   Let the snowflake ballots shower,
Bury 'neath a freeman's power
   Liquor's cruel band.

2. Hear the children while they plead,
   Pity all the hearts that bleed,
Bless the tempted in their need,
   By your ballot true.
Prohibition is our prayer,
   Hunt the lion in his lair,
Let no horrid dramshop dare
   Look for help to you.

3. When we're men and women grown,
   And are seated on the throne,
If the drink fiend has not flown,
   And men are not true;
We for God and Home will stand,
   We will fight for Native Land,
We will win the battle grand,
   But now's the time for you.[57]

Campaign Song
(G. E. Thrall)

1. Home protectors, hold your ground,
   Girt with enemies around,
Let your ranks be firm and sound,
   Not a coward there.
Parties strong in worldly power,
   Brewers' millions as their dower,
This their day and this their hour,
   Learn to stand and bear.

2. You are few and scorned and poor,
   Called to suffer and endure,
Slandered when they can't allure,
   Burned in effigy.
But your boy—a drunkard's life?
   That sweet girl—a drunkard's wife?
Never! Struggle to the knife
   Sooner let it be.

3. Lo! you sires burst England's cords
   You felled slavery with your swords,
Will ye now to liquor lords
   Bend the suppliant knee?
You are few but not forlorn,
   Israel's hosts the heights adorn,
Dark the night, but soon the morn,
   Then the victory.[58]

The Campbells Are Coming

The Sailors Are Coming

Chorus
The Sailors are coming, oho! oho!
   The Sailors are coming, oho! oho!
The Sailors are coming from hither and
      thither,
   The Sailors are coming, oho! oho!

1. The Washingtonians are the boys,
   They offer such alluring joys,
That all who hear their merry song
   Join in, and thus the strain prolong.
      To Chorus

2. The noble tars that brave the seas,
   We love recruits from such as these;
They come with gallant hearts and warm,
   To help our vessel through the storm.
      To Chorus

3. The temp'rance ship sails nobly on,
   Her colors waving strike to none,
She's triumphed o'er her enemy,
   Poor old King Alcohol is he! *To Chorus*

4. Our ship must sail from pole to pole,
   Till we have rescued every soul,
Till all who now are slaves to rum,
   Their enemy have overcome. *To Chorus*

5. Then anchored safe, O, may we be
   Where all from sin and pain are free
And, every toil and danger past,
   O, may we meet in Heaven at last.
      To Chorus[59]

---

57. Gordon, *Marching Songs*, 10.
58. *Prohibition Campaign Song Book*, 4.
59. Dana, *Temperance Lyre*, 9–10.

Shun the Red Wine

(Thomas Frazer)

1. Oh! shun the red wine if you're wise,
    young man,
    For it is but a fiend in disguise, young
    man,
Ever luring to wrong both the frail and the
    strong,
    And filling fair earth full of sighs, young
    man.

2. O, heed not his smirks and his smiles,
    young man,
    For he sports with the hearts he beguiles,
    young man,
And he laughs at the wrecks, be whatever the
    sex,
    That have foundered and sunk through
    his wiles, young man.

3. Never dream of his light-hearted toasts,
    young man,
    But think what his merriment costs,
    young man,
Of the heart-aches and fears, of the sad
    mother's tears,
    O then count how poor are his boasts,
    young man.

4. O what's his wild mirth and its worth,
    young man,
    When it brings sorrow home to the
    hearth, young man,
Breaking hearts that we love, and as silent
    graves prove,
    Spreading ruin and wrong round the
    hearth, young man.[60]

The Doings of Jerry

1. Can drink make you merry? It may be for
    night,
    But in a great hurry the pleasure takes
    flight,
Today it brings laughter, makes enemies
    friends,

But, oh, the day after, what sorrow
    attends!

2. Still Jerry pursuing rank madmen you
    prove,
    But stung with the ruin of all you should
    love,
The knife and the halter next ready you
    find;
    But there your hands falter, for hell is
    behind!

3. Is this to be merry? oh fie! oh fie!
    I tell you what, Jerry, you lie, you lie;
You heighten the fever while proffering relief,
    You bare-faced deceiver—you legalized
    thief!

4. While poverty scatters your last spark of
    pride,
    And patches and tatters your skinny ribs
    hide,
These beer-selling gentry, as if by design,
    Have spick and span garments, how
    spruce and how fine!

5. And while you sit grumbling, alive, and
    but just,
    Voraciously mumbling a butterless crust,
With your hard-earned money the landlords
    command
    The milk and the honey—the fat of the
    land.

6. Your figs are but thistles, I fear, I fear;
    You pay for your whistles too dear, too
    dear;
The price makes you tremble—health, money,
    and peace,
    And you just then resemble so many
    plucked geese.[61]

Rum's Infection

1. There is wide spread infection in every
    direction,
    Infusing its poison from pole to pole;

---

60. Hart, *Juvenile Temperance*, 23–24. This song uses only the chorus.
61. *Crusaders' Temperance*, 60. This song uses only the chorus.

It seizes its victim by an organized system,
    And carries destruction to thousands of
        souls;
They say it is warming, and then it is cooling,
    While all are agreeing it makes them feel
        wise,
And keeps them from freezing, and blood
        circulating,
    So they don't often mind when it
        blackens their eyes.

2. They see the great fury and havoc it makes,
    The cruelties, suicides, premature graves,
They see, but don't care if the last penny
        takes,
    'Tis their money they want, if in poverty
        leaves.
It is strange that a people with Bible in hand,
    With churches and sabbath schools
        having no end,
Having preachers and teachers all over the
        land,
    So little accomplish the evil to mend.

3. We are creatures of habit, you all well
        know,
    And if this infection should deal you a
        blow,
Come over to temperance; I can easily show
    The greatest of blessings on you will
        bestow.
And if I must tell you what is certainly true,
    You follow up drinking, and selling it
        too,
No ribbon or pledge can ever save you,
    For the fangs of the serpent will pierce
        through and through.

4. Then let us all rally, join hand in hand,
    To strengthen our strong cords, and
        tighten the band
That around this great army so wisely
        planned,
    With banners unfurled look ever so
        grand.
We'll onward go marching, and not be
        outdone,

And strike down our foe, if it's one by
        one;
The weapons we use, so near our hearts
        hung,
    Is "Charity for all and malice towards
        none."[62]

Comin' thro' the Rye

The Better Plan
(Mary H. Mather)

1. If a body meet a body, who won't sign the
        pledge,
    Shall a body wound a body with
        contempt's cold edge?
Should not that same body rather
        strenuously try
    To show the t'other body that he'd better
        join the "Y"?

2. If a body meet a body, who at temp'rance
        jeers,
    Shall a body box a body on a body's ears?
Would it not be better rather jeering to pass
        by,
    The while the body sayeth sweetly, "Come
        and join our 'Y'"?

3. Well, the time is coming surely when a
        body'll see
    That a temp'rance pledge is something
        made to set one free,
And there'll be no need for workers,
        furthermore to try— .
    For ev'ry body'll be a member of a
        temp'rance "Y."[63]

Help a Bit
(Frances B. Damon)

1. Eager, able money-getter, with your magic
        power,
    Come and help the world grow better, for
        one little hour.
Yes, whatever your condition, here's a work
        to-day—

---

62. Nichols, *Iron Door*, 16.
63. Gordon, *Songs of the Young Woman's*, 12; Gordon, *Temperance Songster*, no. 19.

Help to bring in prohibition all along the way.

2. Scholar, bending to the letter, scanning glory's way,
   Up, and help the world grow better, for one little day.
Yes, whatever your condition, *etc.*

3. Idler, wearing habit's fetter, pleasures that beguile,

Leave, and help the world grow better for a little while.
Yes, whatever your condition, *etc.*

4. Each is to his race a debtor; would you this forget?
   Up, and help the world grow better. Pay an honest debt.
Yes, whatever your condition, *etc.*[64]

64. Gordon, *Popular Campaign*, 33.

5. Popular Songs

A number of factors came together to create the climate in which popular music began to thrive in nineteenth-century America. Lowell Mason and the Boston Academy of Music successfully made the case for the introduction of music in the Boston Public Schools in 1838, and a number of other cities soon followed. As a result a growing body of talented amateur musicians demanded more instruments and sheet music. Piano manufacturing increased in the United States from 2,500 pianos in 1829 to more than 9,000 in 1851 and 21,000 in 1860; meanwhile, the development of steam-powered printing and typesetting machinery revolutionized the American sheet music publishing industry. The temperance movement took advantage of this explosion of popular music to advance its cause. Sentimental songs like "Home, Sweet Home" and "Long, Long Ago," and songs from the minstrel show tradition, including "Old Dan Tucker" and "Wait for the Wagon," were familiar to the American public and helped temperance reformers reach out to a broader audience.[1]

Home, Sweet Home

"Home, Sweet Home" was a collaborative effort of English composer Sir Henry R. Bishop and the American actor and playwright John Howard Payne. Payne went to London as a young man and while there worked with Bishop on the opera *Clari, or The Maid of Milan*, which included the song "Home, Sweet Home." The opera opened in London on May 8, 1823, and in New York on November 12 of the same year. "Home, Sweet Home" quickly gained popularity both in England and America. Not surprisingly, the dominant themes in

---

1. Branham and Hartnett, *Sweet Freedom's Song*, 69, 131; H. Wiley Hitchcock, *Music in the United States: A Historical Introduction*, 67–70; Stecker, "Respectable Revolution," 48.

Home, Sweet Home

John Howard Payne

Sir Henry R. Bishop

'Mid pleas - ures and pal - a - ces though we may

roam, Be it ev - er so hum - ble there's no place like

home; A charm from the skies seems to hal - low us

there, Which, seek through the world, is ne'er met with else -

Chorus

where. Home, home, sweet, sweet, home, There's

no place like home, Oh, there's no place like home.

One Hundred and One Best Songs, no. 59.

the temperance versions of this song relate to the influence of drinking on home life, with nine of the fifteen versions explicitly referring to the home, including "The Temperance Home."[2]

The Temperance Home

> 1. 'Mid wealth and 'mid luxury though we may roam,
>   There's no place so sweet as a temperance home;
>   Where the drink that destroys has no place on the board,
>   And the libations of only cold water are poured.

2. Ewen, *All the Years*, 53; Dallin and Dallin, *Heritage Songster*, 144; Spaeth, *History of Popular Music*, 55–58.

Chorus
Home, home, sweet fair home,
    There's no place so fair as a temperance home.

2. Oh, sweet 'tis to list in the morning to prayer
    From the lips of a father who offers it there!
And dear, too, at evening, when labor is o'er,
    To join in a temperance circle once more. *To Chorus*

3. No curses are heard to disturb or distress,
    But the accents of love, that soothe, soften, and bless.
Enough, and to spare, for the needy is found,
And the music of thankfulness echoes around. *To Chorus*

4. How different the home where, 'mid terror and strife,
    The children are ragged—heart-broken the wife;
Where the steps of the father make families shrink,
    And the cry is unceasing for soul-killing drink. *To Chorus*

5. But temperance may change to a dwelling of mirth,
    This scene of destruction—this tophet on earth;
And peace again come, from it never to roam,
    To bless and to gladden a temperance home. *To Chorus*[3]

The sentimental quality of Bishop's music lends itself particularly well to suasive lyrics. However, the following selection encouraging listeners to vote liquor out demonstrates that coercive and suasive elements can be effectively blended when set to this nostalgic tune.

The Plea of Mothers and Children
(E. A. Hoffman)

    1. O men of our country, ye loyal and true!
        Your wives and your children are pleading with you;
    The curse of the drink-shop we bitterly feel,
        And for your protection and help we appeal.

    Chorus
    Hear us, patriots leal,
        For help and protection to you we appeal.

    2. You hold in your pow'r both our weal and our woe,
        You can by your votes the saloon overthrow;
    By all of the sorrow and pain that we feel,
        For help and protection to you we appeal. *To Chorus*

3. Stearns, *National Temperance*, 44. Reprinted in Hudson, *Temperance Songster*, no. 69; and Leslie, *Good Templar* (1888), 86, without verses 4 and 5.

3. Our homes are unhappy, our children unfed,
   We suffer for comfort, we suffer for bread;
O see how in dust and in ashes we kneel
   And, bathed in our tears, for protection appeal. *To Chorus*

4. Why should we thus suffer, our children and we,
   In this blessed land of the brave and the free?
O come to our rescue and vote for our weal!
   It is to God's freemen the women appeal. *To Chorus*[4]

Long, Long Ago

Like "Home, Sweet Home," the sentimental quality of "Long, Long Ago" is particularly well suited to the suasionist efforts of temperance reformers. The words and music by Thomas H. Bayly were very familiar in nineteenth-century America. "Long, Long Ago" later provided the melodic basis for the World War II song "Don't Sit under the Apple Tree." Although only three temperance settings of this tune were located, two of those appeared in several songbooks. The lyrics for "Touch Not the Cup" were attributed to the great temperance orator John Gough, who often sang the song at temperance meetings.[5]

Touch Not the Cup

1. Touch not the cup; it is death to thy soul;
   Touch not the cup, touch not the cup!
Many I know who have quaffed from the bowl:
   Touch not the cup, touch it not.
Little they thought that the demon was there;
   Blindly they drank, and were caught in the snare:
Then of that death-dealing bowl, O beware!
   Touch not the cup, touch it not.

2. Touch not the cup when the wine glistens bright;
   Touch not the cup, touch not the cup.
Though like the ruby it shines in the light,
   Touch not the cup, touch it not.
The fangs of the serpent are hid in the bowl;
   Deeply the poison will enter thy soul:
Soon will it plunge thee beyond thy control.
   Touch not the cup, touch it not.

---

4. *Anti-Saloon Campaign*, no. 8; Hoffman, *Woman's Christian Temperance*, no. 8.
5. Spaeth, *History of Popular Music*, 85.

Long, Long Ago

Thomas H. Bayly   Thomas H. Bayly

Tell me the tales that to me were so dear, Long, long a-go,

Long, long a-go; Sing me the songs I de-light-ed to hear,

Long, long a-go, long a-go. Now you are come, all my

grief is re-moved, Let me for-get that so long you have roved,

Let me be-lieve that you love as you loved, Long, long a-go, long a-go.

Osbourne McConathy, ed., *The School Song Book*, 73.

3. Touch not the cup, young man, in thy pride;
    Touch not the cup, touch not the cup.
Hark to the warnings of thousands who've died:
    Touch not the cup, touch it not.
Go to their lonely and desolate tomb;
    Think of their death, of their sorrow and gloom;
Think that perhaps thou may'st share in their doom!
    Touch not the cup, touch it not.

4. Touch not the cup; O drink not a drop;
    Touch not the cup, touch not the cup;
All that thou lovest entreat thee to stop:
    Touch not the cup, touch it not.
Stop for the home that to thee is so near;
    Stop for thy friends that to thee are so dear;
Stop for thy country, the God that you fear;
    Touch not the cup, touch it not.[6]

6. *Union Temperance*, 74–75; Potter, *Boston Temperance*, 1:18–19; Bonner, *Mountain Minstrel*, 70; Hart, *Juvenile Temperance*, 28–29; Thompson, *Thompson's Band*, 17; *Crusaders' Temperance*, 23–24;

A Life on the Ocean Wave

Composer and performer Henry Russell wrote the tune for "A Life on the Ocean Wave" in 1838 to words by Epes Sargent. Although born in England, Russell spent more than eight years in America touring as a singer and serving as the organist at the First Presbyterian Church of Rochester, New York. He composed more than eight hundred songs during his career. "A Life on the Ocean Wave" was one of the best-known sea songs both here and abroad, becoming the official march of the British Royal Marines in 1889. Temperance reformers used this tune to advocate a "Life of Temperance" in all six versions of this song. Marsh's "A Life on the Tidal Wave" also illustrates the strong religious beliefs of many temperance writers.[7]

A Life on the Tidal Wave
(Wm. B. Marsh)

1. A life on the tidal wave,
   A fearless and hardy crew,
The winds and the tempests brave
   In a vessel just launched anew.
Plain temperance of the past
   To stem the current tried,
But found that something fast
   Must be built to stem the tide.

Chorus
Prohibition is her name,
   She sails with a brand new crew,
To meet Rum's hulk her aim,
   And quickly sink her, too!

2. Commanded by our God,
   This ship we'll navigate,
And drive the rebel horde
   Dishonored from our State.
Their battle dogs may frown,
   In fury they may speak,
We'll cut their colors down,
   And fly ours from their peak. *To Chorus*

Stearns and Main, *Trumpet Notes*, 87. Fillmore, *Temperance Musician*, 170–71, and Perkins, *Crystal Fountain*, 107, omit verse 4. Stearns, *National Temperance*, 59, omits verse 3. Herbert, *Young Volunteer*, 29, omits verses 1 and 3. Saunders, *Temperance Songster*, 25, omits verse 2 and makes several changes to verse 3.

7. Ewen, *All the Years*, 52; Spaeth, *History of Popular Music*, 78–81.

A Life on the Ocean Wave

Epes Sargent

Henry Russell

A life on the o - cean wave! A home on the roll - ing deep! Where the scat - tered wa - ters rave, And the winds their re - vels keep. Like an ea - gle caged, I pine, On this dull un - chang - ing shore, Oh give me the flash - ing brine, The spray and the tem - pest's roar.

Chorus

A life on the o - cean wave! A home on the roll - ing deep! Where the scat - tered wa - ters rave, And the winds their re - vels keep.

Heart Songs Dear to the American People (Boston: Chapple Publishing, 1909), 431.

3. God takes the helm in hand,
  To guide our privateer,
Our Prohibition band
  Will meet Rum with a cheer.
Give us the strength to cope
  With those for Satan fight,
Buoy up our hearts with hope,
  Till rum sinks out of sight. *To Chorus*[8]

Old Dan Tucker

Daniel Decatur Emmett, the composer of "Dixie Land" and a leading figure in establishing the minstrel tradition, also contributed the words and music to the humorous song "Old Dan Tucker." First published in 1843 and still familiar today, "Old Dan Tucker" was also borrowed for abolitionist songs, during the Mexican-American War, by the Forty-niners during gold rush days, and in presidential campaigns. The comic tone of the tune becomes more serious in the twelve verses of "Old Sir Toddy."[9]

Old Sir Toddy

1. Come all ye who are fond of singing,
  Let us set a song a-ringing;
Sound the chorus strong and hearty,
  And we'll make a jovial party.
Get out the way, old Sir Toddy,
  You're a drunken thievish body.

2. Some love rum, and some love brandy,
  And some drink whate'er comes handy;
But we'll lump it in a body,
  And we'll call it old Sir Toddy.
Get out the way, old Sir Toddy,
  You're a drunken thievish body.

3. He who drinks cold water only,
  Ne'er will leave his fireside lonely;
But his home a happy place is,
  With its cleanly smiling faces.
Get out the way, old Sir Toddy,
  You're a drunken thievish body.

8. Perine and Mash, *National Prohibition Hymnal*, 56.
9. Dallin and Dallin, *Heritage Songster*, 35; Ewen, *All the Years*, 38, 57, 61; Spaeth, *History of Popular Music*, 94.

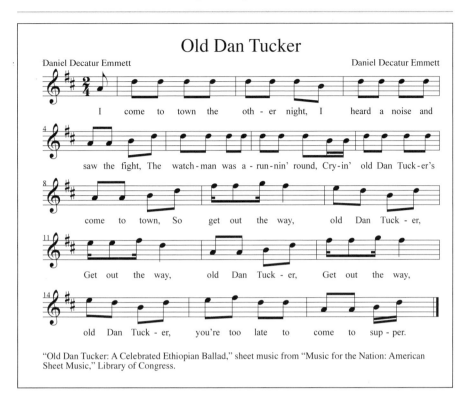

Old Dan Tucker

Daniel Decatur Emmett   Daniel Decatur Emmett

I come to town the oth - er night, I heard a noise and

saw the fight, The watch - man was a - run - nin' round, Cry - in' old Dan Tuck - er's

come to town, So get out the way, old Dan Tuck - er,

Get out the way, old Dan Tuck - er, Get out the way,

old Dan Tuck - er, you're too late to come to sup - per.

"Old Dan Tucker: A Celebrated Ethiopian Ballad," sheet music from "Music for the Nation: American Sheet Music," Library of Congress.

4. Toddy steals a man's good feelings,
     He's a rough in all his dealings;
Smirks and smiles until he's bound you,
     Then oh, cracky, how he'll pound you.
Get out the way, old Sir Toddy,
     You're a drunken thievish body.

5. All who wish for homes to bless them,
     All who wish for girls to kiss them;
Hark, while soberness is over us,
     Here's the song and this is the chorus.
Get out the way, old Sir Toddy,
     You're a drunken thievish body.

6. Then we used to get all merry,
     Drunk on rum, or corned on cherry;
Now we've a drink as sweet as honey,
     Without price and without money.
Get out the way with your brandy,
     We've a drink that's just the dandy.

7. Time was once when every body
     Drank their gin or brandy toddy;

But now a new reform's beginning,
  Drinking liquor now is sinning.
Get out the way with your brandy,
  We've a drink that's just the dandy.

8. Rum, it makes a botheration,
  Deadens all the circulation;
Kills the soul and kills the body,
  All is done by drinking toddy.
Get out the way, old Sir Toddy,
  You're a drunken thievish body.

9. Mitchell set the ball a-running,
  And gave notice of its coming;
Now it's rolled to every station,
  In our own great Yankee nation.
Push it along, keep it moving,
  The temp'rance cause is still improving.

10. Satan saw his trade was failing,
  Heard no more the widow's wailing;
Sent his imps around us yelling,
  "Don't stop, don't stop! keep on selling,"
Get out of the way, you rum-sellers,
  You are mean intriguing fellows.

11. Now, my friends, come stop your drinking
  Health is gone, your fortune's sinking;
Come and own that you're mistaken,
  Sign the pledge and save your bacon,
Push it along, keep it moving,
  The temp'rance cause is still improving.

12. I ask one thing more, my joys to crown,
  That is to see old alchy done up brown;
And when he's banished from our shore,
  Then, my friends, we'll ask no more.
Push it along, keep it moving,
  The temp'rance cause is still improving.[10]

"The Temperance Car" employs the image of a train car to warn opponents to clear the way for reform. It also addresses the perceived failure of suasion alone as a solution to the alcohol problem.

---

10. *Women's Temperance*, 11–12. The first three verses are the same as "Get Out the Way," reprinted later in this chapter.

The Temperance Car
(O. Whittlesey)

1. See! the Temperance car is moving,
    Lightning-like she's onward roving;
Red-nosed topers filled with wonder,
    Save your bacon, run like thunder.
Clear the track!
    Clear the track!
Clear the track, don't stop running,
    Jump for your lives, the cars are coming.

2. See our flag at every station!
    Waving o'er our happy nation;
What though traitors do desert us,
    Fire up! fire up! they can't hurt us.
Put on the steam!
    Put on the steam!
Put on the steam! the bell is sounding—
    All our enemies confounding.

3. Rummies now, on all occasions,
    Always preaching "moral suasion,"
And it makes them groan and wonder,
    When they hear of *legal thunder.*
Clear the track!
    Clear the track!
Clear the track for "legal suasion!"
    For it now, there's much occasion.

4. See the topers fly before us!
    While our flag waves proudly o'er us;
See the venders strive to aid 'em
    Clear the track, boys, you can't save 'em.
Bring out the gun!
    Bring out the gun!
Level all the rum-shops yonder!
    They cannot stand our temperance thunder.[11]

The Old Oaken Bucket

Samuel Woodworth's lyrics to "The Old Oaken Bucket" were written in 1817 and first published in the *Republican Chronicle* in New York, June 3, 1818. In 1843 the lyrics were set to the tune "Araby's Daughter" in *The Amateur Song*

11. *Women's Temperance,* 6.

The Old Oaken Bucket

Samuel Woodworth

George Kaillmark

How dear to my heart are the scenes of my child-hood, When
The or - chard, the mead - ow, the deep tan-gled wild-wood, And

fond rec - ol - lec - tion pre - sents them to view! The
ev - 'ry loved spot which my in - fan - cy knew;

wide - spread - ing pond, and the mill that stood by it. The bridge and the

rock where the cat - a - ract fell; The cot of my fa - ther, the

dai - ry - house nigh it, And e'en the rude buck - et that hung in the

well. The old oak - en buck - et, the i - ron - bound buck - et, The

moss - cov - ered buck - et that hung in the well.

One Hundred and One Best Songs, no. 90.

Book. This tune, by English composer George Kaillmark, was so named because of its use with a Thomas Moore poem of that name, first published in
London in 1822. "The Old Oaken Bucket" also found a place in the temperance movement because it was seen as a tribute to benefits of cold water. It was
printed in its original version in *The Cold Water Melodies and Washingtonian
Songster* (1842), *The Band of Hope Songster* (1885), and many other temperance
collections. This tune was also combined with lyrics about alcohol's influence
on the home and family as in "The Contrast," one of the few temperance
songs to present the viewpoints of multiple characters.[12]

12. Ewen, *All the Years,* 52–53; Spaeth, *History of Popular Music,* 60–61.

The Contrast

1. Solo—*The Wife*

Oh, when I remember the sorrow and sadness,
    Which reign'd in the hut that was not e'en our own—
When night had no solace, and day brought no gladness,
    For husband, and father and friend we had none—
Those dark clouds of woe, are to this scene of splendor,
    As midnight's meridian to day's brightest noon,
A husband reclaimed, and a father all tender,
    And friends smiling here in this home of our own!

2. Duett—*Daughters*

Oh, sad is the story that mem'ry's yet telling!
    It weighs on the heart, it still rings in the ear,
Like the chill blast that howl'd round our desolate dwelling,
    Cold hunger within, when no succors were near!
Our mother—at midnight—her heart almost broken,
    How often she hush'd on her bosom our sighs!
Well—well may she cherish that pledge—dearest token!
    A father reformed wipes all tears from our eyes.

3. Trio—*Sons*

Yes, we who now eagerly run for his blessing,
    Or nightly, in rapture, recline on his knee;
Familiar with blows, in place of caresses,
    Away from our father how oft we did flee!
'Twas drink—'twas the drink—else how could that fond father
    Have treated unkindly his children and wife!
But forgot be the past, and now dwell we much rather
    On the present, the happiest time of our life.

4. Solo—*Husband*

Yes, yes, 'twas the drink that my mind had been stealing,
    Intemp'rance had seared all my heart-fibres o'er;
And conscience to smother—to hush all appealing—
    I drank, till I raved and abused you all sore.
But thanks be to HIM, who hath never forsaken!
    And thanks to his agents, who ne'er gave me o'er—
[*All Sing*] The tee-total Pledge, that we all have now taken,
    We'll keep, Washingtonians, till life is no more![13]

---

13. Bonner, *Mountain Minstrel*, 95.

Wait for the Wagon

Originally credited to George Knauff when it was published in 1851, "Wait for the Wagon" was later attributed to R. Bishop Buckley of the minstrel group the Buckley Serenaders. Both Union and Confederate troops sang this lively tune during the Civil War, and both sides contributed their own parodies. The tune was also used for a number of political campaigns, beginning in 1852 and ending with Theodore Roosevelt's election campaign in 1912. Temperance settings of the rousing chorus to "Wait for the Wagon" spurred listeners to raise the temperance banner, vote for the Prohibition party, ride the prohibition wagon, or throw down the bottle, as in the following setting from *The Temperance Songster* (1867).[14]

Throw Down the Bottle

1. Will you sign the pledge, poor drunkard?
   We wish to set you free
From appetite and passion,
   And custom's slavery;
Strong drink has been your ruin.
   We ask you to abstain;
Come throw down the bottle,
   And never drink again.

Chorus
Throw down the bottle,
   Throw down the bottle,
Throw down the bottle,
   And never drink again.

2. Oh, your wife will smile with gladness
   To know that you have signed:
She'll bid adieu to sadness,
   For comfort she will find;
Within your home what pleasure,
   What happiness will reign;
Then throw down the bottle,
   And never drink again. *To Chorus*

3. Oh, your children, too, will bless you,
   They'll dance with very glee,
And joyfully caress you,
   As they climb upon your knee;

---

14. Dallin and Dallin, *Heritage Songster*, 6; Ewen, *All the Years*, 58–59; Silber, *Songs of the Civil War*, 169–71.

Wait for the Wagon

R. Bishop Buckley   R. Bishop Buckley

Will you come with me, my Phyl-lis dear to yon blue moun-tain

free, Where the blos-soms smell the sweet-est, come

rove a-long with me. It's ev-'ry Sun-day morn-ing, when

I am by your side, We'll jump in-to the wag-on, and all take a

Chorus

ride. Wait for the wag-on, wait for the

wag-on, Wait for the wag-on, and we'll all take a ride.

Wm. B. Bradbury and J. N. Stearns, *Temperance Chimes* (1878), 93.

Their little eyes will sparkle,
    As they sing the joyous strain,
We've thrown down the bottle,
    And we'll never drink again. *To Chorus*

4. Then come along, my brother,
    Though fallen you may rise;
You then may help another
    Who now in bondage lies;
The best of men will bless you;
    You will not live in vain;
So, throw down the bottle,
    And never drink again. *To Chorus*[15]

15. Saunders, *Temperance Songster*, 22–23; Mowatt, *Mowatt's Temperance Glee*, 8.

Home, Sweet Home

The Prodigal's Return

1. Too long have I stray'd, yet no more will I
   roam;
   I'll return, for my Father is calling me
   home.
   The richest of banquets his love will prepare,
   And the best of his robes is awaiting me
   there.

Chorus
Home, home, sweet heavenly home;
   There's no place on earth like my sweet
   heavenly home.

2. By the smile of the harlot, her song and
   her wine,
   I've been made to lie down, and eat husks
   with the swine.
   But now she may smile, and her goblet may
   foam
   In fain, for I'm bound to my sweet
   heavenly home. *To Chorus*

3. O, Father, though long hath thy prodigal
   child,
   Gone astray where the cup of the tempter
   hath smiled;
   Yet, now he hath broken the charm and the
   snare,
   To thy mansion receive him to sing to
   thee there. *To Chorus*[16]

Rum, Curst Rum

1. 'Mid charnels and pest houses though we
   may roam,
   Be it ever so frightful, there's no plague
   like Rum!
   A charm from below seems to lead to the
   snare,
   And leaves us in darkness, and gloom,
   and despair.

Chorus
Rum, Rum, curst, curst Rum,
   There's no plague like Rum, there's no
   plague like Rum.

2. Farewell, thou destroyer! farewell cursed
   Rum,
   The time for our parting forever, is come;
   This heart shall lie silent and cold in the
   tomb,
   Ere again thou enslav'st me, foul Demon
   of Rum. *To Chorus*

3. When we banish Rum, peace smiles on us
   again,
   And virtue resumes o'er the soul her mild
   reign;
   Hope's voice, like the Syren, shall charm us
   once more,
   And the reign of the Tyrant forever be
   o'er. *To Chorus*[17]

Happy Home #1

1. "'Mid scenes of confusion" the drunkard
   did roam,
   His heart was estranged from his fireside
   and home;
   And when from these scenes of mad folly he
   came,
   He felt all the world, but *himself* was to
   blame.
   Blame, blame, himself was to blame,
   [He felt all the world, but *himself* was to
   blame.]

2. Oh! sad was the heart of his grief-stricken
   wife,
   Whom he vowed at the altar to cherish
   through life;
   His children once fondled, now trembled
   with fear,
   As the sound of his footsteps fell sad on
   their ear.
   Ear, ear, fell sad on their ear, *etc.*

---

16. Pierpont, *Cold Water Melodies*, 91; Plimpton, *Washingtonian Choir*, 78–79; Bonner, *Mountain Minstrel*, 89.
17. Bensel, *Temperance Harp*, 21.

3. Oh! drear was their dwelling unsheltered
   from cold,
   There rude Boreas unchecked, nightly
   revels did hold;
The heart of its inmates were sunk in despair,
   When joy came among them, their
   sadness to cheer.
Cheer, cheer, their sadness to cheer, *etc.*

4. A band of *true freemen* did proudly arise,
   And the scales of delusion quick fell from
   their eyes;
So bright and so pure did their vision become
   That naught seemed so pleasant to them,
   as their home.
Home, home, sweet, sweet home, *etc.*

5. No secret, no mystery is theirs to reveal,
   "Sign the Pledge" is the charm which
   gives Washington's zeal;
Then ye drinkers, from vice and from misery
   come,
   And renew the delights of your once
   happy home,
Home, home, sweet, sweet home, *etc.*

6. Come, arouse Washingtonians! with
   confidence say,
   The haunts of inebriates shall vanish
   away;
The day is fast dawning, and surely will come,
   When their hearts shall delight in wife,
   children and home.
Home, home, sweet, sweet home, *etc.* 18

The Drunkard's Lament

1. 'Mid sorrows and sadness I'm destined to
   roam,
   Forlorn and forsaken, deprived of my
   home,
Intemp'rance hath robbed me of all that was
   dear,
   Of my home in the skies, and my
   happiness here,
Home! home! sweet, sweet home!
   An exile from God, I shall ne'er find a
   home.

2. I vainly presumed, when I first took the
   cup,
   I could drink if I chose, or I could give it
   up;
But I tampered too long, too long tempted
   heaven,
   'Till an outcast from God and his
   presence I'm driven.
Home! home! sweet, sweet home,
   On earth or in heaven, I shall ne'er find a
   home.

3. My heart broken wife in her grave hath
   found rest;
   And my children have gone to the land of
   the blest;
While I a poor wretch, a vile wanderer like
   Cain,
   With the "mark" of the beast on the earth
   still remain.
Home! home! sweet, sweet home!
   How happy was I with my loved ones at
   home.

4. Farewell to the social endearments of
   home,
   Justly loathed by my fellows I wander
   alone,
For presumptuously sinning and tempting
   the Lord,
   Of the fruit of my ways, I must reap the
   reward,
Home! home! sweet, sweet home!
   An exile from God, I shall ne'er find a
   home. 19

Happy Home #2

1. "'Mid scenes of confusion," from morning
   till eve,
   With no heart to pity, no hand to relieve,
The drunkard abandoned was once left to
   roam,
   His fam'ly neglected, deserted his home.
Home, home, sweet, sweet home,
   Oh, what drunkard's dwelling was ever a
   home?

---

18. Bigelow and Grosh, *Washingtonian Pocket*, 89.
19. *Collection of Hymns and Songs*, 16–17; Bonner, *Mountain Minstrel*, 78.

2. Oh, sad was the heart of his grief-stricken
wife,
   Whom he vow'd at the altar to cherish
   through life;
His children, once fondled, 'neath heaven's
wide dome,
   Roamed hungry and naked, unknowing a
   home.
Home, home, sweet, sweet home,
   Oh, what drunkard's dwelling was ever a
   home?

3. For drear was their dwelling, unsheltered
from cold,
   There Boreas uncheck'd, nightly revels did
   hold;
The hearts of its inmates were sadden'd and
lone,
   When hope came once more to brighten
   their home.
Home, home, sweet, sweet home,
   Even hope, fondly cherished, can sweeten
   our home.

4. A band of *true freemen* did proudly arise,
   And scales of delusion quick tore from
   their eyes;
Now sober'd, to them soon fair Plenty did
come,
   And Virtue and Peace again sweet made
   their home.
Home, home, sweet, sweet home,
   Peace, plenty and joy can make *any* place,
   home.

5. No secret, deep hidden, is theirs to reveal,
   "Sign the pledge," Washingtonians cry, in
   their zeal,
"Ye drinkers, from vice and from misery
come,
   And renew the delights of your once
   happy home.
Home, home sweet, sweet home,
   Oh, renew the delights of your once
   happy home!"

6. Come, arouse, Washingtonians! with
confidence say,
   The haunts of inebriates shall vanish
   away;

The day is fast dawning, and surely will come,
   When their hearts shall delight in wife,
   children and home.
Home, home sweet, sweet home,
   Oh, renew the delights of your once
   happy home![20]

Lament of the Reformed

1. 'Mid scenes of reflection on times which
are past,
   Remorse fills my bosom, and clouds
   overcast;
The monster, Intemperance, has robbed me
of all
   In the morning of manhood he doomed
   me to fall.
Home, home, sweet, sweet home,
   Remorse fills my bosom whenever I roam.

2. That *first, fatal glass* in my memory
remains,
   It soon sealed my fate and confined me in
   chains;
In the chains of Intemperance my soul long
was bound,
   But Heaven has broke them, and freedom
   I've found.
Home, home, sweet, sweet home,
   I am now blest with freedom, with friends
   and with home.

3. But I ne'er can forget her I promised to
love,
   Who now dwells in glory with angels
   above;
And four tender offspring, that Heaven
bestowed,
   Now sing with their mother in blissful
   abode.
Home, home, sweet, sweet home,
   There are charms in the skies, where their
   souls are at home.

4. Yes, she sleeps with the dead in her lone
mountain grave,
   Where the sweet summer flowerets in soft
   breezes wave;
Entombed with her loved ones, her trials are
o'er,

20. Bonner, *Mountain Minstrel*, 115. Note similarities to "Happy Home #1."

And sickness and sorrow shall reach her
no more.
Home, home, sweet, sweet home,
There are charms in the skies where no
sorrow can come.

5. Sweet blooms the wild rose and soft fall
the show'rs,
In the vale where she resteth—beneath the
green bow'rs;
By the home of her childhood—near
Chester's sweet stream,
Where my soul often wafts me in the lone
midnight dream.
Home, home, sweet, sweet home,
Yes! her spirit now rests in her bright
heavenly home.[21]

No Place Like This
(F. M. Adlington)

1. Through all our wild rambles in search
after bliss,
Experience informs us there's no place
like this;
A charm for the soul seems to hallow this
place,
And open our hearts to the whole human
race.

Chorus
This, yes, this, 'tis this,
There's no place like this,
There's no place like this.

2. A brother who breaks from his festering
chain,
And seeks for that freedom he scarce
hopes to gain,
Kind friends, and protection, will find in this
Hall,
And freedom of speech that's awarded to
all. *To Chorus*

3. The slave of intemperance, though chained
to the car,
As victors of old dragged their trophies of
war,

If he would be free, let him whisper our call;
We'll tender the pledge, and his fetters
will fall. *To Chorus*

4. To all we the hand of affection extend,
And hail ev'ry man as a brother and
friend;
The seal of our God on his forehead we
trace,
And ask not his title, his sect, or his race.
To Chorus[22]

The Home of Young Mary

1. Oh, sweet was the home of young Mary
the fair,
For love and contentment were found
ever there;
When evening spreads over the earth, her
dark wing,
Then William and Mary together would
sing—

Chorus
Home, home, sweet, sweet home;
There's no place like home, There's no
place like home.

2. But dark was the cloud that o'ershaded
that home,
When William had learned to the
alehouse to roam;
When came the long evening, no joy did it
bring,
For the wife and the children no longer
could sing—*To Chorus*

3. But joy came again—the gaunt demon had
fled—
The husband and father the promise had
made
To touch not, to taste not, the poisonous
thing,
And now every evening with transport
they sing—*To Chorus*[23]

---

21. Ibid., 93.
22. Potter, *Boston Temperance*, 2:49.
23. *Crusaders' Temperance*, 18–19.

Pure Water Be Mine

1. 'Mid the sparkling of glasses, or goblets of
      wine,
   Look they ever so tempting, pure water be
      mine;
It gives neither headache, nor heartache, nor
      pain,
   No trouble attends it, no loss, but all gain.
Hail, hail water, hail!
   'Twill make the cheeks rosy which wine
      has made pale.

2. For wine, rum, or brandy, no charm hath
      for me;
   In their fumes or their color no beauty
      I see;
My drink is transparent, sent down from
      above,
   Gushing forth from the mountain,
      directed by love.
Drink, drink, water drink,
   Nor swallow more poison, but now stop
      and think.

3. It will strengthen and purify body and
      mind;
   Make the careless one thoughtful, the
      cruel more kind.
'Twill give you more leisure to read, think,
      and pray;
   Sobriety surely's the happier way.
Water give to me,
   'Tis simple, 'tis wholesome, and God
      sends it free.[24]

First Debauch

1. O, I am sometimes crazy, not knowing
      what to do,
   My eyes and cheeks are swollen, as you all
      can see and know;
I feel there's none to pity me, my character all
      gone,
   No friends have I, nor money to carry me
      along.

Chorus
O Christie, darling Christie,
   Cannot you forgive me,
   And I will drink no more.

2. O, well do I remember when first I learned
      to sip,
   In the grog-shop of my neighbor, where
      the bottles used to tip,
'Twas on a boisterous evening, the wind was
      blowing cold,
   My uncle's son says, Billy, let's o'er to
      Goutie's stroll! *To Chorus*

3. A jolly set of fellows had already gathered
      there,
   For Hansie's, Scobie's, Rignie's, would all
      a portion bear;
And while the ball was rolling, Billy, says,
      Tom, to me,
   Let's have a sling or toddy and we'll all get
      on a spree. *To Chorus*

4. No friend was there to tell me of the
      tempter's aim to catch
   A sober son of Adam, and convert him to
      a wretch;
I soon was all bewildered, and staggered to
      my home,
   To meet my dear, poor Christie, all, all
      disguised with rum. *To Chorus*

5. As I tottered to the bedside, my wife awoke
      with fright,
   And says to me, my Billy? why, what a
      looking sight;
Now, all that I remember of that first night's
      debauch
   Would flit before my vision as a dream of
      tigers fought. *To Chorus*

6. Let all from this a lesson take, and never,
      never touch
   The least that will intoxicate, if any offer
      such;
And if perchance a lady should offer you
      some wine,
   Say no, and bow politely, then sing her
      "Auld Lang Syne." *To Chorus*[25]

24. Ibid., 19.
25. Nichols, *Iron Door*, 10.

Despair Not

1. O, heart-broken brother, despair not, I pray,
    The gloom of thy soul but presageth the
        day;
There's light in the future, resplendently fair,
    And fond, loving spirits are waiting thee
        there.

Chorus
Come, come, dear one blest,
    In the ranks of the faithful there only is
        rest.

2. How deeply you suffer, each heart knoweth
        well,
    Your sorrow and anguish, the tongue
        cannot tell;
In pain and in darkness the foe chains thy
        soul,
    But look! fainting brother, right yonder's
        the goal. *To Chorus*

3. Hopes bright as the morning, have
        vanished away,
    The idols of manhood have crumbled to
        clay;
The bright beams of promise that fell on thy
        sight,
    Have faded in vapor like songs of the
        night. *To Chorus*

4. Thy wife and thy children with sorrow are
        dumb;
    Their lives have been blighted by
        death-dealing rum;
In faith they are praying, with light on each
        brow,
    "Save husband and father! O God, save
        him now!" *To Chorus*

5. Thou canst not resist them! their
        love-laden tears,
    Their faith all unchanging, have lived
        through the years;
Their prayers God will answer 'mid thrills of
        delight.
    He'll answer, will answer! thou'lt sign her
        to-night! *To Chorus*

6. He comes, the dear brother! comes bearing
        a cross;
    He views his past conduct as worthless as
        dross;
He comes, firm in purpose, regardless of jeers,
    While dear wife and children are shouting
        through tears. *To Chorus*26

Happy Temperance Men

1. Sweet home is a treasure, naught else can
        compare,
    When temperance governs, 'tis fruitful
        and fair,
'Tis precious and hopeful, a refuge in life,
    When free from temptation and sorrow
        and strife.

Chorus
Home, home, home, sweet home!
    The total abstainer finds pleasure at home.

2. Not so with the drunkard, not so with the
        sot,
    Whose sorrowing wife weeps for him who
        is not,
She knows not the pleasures or comforts of
        life,
    No! sad is the fate of the poor drunkard's
        wife. *To Chorus*

3. O "haste to the rescue," abstainer, and give
    A proof to the drunkard, for him thou
        canst live;
The fallen to ransom from folly and shame,
    And wipe out, forever, the drunkard's
        foul name. *To Chorus*27

Strength, Health, and Wealth

1. 'Tis Temp'rance that gives us our strength
        and our health
    And leads us straight on in the pathway of
        wealth,
A wealth of the soul and a wealth of the
        mind,
    And true wealth of love to our God and
        mankind.

26. Moffitt, *National Temperance*, 17.
27. Leslie, *Good Templar* (1888), 87.

Chorus
Strength, health, true, true wealth,
   'Tis Temp'rance that gives us strength,
   health, and true wealth.

2. To Temperance we'll give then our lives
   one and all,
   And find that true wealth which will
   come at her call.
In virtue and happiness we'll be secure
   And find such true pleasure will ever
   endure. *To Chorus*

3. Thus Temp'rance in all things we'll ever
   perform,
   And lead others on in the path of reform,
That they may enjoy all the wealth that we
   find,
   The true wealth of love to our God and
   mankind. *To Chorus*28

Long, Long Ago

Where Are the Friends!

1. Where are the friends that to me were so
   dear,
   Long, long ago—long, long ago?
Where are the hopes that my heart used to
   cheer,
   Long, long ago—long ago?
Friends that I loved in the grave are laid low—
   Hopes that I cherished have fled from me
   now—
I am degraded, for rum was my foe—
   Long, long ago—long ago.

2. Sadly my wife bowed her beautiful head—
   Long, long ago—long, long ago.
O, how I wept when I knew she was dead!
   Long, long ago—long ago.
She was an angel—my love and my guide—

Vainly to save me from ruin she tried;
Poor broken heart! it was well that she died—
   Long, long ago—long ago.

3. Let me look back on the days of my
   youth—
   Long, long ago—long, long ago.
I was no stranger to virtue and truth,
   Long, long ago—long ago.
O for the hopes that were pure as the day!
   O for the joys that were purer than they!
O for the hours that I've squandered away!
   Long, long ago—long ago.29

Song of the Redeemed
(P. H. Sweetser)

1. Joyful, the season, and blest was the hour,
   When, long ago, long, long ago,
We broke from the tyrant's dominion and
   power,
   Long, long ago, long ago!
Farewell to the days of our sorrow and
   shame—
   The Pledge has redeemed us—the tidings
   proclaim—
Let earth swell the chorus of praise to thy
   name!
   Gloria Patri below!

2. Husbands, and wives, and children,
   rejoice;
   All happy now—happy now!
Join in the chorus with heart and with
   voice—
   All happy now—happy now!
Old Bacchus is spoiled of his magical charm;
   The wine-god of revels no more shall
   alarm—
Then join in the chorus with hearts ever
   warm;
   All happy now—happy now!

---

28. Hudson, *Temperance Songster,* no. 6.

29. Dana, *Temperance Lyre,* 60–61. Asa R. Trowbridge, *The Temperance Melodeon,* 52, Potter, *Boston Temperance,* 1:55–56, *Crusaders' Temperance,* 9, and Gordon, *White Ribbon,* 60–61, name this song "The Inebriate's Lament." Fillmore, *Temperance Musician,* 177, entitles the song "Long, Long Ago." Alexander Auld, *The Ohio Harmonist,* 193, entitles this song "The Drunkard Lamenting His Wife," and *Women's Temperance,* 50, names it "The Drunkard's Lament." Bonner, *Mountain Minstrel,* 67, entitles this song "Lamentation" and includes an additional verse between verses 1 and 2.

3. Blessings attend us, and peace from on
   high;
   Gladness for woe—joy for woe!
Angels repeat the glad song from the sky—
   Gladness for woe—joy for woe!
The Pledge shall protect us from sorrow and
   pain;
   The vow is recorded—we'll keep it like
   men,
Nor yield to the spell of the tempter again—
   Gladness for woe—joy for woe!

4. Token of peace and of mercies in store—
   Witness the vow, God above!
Gloria Patri hence evermore;
   Grant us the spirit of love!
Our holiest mem'ries round it throng,
   Our heart's affections, pure and strong—
To thee all the praise and the glory belong,
   Gloria Patri—above![30]

A Life on the Ocean Wave

A Life of Temperance
(Charles Marsh)

1. A life of temperance,
   And a home of peace and joy,
Where bounteous blessings dwell,
   And love without alloy!
Like a stricken bird I pined,
   When the rosy wine did rule,
An aching head was mine,
   And reason never cool:

Chorus
A life of temperance,
   And a home of peace and joy,
Where bounteous blessings dwell,
   And love without alloy.

2. The nights in revelry,
   And the days in foolishness,
Were always spent by me,
   With no one near to bless;
My aching heart would throb,
   My burning brain would reel,

My fevered hand would shake
   Like the warrior's glistening steel:
   To Chorus

3. But now I've signed the pledge,
   And meet with no reproof:
With blessings I am crowned,
   Beneath this Temperance roof;
Then give a glorious shout;
   Let the bells be merrily rung;
The "Monster's" lease is out,
   And his death-dirge we have sung:
   To Chorus[31]

A Life in the Temperance Cause

1. A life in the temperance cause,
   Afar from the drunkard's woes,
Where pure cold water pours,
   And a healthful stream o'erflows,
I've felt the woe and pain
   Of a drunkard's fearful life,
But now I'm free again,
   With joy and peace I'm rife.

Chorus
A life in the temperance cause,
   Afar from the drunkard's woes,
Where pure cold water pours,
   And a healthful stream o'erflows.

2. Once more as a man I stand.
   No more in grief I pine;
Farewell ye jovial band,
   Your doom is no more mine;
Like the mountain birds set free,
   Far behind I've left your thrall—
Brighter scenes I hope to see,
   My home among them all. *To Chorus*

3. E'en now my joys o'erflow,
   My home is bright and fair;
The tearful ones I know
   Now smile to meet me there.
Then join each sorrowing one
   With me, and gladly ring
"The song triumphant round,"
   While joyfully we sing—*To Chorus*[32]

---

30. Potter, *Boston Temperance*, 1:60–61.
31. Ibid., 1:50–51.
32. Bonner, *Mountain Minstrel*, 28.

Hurrah for the Temperance Cause

1. Hurrah for the Cause we love!
   Hurrah for the Pledge we keep!
Our Banner is nailed above,
   And our Faith is anchored deep!
Then away with wine and beer
   And brandy and rum and gin!
And give us a table clear
   From the drinks which lead to sin!

Chorus
Then hurrah for the Cause we love!
   And hurrah for the Pledge we keep!
Our Banner is nailed above,
   And our Faith is anchored deep!

2. Let Temperance Banners wave!
   And Temperance Unions grow!
With brothers yet true and brave,
   We will conquer every foe!
We expect some bitter strife,
   But we will never give up the field!
We have volunteered for life,
   And we don't intend to yield! *To Chorus*

3. Our enemy's fort is strong,
   But we're never afraid to fight
'Gainst evil and sin and wrong,
   For we know our cause is right!
Let the Gospel Trumpet blow!
   As we steadily onward press;
In the name of the Lord we go!
   "In Christ is our success!" *To Chorus*[33]

I Never Again Will Drink

1. I never will drink again,
   I never will touch the cup,
I will bid adieu to wine,
   And will give its pleasures up;
For its pleasures they are false,
   And as fickle as the wind,
Bid joy for a moment flow,
   Yet they leave a pang behind.

Chorus
I will never drink again,
   I never will touch the cup,

I will bid adieu to wine,
   And will give its pleasures up.

2. Too long I have bowed beneath
   Its gentle alluring sway;
Too long I have walked within
   Its false yet glittering way,
But now I bid adieu
   To the wine-cup and its ills,
Once more like a man I stand,
   To "work with a freeman's will."
      To Chorus

3. I never again will drink,
   Except from the crystal spring,
For that which God hath given,
   Can never a sorrow bring;
Farewell to the well-filled cup,
   Farewell to the ruby wine,
The sorrow and pain they bring,
   Shall never again be mine. *To Chorus*[34]

Contest Song
(Emma E. Page)

1. We're contesting for the truth,
   If truth be lifted up,
"Prohibition shall prohibit,"
   We'll break the drinking cup;
From ev'ry land they come,
   Their banners gleam and wave,
Protection to the home,
   The girl and boy to save.

Chorus
Contesting for the truth,
   And the truth shall make us free;
"Prohibition shall prohibit,"
   And ours the vict'ry shall be.

2. We're contesting for the truth,
   And truth shall make us free,
"Prohibition shall prohibit,"
   And ours the victory;
Six hundred thousand strong,
   We wage our peaceful war;
God's errands never fail,
   They come from near and far.
      To Chorus

33. Stearns, *National Temperance*, 46.
34. Ibid., 23.

3. We're contesting for the truth,
    The truth without a flaw,
"Prohibition shall prohibit,"
    And love shall be the law;
The love that never fails
    Toward any living thing,
Makes men and women fair,
    Fair children of the King. *To Chorus*[35]

Old Dan Tucker

Get Out the Way

1. Come, all ye who're fond of singing,
    Let us set a song to ringing;
Sound the chorus, strong and hearty,
    And we'll make a jovial party.

Chorus
Get out the way—
    Get out the way—
Get out the way with your liquor;
    We've a drink a great deal slicker.

2. Some love rum, and some love brandy,
    And some drink whate'er comes handy,
But we'll lump it in a body,
    And we'll call it all Sir Toddy. *To Chorus*

3. He who drinks cold water only
    Ne'er will leave his fireside lonely;
But his home a happy place is,
    With its clearly, smiling faces. *To Chorus*[36]

Happy Day
(P. H. Sweetser)

1. We greet with joy this happy day,
    And we will drive dull care away;
Hearts full of cheer we'll never fear,
    While we for Temperance appear.

Chorus
Hurrah! hurrah! hurrah! hurrah!
    Hurrah! hurrah! hurrah! hurrah!
Hurrah! hurrah! swell the chorus,
    Happy days are yet before us!

2. The Temp'rance cause we dearly love,
    Our vow is registered above;
United all in heart and hand,
    Oh, are we not a happy band? *To Chorus*

3. From morn to noon, from noon to night,
    O may the cause our hearts delight;
And when our daily task is o'er,
    We'll sing the song we sung before.
        To Chorus

4. The Temp'rance Star is rising high,
    It shines in splendor from the sky;
Its beams shall light the drunkard's cot,
    And pierce the darkness of his lot!
        To Chorus

5. O we will love the Temp'rance Pledge,
    It blesses youth and riper age;
It gives to all the joys of home,
    And earnest of the peace to come!
        To Chorus

6. And science fair, and learning bright
    Shall shed a pure and holy light;
And *Temp'rance, Love, and Liberty*,
    Our watchword ever more shall be!
        To Chorus[37]

The Temperance Ship

1. The Temperance Ship is now afloat;
    She is called by all a splendid boat;
With Washingtonians we will man her,
    And on her raise the temp'rance banner.

Chorus
Huzza! we'll raise the temp'rance banner,
    Huzza! we'll raise the temp'rance banner,
Huzza! we'll raise the temp'rance banner,
    From the old Bay State to Indiana.

2. Behold her riding on the gale;
    The wind is filling every sail,
The crew are shouting loud Hosanna,
    And proudly waves the temperance
        banner. *To Chorus*

35. Gordon, *Temperance Songster*, no. 74.
36. Potter, *Boston Temperance*, 1:41–43.
37. Ibid., 2:21.

3. This ship has sailed four years or more;
   She never was beached or run ashore;
The worst of storms she has outbraved,
   And hosts of deathless drunkards saved.
   To Chorus[38]

Get off the Track

1. Ho, the car of Reformation
   Rides majestic through the nation;
Bearing in its train the story—
   Temperance, a nation's glory.
Roll it along thro' the nation,
   The temperance car of Reformation.
[Roll it along, *etc.*]

2. Men of various predilections,
   Frightened run in all directions,
Landlords, Squires and Supervisors,
   And their tippling law advisers.
Get out the way, every station—
   Clear the track for Reformation.
[Get out the way, *etc.*]

3. Moderate drinkers in the churches,
   Leave behind intemperate lurches—
Hasten without hesitation,
   Get on the car of Reformation.
Sound the alarm, pulpit's thunder,
   Ere too late you see your blunder.
[Sound the alarm, *etc.*]

4. Boards of License gazed astounded,
   When at first our bell resounded—
Freight trains coming, tell these foxes,
   With our votes and ballot boxes.
Jump for your lives, ruination
   Awaits your shameful false position.
[Jump for your lives, *etc.*]

5. All true friends of Reformation,
   Haste unto the temperance station—
Quick into the car get seated,
   All is ready and completed.
Put on the steam, all are crying,
   While teetotal flags are flying.
[Put on the steam, *etc.*]

6. On triumphant see them bearing,
   Through intemperate flood-trash tearing.
The bell, the whistle and the steaming,
   Startle thousands from their dreaming.
Look out for the cares, while the bell rings,
   Ere the sound your funeral knell rings.
[Look out for the cares, *etc.*]

7. See the people run to meet us,
   At the depots thousands greet us—
All take seats with exultation,
   In the car of Reformation.
Hurrah, hurrah, Reformation
   Soon will bless our happy nation.
[Hurrah, hurrah, *etc.*][39]

Temperance Song
(W. H. Gove)

1. Our Forefathers—heaven bless them!
   When Old England would oppress them,
Signed a pledge against taxation—
   Calling it the Declaration.
Liberty was their motto;
   So they signed, just as they ought to.
[Liberty was their motto, *etc.*]

2. They, when John Bull tried to cheat 'em,
   Fought the red coats and they beat 'em;
And our warfare never closes,
   Till we've conquered the red noses,
Clear the track with your humbugs,
   Cider cans, and filthy rum jugs!
[Clear the track, *etc.*]

3. Whisky is an intermeddler,
   Retail scandal, mischief peddler;
Haunts all dark and wretched places,
   Breaks men's bones, and paints their
      faces,
Clear him out—the old villain—
   Every mischief he has skill in!
[Clear him out, *etc.*]

4. He makes strife 'twixt friends and brothers,
   Laughs at broken-hearted mothers,
Steals the children's bread and butter,
   Lays their fathers in the gutter!

38. Ibid., 2:48–49.
39. Bonner, *Mountain Minstrel*, 26–27.

Kill him dead with cold water;
  Hang him first—don't cheat the halter.
[Kill him dead, *etc.*]

5. And he comes, with many dresses
  From the shills and cider presses,
White, and red, and brown and yellow;
  But it's all the same old fellow;
Pull them down, cider grinders,
  You can't see behind such blinders!
[Pull them down, *etc.*]

6. Into every place he's creeping,
  Constant noise and uproar keeping,
And for power he's truly wond'rous
  More than once he's been to Congress.
Turn him out—the defaulter—
  Hang him up—don't cheat the halter!
[Turn him out, *etc.*]

7. O, for shame! all you rumsellers,
  You're offensive to your smellers;
Never more in open day go,
  For New Hampshire ladies say so!
Quit the trade, or we'll hit you
  With a drubbing that shall fit you!
[Quit the trade, *etc.*]

8. Some one threatening us with trouble,
  But the rummies all see double;
Armed with brandy, rum and cider,
  Off the mark men ne'er shot wider,
Let them come—fires much hotter,
  We can quench with pure cold water!
[Let them come, *etc.*]

9. Then fling out the Temperance Banner,
  Let the mountain breezes fan her,
For our strife is great and glorious,
  And we yet shall be victorious!
Drinking's wrong—you all know it—
Sign the pledge, and then you'll go it.
  [Drinking's wrong, *etc.*]

10. Every Granite son and daughter,
  Give three cheers for clear cold water,
While it gushes and rejoices,
  Like the music of your voices!
Then hurrah for cold water,

Every Temperance son and daughter.
[Then hurrah, *etc.*]40

United in a Joyous Band

1. United in a joyous band,
  We'll sign the pledge with heart and
  hand,
The ruby wine we'll lay aside
  And be our country's hope and pride.

Chorus
Then sign the pledge, yes, sign the pledge,
  And choose the clear and sparkling water;
Sign the pledge, each son and daughter,
  And choose the clear and sparkling water.

2. 'Twill keep the roses on your cheek,
  Preserve your spirits, mild, and meek,
Your eye will beam expression bright,
  Your mind improve in wondrous light.
    To Chorus

3. It makes the home of labor sweet,
  And happy faces there you'll greet;
It leads the way to honest wealth,
  And gives earth's choicest blessing, health.
    *To Chorus*41

The Prohibition Train

1. Ho! the engine, Prohibition,
  Grandly rushing through the nation,
Bearing on the train its story,
  Temperance, the Nation's glory.
Put on the steam, all are crying,
  Put on the steam, all are crying,
Put on the steam, all are crying,
  And the Temperance flag is flying.

2. Men of various predilections
  Hurrying come from all directions
Merchants, lawyers, and physicians,
  Farmers, Priests, and politicians.
Clear the track of party humbugs,
  Clear the track of party humbugs,
Clear the track of party humbugs,
  With platforms built on beer and
  rum-jugs.

40. Ibid., 102.
41. *Crusaders' Temperance*, 62.

3. First of all the cars in line see
   "State of Maine," whose rock and pine tree
Give the world, in its lost condition,
   General Dow and Prohibition.
Clear the track of false staticians,
   Clear the track of false staticians,
Clear the track of false staticians,
   Time-serving Priests, and politicians.[42]

Got No Life Preservers

1. Rum parties now are looking blue,
   And do not know just what to do;
Republicans "high license" see,
   The Democrats want whisky free.

Chorus
So what will you do, old rum-servers?
   So what will you do, old rum-servers?
So what will you do, old rum-servers?
   You have got no life preservers.

2. The Democrats, with too much rum
   Will presently so sicken some,
That in disgust they'll leave beer tanks,
   And enter Prohibition ranks. *To Chorus*

3. With license and with "temp'rance" mixed,
   Republicans are sadly fixed;
Saloon and church is such a load,
   They will break down upon the road.
      To Chorus

4. They tried it in Ohio, once,
   And felt thereafter like a dunce;
Then tried the Prohibition game,
   Just lately, with results the same.
      To Chorus

5. Republican brands Democrat,
   With drinking, selling and all that,
But if they do, we want to know
   Who gives them license to do so.
      To Chorus

6. Of course the ruling party gives
   Them license for by that it lives;
Which is the guiltier of the two?
   We leave the answer, sir, to you. *To Chorus*

7. Both parties, when the facts are weighed,
   Are partners in the liquor trade,
But we expect 'most any day,
   The firm will "bust" and run away.
      To Chorus

8. Old parties so allied to drink,
   Of Prohibition need not think;
And they may cheat and steal and lie,
   But such thin tricks they need not try.
      To Chorus[43]

The Old Oaken Bucket

The Inebriate's Farewell to His Cup

1. Farewell, farewell thou dark spirit of evil!
   Farewell, thou destroyer of body and soul!
No curse o'er what hatred in the brain of the
      devil
   So destructive to man, as "the full flowing
      bowl."
Thy influence poisons the pure font of feeling,
   And robs us of every enjoyment below;
While thy cursed enchantment around us is
      stealing,
   Entangling the soul in the meshes of woe!

2. Oh, ne'er will the heaven-redeemed one
      forget thee.
   Thou curse of humanity, reason, and life!
Deep, deep in the list of earth's curses he'll
      set thee,
   Thou fruitful promoter of rapine and
      strife.
Around thee still gathers the thoughtless,
      delighted
   To madly carouse, and thy poison to quaff—
But soon will they mourn over fondest hopes
      blighted;
   Too soon will be turned into grief the
      loud laugh.

3. Arouse from your stupor! The poisonous
      chalice
   Dash, dash from your lips while your
      reason remains!

---

42. Stearns, *National Temperance*, 52.
43. Durant, *Prohibition Home*, 10–11.

Tear away from your heart the foul demon of malice!
    Nor be your robes soiled by its blood-colored stains.
Oh firm be my heart in its blest resolution,
    To put from my lips the curst bev'rage away;
That when death triumphs over the frame's dissolution,
    The soul may rejoice in the bright light of day.[44]

The Banner of Temperance
(Dedicated to the Ladies' Cold Spring Society)

1. The Banner of Temp'rance invites to the fountain
    That springs from the earth 'neath its sheltering fold,
It waves o'er the valley, the plain and the mountain,
    Conveying dismay to the drunkard's strong hold.
See how the poor lost one retreats from pollution,
    Impelled by the voice of the Temperate man,
He leaves the foul den with a firm resolution,
    To stand by the Banner of Temp'rance again.

Chorus
That beautiful banner, that soul-cheering banner,
    That glorious banner, that floats o'er the plain.

2. Oh, who would not seek that proud banner's protection
    That guards us from tyranny, sorrow and woe?
Oh, who would not trust to that banner's direction
    Which points to all blessings enjoyed here below?
Oh, follow its guidance, 'twill lead you to glory,

And save from perdition the soul that obeys;
The hearts that embrace it shall long live in story,
    And joy in the light of its life-giving rays,
    To Chorus[45]

Woes of Intemperance

1. Hark! hark ye! O listen the sorrow and weeping
    Which rise from the hovel where misery reigns,
To the howl of the winds a wild harmony keeping,
    Which chills the war life-blood that speeds through our veins:
Sad, sad is the story those accents are telling,
    Like the wail of the dying, it pierces the air,
Oh, what has so blasted that comfortless dwelling?
    The monster intemperance is rioting there.

2. The wife worse than widowed, forlorn and heart-broken,
    While hunger and want make her little ones cry;
All trembling and pale, hears the terrible token
    Of anguish, the steps of her husband are nigh!
Those sounds once she caught with unspeakable gladness,
    While lit with affection her eye brightly shone,
Now sunken, her bosom o'erburdened with sadness,
    Like the funeral knell or the dirge's low moan!

3. He comes! see he comes! but no fond salutation
    Breaks forth from his lips which once murmured of love:
Those eyes, once accustomed to smile approbation,

---

44. Bensel, *Temperance Harp*, 17. The chorus is not used with this song.
45. Ibid., 22.

Look dark as the storm-cloud which
    mutters above;
With oaths and reproaches he vents his
    displeasure,
    And smites the frail form he has vowed to
    protect;
Her tears and entreaties avail in no measure;
    He treats them with scorn or with cruel
    neglect.

4. His babes who once crowded around for
    his blessing,
    Or sat gaily prattling for joy on his knee,
Familiar with blows in the place of caressing,
    Away from their father instinctively flee.
O! the withering curse and the ruin
    appalling,
    Which ALCOHOL wreaks on a suffering
    world!
Let the people's rebuke, like hot
    thunder-bolts falling,
    Shower fierce on the fiend 'till from earth
    he is hurled.[46]

My Mother's White Ribbon
(S. R. Graham Clark)

1. She's gone, and I miss her, shall miss her
    forever,
    The mother who loved me, who taught
    me to pray;
The mother who wore on her breast a white
    ribbon,
    The mother whose teachings have saved
    me today.
I dream of her love in the quiet night-watches,
    I wake with a yearning no tongue can
    repeat;
And think of the ribbon, the little white
    ribbon,
    As pure as the heart which beneath it did
    beat.

Chorus
The ribbon, the ribbon, the little white
    ribbon,
    The modest white ribbon she wore on her
    breast.

2. I strayed from her side, I tried hard to
    forget her;
    I sinned, I betrayed all the trust of her
    heart;
Yet the sight or the thought of a little white
    ribbon
    Had always the power home-longings to
    start.
Life wasted and ruined, I vowed I would end
    it;
    I sought a lone river—a woman passed by;
The wind caught her mantle—I saw a white
    ribbon—
    I thought of my mother—I dared not thus
    die. *To Chorus*

3. All ruined and soiled, that white ribbon
    yet drew me
    Back gently to mother who loved me so
    well;
It painted the past with a beauty alluring;
    I followed its lead, I was under its spell.
She lay on a sick-bed, they said she was dying,
    Yet bright grew her face as I knelt by her
    side
And whispered my story—she murmured
    thanksgiving,
    And then to my coat the white ribbon she
    tied. *To Chorus*

4. I closed her dear eyes—I the washed and
    forgiven,
    With tears to her shroud did I pin a white
    bow;
As in life, so in death she should wear the
    white ribbon;
    She will wear a white ribbon in heaven, I
    know.
Not for temp'rance alone, but for God stands
    that ribbon,
    For manhood redeemed, earth made safe
    for his soul;
O mother, I follow, I know where it leadeth,
    Christ, heaven, and thee, these the goal,
    blessed goal. *To Chorus*[47]

---

46. Ibid., 42.
47. Gordon, *Temperance Songster*, no. 63.

Wait for the Wagon

Come, Join Our Social Band

1. O, come and join our social band,
   And leave the treacherous wine;
O, come and join, with heart and hand,
   Our temperance cause divine.
For to us 'tis cheering
   When we see our efforts crowned,
Each to each endearing,
   And in friendship bound.

Chorus
Hurrah for the cause of temperance!
   Hurrah for the cause of temperance!
Push on for the cause of temperance!
   For we are a temperance band.

2. We all invite to join our host,
   In accents loud and clear;
For joy and happiness we boast
   Without alloy or fear.
For to us 'tis cheering
   When we see our efforts crowned,
Each to each endearing,
   And in friendship bound. *To Chorus*

3. No longer then neglected
   Let our friendly warning fall;
No longer be neglected now
   The friendly temperance call.
For to us 'tis cheering
   When we see our efforts crowned,
Each to each endearing,
   And in friendship bound. *To Chorus*[48]

Up with the Banner
(J. B. Dunn)

1. To greet our "Banner" rightly,
   Its love shall be our law,
So chorus out its welcome—
   Hurrah—once more—hurrah!
Though tiny as ourselves,
   Yet it is our rising sun,
And while we've life, we'll rally
   Around it, every one.

Chorus
Up with the Banner!
   Up with the Banner!
Up with the Banner!
   Till it waves far and wide!

2. Come, brothers, round it gather—
   Come, sisters, help our hands,
To bear before us lightly
   The Banner of our bands:
'Tis all our own to follow,
   Our own to guard and guide,
Presager of our conquest,
   While we march side by side. *To Chorus*

3. Our hearts are with our Banner,
   And though our hearts are young,
Let every little heart's love
   Be o'er its emblems flung;
And hope, bright bird of promise,
   Our own young hope will sing
Among the olive branches,
   That round our Banner cling. *To Chorus*

4. A shout then for our Banner!
   Let one and all unite
To shower its radiance round us
   Till every home is bright,
And every home will bless it,
   And every mother's hand
Will aid our sturdy fathers
   To bear it round the land. *To Chorus*[49]

Vote for Our Party

1. Six hundred thousand victims,
   Drink yearly binds in chains;
That deadly still and dram-shop,
   May reap their guilty gains;
We want no license party,
   A bloody flag that waves
O'er sixty thousand drunkards,
   It yearly sends to graves.

Chorus
Vote for our Party,
   Vote for our Party,
Vote for our Party,
   And we'll put rum away.

48. Thompson, *Thompson's Band*, 33–34.
49. Bradbury and Stearns, *Temperance Chimes* (1867 and 1878), 93.

2. Away with party, boasting
    Its crime-cursed revenue,
That costs a thousand millions,
    For ev'ry million due!
We are determined fully,
    That rum no more shall rule,
And that its crime-cursed money,
    Shall not support the school. *To Chorus*

3. Within the nation's councils,
    Controlling at its will,
Rum legislates to suit it,
    While party runs the still:
Shall Government be partner
    Engaged in liquor trade,
Both licensing the traffic,
    And sharing profits made? *To Chorus*

4. That is no honest business,
    That honest business kills,
And, without skill or labor,
    Its bloated coffers fills.
Shall longer, soul and body
    By license laws be sold,
That Government and dram-shop
    May get their price in gold? *To Chorus*

5. Hurrah, for Prohibition!
    We'll put this rum away,
If we go firmly forward,
    And vote just as we pray:
Hurrah! The mighty ballot
    Is never known to fail!
Then sturdily we'll wield it,
    And over rum prevail. *To Chorus*[50]

The Prohibition Wagon
(Herbert Whitney)

1. The good old party wagons
    in which we used to ride—
Republican and Democrat—
    must soon be thrown aside;
They've taken too much freight on board,
    and soon there'll be a break,
And anxiously we're asking,
    "What wagon shall we take?"

Chorus
Hurray for the wagon,
    the Prohibition wagon,
Wait for the wagon
    and we'll all take a ride!

2. They say it doesn't travel fast,
    but it is true and tried;
'Twont catch the offices just yet,
    but then we'll have the ride.
So let's hold on for principle
    with all our strength and might,
And just drive on straight forward,
    for we know the road is right. *To Chorus*

3. The road is clear before us,
    and will not turn aside,
Till we drive up to the White House,
    and there we'll end our ride;
We'll rule this Yankee land awhile
    and banish the saloon,
So get on board if you will go,
    we start off very soon![51]

50. Durant, *Prohibition Home*, 20–21.
51. Silver Lake Quartette, *Prohibition Bells*, 79.

6. Civil War Songs

With the onset of the Civil War, attention turned briefly from temperance, woman suffrage, and other social issues to the conflict between the Union and the Confederacy. No war in our history has produced such a large number of songs. Silber located some ten thousand songs in the process of compiling *Songs of the Civil War*. Many borrowed their tunes from earlier songs and the North and South freely borrowed tunes from each other. Since the Civil War fell within the period of temperance reform, it is not surprising that the tremendous output of Civil War songs soon fed the flames of temperance by providing new song material from which to draw.[1]

Particularly preferred among temperance writers were those Civil War songs with a strong martial spirit that supported coercive themes such as "Battle Cry of Freedom," "Battle Hymn of the Republic," "Marching through Georgia," and "Tramp, Tramp, Tramp." Although none of these Civil War songs became ammunition for the temperance cause until 1867, their familiarity inspired numerous settings of temperance lyrics well into the 1900s.

Maryland, My Maryland

"Maryland, My Maryland" employs the tune for "O Tannenbaum," which first appeared in print in 1824; the tune may originally date from the twelfth century. In creating "Maryland, My Maryland," Jenny Cary of Baltimore set James Ryder Randall's text to this tune in 1861, but she actually knew the tune not as the familiar Christmas song "O Christmas Tree," but as the rousing Yale college song "Lauriger Horatius." "Maryland, My Maryland" was one of the most familiar Southern songs of the war, and there were also scores of Union settings of this tune. Like those tunes mentioned earlier, temperance writers

1. Branham and Hartnett, *Sweet Freedom's Song*, 163; Silber, *Songs of the Civil War*, 4.

Maryland, My Maryland

James Ryder Randall   German Folk Song

The des-pot's heel is on thy shore, Ma-ry-land, my Ma-ry-land! His

torch is at thy tem-ple door, Ma-ry-land, my Ma-ry-land! A-

venge the pa-tri-ot-ic gore That flocked the streets of Bal-ti-more, And

be the bat-tle-queen of yore, Ma-ry-land, my Ma-ry-land!

One Hundred and One Best Songs, no. 66.

used "Maryland, My Maryland" exclusively for coercive purposes with the notable exception of Dwight Williams's "Touch Not, Taste Not."[2]

Touch Not, Taste Not
(Dwight Williams)

> 1. There's danger in the flowing bowl!
>   Touch not, taste not, handle not!
> 'Twill ruin body, ruin soul!
>   Touch not, taste not, handle not!
> 'Twill rob the pocket of its cash;
>   'Twill scourge thee with a cruel lash;
> And all thy hopes of pleasure dash,
>   Touch not, taste not, handle not!
>
> 2. "Strong drink is raging," God hath said:
>   Touch not, taste not, handle not!
> And thousands it hath captive led!
>   Touch not, taste not, handle not!

2. Dallin and Dallin, *Heritage Songster*, 76; Ewen, *All the Years*, 70–71; Silber, *Songs of the Civil War*, 54–55; Spaeth, *History of Popular Music*, 144.

It leads the young, and strong, and brave;
　　It leads them to a drunkard's grave;
It leads them where no arm can save—
　　Touch not, taste not, handle not!

3. Come, let us join each heart and hand,
　　Touch not, taste not, handle not!
To drive the traffic from the land;
　　Touch not, taste not, handle not!
We need the strongest, bravest hearts
　　To foil the cruel tempter's arts,
And heal his fearful wounds and smarts—
　　Touch not, taste not, handle not![3]

　　E. O. Excell adds the following fourth verse anticipating the "happy time" when Prohibition would rule the day:

4. Oh, hasten, then, the happy time!
　　Touch not, taste not, handle not!
When joyful bells the notes will chime;
　　Touch not, taste not, handle not!
Then raise the temp'rance flag on high,
　　And lift your voices to the sky—
Sing, glory be to God on high—
　　Touch not, taste not, handle not![4]

Battle Hymn of the Republic

　　"Battle Hymn of the Republic" employs the tune, "Glory Hallelujah" or "Say, Brothers, Will You Meet Us?" which was composed by William Steffe around 1856, but Julia Ward Howe knew the melody as "John Brown's Body," a parody introduced by glee club members from a battalion stationed at Fort Warren in Boston Harbor. Upon hearing the song at a Union army camp, Mrs. Howe, who accompanied her husband, Samuel, and Rev. James Clarke on the visit, was encouraged by Clarke to write a more worthy text for the air. Howe wrote "Battle Hymn of the Republic" in response to this suggestion. She sold her lyrics to the *Atlantic Monthly* for five dollars, and the song first appeared on the cover of that magazine in February 1862. "Battle Hymn of the Republic" was reprinted in a number of newspapers and later became the marching song of the Union army. Its melody also served several political campaigns.[5]

3. Stearns, *National Temperance*, 51–52.
4. E. O. Excell, *Inspiring Hymns*, no. 358; E. O. Excell, *Joy to the World*, no. 328.
5. Dallin and Dallin, *Heritage Songster*, 27; Ewen, *All the Years*, 73–74, Silber, *Songs of the Civil War*, 10–11; Spaeth, *History of Popular Music*, 147–50.

Battle Hymn of the Republic

Julia Ward Howe

Attr. William Steffe

One Hundred and One Best Songs, no. 44.

During the temperance movement, the tune to "Battle Hymn of the Republic" was often used in the songbooks of the Woman's Christian Temperance Union. Gordon's *Popular Campaign Songs* offers the following "roll call" of the nineteen states that voted to ban alcohol by 1915 in "The Nation's Going Dry."

The Nation's Going Dry

1. We've got them out of Georgia, and we've got them out of Maine.
   We've got them out of Tennessee, to ne'er come back again;
   And on the liquor traffic we will place the mark of Cain.
   The nation's going dry.

Chorus
Glory, glory, hallelujah,
   Glory, glory, hallelujah,

Glory, glory, hallelujah,
    The nation's going dry.

2. They're out of Oklahoma and they're out of Kansas, too.
    Mississippi, North Dakota's in the Prohibition Crew;
The coast is on the program and the Wets are looking blue—
    The nation's going dry. *To Chorus*

3. They are out of West Virginia and Virginia's dry to-day.
    Carolinas both have chased them, and the South is dry to stay;
And the people are rejoicing, for they see a better day—
    The nation's going dry. *To Chorus*

4. They are gone from Alabama and from Arkansas to-day;
    Yes, and Oregon and Washington have put them far away;
And the other states will follow if we work for them and pray—
    The nation's going dry. *To Chorus*

5. Colorado, too, and Idaho, have taken up the plan,
    Arizona joins Iowa in a ride upon the van;
So you see nineteen in all agree to put them under ban—
    The nation's going dry.

6. We are out for prohibition clear across our native land,
    For the North and South united now for prohibition stand;
The Atlantic and Pacific are together heart and hand—
    The nation's going dry.[6]

Included among the additional lyrics are several other WCTU selections set to this tune including "Welcome Song," "The 'Y' Is Marching On," "YWCTU Marching Song," "In His Name We Conquer," and "WCTU Battle Hymn." The following WCTU song is another of those rare examples of temperance/suffrage songs.

Help Us Win the Vote

1. We have heard a song of triumph, it has rolled from shore to shore,
    A song of joy and gladness which we'll sing forevermore;
"Woman suffrage sure is coming to the land which we adore,"
    Come help us win the *Vote*.

Chorus
Soon the women will be voting,
    Soon the women will be voting,
Soon the women will be voting,
    Come help us win the *Vote*.

6. Gordon, *Popular Campaign*, 31.

2. Come, sisters of the sunny south, we need your help to-day;
 Come, comrades of the eastern states, we know you're on the way;
Our western sisters join us, and they sing this happy lay,
 "You soon will win the *Vote*." *To Chorus*

3. There is much of wrong that we would right, there's work for
  each to do;
 The license shame we'll put to rout and all that is untrue;
For prohibition is our goal, the challenge comes to you,
 To help us win the *Vote. To Chorus*[7]

Dixie Land

Several sources maintain that Daniel Decatur Emmett, a Northerner who performed with Bryant's Minstrels, wrote "Dixie Land" at a New York boardinghouse in November of 1859 as a final number for a minstrel show. However, Hitchcock argues that "Dixie" was derived from a number of sources including English and Scottish dance tunes, a minstrel song of the 1830s entitled "Gumbo Chaff," and a tune from Emmett's *Fife Instructor.* Hamm also questions the origins of many of Emmett's compositions: "the origins of many of his songs are cloudy; some are also claimed by other composers, and some seem to have been known before he performed them and published them under his own name. They were undoubtedly drawn from traditional Anglo-American melodies stored in his memory, single tunes or several patched together; if any were original, they were patterned closely on the same tune tradition. . . . Thus Emmett and other early minstrel performers were more adapters than composers." More recently, Sacks and Sacks make a compelling case that "Dixie" originated with the Snowdens, a family of African American musicians and farmers who lived in Emmett's hometown of Mount Vernon, Ohio. In contrast, Chase explains that questions regarding authorship of the song were largely due to publishers clashing over copyright, and Paskman and Spaeth maintain that "there has never been any real doubt as to the origin of the song" because Emmett retained the original manuscript.[8]

Regardless of its origins, the tune's influence is undisputed. "Dixie" was first introduced in the South as a "walk-around," or closing number, for a

---

7. Gordon, *Popular Campaign*, 25. Reprinted in Dailey and Mead, *Prohibition Chimes*, no. 81, with minor alterations.

8. Dallin and Dallin, *Heritage Songster*, 138; Ewen, *All the Years*, 38–40; Dailey Paskman and Sigmund Spaeth, *"Gentlemen, Be Seated!" A Parade of the Old-Time Minstrels*, 185–86; Silber, *Songs of the Civil War*, 50–52; Hitchcock, *Music in the United States*, 123; Hamm, *Yesterdays*, 130; Howard L. Sacks and Judith Rose Sacks, *Way up North in Dixie: A Black Family's Claim to the Confederate Anthem*; Chase, *America's Music*, 242.

Dixie Land

Daniel Decatur Emmett · Daniel Decatur Emmett

I wish I was in the land of cot - ton, Old times there are not for - got - ten, Look a - way! Look a - way! Look a - way! Dix - ie Land. In Dix - ie Land where I was born in, Ear - ly on one frost - y morn - in', Look a - way! Look a - way! Look a - way! Dix - ie Land.

Chorus Then I wish I was in Dix - ie, Hoo - ray! Hoo - ray! In - Dix - ie Land I'll take my stand to live and die in Dix - ie; A - way, A - way, A - way down south in Dix - ie; A - way, A - way, A - way down south in Dix - ie.

One Hundred and One Best Songs, no. 74.

burlesque about Pocahontas in New Orleans in 1860, and it became an immediate hit. It was sung at Jefferson Davis's inauguration in Montgomery, Alabama, in 1861 and became the best-known Confederate song of the Civil War. This Southern song by a Northern composer was also the source for numerous parodies both in the South and the North during the Civil War. Temperance writers often capitalized on the popularity of "Dixie" to encourage Southerners to vote for prohibition. "The Saloonocrat" further warns Southern listeners to beware of dishonest politicians who argue that personal liberty is threatened by the prohibition of alcohol consumption.[9]

The Saloonocrat
(R. H. Cornelius)

1. The saloonocrat is in the land,
   He's prying around to catch you if he can,
Better watch, better watch,
   Better watch in Dixie Land.
On election day he has his man,
   He'll pull your vote ev'ry time that he can,
Better watch, better watch,
   Better watch in Dixie Land.

Chorus
Just vote for Prohibition, better watch, better watch,
   Saloonocrats are very sly, they know just when to try,
Better watch, better watch,
   Better watch your vote in Dixie.

2. The Saloonocrat is ev'rywhere,
   You'll find him here, you'll find him over there,
Better watch, better watch,
   Better watch in Dixie Land.
And his "Personal Liberty" farce he'll tell
   "It won't prohibit!" you'll hear him loudly yell,
Better watch, better watch,
   Better watch in Dixie Land. *To Chorus*

3. On election day just take your stand,
   And vote as you pray, don't join the whiskey clan,
Better watch, better watch,
   Better watch in Dixie Land.
For the judgment day is sure, you know,
   Your whiskey vote will meet you when you go,
Better watch, better watch,
   Better watch in Dixie Land. *To Chorus*[10]

---

9. Dallin and Dallin, *Heritage Songster,* 138; Ewen, *All the Years,* 38–40; Paskman and Spaeth, *"Gentlemen, Be Seated!"* 185; Silber, *Songs of the Civil War,* 50-52.
   10. Cornelius, *Cornelius' Prohibition,* no. 31.

When Johnny Comes Marching Home

The famous Union army bandsman Patrick Gilmore wrote the words to "When Johnny Comes Marching Home" under the pen name of Louis Lambert early in the Civil War, but the origins of the melody are uncertain. Spaeth attributes the tune to Gilmore, but Gilmore himself claimed that it was a traditional Negro air. Dallin traces the origins of the melody to an Irish antiwar song. "When Johnny Comes Marching Home" was extremely well known during the Spanish-American War and was refashioned as a fox-trot during World War I.[11]

Temperance writers used "When Johnny Comes Marching Home" both to persuade and to coerce. "Come Friends and Brothers" encourages listeners to take the pledge:

Come Friends and Brothers

1. Come, friends and brothers, all unite; Hurrah! hurrah!
   Come out and take the Pledge to-night, Hurrah! hurrah!
Come out and join our Temp'rance band,
   And nobly to our colors stand!
   And you'll all feel gay as you go marching home.

2. Too long Old Alcohol has reigned; Hurrah! hurrah!
   And many noble ones he's slain; Hurrah! hurrah!
Come out and break his chains to-night,
   And stand up with us for the fight;
   Then you'll all feel gay as you go marching home.

3. This Pledge was made for every one; Hurrah! hurrah!
   By Erin's brightest, noblest son; Hurrah! hurrah!
And in your name to this be signed,
   True happiness you'll surely find,
   And you'll all feel gay as you go marching home.

4. Come friends and brothers, every one; Hurrah! hurrah!
   Come join us in our Temp'rance song; Hurrah! hurrah!
The cold water flag we will unfurl,
   And shout for Temp'rance through the world!
   And we'll all feel gay as we go marching home.[12]

In contrast, "Rally round the Polls" takes the alcohol issue to the voting booth despite the wishes of political parties and the "hooting" of politicians to

11. Dallin and Dallin, *Heritage Songster,* 178; Ewen, *All the Years,* 74; Silber, *Songs of the Civil War,* 174–75; Spaeth, *History of Popular Music,* 154–55.

12. Leslie, *Good Templar* (1886), 49. Verses 1 and 4 are reprinted in Perkins, *Crystal Fountain,* 108.

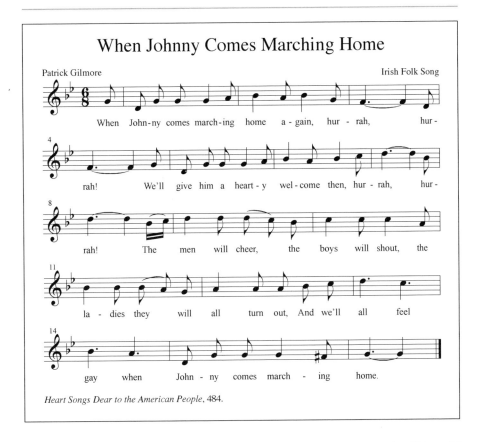

When Johnny Comes Marching Home

Patrick Gilmore   Irish Folk Song

When John-ny comes march-ing home a-gain, hur-rah, hur-rah! We'll give him a heart-y wel-come then, hur-rah, hur-rah! The men will cheer, the boys will shout, the la-dies they will all turn out, And we'll all feel gay when John-ny comes march-ing home.

Heart Songs Dear to the American People, 484.

the contrary. This setting is one of the few that does not borrow the "Hurrah! Hurrah!" response from Gilmore's original lyrics.

Rally round the Polls

1. Our voters come to put all rum
    Away, away!
And take old license party's plum
    Away, away!
The still must go, with all its woe,
    And liquor men, may brag and blow—
We'll vote all drink down,
    Then rally round the polls!

2. We'll banish years of blood and tears,
    Away, away!
And when the smoke of battle clears
    Away, away!
We shall be free, from sea to sea,
    From rum's accursed slavery—

We'll vote all drink down,
    Then rally around the polls!

3. From heart and soul, the gloom shall roll,
    Away, away!
And reason rise from rum's control,
    Away, away!
No tearful eyes, no hopeless sighs,
    When drink that cruel monster dies—
We'll vote all drink down,
    Then rally round the polls!

4. Let party growl, and rum-dens howl
    Away, away!
And politicians hoot like owl,
    Away, away!
Rum-party cry, of license "high,"
    Cannot deceive, it now must die—
We'll vote all drink down,
    Then rally around the polls!

5. For God and Right, work with your might,
    Away, away!
Straight onward march and valiant fight
    Away, away!
The end is near, the day is here,
    Lo! Signs of victory appear!
We'll vote all drink down—
    Then rally around the polls![13]

Battle Cry of Freedom

George F. Root wrote "Battle Cry of Freedom" in 1862, and it is still counted among the best military tunes ever written. The song was such an inspiration to the Union soldiers that President Lincoln once told Root, "You have done more than a hundred generals and a thousand orators." Southern lyricists commonly borrowed "Battle Cry of Freedom" for their own versions, and it provided the tune for several political songs, including "Rally for Old Abe" during Lincoln's second bid for presidency and "Ulysses Forever" for Grant's presidential campaign.[14]

13. Durant, *Prohibition Home*, 29–30.

14. Quoted in Ewen, *All the Years*, 77. Richard Crawford, ed., *The Civil War Songbook*, vi, x; Ewen, *All the Years*, 77; Silber, *Songs of the Civil War*, 8–9, 13–15, 50–52; Spaeth, *History of Popular Music*, 126–27.

Battle Cry of Freedom

George F. Root

George F. Root

Yes, we'll ral - ly round the flag, boys, we'll ral - ly once a - gain,

Shout - ing the bat - tle cry of Free - dom; We will ral - ly from the hill - side, we'll

gath - er from the plain, Shout - ing the bat - tle cry of

Chorus

Free - dom. The Un - ion for - ev - er, hur - rah, boys, hur - rah!

Down with the trai - tor, Up with the star; While we ral - ly round the flag, boys,

ral - ly once a - gain, Shout - ing the bat - tle cry of Free - dom!

One Hundred and One Best Songs, no. 28.

Of the temperance settings for George Root's well-known tune, seven borrow his phrase "shouting the battle cry of freedom," reflecting the view of reformers that they were freeing drinkers and their families from slavery to alcohol. Seven other settings modify this phrase to "shouting the battle cry of temperance" or some variation on that theme, and two settings shout for total Prohibition including "Yes, We'll Rally for the Right" by the composer of the original song.

Yes, We'll Rally for the Right
(G. F. Root)

> 1. Yes, we'll rally for the right, friends,
>   We'll rally once again,

This time for total Prohibition;
    We will rally from the hillside,
We'll gather from the plain,
    This time for total Prohibition.

Chorus
    United forever! Hurrah, all, hurrah!
Down now and ever, the still and the bar;
    While we rally for the right, friends,
Rally once again,
    Shouting for total Prohibition.

2. We are springing to the call
    Of our brothers in the field,
Shouting for total Prohibition;
    And we'll never quit the fight
'Till the enemy shall yield,
    Shouting for total Prohibition. *To Chorus*

3. We will welcome to our numbers
    The loyal, true and brave,
Shouting for total Prohibition;
    And although they may be poor,
Not a man shall be a slave,
    Shouting for total Prohibition. *To Chorus*

4. So we're springing to the call
    From the east and from the west,
Shouting for total Prohibition;
    And we'll drive the worst of foes
From the land we love the best,
    Shouting for total Prohibition. *To Chorus*[15]

Tramp! Tramp! Tramp!

Root's "Tramp! Tramp! Tramp!" written in 1863, was originally published to fill an empty page in the Christmas catalog from Root and Cady publishers, but it became Root's second most familiar Civil War song. It was appropriated not only by Confederate authors but also by the Irish for the song "God Save Ireland." The repeated verb *tramp* in the song's refrain provided temperance writers an opportunity not only to encourage action, but also to further emphasize that action through repetition. Nine writers borrowed the original

15. G. F. Root, *The Glorious Cause*, 114–15; *Prohibition Campaign Songster*, 114–15.

Tramp! Tramp! Tramp!

George F. Root   George F. Root

In the pris - on cell   I sit,   Think - ing, Moth - er dear, of you, And our

bright and hap - py home so far   a - way;   And the   tears they fill my eyes Spite of

all that I can do, Though I   try to cheer my com - rades and be   gay.

Chorus

Tramp! tramp! tramp! the boys are   march - ing,   Cheer up, com - rades, they will

come,   And be - neath the star - ry flag We shall   breathe the air a - gain Of the

free   land in   our own   be - lov - ed   home.

One Hundred and One Best Songs, no. 26.

words "tramp! tramp! tramp!" from the title of the song. Others employ different action verbs, including *work, come, hark,* and *vote*.[16]

Root's interest in the temperance movement was exceptional among the established composers of his day. He compiled two temperance songsters, *The
Musical Fountain* (1867) and *The Glorious Cause* (1888). As noted earlier, he wrote
temperance lyrics for "Battle Cry of Freedom," and in his temperance setting
of "Tramp! Tramp! Tramp!" he paints the emotional picture of a mother's concern for her sons.

16. Ewen, *All the Years*, 78; Silber, *Songs of the Civil War*, 13–14.

In Her Home the Mother Sits
(G. F. Root)

1. In her home the mother sits thinking anxiously and long
   Of the dangers to the sons she loves so well;
For despite her prayers and tears, men have done the cruel wrong,
   To establish at her door a licensed hell.

Chorus
But, cheer up, mothers, in your sorrow,
   Help to you will surely come!
For so true as God is just, He will hear your prayer at last,
   And your hand shall hold, Protection for your Home.

2. Though she try with all her powers to restrain them in their course,
   They will seek the haunts of revelry and mirth;
And she knows that once begun they will go from bad to worse,
   'Till the light of hope has left her wretched hearth. *To Chorus*

3. Then her weary eyes must wake while she waits through anguished
      hours
   For the steps that come unsteadily and slow;
And she notes the shameful change wrought by Satan's licensed powers,
   Till she sinks in utter helplessness and woe.[17]

One rather unusual setting of this tune, "The Conflict Is Past," gives every indication that National Prohibition has been achieved. However, its publication in *Anti-Saloon Campaign Songs* in 1909 falls a decade too early to make that claim.

The Conflict Is Past

1. O the conflict now is past, we have gained the day at last,
   And we celebrate a glorious victory;
Let us heartily rejoice, and with thankful heart and voice
   Praise the Lord whose arm has made His people free.

Chorus
Glory, glory, hallelujah
   For the glorious victory!
By a loyal people's votes now the flag of freedom floats
   O'er a nation that is honored, pure and free.

2. All the skirmishing is done, and the victory is won,
   And a million homes with happiness are bright;

---

17. Root, *Glorious Cause*, 108-9.

All the sorrowing is o'er, drink will crush their lives no more,
 Praise the Lord for giving triumph to the Right. *To Chorus*

3. We at last have gained the day, it could go no other way,
 God had waited long for this auspicious hour;
He was ready long ago, we to follow on were slow,
 Now our God has shown His hand of wondrous power. *To Chorus*[18]

We're Tenting Tonight

"We're Tenting Tonight" was a unique exception to the practice of writing new lyrics to tunes borrowed from the enemy. Walter Kittredge's lyrics and mournful tune had such universal appeal that they were often sung by Northerners and Southerners alike without modification. In contrast to the martial spirit of many Civil War songs, the sentimental nature of "We're Tenting Tonight" is more conducive to suasion than coercion. Pleas to take the pledge, think of wives and children, and pray outnumber the more militant lyrics for this tune. "On the New Camp-Ground" from *Prohibition Chimes* borrows Kittredge's lyrics with only minor alterations.[19]

On the New Camp-Ground

1. We're tenting to-night on the new camp-ground;
 Give us a song to cheer
Our earnest hearts; a song for home
 And friends we love so dear.

Chorus
Many are the hearts that are hopeful to-night,
 Praying for this woe to cease;
Many are the hearts looking to the right,
 To bring the dawn of peace,
Tenting to-night, tenting tonight,
 Tenting on the new camp-ground.

2. We were tenting of late on the old camp-ground,
 Enduring all the wrong
To loved ones and home in this free land,
 Thinking not it would be long. *To Chorus*

---

18. *Anti-Saloon Campaign*, no. 36; Hoffman, *Local Option*, no. 36; Hoffman, *Woman's Christian Temperance*, no. 36.

19. Ewen, *All the Years*, 75; Silber, *Songs of the Civil War*, 167–68; Spaeth, *History of Popular Music*, 152–53.

We're Tenting Tonight

Walter Kittredge   Walter Kittredge

We're tent - ing to - night on the old camp - ground,

Give us a song to cheer Our wear - y hearts, a

song of home, And friends we love so dear.

Man - y are the hearts that are wear - y to - night, Wish - ing for the war to

cease, Man - y are the hearts that are look - ing for the right, To

Chorus

see the dawn of peace. Tent - ing to - night,

Tent - ing to - night, Tent - ing on the old camp ground.

One Hundred and One Best Songs, no. 89.

3. But we're tired of deceit on the old camp-ground;
   Many are the dead and gone
Of the brave and true whom the arch-fiend Rum,
   Had held in bondage long. *To Chorus*

4. So we're fighting to-day for our new camp-ground;
   Many are falling near,
Thro' the power of this curse, while some are dead,
   Many are in tears.

Final Chorus
Many are the hearts that are wary to-night,
 Longing for this woe to cease;
Many are the hearts looking for the right,
 To bring their sure release.
Dying to-night, dying to-night,
 Dying on the old camp-ground.[20]

Marching through Georgia

Henry Clay Work's "Marching through Georgia" depicts Sherman's march to the sea in 1864. Although a cheerful tune, Southerners, and Georgians in particular, despised the song and chose not to use it for their own parodies, in part because it reminded them of the destruction in their state during the months before the war ended. However, "Marching through Georgia" later provided support for the Populist party and for the presidential races of William McKinley and Theodore Roosevelt.[21]

Thirty-three of the thirty-six temperance settings for this tune—including "Dry Ohio," which employs another of the many pseudonyms for the alcohol problem, "John Barleycorn"—borrow the "Hurrah! Hurrah!" from the beginning of the chorus.

A Dry Ohio
(L. Moore)

 1. Lift up the temp'rance banner, boys, and let it float on high;
  Arise, you anti-liquor hosts, and make Ohio dry.
 "John Barleycorn must leave our state," be this our battle cry.
  Fighting to make a dry Ohio.

Chorus
Hurrah! Hurrah! We're in the fight to win!
 Hurrah! Hurrah! We'll down the liquor sin!
We'll rise en masse and crowd the booths to cast our ballots in,
 Fighting to make a dry Ohio.

 2. The liquor gang began the fight on Independence Day,
  With purpose high to take the laws of temperance away;
 But He who is the God of Hosts will help us in the fray,
  Fighting to make a dry Ohio. *To Chorus*

20. Dailey and Mead, *Prohibition Chimes*, n.p.
21. Crawford, *Civil War Songbook*, vii; Ewen, *All the Years*, 78; Silber, *Songs of the Civil War*, 16; Spaeth, *History of Popular Music*, 156–57.

Marching through Georgia

Henry Clay Work   Henry Clay Work

Bring the good old bu - gle, boys, we'll sing an - oth - er song,

Sing it with a spir - it that will start the world a - long;

Sing it as we used to sing it fif - ty thou - sand strong,

While we were march - ing through Geor - gia. *Chorus* Hur - rah! Hur - rah! we

bring the ju - bil - lee! Hur - rah! Hur - rah! the

flag that makes you free! So we sang the cho - rus from At -

lan - ta to the sea, While we were march - ing through Geor - gia.

Osbourne McConathy, ed., *The School Song Book*, 130.

3. With bleary eye and maudlin tongue they'll make the liquor plea,
   Then back it up with legal lore and twisted Scripture, See?
But mighty soon they'll understand that on the job we'll be,
   Fighting to make a dry Ohio. *To Chorus*

4. Go call the undertaker up and have him right at hand,
   For poor old Johnny Barleycorn is sick, you understand.
We'll make him pass his checks in soon in our own Buckeye land,
   Fighting to make a dry Ohio. *To Chorus*[22]

22. *Ohio State Prohibition*, 14.

One of the few songs not borrowing Work's *hurrahs* chooses instead to put forth "Our Homes" as a "Shibboleth," or slogan, to identify those who fight the battle against alcoholism:

Our Homes Our Shibboleth Shall Be

1. Come and swell the chorus friends, and let us sing this song,
    Sing it as the battle cry of Right against the Wrong;
Sing it with the spirit that will move the world along,
    Away from saloons and the grog shop.

Chorus
"Our Homes! Our Homes!" our Shibboleth shall be;
    "Our Homes! Our Homes!" shall sweep from sea to sea,
Until our flag no longer as the emblem of the free,
    Waves o'er the slaves of the grog shop.

2. Come and save the loved ones whom the tempter may deprave,
    Come and rescue neighbors ere they sink beneath the wave,
Come as loyal freemen who their native land would save–
    Save from saloon and the grog shop. *To Chorus*

3. See the countless evils follow where the curse appears,
    Look upon the ruins it has strown along the years,
Hear the voice of sorrow and behold their tide of tears
    Caused by the saloon and the grog shop. *To Chorus*

4. Who that loves his fellow will not raise him if he fall?
    Who that loves his fam'ly will not war with alcohol?
Who loves God and country that will falter when they call,
    Call him to war with the grog shop. *To Chorus*[23]

23. Cake, *Popular Campaign*, n.p.

We Are Friends.

Maryland, My Maryland

We Will Redeem All Maryland
(Samuel Jarden)

1. To arms! to arms! gird on your sword,
    Ye gallant sons of Maryland;
Come join our band, with one accord,
    And banish rum from Maryland,
We'll make the hills and valleys ring,
    Proud Alcohol shall not be King;
For Local Option's just the thing,
    To break his power in Maryland.

Chorus
O come and join our glad refrain,
    And send the echo back again,
We'll break the tyrant's slavish chain,
    In Maryland, dear Maryland.

2. Let Local Option be endorsed,
    In Maryland, dear Maryland;
And Prohibition be enforced,
    Throughout the State of Maryland,
Ye men of Howard, form in line,
    With Calvert, Kent and Caroline,
Let every district now combine
    To break his power in Maryland.
        To Chorus

3. Hark! hear ye not the mother's cry?
    Oh, save our sons in Maryland;
Come to their rescue, or they die,
    Ye noble sons of Maryland,
They can't resist the tempter's power,
    Save, save in this, their needful hour,
Trust in the Lord, your strength and tower,
    And banish rum from Maryland.
        To Chorus

4. Ye doubting souls, fresh courage take,
    We will redeem all Maryland;
Our lives, our fortunes, we will stake,
    On the results of Maryland,
We'll win the East and Western shore,
    Then one grand strike for Baltimore—
Our glorious work will not be o'er,
    Till we redeem all Maryland. *To Chorus*

5. And now dear friends, I've one request—
    One plea for dear old Maryland—
That you will do your level best,
    To help our cause in Maryland;
Come man this Local Option boat,
    Her sails are set, she's now afloat,
And when the time comes cast your vote,
    To banish rum from Maryland.
        To Chorus[24]

Rally the Clans
(G. H. McLeod)

1. 'Tis sunrise on the mountain-top,
    Rally now, the Temp'rance Band!
Our onward march must know no stop,
    Until victors, crowned we stand.
From mountain, vale, and city home,
    Dear girls and boys, come with us come,
Our aim, our work, our cause is one,
    Banish Rum from this fair land!

2. No footstep falters on the way,
    Rally now the Temp'rance Band!
We're coming into perfect day,
    Soon as victors glad we'll stand,
And shout for joy, when sins dark sway,
    Shall pass forevermore away,
December cold, give place to May,
    When Rum's banished from the land!

3. Our banner proud waves on the air,
    Rally now the Temp'rance Band!
The battle won, how bright and fair,
    With the victors we shall stand,
The W.C.T.U. with pride,
    Each girl will claim, and joy betide,
The boys with brave men, side by side
    Shout, Rum's banished from the land![25]

Brave Temperance Men

1. The foe is great, but ye are strong,
    Temperance Men! Brave Temperance
        Men!
The fight is fierce and may be long,
    Temperance Men! Brave Temperance
        Men!

24. Jarden, *Prohibition Banner*, 6–7.
25. Gordon, *Marching Songs*, 37.

Remember Haddock's sacred dust,
    Remember Dow's incisive thrust,
Remember all the heroes just,
    Temperance Men! Brave Temperance
    Men!

2. Then strike the foe with all your soul,
    Temperance Men! Brave Temperance
    Men!
Ye must not yield to his control,
    Temperance Men! Brave Temperance
    Men!
A martyr's fate you may receive,
    'Twere better thus souls to receive,
That rum should live souls to deceive,
    Temperance Men! Brave Temperance
    Men!

3. I see your courage in the eye,
    Temperance Men! Brave Temperance
    Men!
Though meek you're not afraid to die,
    Temperance Men! Brave Temperance
    Men!
For life or death, for weal or woe,
    Seize now the sword of truth and show
Your courage 'gainst this deadly foe.
    Temperance Men! Brave Temperance
    Men!

4. I hear the distant thunder hum,
    Temperance Men! Brave Temperance
    Men!
We soon shall banish wine and rum,
    Temperance Men! Brave Temperance
    Men!
Come to thine own heroic throng
    That stalks with liberty along,
And ring this dauntless slogan song,
    "Rum shall go, yes, rum shall go."26

We Shall Win
(J. R. Norris)

1. We're marching on to vict'ry grand,
    We shall win, yes, we shall win;
Ours is a brave and loving band,
    We shall win, yes, we shall win;

No compromise with wrong we'll know,
    With sword of truth we'll meet the foe.
At God's command we'll onward go,
    We shall win, yes, we shall win.

2. Defeat we never will confess,
    We shall win, yes, we shall win;
Because we fight for righteousness.
    We shall win, yes, we shall win;
Though enemies may all unite
    Our holy purposes to blight,
They all shall flee before the light,
    We shall win, yes, we shall win.

3. Whate'er the cost, the lost we'll save,
    We shall win, yes, we shall win;
We'll snatch them from a drunkard's grave,
    We shall win, yes, we shall win;
While marching on our hearts grow strong
    To hate and conquer ev'ry wrong,
We soon shall sing the victor's song,
    We shall win, yes, we shall win.

4. Our leader is the mighty Lord,
    We shall win, yes, we shall win;
'Tis thus recorded in His word,
    We shall win, yes, we shall win;
He'll help us save the rising race,
    His coming kingdom grows a-pace,
Ere long we'll see His blessed face,
    We shall win, yes, we shall win.27

What's the News?
(E. A. Hoffman)

1. Where'er we go the people say,
    What's the news? O, what's the news?
What are the tidings of the day?
    What's the news? O, what's the news?
O, we have gladsome news to tell,
    The cause of Right is going well,
And wrong now hears its funeral knell,
    That's the news. O, that's the news.

2. The world is asking far and near,
    What's the news? O, what's the news?
What brings the message, hope and cheer?
    What's the news? O, what's the news?

We tidings bring of joy and cheer,
  The hour of triumph now is near,
The curse of drink must disappear,
  That's the news, O, that's the news.

3. The temp'rance armies march along,
  That's the news, O, that's the news.
They muster millions, brave and strong,
  That's the news, O, that's the news.
Their hearts are set on victory,
  A triumph that complete will be,
Then will they shout their jubilee,
  That's the news, O, that's the news.[28]

A Foe to Fight

1. We have a foe we mean to fight,
  Within our state, within our state,
An enemy to God and right,
  Within our state, within our state,
Arise, ye people, take your stand,
  And work together, hand in hand
For God, and home, and native land,
  Within our state, within our state.

2. The counties small and counties great,
  Within our state, within our state,
Will vote on Prohibition straight,
  Within our state, within our state,
Arise, ye people, in your might,
  For God is on the side of Right,
And He will help us win the fight
  Within our state, within our state.

3. Saloons are warned that they must go,
  Go from our state, go from our state;
Good thinking people will it so,
  Within our state, within our state,
We'll win the day, for God we'll trust,
  We'll win the day, our cause is just;
We'll win the day, but fight we must
  Within our state, within our state.[29]

Vote It Out

1. What shall we do with the saloon?
  Vote it out, we'll vote it out;
The evil thing must perish soon,
  Vote it out, we'll vote it out;
So great a wrong should never stand
  A single day in this fair land,
The home of freemen brave and grand,
  Vote it out, we'll vote it out.

2. This is what we propose to do,
  Vote it out, we'll vote it out;
For help we must depend on you,
  Vote it out, we'll vote it out;
The homes have suffered much and long,
  Through this unjust and cruel wrong,
And now, O patriots, true and strong,
  Vote it out, we'll vote it out.

3. The signs of victory are bright,
  Vote it out, we'll vote it out;
The wrong cannot withstand the right,
  Vote it out, we'll vote it out;
Why shall we longer then delay?
  The curse should not remain a day,
An earnest fight will win the day,
  Vote it out, we'll vote it out.[30]

Pass the News Along

1. The days are full of joy and cheer,
  Pass the glorious news along;
The hour of victory is near,
  Pass the glorious news along;
The hard campaign will soon be past,
  The winning ballots will be cast,
The battle will be ours at last,
  Pass the glorious news along.

2. Our cause is gaining volunteers,
  Pass the happy news along;
They join the ranks with rousing cheers,
  Pass the happy news along;

28. *Anti-Saloon Campaign*, no. 26; Hoffman, *Local Option*, no. 26; Hoffman, *Woman's Christian Temperance*, no. 26.

29. *Anti-Saloon Campaign*, no. 30, and Hoffman, *Woman's Christian Temperance*, no. 30, suggest that singers insert the name of their state in place of "our state." Hoffman, *Local Option*, back cover, entitles this song "Michigan, My Michigan" and modifies the text as suggested by the other sources.

30. *Anti-Saloon Campaign*, no. 32; Hoffman, *Local Option*, no. 32; Hoffman, *Woman's Christian Temperance*, no. 32.

With faith and courage moves our band,
    Inspired with purpose holy grand,
To drive saloons from out the land,
    Pass the happy news along.

3. The outlook brighter grows each day,
    Pass the splendid news along;
The tide is turning now our way,
    Pass the splendid news along;
The arm of God has been made bare,
    The cry of victory fills the air,
And prayer is offered everywhere,
    Pass the splendid news along.[31]

Ohio! My Ohio

1. A blighting curse stands at each door,
    Ohio, my Ohio!
From river bank to Erie's shore,
    Ohio, my Ohio!
Strike! in the name we all adore,
    Strike! for the flag our fathers bore;
For freedom now and evermore;
    Ohio, my Ohio!

2. They come—the sons with loud acclaim,
    Ohio, my Ohio!
'Neath Prohibition's oriflamme,
    Ohio, my Ohio!
While truckling statesmen, who defame,
    With graft and greed, thy glorious name,
Sink 'neath the burden of their shame,
    Ohio, my Ohio!

3. Hail, Glorious State! the whole earth
        'round,
    Ohio, my Ohio!
With Hallelujahs shall resound!
    Ohio, my Ohio!
She's been redeemed! She's hallowed ground
    Where Truth and Temperance abound;
Let all her sons her praises sound;
    Ohio, my Ohio![32]

The Tide Rolls In
(H. Anna Brunner)

1. The prohibition tide comes on,
    It's rolling in, it's rolling in;

The liquor dealers must be gone,
    They see with fear the tide roll in.
The tide rolled in, the tide rolled in,
    The prohibition tide rolled in;
On wet and dry the tide ran high,
    The prohibition tide rolled in.

2. The liquor dealers took their stand,
    And vowed to drive us from the land;
But soon we drowned their noise and din,
    The prohibition tide rolled in.
The tide rolled in, the tide rolled in,
    The prohibition tide rolled in;
On wet and dry the tide ran high,
    The prohibition tide rolled in.

3. The northern states long heard the roar
    Of prohibition on their shore;
And then the tide so grandly came,
    Before the ebb—the South to claim.
The tide rolled in, the tide rolled in,
    The prohibition tide rolled in;
On wet and dry the tide ran high,
    The prohibition tide rolled in.

4. And now we want this mighty tide
    Of prohibition nationwide,
To lap the world that we may cry,
    The whole wide world has now gone dry.
It's rolling in, it's rolling in,
    The prohibition tide rolls in;
We'll live to hear the glorious cry—
    The whole wide world has now gone
        dry![33]

Battle Hymn of the Republic

On to Meet the Foe
(Asa Hull)

1. On, Brothers, on, to meet the foe that we
        abhor!
    Rise and put your armor on, and hasten
        to the war;
Never dare to think that your fighting days
        are o'er,
    Until the battle's won.

31. Hoffman, *Woman's Christian Temperance*, no. 46
32. *Ohio State Prohibition*, 15.
33. Gordon, *Jubilee Songs*, 16.

Chorus
Glory, glory hallelujah!
   Glory, glory hallelujah!
Glory, glory hallelujah!
   Our cause is marching on.

2. See how the banners gleam along his ranks
   today!
   See! he hides his horrors 'neath a
      glittering display;
Husband, Wife, and Children are caught and
   lured away,
   To join the hosts of sin. *To Chorus*

3. On to the rescue now, before it is too late;
   Let us save a comrade from so terrible a
      fate;
Death may be his portion, if we the morrow
   wait;
   So fill the ranks to-day. *To Chorus*

4. Strike for the homes where peace does
   never enter in;
   Strike for the many souls that you may
      help to win;
Strike for love of right, and against the power
   of sin,
   And God shall nerve the arm.
   To Chorus[34]

General Invitation Song
(Frank C. Filley)

1. Come and sign our pledge tonight and
   take the badge of Blue,
   Come and sign our pledge tonight and
      take the badge of Blue,
Come and sign our pledge tonight and take
   the badge of Blue,
   And join our Gospel Temperance Band.

Chorus
Glory! Glory! Hallelujah!
   Glory! Glory! Hallelujah!
Glory! Glory! Hallelujah!
   Our cause goes bravely on.

2. Let not a single soul despair, there's hope
   for one and all,

Let not a single soul despair, there's hope
   for one and all,
Let not a single soul despair, there's hope for
   one and all,
   If you join our Gospel Temperance Band.
   To Chorus

3. Though low you may have fallen, your life
   you can renew,
   Though low you may have fallen, your life
      you can renew,
Though low you may have fallen, your life
   you can renew,
   If you join our Gospel Temperance Band.
   To Chorus

4. God's precious grace is free to all; the offer
   don't refuse,
   God's precious grace is free to all; the
      offer don't refuse,
God's precious grace is free to all; the offer
   don't refuse,
   Come, join our Gospel Temperance
   Band. *To Chorus*[35]

The Coming of the Lord

1. Mine ears have caught the footfalls of the
   coming of the Lord,
   He is marshaling his squadrons, He has
      girded on His sword;
The timid and the silent, they are mustering
   at His word,
   Our God is marching on!

Chorus
Glory, glory, hallelujah!
   Glory, glory, hallelujah!
Glory, glory, hallelujah!
   Our God is marching on.

2. There were faint and distant steppings that
   our dull ears scarce could hear,
   There were nearer sounds of tramping,
      there were signs of boding fear;
There's a mighty, rushing onset, for the Lord
   Himself is here,
   His day is marching on! *To Chorus*

34. Hull, *Hull's Temperance*, 36. Perkins, *Crystal Fountain*, 108, omits verse 2 and makes minor word changes in the three remaining verses.
35. Filley, *Red, White, and Blue*, 3–4.

3. From the closet and the prayer-room, tones
   of hallowed wrestling swell;
   Up from "sample-room" and "cellar" ring
   the maddened cries of hell,
Where shall wave the victor's banner,
   grandest words of promise tell;
   'Tis God that's marching on! *To Chorus*

4. Sisters up, for he is passing. Rise, today He
   calls for *thee*;
   Yours has been the heavy anguish,
   you shall share the victory;
Lo, the might of God is in you, ye shall
   triumph gloriously,
   For He is marching on! *To Chorus*[36]

The Angel of Temperance

1. God hath sent a glowing angel, to unbar
   the gates of sin,
   And to wrestle with the tempter, who
   entices souls therein,
'Tis the Temperance Angel leading on the
   armies that shall win,
   Where right is marching on.

Chorus
Glory, Glory, Hallelujah
   Glory, Glory, Hallelujah,
Glory, Glory, Hallelujah,
   When right is marching on.

2. Every loyal son and daughter is enrolling
   for the fray,
   And the tramp of marching armies echoes
   near and far away,
Some to mingle in the contest, some to wait,
   and watch, and pray,
   While right is marching on! *To Chorus*

3. Through the thoroughfares of traffic,
   through the flowery paths of ease,
   In the haunts where crime and sorrow,
   sow the upas of disease,
The Temperance Angle moves, as Christ trod
   the angry seas,
   While right is marching on! *To Chorus*

4. Homes shall brighten, hearts shall lighten,
   when the Temperance Angel comes,
   And the lives that grope in darkness, turn
   again to brighter suns.
Crime shall languish, wrong shall perish, and
   a glorious cause be won,
   When Temperance work is done!
   To Chorus[37]

Battle Song of Prohibition

1. Prohibition Home Protection! we have
   waited for it long;
   Now its hosts are forward marching, lo!
   we see them sweep along—
Rank and file, with plume and banner,
   marching on to conquer wrong:
   The Right is marching on.

Chorus
Prohibition Home Protection!
   Prohibition Home Protection!
Prohibition Home Protection!
   The Right is marching on.

2. Nearer draws the hour of conflict, when
   the haughty liquor-foe,
   Soul and body both destroying, vengeance
   swift shall overthrow!
God is marshaling his legions, he is calling us
   to go;
   His wrath is marching on. *To Chorus*

3. In the councils of the nation, rum is ruling
   at its will,
   While its revenue of sorrow, flows from
   crime producing-still;
Thus enslaved, rum-license party, Heaven's
   cup of wrath shall fill:
   Its doom is marching on. *To Chorus*

4. Ev'ry year, six hundred thousand of the
   nation, rum enslaves,
   Sixty thousand yearly, going down to sad
   and lonely graves;
Revenue from rum, they tell us, thus a
   hundred million saves:
   But Right is marching on. *To Chorus*

36. Stearns, *National Temperance*, 29.
37. Daniels, *Temperance Songster*, 19–20.

5. Will this pay for thousands slaughtered,
	life and hope and fortune wrecked?
	Must we still reap crime and sorrow, while
	rum slav'ry we protect?
Look upon the hideous picture; as ye pray or
	vote, reflect,
	The truth is marching on. *To Chorus*

6. There is coming, swiftly coming down on
	all the guilty land,
	Mighty tempest and convulsion,
	rum-made laws can not withstand;
Like the empty chaff, in fury guilty party shall
	be fanned,
	In doom is marching on. *To Chorus*

7. We are marching! Lo, our banner, free
	from rum's accursed stain!
	Rally, if ye would be freemen, from hill,
	valley, mountain, plain;
Down with drink, in gladness hailing
	Prohibition's blessed reign;
	Its truth is marching on. *To Chorus*38

Never Cease the Conflict

1. There's a mighty conflict coming o'er the
	rum-cursed land;
	Face to face, those foemen, Rum and
	Prohibition stand;
To begin the battle, they are waiting the
	command:
	The Right shall surely win.

Chorus
Never, never cease the conflict!
	Never, never cease the conflict!
Never, never cease the conflict!
	The Right shall surely win.

2. Listen how the fetters of the dire
	rum-slav'ry clank;
	Never mind its "hobby" and never mind
	its "crank";
Smite its bloated center, and turn its reeling
	flank:
	The Right shall surely win. *To Chorus*

3. Never heed the clamor raised from pulpit
	and from press,
	License party aiding, Prohibition to distress;
Heed not non-committal views such
	hypocrites express:
	The Right shall surely win. *To Chorus*

4. Heed them not—these hirelings in the
	sinking cause of rum;
	At the battle's turning, the craven cowards
	shall be dumb;
To the winning side then, cheering loudest
	they will come!
	The Right shall surely win. *To Chorus*

5. Thus it has been ever, with a struggling,
	righteous cause;
	Scornful pride and bitter jealousy
	withhold applause,
'Till at last it conquer, then they give it loud
	huzzas!
	The Right shall surely win. *To Chorus*39

Soldiers of the King
(Mary Lowe Dickinson)

1. In His name, whose voice has called us, in
	the morning of our day,
	We have joined the mighty army, of the
	souls who work and pray,
We will follow Christ our leader, however
	hard the way,
	Young soldiers of the King.

Chorus
Shining, shining, shining there above us.
	Cheering, cheering, cheering all who love
	us,
White gleams the snowy cross to prove us,
	True soldiers of the King.

2. It will guide us o'er the waters, when the
	waves of evil toss,
	It will help us to be victors over sin and
	shame and loss,
And to gather many a follower, beneath the
	snowy cross,
	New soldiers for the King

38. Durant, *Prohibition Home,* 9.
39. Ibid., 34.

Chorus
Rally, rally, rally round the banner,
Singing, singing, singing our hosanna,
Rally, rally, rally round the banner,
Young soldiers of the King.

3. Our foes are brave and mighty, and our
strength sometimes is small;
Yet swift before our leader's face, must evil
flee or fall;
For all the shining hosts of God are waiting
for his call,
True soldiers of the King.

Chorus—Rally, rally, rally, *etc.*
True soldiers of the King.

4. Our march is forward ever, with weapons
gleaming bright;
Our warfare is with sin and wrong; our
watchword, "For the Right."
And above us, beckoning ever, the cross of
snowy white,
Young soldiers of the King.

Chorus—Rally, rally, rally, *etc.*
Young soldiers of the King.[40]

Welcome Song
(Anna A. Gordon)

1. In the name of God, our Father, do we
welcome you to-night.
We are only little children, but we know
your cause is right,
We have learned the precious letters, that are
on your banner bright,
The W.–C.–T.–U.

Chorus
Glory, glory, hallelujah;
Glory, glory, hallelujah;
Glory, glory, hallelujah;
Our Cause is marching on.

2. For the sake of Home, we welcome you,
White Ribbon army true;
May the homes we love be purer for the
work that you shall do,

Till the name that is more famous than the
beer that now we brew
Is W.–C.–T.–U. *To Chorus*

3. You are welcome to our city, in the name
of Native Land,
Loyal daughters of your country, as you
labor hand in hand,
Old King Alcohol must tremble, for he
cannot long withstand
The W.–C.–T.–U. *To Chorus*

4. Now "For God, and Home and Native
Land" thrice welcome is our song.
We are all cold water children, won't that
help the cause along?
Home Protection soon is coming, right must
triumph over wrong,
Since God is marching on. *To Chorus*[41]

Glory, Hallelujah!
(J. C. Macy)

1. Old Whiskey's going where all evil things
must go;
We're bound to make him pay the debts
of misery and woe!
He'll find that Temp'rance people are a stern,
unyielding foe,
As they go marching on!

Chorus
Glory! Glory Hallelujah!
Glory! Glory Hallelujah!
Glory! Glory Hallelujah!
As we go marching on!

2. Our banner's waving now throughout the
union grand,
The battle cry of Temperance is ringing
through the land!
Oh, see the legions rally to support the
Temp'rance band,
As they go marching on! *To Chorus*

3. Then struggle bravely in the work of doing
right!
The Temp'rance star is shining with a
never fading light!

---

40. Gordon, *Marching Songs*, 19.
41. Ibid., 17.

From North, and South, from East and West,
we're coming in our might,
Oh, yes! we're marching on! *To Chorus*42

Good Time Coming

1. Pass the word along the column, boys, and
sound it with a will;
"No saloon down in the valley, but a
school on every hill."
Ever let it be our watchword, then, and for it
labor still,
As we go marching on.

Chorus
There's a good time a-coming, hallelujah!
No saloon in the valley, hallelujah!
But a school on every hill, hallelujah!
As we go marching on.

2. Despair not, weeping mothers, for there
still is hope for you;
Hope for the drunkard's starving wife, his
ragged children, too.
Cheer up! The clouds are breaking; there are
brighter stars in view,
As we go marching on. *To Chorus*

3. Cheer up, ye weak and erring ones,
to drink enslaved so long;
Come aid us bind the demon, now, in
fetters fast and strong;
For God will ever help us as we battle against
the wrong.
As we go marching on. *To Chorus*

4. Guard well your home, your own sweet
home, where'er that home may be;
Strike felling blows 'gainst all our foes—till
from the traffic free.
We raise our hallelujahs high in songs of
victory,
As we go marching on. *To Chorus*43

Fill the Ranks with Voters
(G. F. Root)

1. Fill the ranks with voters and be ready for
the fray,
For the only battle is upon election day.
Liquor folks would like to have us try some
other way,
As we go marching on.

Chorus
Glory, glory, hallelujah!
Glory, glory, hallelujah!
Glory, glory, hallelujah!
As we go marching on.

2. Yes, the liquor folks proclaim that license
is the best,
But, where'er we've tried it, it has never
stood the test.
So we'll give the license scheme where'er we
can, a rest,
As we go marching on. *To Chorus*

3. Does it help the mother when she's lost
her only son,
To be told that by the law the cruel deed
was done?
No! and that is why we take the vote and not
the gun,
As we go marching on. *To Chorus*

4. Ah, if at the ballot box the mother could
be heard,
How the hearts of suff'ring ones with
gladness would be stirred!
How the feeble wail would cease and
Triumph be the Word!
And we'd go marching home. *To Chorus*44

Rally round the Standard

1. Fill the ranks with soldiers and be ready
for the fight,
Let the world behold us with our colors
waving bright;
We're the temp'rance army and we battle for
the right,
As we go marching on.

42. Macy, *Temperance Song-Herald*, 40.
43. Leslie, *Good Templar* (1888), 37.
44. Root, *Glorious Cause*, 104–5; *Prohibition Campaign Songster*, 104–5.

Chorus
Rally, rally, round the standard!
  Rally, rally, round the standard!
Rally, rally, round the standard!
  As we go marching on.

2. Fill the ranks with soldiers, and, oh, never
    be afraid,
   First in ev'ry conflict where the tempter
    would invade;
Bringing back the sunlight o'er the ruin he
    has made,
   Oh, we'll go marching on. *To Chorus*

3. Water, crystal water, from the quiet
    mountain rill,
   Cool and sparkling water, that with joy
    the heart can fill,
Merry, laughing water, let it be our chorus
    still,
   As we go marching on. *To Chorus*[45]

The "Y" Is Marching On

1. We have heard the cry arising from the
    mountain and the plain,
   Mourning for the lives of millions by the
    deadly rum power slain.
But with voices sweetly blending will we sing
    the glad refrain,
   The "Y" is marching on.

Chorus
Glory! glory! hallelujah!
  Glory! glory! hallelujah!
Glory! glory! hallelujah!
  The "Y" is marching on.

2. In the glory of our girlhood have we joined
    the loyal band,
   Marching on beneath the banner, "God
    and Home and Native Land,"
With a consecrated courage that the foe
    cannot withstand,
   The "Y" is marching on. *To Chorus*

3. And when free from sin's dominion, loved
    America we see,
   Our fair land shall be a temple, sacred
    Temperance, to thee;
And its "cornerstones" unyielding, may the
    "Ys" forever be,
   The "Y" is marching on. *To Chorus*[46]

Glory Hallelujah
(M. H. Evans)

1. The White Ribbon army stands "for Home
    and Native Land,"
   The White Ribbon army stands "for
    Home and Native Land,"
The White Ribbon army stands "for Home
    and Native Land,"
   As we go marching on.

Chorus
Glory, glory hallelujah,
  Glory, glory, hallelujah,
Glory, glory, hallelujah,
  As we go marching on.

2. With Prohibition banners we will rally for
   fight, *etc. To Chorus*

3. With ballots for our bullets we can shoot
   the traffic down, *etc. To Chorus*

4. We will never grant a license for the sale of
   alcohol, *etc. To Chorus*[47]

Sign the Pledge
[*Chorus Only*]
1. Come and sign the pledge tonight, boys!
   Come and sign the pledge tonight, boys!
Come and sign the pledge tonight, boys!
   Be slaves to drink no more!

2. God will give you strength to keep it,
   God will give you strength to keep it,
God will give you strength to keep it,
   If you his grace implore.[48]

45. Leslie, *Good Templar* (1888), 94.
46. Gordon, *Songs of the Young Woman's*, 54–55.
47. Cassel, *White Ribbon*, no. 41. The author suggests, "let a single voice sing the first line and then have the audience take it up. Make your own verses. . . . Ask the audience to add lines. . . . Try this as a pastime while the crowd is gathering. Try it when clubs are marching."
48. McCauley, *Anti-Saloon Songs*, 41; Lorenz, *New Anti-Saloon*, 41; *Songs of the Temperance Reform*, 41.

The Whisky Shops Must Go

1. O, comrades in this conflict of the right
       against the wrong.
    To the battle of the ballots come with
       shouting and with song;
And this shall be our slogan as the legions
       march along—
    "The whisky shops must go."

Chorus
Rally! Rally! O, ye freemen!
    Rally! Rally! O, ye freemen!
Rally! Rally! O, ye freemen!
    The whisky shops must go.

2. Jehovah's wrath is kindled, and His arm is
       lifted high,
    For from out the dust of ages He has
       heard the martyr's cry;
The cup of wrath is brimming, and His
       vengeance draweth nigh—
    "The whisky shops must go." *To Chorus*

3. From the silence and the shadows, where
       our mothers weep and pray,
    With their patient hands uplifted 'gainst
       the woe they cannot slay,
We have heard a voice entreating us to sweep
       the curse away—
    "The whisky shops must go." *To Chorus*

4. Hear the children cry for pity from the
       cruel heart of greed;
    See them trampled into silence by the
       monster while they plead!
Be quick, my patriot brothers, to the rescue
       let us speed—
    "The whisky shops must go." *To Chorus*

5. We are coming, we are coming for the light
       has dawned at last,
    Hark! the battle-cry is ringing, and our
       lines are length'ning fast,
For God, and Home, and Native Land, our
       ballots shall be cast—
    "The whisky shops must go." *To Chorus*[49]

YWCTU Marching Song
(Bertha C. Thorne)

1. Mine eyes have seen the glory of a banner
       white unfurled,
    And it bears a God-sent message to all
       nations of the world;
It will float till liquor's legions from their
       stronghold shall be hurled;
    Our cause is marching on.

Chorus
Glory, glory, hallelujah!
    Glory, glory, hallelujah!
Glory, glory, hallelujah!
    Our cause is marching on.

2. A million rain-drops glisten in the bow
       that spans the skies;
    A million bands must help us if our
       banner still shall rise;
If your hands are weak or weary let your
       hearts be with the "Ys,"
    And join them—marching on.

Chorus
Glory, glory, hallelujah! etc.
    And join them—marching on.

3. Oh, the false notes in life's harmony; the
       discords and the tears!
    Could we make the notes ring truer with
       the swiftly passing years,
Our work would find an echo in the music of
       the spheres,
    For Truth is marching on,

Chorus
Glory, glory, hallelujah! *etc.*
    For Truth is marching on.[50]

A Day of Wrath

1. A day of wrath is waiting for the hosts of
       sin and shame,
    The lord of righteousness shall rise and
       glorify His name,
He's coming to deliver as in days of old He came,
    With glory and with power!

49. Fillmore and Fillmore, *Fillmores' Prohibition*, no. 153; Biederwolf and Lawson, *Best Temperance Songs*, no. 15. Gordon, *Popular Campaign*, 32, changes the title to "The Liquor Traffic Goes" and ends each verse and the chorus with these words; verse 2 is omitted.

50. Gordon, *Temperance Songster*, no. 123.

Chorus
Glory, Glory, Hallelujah!
　Glory, Glory, Hallelujah!
Glory, Glory, Hallelujah!
　Our God will come with power!

2. No more our Sabbaths shall for work of
　　sin and death be sold,
　No more our treasuries be cursed with
　　sin-polluted gold,
No more our prisons shall the fruits of
　　licensed liquor hold,
　For God in justice reigns! *To Chorus*

3. The wall of suff'ring ones has reached
　　th' Omnipotent on high,
　And He who never fails to hear the
　　burdened when they cry,
Hath sounded forth the order that the
　　cursed saloon must die,
　For God in mercy reigns! *To Chorus*

4. Down from the battlements of heav'n has
　　been heard the trumpet call,
　That summons forth an army on the
　　hosts of sin to fall,
And the sword of God in righteousness shall
　　break the despot's thrall,
　For God in triumph reigns! *To Chorus*[51]

Light of Truth Is Breaking

1. The light of truth is breaking, on the
　　mountain tops it gleams;
　Let it flash along the valleys, Let it glitter
　　on our streams,
Till all the land awakens, In its flush of
　　golden beams;
　Our God is marching on.

Chorus
Glory, Glory, Hallelujah!
　Glory, Glory, Hallelujah!
Glory, Glory, Hallelujah!
　Our God is marching on.

2. With purpose strong and steady in the
　　great Jehovah's name,

We rise to snatch our kindred from the
　　depths of woe and shame;
And the jubilee of freedom to the slaves of
　　sin proclaim:
　Our God is marching on. *To Chorus*

3. Our strength is in Jehovah, and our cause
　　is in his care;
　With Almighty God to help us, we have
　　faith to do and dare,
While confiding in the promise that the Lord
　　will answer prayer:
　Our God is marching on. *To Chorus*[52]

New Battle Hymn of the Republic
(Herbert Whitney)

1. We have lifted up our banner in a just and
　　righteous cause,
　We have set our faces forward and we will
　　not idly pause
Till we've cleansed our land from evil and
　　have purified our laws,
　For God is marching on.

Chorus
Glory, glory, hallelujah!
　Glory, glory, hallelujah!
Glory, glory, hallelujah!
　Our God is marching on.

2. Never more in any measure will we touch
　　the cursed thing,
　It can only loss and sorrow to the State
　　and people bring,
For it biteth like a serpent, like an adder's is
　　its sting,
　But God is marching on. *To Chorus*

3. He is marching on to battle, and he calleth
　　not in vain,
　That his chosen follow onward, for his
　　hosts fill all the plain,
Where the last great cause is tested and the
　　monster will be slain,
　For God is marching on. *To Chorus*

51. Miller, *Patriotic No-License*, no. 13.
52. Stearns, *National Temperance*, 10. Miller, *Patriotic No-License*, no. 25, replaces the phrase "Our God is marching on" with "Our cause is marching on" and adds a verse 4.

4. The first dawning light is breaking, the
full day we yet shall see,
When the cause of all our sorrow will
be banished utterly,
And our homes be pure as heaven, and our
sons be brave and free,
For God is marching on. *To Chorus*[53]

WCTU Battle Hymn

1. We're a band of Christian women
marching at the Captain's word
With our Christian Temp'rance Union
holding high the Spirit's sword;
And through faith we're bound to conquer
with the help of Christ, our Lord,
As we go marching on.

Chorus
Glory, Glory, Hallelujah!
Glory, Glory, Hallelujah!
Glory, Glory, Hallelujah!
Our cause is marching on.

2. Our mission is to educate the people of
our land,
To fight the liquor traffic, and for
temp'rance boldly stand,
For all the moral forces should unite both
heart and hand,
As right goes marching on. *To Chorus*

3. Jesus on His throne in glory, sends this
message from above,
By the Holy Spirit's coming in the
likeness of a dove,
Bidding us to save our children, precious
jewels that we love,
For God is marching on. *To Chorus*

4. In the name of Christ, the Conqueror,
we plead and fight and pray,
That the evils of intemp'rance may be
driven all away;
Lo! the night of sin is passing—dawns the
prohibition day,
And God is marching on. *To Chorus*[54]

LTL Battle Hymn

We're a band of youthful soldiers marching
to the battle-field,
With our Loyal Temp'rance Legion armed
with helmet, sword and shield;
To the pow'rs of sin and darkness, we're
determined not to yield,
While God is marching on.

Chorus
Glory, Glory, Hallelujah!
Glory, Glory, Hallelujah!
Glory, Glory, Hallelujah!
Our cause is marching on.

2. In the cause of truth and justice, God, our
Father, bids us shine,
Like the angels up in glory, radiant with
light divine;
Bids us save our home and nation from the
sparkle of the wine,
As we go marching on. *To Chorus*

3. We have heard the cries of children in the
drunkard's lowly home,
Caused by pain, distress and poverty
wrought by the demon, rum,
Oh! thou mighty God of battles help us to
their rescue come:
May right go marching on. *To Chorus*

4. There'll be joy among the angels o'er the
hosts who're saved by grace,
When at last we're crowned with vict'ry
and with Christ have found a place,
Then forevermore in heaven, we shall see
Him face to face,
For God is marching on. *To Chorus*[55]

Temperance Marching Song

1. From the boundless starry heavens comes
the Saviour's great command,
Calling forth the Christian people all in
one strong temp'rance band;

53. Silver Lake Quartette, *Prohibition Bells*, 81.
54. Roush, *Temperance Rally*, 18.
55. Ibid., 25.

Let us then press on to battle for God,
    home and native land,
    As right goes marching on.

Chorus
Glory, Glory, Hallelujah!
    Glory, Glory, Hallelujah!
Glory, Glory, Hallelujah!
    Our God is marching on.

2. We are marching in the cause of right with
    banner bright unfurled,
    For King Alcohol with all his force must
    from his throne be hurled;
Then we'll join in happy chorus with the
    nations o'er the world,
    While God is marching on. *To Chorus*

3. Angels from the heights of glory bid us win
    the victory;
    Christ will help us in the conflict if we
    vote for liberty;
He will crown us honest victors in the battle
    of the free,
    For God is marching on. *To Chorus*

4. God will hasten prohibition if our youth
    we try to save,
    From the curse of rum dominion with an
    army true and brave,
Then we'll wave the flag in triumph o'er a
    land without a slave,
    As we go marching on. *To Chorus*56

Temperance Battle Hymn of Victory

1. We're an army marching in the paths of
    justice, truth and right;
    Battling with the pow'rs of evil, shielded
    by Jehovah's might;
Waving high our starry banner with her
    colors shining bright,
    We're sure of victory.

Chorus
Waving high the starry banner!
    Waving high the starry banner!
Waving high the starry banner!
    Our grand Red, White and Blue.

2. We've beheld the fearful ravage of the
    awful curse of rum,
    How it wrecks the very souls of men and
    threatens every home;
Oh! may we to the rescue of its victims
    quickly come;
    And grant them liberty. *To Chorus*

3. With courage true and steadfast in the
    Saviour's blessed name,
    We rise to save our native land from
    poverty and shame,
And destroy the force of Satan, bringing in
    the temp'rance reign
    Of love and purity. *To Chorus*

4. When the Lord descends from heaven and
    our earthly work is o'er;
    He will take us home to glory—that
    celestial, golden shore,
And with angel bands around His throne,
    we'll wear forevermore,
    Bright crowns of victory. *To Chorus*57

Our Cause Is Gaining Ground
(G. W. Dungan)

1. There's a glorious morning dawning for
    the cause of truth and right,
    And our temperance flag is gleaming in
    the rays of glory bright,
While our army marches onward to the cry of
    God and right:
    Our cause is gaining ground.

Chorus
All for God and Home and Country,
    All for God and Home and Country,
All for God and Home and Country,
    Our cause is gaining ground.

2. See the smile of happy childhood as we
    march along the way;
    And the beaming face of mother for the
    dawning of the day,
When drink, the fell destroyer, is forever put
    away;
    Our cause is gaining ground. *To Chorus*

56. Ibid., 6.
57. Ibid., 9.

3. We will vote for men who help us and will
   leave the others home
   Who obey behest of brewers and distillers
   till they come
To remember we are sovereigns and will read
   in this their doom!
   Our cause is gaining ground. *To Chorus*[58]

Saloons Shall Surely Go
(Thomas B. Roberts)

1. In a thousand hearts are waking visions of
   futurity;
   While from loyal lips are breaking songs
   of joyful jubilee,
Singing of this crowning conquest of this
   hope-filled century,
   Saloons shall surely go!

Chorus
Glorious, glorious prohibition!
   Glorious, glorious prohibition!
Glorious, glorious prohibition!
   Saloons shall surely go!

2. In the might and light of youth-time
   forward, onward, upward we;
   Where the path of human progress leads
   to set the captive free,
Where Jehovah's pillared presence leads us
   on to victory;
   Saloons shall surely go! *To Chorus*

3. I have seen the mother smitten with the
   tear drops in her eye,
   I have seen the serpent bitten looking to
   the Lord on high;
I have seen His promise written in the
   rainbow of the sky;
   Saloons shall surely go! *To Chorus*

4. In the rumbling of the thunder God has
   spoken forth his wrath;
   He hath written with forked lightning in
   the storm-king's lurid path;
And the mighty powers of darkness melt before Jehovah's breath;
   Saloons must surely go! *To Chorus*

5. O'er the hilltop breaks the glory of the
   coming of the dawn;
   O'er the valley sounds the music of the
   marshaled legions strong,
Till my raptured soul re-echoes back their
   hope-inspiring songs;
   Saloons shall surely go! *To Chorus*[59]

In His Name We Conquer
(Anna G. Curtis)

1. We are glad the "loyal women" of our state
   are here to-day
   Gathered here in this convention thus to
   sing, to work, and pray;
In the service of the Master it is glory all the
   way,
   We shall conquer "in his name."

Chorus
Glory, glory hallelujah!
   Glory, glory hallelujah!
Glory, glory hallelujah!
   We'll conquer in his name.

2. We are only Christian women, who will
   wear the "ribbon white"
   But it binds our hearts together in the
   holy cause of right;
And it represents the whiteness of the work
   we plead to-night,
   Hallelujah to His name. *To Chorus*

3. We are here to plead redemption for our
   loyal state so true,
   Which has stood so brave for freedom,
   with rebellion's flag in view
Will it stand for "Prohibition?" It must
   answer me and you.
   "For truth is marching on." *To Chorus*

4. Can our fathers, sons and brothers turn a
   deaf ear to our cry,
   While so many of rum's victims sadly sink
   with shame and die;
With freedom and the ballot, can they tell
   the reason why?
   Since God is marching on. *To Chorus*[60]

58. Dungan et al., *Acorn Temperance*, no. 27.
59. Law, *Temperance Bells*, no. 46.
60. Ibid., no. 48.

Are You in the Ranks?

1. Do you hear the songs of children in the
   valleys, on the hills,
   And the tones of men and women louder
   than a thousand rills?
   O, their battle cry of freedom every heart
   with rapture thrills,
   For God is marching on.

Chorus
Glory, glory, hallelujah! etc.

2. Everywhere there is a stir among the
   legions of the free,
   Who have vowed that from intemperance
   our land shall rescued be;
   And they march in solid column singing
   freedom's jubilee,
   While God is marching on. *To Chorus*

3. Are you in the ranks, a soldier, with your
   shield and armor on?
   Are you consecrated to the work so
   valiantly begun?
   Will you fight beneath the colors till the
   victory is won?
   Our God is marching on. *To Chorus*[61]

Rally, Freemen!
(W. W. Pinsar)

1. O my comrades, in this conflict of the
   right against the wrong,
   To the battle of the ballots come with
   shouting and with song;
   And this cry shall be our slogan as the
   legions march along,
   A victory is at hand!

Chorus
Rally, rally, O ye freemen!
   Rally, rally, O ye freemen!
Rally, rally, O ye freemen!
   For victory is at hand.

2. From the silence and the shadows where
   our mothers weep and pray,
   With their patient hands uplifted 'gainst
   the woe they cannot stay,
   We have heard a voice entreating us to sweep
   the curse away.
   And victory is at hand. *To Chorus*

3. Hear the children cry for pity from the
   cruel heart of greed,
   See them trampled into silence by the
   monster while they plead;
   O be quick, my patriot brothers, and unto
   the rescue speed,
   The victory is at hand. *To Chorus*[62]

A Triumph Hymn
(S. B. McManus)

1. What a hallelujah chorus shall go ringing
   through the land,
   From Atlantic to Pacific, from the North
   to Southern strand,
   And the mountains they shall shout it over
   dales and desert sands,
   Saloons shall be no more.

Chorus
Glory, glory hallelujah,
   Glory, glory hallelujah,
Glory, glory hallelujah,
   Saloons shall be no more.

2. Then no more the drunkard's hand shall
   smite the ones he loves the best,
   Then no more the babe shall die of want
   upon the mother's breast,
   Then no more the drunkard, trembling,
   stand a murderer confessed,
   Saloons shall be no more. *To Chorus*

3. O ye men and women, work and pray that
   soon the day may come!
   O be up and doing with a zeal and stand
   not idle, dumb!
   Work that this republic may be rescued from
   the curse of rum,
   Saloons shall be no more. *To Chorus*[63]

---

61. *Anti-Saloon Campaign*, no. 35; Hoffman, *Woman's Christian Temperance*, no. 35.

62. Hoffman, *Woman's Christian Temperance*, no. 33.

63. Ibid., no. 45. Biederwolf and Lawson, *Best Temperance Songs*, no. 14, entitles this "Saloons Shall Be No More."

We'll Rout John Barleycorn

(John R. Clements)

1. We stand at Armageddon and we battle for
      the Lord
    We stand amid the wrecks of time that
      wars of right afford;
  We stand a mighty army and we fight with
      one accord
    To rout John Barleycorn.

Chorus
Fighting, fighting for our homeland;
    Voting, voting as we're praying;
Singing, singing hallelujah!
    We're bound to win the day.

2. We stand at Armageddon and we bare to
      God our heads;
    The very cause is sacred as the ground the
      martyr treads;
  In willing human sacrifice the cause of right
      e'er spreads;
    We'll rout John Barleycorn. *To Chorus*

3. We stand at Armageddon for this fiercest
      fight with rum;
    The mighty hosts are marshaled, and we
      beat the charging drum;
  The free-born sons of every state are to the
      colors come;
    We'll rout John Barleycorn. *To Chorus*[64]

National Prohibition

(Annie Jones Pyron)

1. Most joyfully we gather as a great white
      ribbon throng,
    For God and Home and Native Land, and
      this shall be our song:
  "With national prohibition we will right a
      world-wide wrong;
    Our righteous cause shall win."

Chorus
Glory! Glory! man's awakening;
    Glory! Glory! votes we're making;
Glory! Glory! states we're taking;
    Our righteous cause shall win.

2. With purpose strong and steady, in the
      great Jehovah's name,
    We work to save our country from the
      depths of sin and shame;
  For national prohibition with its truth we do
      proclaim—
    Our righteous cause shall win. *To Chorus*

3. Our strength is in Jehovah and our cause
      is in His care,
    And with Him to lead us forward we will
      work and fight and dare;
  For national prohibition shall be our daily
      prayer,
    Our righteous cause shall win.
      To Chorus[65]

The Battle Hymn of Ohio

(S. E. Sears)

1. My faith has caught the vision of the
      dawning of the day
    When the manhood of our Buckeye State
      shall stop Rum's deadly sway,
  And the members of our Churches shall all
      vote just as they pray,
    Our God is Marching on!

Chorus
Be Ohio's great defender!
    Smite the brewers next November,
Smite them so they will remember
    That God is marching on!

2. I have seen it in the protests of the people
      of our state,
    In the local option voter where, with
      manly strength and great,
  He, David-like, is smiting the Goliath
      Whisky's pate.
    Our Cause is marching on! *To Chorus*

3. I hear it in the heart-throbs of the
      independent man,
    Who never will be saddled by the brewers'
      liquor plan,
  And be ridden like a donkey from Beersheba
      unto Dan.
    The Truth is marching on! *To Chorus*

64. Clements, *Shaw's Campaign*, 3.
65. Gordon, *Popular Campaign*, 29.

4. God is calling to Ohio, and Ohio shall be free,
    And the state once ruled by liquor shall soon have its liberty;
The tide is set against them, O my brother, can't you see
    That God is marching on? *To Chorus*

5. The rum-bought press would drive us to the slaughter as an ox.
    But the Prohibition vote is not training for the stocks.
And we'll smite the reign of liquor with our ballots in the box.
    Our God is marching on! *To Chorus*[66]

Democratic Dead March in Sobs

1. We the Democratic party met the people at the polls;
    So hot they made it for us that we took some awful colds;
We're bound for an excursion where th'old Salt River rolls
    So we go marching on.

Chorus
Going, going up Salt River,
    Going, going up Salt River,
Going, going up Salt River,
    For we're set down upon.

2. Our platform was the stomach, and was built with longing pains,
    To catch the Dutch and Irish and the Germans, Swedes and Danes,
We undersized them sadly, for they voted with their brains
    The stomach "didn't catch on." *To Chorus*

3. They voted the Amendment Eighteen Hundred Eighty-two
    So what the people wanted ev'ry politician knew;
We said they shouldn't have it, but we learned a thing or two;
    We were set down upon. *To Chorus*

4. The people met us Bourbons and they voted for their homes,
    They turned the tide against us that most always sometimes comes,
They watered beer and whisky till it neither beads nor foams.
    And our "main holt" is gone. *To Chorus*

5. With all our Bourbon blowing we're too late to catch the train,
    We're born behind the season and we can't catch up again,
We're going up Salt River as we do each fall campaign,
    For we're sat down upon. *To Chorus*[67]

Dixie Land

Look Away! Look Away!

1. Away down east in the land of mountains,
    College groves and sparkling fountains,
Look away, look away,
    Look away, noble land;
They never will grant "license," oh no! oh no!
    In Yankee land they'll take the stand,
To live or die for Temp'rance.
    For aye, for aye, For aye to stand for Temp'rance.
    For aye, for aye, For aye to stand for Temp'rance.

2. Away out West, in the land of prairie,
    Cornfields broad, the stock and dairy,
Look away, look away
    Look away, Temp'rance land;
They're checking now Rum's progress! oh yes, oh yes!
    The prairied West will do its best
For honor, right and Temperance.
    The West, proud West, the West will stand for Temp'rance.
    The West, proud West, the West will stand for Temp'rance.

3. Away down South in the land of cotton,
    Now that slav'ry is forgotten—

---

66. *Ohio State Prohibition*, 13.
67. Cake, *Popular Campaign*, n.p.

Look away, look away,
  Look away, sunny land;
To duty they are waking, oh yes, oh yes!
  In Dixie's land they'll take the stand,
To live and die for Temperance.
    The South, brave South, the South will
      stand for Temp'rance.
    The South, brave South, the South will
      stand for Temp'rance.

4. Around the earth and among all nations,
  In the high and lowly stations,
Look away, look away,
  Look away, vision grand;
Truth's sunlight now is glowing, oh yes, oh
  yes!
  Around the world shall be unfurled
The fadeless light of Temperance.
    This world, God's world, this world shall
      stand for Temp'rance.
    This world, God's world, this world shall
      stand for Temp'rance.[68]

Out for Prohibition
(Fannie B. Damon)

1. Quit your ease, forget your sorrow,
  Give today and save tomorrow,
Come out, come out,
  Come out for Prohibition.
Waste no more of wheat and barley,
  Down with compromise and parley,
Come out, come out,
  Come out for Prohibition.

Chorus
We're out for Prohibition! Hurrah! Hurrah!
  We're out for Prohibition! Yes, we're out
    for Prohibition!
Hurrah! Hurrah! We're out for Prohibition!
  Hurrah! Hurrah! We're out for
    Prohibition!

2. Traitors' money take no longer,
  License makes the evil stronger.

Come out, come out,
  Come out for Prohibition!
Don't you know from the beginning
  There's one way to deal with sinning?
Come out, come out,
  Come out for Prohibition! *To Chorus*[69]

Dixie Land for Temperance

1. The Temperance wave o'er the South is
    spreading;
  It is what saloons are dreading.
Look away! look away!
  Look away! Dixie land.
In Dixie land where I was born in,
  People are 'gainst rum a-stormin'
Look away! look away!
  Look away! Dixie land.

Chorus
Then I wish I was in Dixie, Hooray! Hooray!
  In Dixie land, I took my stand, to live
    and die in Dixie,
Away, away, away down South in Dixie.
  Away, away, away down South in Dixie.

2. The masters used to have liquor plenty
  All young bloods drank gin at twenty,
Look away, *etc.*
  But things down there are all a-changin',
Temperance guns 'gainst rum are rangin',
  Look away, etc. To Chorus

3. Down South they fight it by local option;
  "No rum sold by our adoption."
Look away, *etc.*
  That motto should all men inspire
To rise and fight this rum-fiend's fire,
  Look away, *etc. To Chorus*[70]

Cutting It Out
(E. Norine Law)

1. Away down south in the land of cotton,
  Rum and gin are being forgotten.

---

68. Moffitt, *National Temperance*, 29–30. To conform to the tune, singers must either repeat the first four lines of text for each verse or skip immediately from the verse to the chorus without repeating the music for the verse.

69. Gordon, *Temperance Songster*, no. 128; Law, *Temperance Bells*, no. 69; *Anti-Saloon Campaign*, no. 57; Gordon, *Popular Campaign*, 12.

70. Miller, *Patriotic No-License*, no. 38.

Look away, Look away,
  Look away to Dixie Land.
Rum and crime shall reign no longer.
  No license laws to make it stronger.
Look away, *etc.*

Chorus
They're cutting it out in Dixie; O yes, O yes,
  No use to ask for a Scotch High Ball,
    or a gin, or a fizz in Dixie.
O yes, O yes, They're cutting it out in Dixie.
  O yes, O yes, They're cutting it out in
    Dixie.

2. To save their homes from Rum's
    destruction,
  They passed the law of Prohibition,
Look away, *etc.*
  It can't be taxed without sinning.
It keeps their souls from salvation winning.
  Look away, etc. *To Chorus*

3. Rouse ye men and save the Nation.
  Sing it out through all creation.
Look away, *etc.*
  We're out to keep our women from
    sighing.
We're out to keep our children from dying.
  Look away, *etc.*

Final Chorus
We'll cut it out in Pensy, Oh yes, Oh yes.
  It's on the way and some glad day, we'll
    drive the saloons from *Pensy.*
Oh yes, Oh yes, we'll cut it out in *Pensy.*
  Oh yes, Oh yes, we'll cut it out in *Pensy.*71

Drive Him Out
(E. Norine Law)

1. From our dear land so fair and bright,
  King alcohol must take his flight.
Drive him out, Drive him out,
  Drive out the curse of rum.
Too long to him we've loved to kneel,
  But now we've vowed we will be free.
Drive him out, Drive him out,
  Drive out the demon rum.

Chorus
Prohibition is our watchword, O yes, O yes.
  From mountain top to sandy plain,
    Prohibition yet will reign.
O yes, O yes, We'll fight for Prohibition.
  O yes, O yes, We'll fight for Prohibition.

2. In the name of Jesus Christ our King,
  We'll sing our song and make it ring.
Drive him out, Drive him out,
  Drive the demon drink curse out.
For God and home and native land,
  We've pledged our votes and take our
    stand.
Drive him out, Drive him out,
  Drive this awful rum curse out. *To Chorus*

3. The women too will help the fight,
  Because they know our cause is right.
Drive him out, Drive him out,
  Drive out the curse of rum.
When a woman will, she will you know,
  And that is why this curse must go.
Drive him out, Drive him out,
  Drive out the curse of rum. *To Chorus*72

The Saloon Must Be Going
(E. A. Hoffman)

1. All o'er the land there's a great
    commotion,
  And the people have the notion
The saloon, it must go,
  It must go, it must go.
They've seen enough of its shame and
    sorrow,
  And resolved that with the morrow
The saloon, *etc.*

Chorus
There's a wonderful commotion, Hurrah!
    Hurrah!
  The people have the notion the saloon
    should be in motion;
Hurrah! Hurrah! the saloon it must be going.
  Hurrah! Hurrah! the saloon it must be
    going.

71. Law, *Temperance Bells*, no. 70. "Pensy" refers to Pennsylvania. Singers are encouraged to substitute the name of their own state here.
  72. Ibid., no. 71.

2. North, south, east, west, there is strong
    conviction
   The best cure would be eviction.
The saloon, *etc.*
   At this great sin people have been winking,
Now they've done some strenuous thinking.
   The saloon, *etc. To Chorus*

3. Within our own wide-extended borders
   Have gone forth the people's orders.
The saloon, *etc.*
   The cry of each noble son and daughter
Is to give the foe "No quarter,"
   The saloon, *etc. To Chorus*[73]

Dixie Up to Date
(J. C. Dailey)

1. Way down South in de fields of cotton
   Whiskey business sure am rotten;
Run 'em out, run 'em out,
   Run 'em out, run 'em out.
Prohibitionists are out a scoutin'
   Temp'rance folks are all a shoutin',
Run 'em out, run 'em out,
   Run 'em out, run 'em out.

Chorus
We'll run 'em out of Dixie, Hurrah! Hurrah!
   Way over Mason-Dixon's line,
We'll run 'em out of Dixie.
   Hurrah! Hurrah! We'll run 'em out of
      Dixie.
   Hurrah! Hurrah! We'll run 'em out of
      Dixie.

2. Men and women in a fight terrific,
   From de "Lantic" to de "Cific";
Run 'em out, run 'em out,
   Run 'em out, run 'em out.
Been a thinkin' and decide we oughter
   Chase 'em till dey take to water;
Run 'em out, run 'em out,
   Run 'em out, run 'em out. *To Chorus*

3. We remember back in 1860,
   How you helped us down in Dixie;
Run 'em out, run 'em out,
   Run 'em out, run 'em out.

We old Johnnies ain't de least bit cranky,
   We'll come up and help de Yankees,
Run 'em out, run 'em out,
   Run 'em out, run 'em out. *To Chorus*

4. Keep 'em goin' an' a scratchin' gravel
   Up de hill and on de level;
Run 'em out, run 'em out,
   Run 'em out, run 'em out.
Up to Canada we're bound to chase 'em;
   There let Johnny Bull efface an'
Run 'em out, run 'em out,
   Run 'em out, run 'em out. *To Chorus*[74]

When Johnny Comes Marching Home

When Rum Shall Cease to Reign

1. Get ready for the jubilee, hurrah! hurrah!
   When this our country shall be free,
      hurrah! hurrah!
The girls will sing, the boys will shout.
   When Alcohol is driven out:
   And we'll all feel gay when whiskey is no
      more.

2. We're only children now, you know,
      hurrah! hurrah!
   But Temp'rance children always grow,
      hurrah! hurrah!
The girls will all be women then,
   The boys, of course, will all be men,
   And we'll all fight rum till rum shall be
      no more.

3. From Maine to California, hurrah! hurrah!
   From Delaware to Canada, hurrah!
      hurrah!
The struggle now is going on, and,
   When the mighty victory's won,
   We'll all feel gay that whiskey reigns no
      more.

4. It will not do to simply say, hurrah!
      hurrah!
   But do your duty, then you may, hurrah!
      hurrah!

73. *Anti-Saloon Campaign*, no. 16; Hoffman, *Woman's Christian Temperance*, no. 16.
74. Dailey and Mead, *Prohibition Chimes*, no. 78.

Assist the weak, yourself deny,
Stand by the right, and bye-and-bye
We'll all feel gay that whiskey reigns no
more.[75]

Battle Line

1. The Temperance lines are filling fast,
Hurrah! hurrah!
A mighty force will soon be massed,
Hurrah! hurrah!
Of soldiers roused by duty's call to storm the
works of Alcohol,
And we'll all rejoice when the rum curse
is no more.

2. From field and town, from hill and glade,
Hurrah! hurrah!
They're gathering for the new crusade,
Hurrah! hurrah!
They come to fight, and this the way—they
pray and vote, and vote and pray,
And we'll all rejoice when the rum curse
is no more.

3. The hosts of rum are sore dismayed,
Hurrah! hurrah!
In frantic tones they call for aid, Hurrah!
hurrah!
Our parties old in sin and years, whose sand
of life fast disappears,
And we'll all rejoice when the rum curse
is no more.

4. From North to South, from East to West,
Hurrah! hurrah!
From ocean to the wilderness, Hurrah!
hurrah!
The forces muster through the land that swell
the Prohibition band,
And we'll all rejoice when the rum curse
is no more.

5. A joyful shout comes from the soul,
Hurrah! hurrah!
Which East and West its echoes roll,
Hurrah! hurrah!

It is a nation's gladsome cry—the swelling
notes of victory,
And we'll all rejoice when the rum curse
is no more.[76]

Old Adages
(Wm. B. Marsh)

1. Be guarded as to how you're led, hurrah!
hurrah!
Be sure you're right then go ahead,
hurrah! hurrah!
Don't glory in what others do, but lend a
hand to help us through,
To crush this curse its power to undo.

2. Look well before you make a leap, hurrah!
hurrah!
In confidence don't fall asleep, hurrah!
hurrah!
There's danger stalking in our land, to Strike
you down where'er you stand;
A secret foe your freedom to demand.

3. We take a stand, we count the cost,
hurrah! hurrah!
And only think of all we've lost, hurrah!
hurrah!
Our minds made up no toil to shirk although
it may seem up-hill work.
We'll root rum out wherever it may lurk.

4. In North and South, in East and West,
hurrah! hurrah!
The ball is rolling without rest, hurrah!
hurrah!
United we can win for all, divided we must
surely fall.
Then come and join in answer to our call.[77]

The Skies Are Bright
(E. A. Hoffman)

1. The skies are very bright at last, Hurrah!
Hurrah!
The hour of doubt is overpast, Hurrah!
Hurrah!

---

75. Moffitt, *National Temperance*, 39
76. Stearns, *National Temperance*, 48.
77. Perine and Mash, *National Prohibition Hymnal*, 55.

We have the votes to win the day,
    The folks have come to think our way,
    They will cast their votes to put the saloon
        away.

2. We knew when people came to think,
    Hurrah! Hurrah!
    They would destroy the curse of drink,
    Hurrah! Hurrah!
They've done some thinking, sure, of late,
    And learned the evil thing to hate,
    And to drive it out with ballots they only
        wait.

3. This enemy of land and home, Hurrah!
    Hurrah!
    Will at the last be overcome, Hurrah!
    Hurrah!
Its death is up in heav'n decreed,
    And prohibition will succeed,
    And to cast their votes is all that the
        people need.

4. Then one more song of hope and cheer,
    Hurrah! Hurrah!
    The better day is drawing near, Hurrah!
    Hurrah!
For glorious victory we pray,
    We'll win the fight, it looks that way,
    In a few more days we'll put the saloon
        away.[78]

We Have the Votes

1. Rejoice, ye patriots, everywhere, Hurrah!
    Hurrah!
    The ring of victory's in the air, Hurrah!
    Hurrah!
The hosts are lined up for the fray,
    And ready for election day,
    And they have the votes to put the
        saloons away.

2. The hearts of millions will be glad,
    Hurrah! Hurrah!

No more will drunkards' wives be sad,
    Hurrah! Hurrah!
The day of our release will come,
    A day of blessing for each home,
    For we have the votes the evil to
        overcome.

3. At last will end the misery, Hurrah!
    Hurrah!
    At last will dawn the victory, Hurrah!
    Hurrah!
We've waited long for this glad day,
    With courage, faith, and hope alway,
    Now we have the votes, the evil must pass
        away.[79]

Strike the Blow

1. 'Tis settled—the saloon must go, Hurrah!
    Hurrah!
    We've vowed its utter overthrow, Hurrah!
    Hurrah!
The clock of God has struck the hour,
    His arm has nerved our own with pow'r,
    We will strike the blow, and then the
        saloon must go.

2. Our God is with us in the fight, Hurrah!
    Hurrah!
    We know it will be settled right, Hurrah!
    Hurrah!
The clouds have long been gath'ring strength,
    And empty out their wrath at length;
    We will strike the blow, and then the
        saloon must go.

3. Recruits are filling up the ranks, Hurrah!
    Hurrah!
    For this to God we render thanks,
    Hurrah! Hurrah!
If we but push the battle on
    A noble vict'ry will be won;
    Let us strike the blow, and then the
        saloon must go.[80]

78. *Anti-Saloon Campaign*, no. 27; Hoffman, *Local Option*, no. 27; Hoffman, *Woman's Christian Temperance*, no. 27.

79. *Anti-Saloon Campaign*, no. 38; Hoffman, *Local Option*, no. 38; Hoffman, *Woman's Christian Temperance*, no. 38.

80. Hoffman, *Woman's Christian Temperance*, no. 43.

Battle Cry of Freedom

[We Are Gathering]

We are gathering for the conflict,
    With earnest hearts and true,
Shouting the battle-cry of Temperance,
    The world will bless our progress
In the work we have to do;
    Shouting the battle-cry of Temperance.

Chorus
Cold water forever, hurrah! then, hurrah
    Down with the wine-glass—up with our star,
As we gather for a right cause,
    With earnest hearts and true,
    Shouting the battle-cry of Temperance.[81]

Temperance Forever

1. We will rally to the cause, boys,
    Rally here to-night,
Shouting the thrilling cry of Temperance;
    And we'll work like vet'rans true,
In the army of the right,
    Shouting the thrilling cry of Temperance.

Chorus
Temperance forever, hurrah, boys, hurrah,
    Down with the traffic and up with the law,
While we rally to the cause, boys,
    Rally in our might,
    Shouting the thrilling cry of Temperance.

2. From the mountains of the East
    And the prairies of the West,
Shouting the thrilling cry of Temperance;
    They are springing to the call
With a spirit-moving zest,
    Shouting the thrilling cry of Temperance.
        To Chorus

3. We are filling up the ranks
    With the former slaves of Rum,
Shouting the thrilling cry of Temperance;
    We've five hundred thousand now,

Yet in legions still they come,
    Shouting the thrilling cry of Temperance.
    To Chorus

4. The sad mother hears the shout
    As she kneeleth at her prayer,
Swelling the thrilling cry of Temperance;
    "Praise the Lord!" escapes her lips
When she views her eldest there,
    Shouting the thrilling cry of Temperance.
    To Chorus

5. The distiller hears the fife
    And the rattle of the drum,
Sounding the thrilling cry of Temperance;
    The retailer blanching white,
Thinks the judgment day is come,
    Thundering the thrilling cry of
    Temperance. *To Chorus*[82]

Temperance Rallying Song
(Frank C. Filley)

1. Come rally round our flag boys, rally firm
        and true,
    Shouting our battle-cry of Temperance,
Come rally to our standard, our banner of
        dark blue,
    Shouting our battle-cry of Temperance.

Chorus
Temperance forever, Hurrah! boys, Hurrah!
    Down with King Alcohol and up with our
        star,
While we rally round our Blue flag, boys,
        rally once again,
    Shouting our battle-cry of Temperance.

2. We've come to sign the pledge that our
        Brothers signed before,
    Shouting our battle-cry of Temperance.
We'll fill the Gospel Temperance ranks with
        many thousands more,
    Shouting our battle-cry of Temperance.
        To Chorus

81. Bradbury and Stearns, *Temperance Chimes* (1867 and 1878), 107; Sherwin and Stearns, *Bugle Notes*, 118; Leslie, *Good Templar* (1886), 65; Leslie, *Good Templar* (1888), 26; Root, *Musical Fountain*, 106–7. Perkins, *Crystal Fountain*, 196, uses this verse and chorus along with verses 2 and 3 from "The Jubilee of Temperance."
    82. Moffitt, *National Temperance*, 27–28.

3. We will welcome to our numbers the loyal,
    brave and true,
Shouting the battle-cry of Temperance.
Then sign the pledge, and on your breast, pin
    our bright badge of blue,
Shouting our battle-cry of Temperance.
    To Chorus[83]

The Jubilee of Temperance

1. We have met you here again, friends,
    To sing you our refrain,
Shouting the Jubilee of Temp'rance;
    We will join in song together,
And this shall be our strain,
    Shouting the Jubilee of Temperance.

Chorus
Temp'rance forever, hurrah, friends, hurrah!
    Keep from the rum-shop forever and far,
And we'll rally round the pledge, friends,
    United in our Cause,
    Shouting the Jubilee of Temp'rance.

2. We have signed the good old Pledge,
    That our brothers signed before,
Shouting the Jubilee of Temp'rance;
    And will number in our ranks
A million signers more,
    Shouting the Jubilee of Temp'rance.
    To Chorus

3. We are springing to the call,
    The young, and old and all,
Shouting the Jubilee of Temp'rance;
    And we'll banish alcohol
From the parlor, shop, and hall,
    Shouting the Jubilee of Temp'rance.
    To Chorus

4. We will raise the fallen up,
    And will make them sober men,
Shouting the Jubilee of Temp'rance;
    Till the hills and valleys ring,
This Temp'rance song we'll sing,
    Shouting the Jubilee of Temp'rance.
    To Chorus[84]

King Alcohol's Battle Cry of Ruin

1. For eighteen hundred years and more,
    King Alcohol has been
Shouting the Battle Cry of Ruin!
    And all these years in bondage vile,
Has chained the souls of men,
    Shouting the Battle Cry of Ruin!

Chorus
How long shall he reign boys? how long shall
    he reign?
    Sowing destruction and sorrow and
    shame,
O'er the graves of his victims
    He rallies again,
    Shouting the Battle Cry of Ruin!

2. One hundred thousand souls,
    Is the yearly harvest given,
Swelling the Battle Cry of Ruin!
    One hundred thousand souls
Beneath the blue of Heaven
    Shouting the Bitter Cry of Ruin!
    To Chorus

3. One thousand million dollars,
    Is the yearly price of souls,
Lost in the Battle Cry of Ruin!
    One thousand million dollars
The "License law" controls
    Speeding the Battle Cry of Ruin!
    To Chorus

4. Will Temp'rance workers overthrow
    This foul and costly crime?
Shouting the Battle Cry of *Freedom!*
    Invoking every aid on earth
And every power divine,
    Shouting the Battle Cry of Freedom?

Final Chorus
Then Temp'rance shall reign boys,
    Temp'rance shall reign,
    And manhood no longer be trampled in
    shame,
For the whole world shall rally,
    The race to reclaim,
    Shouting the Battle Cry of Freedom![85]

83. Filley, *Red, White, and Blue*, 12–13.
84. Stearns, *National Temperance*, 32; Leslie, *Good Templar* (1886 and 1888), 27.
85. Daniels, *Temperance Songster*, 4–5.

Battle Song

1. We have come to join the army
   And fight for God and Right,
Singing the battle-song of Temp'rance!
   We will march as one to battle
And put old wrongs to flight,
   Singing the battle-song of Temp'rance!

Chorus
Temp'rance forever, hurrah, friends, hurrah!
   Down with the rum-shops, and up with
      the Cross
And we'll rally round the Cross, friends,
   Determined all to win,
   Singing the battle-song of Temp'rance!

2. We have come from hills and valleys
   To heed our Country's call,
Singing the battle-song of Temp'rance!
   We will follow now our Banner
And never shall it fall,
   Singing the battle-song of Temp'rance!
      To Chorus

3. We have pledged ourselves to labor,
   And never will we cease,
Singing the battle-song of Temp'rance!
   We have heard the Master calling
Our brothers to release,
   Singing the battle-song of Temp'rance!
      To Chorus

4. We are armed with Love and Mercy,
   Our weapons cannot fail,
Singing the battle-hymn of Temp'rance!
   We are led by Truth and Justice,
And clad in knightly mail,
   Singing the battle-song of Temp'rance!
      To Chorus[86]

Rally for the Right #1

1. Prohibition triumphs and its conq'ring
      march begins,
   Never to cease from its campaigning,
Until the grandest vict'ry on the moral field
      it wins,
   Over the rum-foe proudly reigning.

Chorus
Away with all liquor! Hurrah, boys, hurrah!
   Down with the rum-curse and rum-party
      law!
Rally for the Right, boys, rally till we win,
   Shouting the cry of Prohibition.

2. Rescue ev'ry drinker struggling hopeless
      with his foe,
   Fettered as slaves in rum's dominions;
Drive earth's fiercest demon to his native
      place below,
   Banish him and his impish minions.
      To Chorus

3. Break the servile fetters binding body,
      heart and soul,
   Help them to rise from degradation;
Let the shout of freedom, loud as thunder
      onward roll—
   Freedom from drink throughout the
      nation. *To Chorus*

4. Rally from the work-shop, rally from the
      busy mill;
   Rally from high and low position;
Banish want and sorrow flowing from the
      deadly still,
   Fall into line for Prohibition.
      To Chorus[87]

Rally for the Right #2

1. We'll rally for the right, men,
   We'll rally once again,
Voting for legal prohibition!
   We will save our boys and men
From the liquor-seller's den,
   Voting for legal prohibition!

Chorus
Our triumph is coming! arise, men! arise!
   Down with the traffic! strike till it dies!
While we rally for the right, men,
   Rally once again,
   Voting for legal prohibition!

2. We will answer to the call
   Of the women of our land,

86. Munson, *Gospel and Maine*, 25.
87. Durant, *Prohibition Home*, 10.

Voting for legal prohibition!
  We will fight in their defense
With a strong and willing hand,
  Voting for legal prohibition! *To Chorus*

3. We will cast away the curse
  That the liquor-sellers bring,
Voting for legal prohibition!
  We will crush the cruel head
Of the alcoholic king,
  Voting for legal prohibition! *To Chorus*

4. We have God upon our side
  And must conquer in the end,
Voting for legal prohibition!
  He is stronger than the foe,
And on Him we will depend,
  Voting for legal prohibition!
    To Chorus[88]

We Are Going to the Polls, Boys

1. We are going to the polls, boys,
  We're going to the fight,
Shouting the battle-cry of freedom!
  And we will cast a vote
In the name of God and Right,
  Shouting the battle-cry of freedom!

Chorus
Temperance forever! Hurrah! boys, hurrah!
  Let virtue triumph, and shout her hurrah!
As we vote for Temperance
  In the name of God and Right,
  Shouting the battle-cry of freedom!

2. With our vote of Temperance,
  We'll strike a mighty blow,
Shouting the battle-cry of freedom!
  And we'll crush the monster evil—
The liquor-traffic low,
  Shouting the battle-cry of freedom!
    To Chorus

3. We will rally to the polls, boys,
  We'll rally once again,

Shouting the battle-cry of freedom!
  We will rally from the hillside,
We'll rally from the plain,
  Shouting the battle-cry of freedom!
    To Chorus[89]

The Battle-Cry of Temperance

1. We will rally in our might
  To the great and glorious fight,
Shouting the battle-cry of Temperance!
  We will deal a final blow
To the mean, insidious foe,
  Shouting the battle-cry of Temperance!

Chorus
Cold water forever! Away with the wine!
  For us its false glitter no longer shall
    shine.
We will rally in our might
  To the great and glorious fight,
  Shouting the battle-cry of Temperance!

2. Long has Alcohol held sway;
  Now we'll drive the fiend away,
Shouting the battle-cry of Temperance!
  We will break the poisoned bowl,
Which will ruin mind and soul,
  Shouting the battle-cry of Temperance!
    To Chorus

3. Now's the day and now's the hour;
  Let us break wine's wicked power,
Shouting the battle-cry of Temperance!
  Gird the armor on anew,
Be in earnest and be true,
  Shouting the battle-cry of Temperance!
    To Chorus[90]

Prohibition Battle Cry
(C. L. Shacklock)

1. We have saved the grand old Union,
  And we'll save it once again;
This is the woman's holy mission;

---

88. *Prohibition Campaign Song Book*, 7. Hudson, *Temperance Songster*, no. 67, omits verse 3.

89. Leslie, *Good Templar* (1886), 27; Stearns, *Prohibition Songster*, no. 51; Dungan et al., *Acorn Temperance*, no. 30; Merryman, *Amendment Songs*, no. 18.

90. Stearns, *Band of Hope*, 63; Leslie, *Good Templar* (1886 and 1888), 27; Miller, *Patriotic No-License*, no. 46.

We will swell the mighty army
And the victory attain,
   Shouting the cry of prohibition.

Chorus
Yes, this is our mission, United we stand,
   Dam up the tide, boys, Sweeping our land;
And we'll save the grand old Union.
   Yes we'll save it once again
   Shouting the cry of Prohibition

2. There are vet'rans of the army,
   Who are foremost in the fight;
This was their motto, Ne'er surrender;
   Round the polls they'll bravely rally
And they'll battle for the right,
   And in their country's need defend her.
   To Chorus

3. There are hosts of little children,
   To the rescue they have come;
Bounded by Hope, by Faith united;
   They are angels of the household
And the light of ev'ry home,
   Soon will the wrongs of earth be righted.
   To Chorus

4. We've no foreign foe to conquer,
   For the enemy is here;
Sweeping a cyclone through the nation,
   In its pathway lies the destiny
Of all we hold most dear,
   No [sic] let us check this desolation.
   *To Chorus*91

The Battle Cry of Temperance
(Harriet D. Castle)

1. Come and join the temp'rance army
   And fight against saloons,
Shouting the battle cry of temp'rance.
   We will fight the mighty evil
That's ruining our homes,
   Shouting the battle cry of temp'rance.

Chorus
Yes, once and forever the grog shop must go;
   Down with the brew'ry, and shut off
      the flow;
And we'll rally 'round our standard

And go for the saloon,
   Shouting the battle cry of temp'rance.

2. Come and fight against the army
   That fills our prison cells,
Shouting the battle cry of temp'rance.
   Come and help us to bombard them
With temp'rance shot and shells,
   Shouting the battle cry of temp'rance.
   To Chorus

3. We are marching on to fight
   As we never fought before,
Shouting the battle cry of temp'rance.
   We are saving from its clutches,
A million loved ones more,
   Shouting the battle cry of temp'rance.
   To Chorus

4. Though our army may be small,
   There are other hosts beside,
Shout ye the battle cry of temp'rance.
   Lo, the chariots of God are
Upon the mountain side;
   Shout ye the battle cry of temp'rance.
   To Chorus

5. It will be a glorious battle,
   What ever may betide;
Shout ye the battle cry of temp'rance!
   And the victory will be ours,
For the Lord is on our side;
   Shout ye the battle cry of temp'rance!
   *To Chorus*92

No License Forever!

1. We are coming to the polls, boys,
   We're coming in our might,
Voting for temp'rance and No license;
   And we bear the stars and stripes
Of the Union and the right,
   Voting for temp'rance and No license.

Chorus
No License forever! Hurrah! boys, Hurrah!
   Drive now the rumshop forever afar,
As we rally round the polls, boys,
   United in our cause,
   Voting for temp'rance and No license.

91. Leslie, *Good Templar* (1888), 80–81.
92. Lorenz, *New Anti-Saloon,* 103.

2. We will soon decide the day, boys
    For honest men and true,
Voting for temp'rance and No license;
    And we'll show what all the world
Has for sober men to do,
    Voting for temp'rance and No license.
        To Chorus

3. Yes, for liberty and order,
    For honor true and bright,
Voting for temp'rance and No license;
    And the vict'ry shall be ours,
For we're coming in our might,
    Voting for temp'rance and No license.
        *To Chorus*93

W.C.T.U. Battle-Cry

1. We're a Woman's Temp'rance Union
    With forces brave and strong,
Shouting the battle-cry of freedom!
    Marching forth to glorious conflict
Against the hosts of wrong,
    Shouting the battle-cry of freedom!

Chorus
Our Union for temp'rance, Hurrah! for the
    cause,
    Down with the traffic, up with our laws!
We'll press onward to the goal
    In the name of Christ, our King,
    Shouting the battle-cry of freedom!

2. Our cause is bound to win
    For we're fighting for the truth,
Shouting the battle-cry of freedom!
    And temptation will be taken
Forever from our youth,
    Shouting the battle-cry of freedom!
        To Chorus

3. For God and home and nation,
    We'll plead and work and pray,
Shouting the battle-cry of freedom!
    Till the earth becomes a heaven
And sin has passed away,
    Shouting the battle-cry of freedom!
        To Chorus

4. We can see within the distance
    The day of liberty,
Shouting the battle-cry of freedom!
    Then the heavens will re-echo
Our notes of victory,
    Shouting the battle-cry of freedom!
        *To Chorus*94

Ohio Battle-Cry of Freedom

1. Yes, we'll fight the pow'rs of rum
    For the morning draweth nigh,
Shouting the battle-cry of freedom!
    When the Christian temp'rance forces
Will vote Ohio dry,
    Shouting the battle-cry of freedom!

Chorus
Ohio for temp'rance! Hurrah boys, Hurrah!
    Down with the traffic, and all its woe!
Yes, saloons will have to go
    For Ohio's going dry,
    Shouting the battle-cry of freedom!

2. We can see rum's wretched victims
    Go down to drunkards' graves,
Shouting the battle-cry of freedom!
    Now, to arms ye Christian soldiers,
And rescue all its slaves,
    Shouting the battle-cry of freedom!
        To Chorus

3. For county Local Option,
    We'll press the temp'rance fight,
Shouting the battle-cry of freedom!
    Our God will lead us through
For we're on the side of right,
    Shouting the battle-cry of freedom!
        To Chorus

4. From our grand old starry flag,
    We'll remove the stain of rum,
Shouting the battle-cry of freedom!
    Then we'll wave her folds in triumph
O'er ev'ry school and home,
    Shouting the battle-cry of freedom!
        *To Chorus*95

93. Miller, *Patriotic No-License*, no. 5.
94. Roush, *Temperance Rally*, 18.
95. Ibid., 2.

L.T.L. Battle-Cry

1. We're a Loyal Temp'rance Legion
    Marching 'gainst the foe,
Shouting the battle-cry of freedom!
    That curses home and nation
With poverty and woe,
    Shouting the battle-cry of freedom!

Chorus
Our nation for temp'rance! forever, Hurrah!
    Down with the traffic, saloons must go!
Yes, King Alcohol must tremble
    For we are growing up,
    Shouting the battle-cry of freedom!

2. God will help us in the conflict
    If we are brave and true,
Shouting the battle-cry of freedom!
    Waving high the starry banner,
Our old Red, White and Blue,
    Shouting the battle-cry of freedom!
        To Chorus

3. We pledge our hearts and hands
    For both home and native land,
Shouting the battle-cry of freedom!
    As we march to victory
So glorious and grand,
    Shouting the battle-cry of freedom!
        To Chorus

4. We'll press onward with our Legion
    Till rum has lost its sway,
Shouting the battle-cry of freedom!
    And we'll see the Prince of Peace
Reigning o'er the land alway,
    Shouting the battle-cry of freedom!
        To Chorus[96]

Temperance Battle-Cry

1. Yes, we'll rally for the cause, boys,
    We'll rally as we pray,
Shouting the battle-cry of freedom!
    We'll unite our temp'rance forces
And drive saloons away,
    Shouting the battle-cry of freedom!

Chorus
Prohibition forever! hurrah boys, hurrah!
    Away with the liquor, up with the cross!
While we rally for the cause, boys,
    Rally every day,
    Shouting the battle-cry of freedom!

2. We will save our boys and girls
    From the sparkle of the wine,
Shouting the battle-cry of freedom!
    And we'll gladden mothers' hearts
With a joy that is sublime,
    Shouting the battle-cry of freedom!
        To Chorus

3. In the name of Christ, our Leader,
    King Alcohol must die,
Shouting the battle-cry of freedom!
    Lo, the dawn of prohibition
Is lighting up the sky,
    Shouting the battle-cry of freedom!
        To Chorus

4. We are marching in the paths
    Of truth and purity,
Shouting the battle-cry of freedom!
    And the conflict ne'er shall cease
Till we're crowned with victory
    Shouting the battle-cry of freedom!
        To Chorus[97]

Arouse Ye, Good People
(E. A. Hoffman)

1. Are you going to the polls
    With a ballot for the Right?
Go in the name of Truth and Freedom;
    Join the legions of reformers
Beneath the standard white;
    Go in the name of Truth and Freedom.

Chorus
Arouse ye, good people, arise in your might,
    Carry to vict'ry your standard so white;
For the battle will be yours,
    Only push along the fight,
    All in the name of Truth and Freedom.

96. Ibid., 24.
97. Ibid., 4.

2. It is but a little thing
   You are called upon to do,
All in the name of Truth and Freedom;
   Just to cast a little ballot
To God and country true,
   All in the name of Truth and Freedom.
      To Chorus

3. We can rid this fairest land
   Of its foulest blot and stain,
All in the name of Truth and Freedom;
   We can cleanse the land of evil
And make it pure again,
   All in the name of Truth and Freedom.
      *To Chorus*98

Battling for God and Home
(E. A. Hoffman)

1. Have you heard the latest news
   From the Temperance Crusade,
Battling for God and Home and Country?
   Do you know that many millions
Are in its lines arrayed,
   Battling for God and Home and Country?

Chorus
For God, Home and Country we join hand
      in hand.
   For God, Home and Country united we
      stand;
And we'll push the conflict on
   Until victory is won,
   Battling for God, and Home, and
      Country.

2. O the prospect is inspiring,
   A triumph is in sight,
Battling for God and Home and Country;
   All the brave and good and true
Are enlisting for the right,
   Battling for God and Home and Country.
      To Chorus

3. Take your places in the ranks
   'Neath the banner of the free,

Battling for God and Home and Country;
   Stand upon the winning side,
Share the coming victory,
   Battling for God and Home and Country.
      *To Chorus*99

Rally round the Flag

1. We're coming from the factory,
   The office, shop and store,
Shouting the battle cry of "Freedom!"
   We're coming from the farmland
      and city more and more,
   Shouting the battle-cry of "Freedom!"

Chorus
Prohibition forever! Hurrah! boys, hurrah!
   Down with the traffic and up with the
      law,
Yes, we'll rally 'round the flag, boys,
   We'll rally once again,
   Shouting the battle-cry of "Freedom!"

2. We hate the liquor traffic;
   Its sorry, sin and crime,
Shouting the battle-cry of "Freedom!"
   We hate its license money,
We hate it all the time,
   Shouting the battle-cry of "Freedom!"
      To Chorus

3. We're bound to save the children,
   Regenerate the race,
Shouting the battle-cry of "Freedom!"
   We exalt the Christ triumphant,
Who saves us through His grace,
   Shouting the battle-cry of "Freedom!"
      To Chorus

4. We'll down the liquor traffic,
   Annihilate it quite,
Shouting the battle-cry of "Freedom!"
   Our God will give the victory;
We conquer in His might,
   Shouting the battle-cry of "Freedom!"
      *To Chorus*100

98. *Anti-Saloon Campaign*, no. 2; Hoffman, *Local Option*, no. 2; Hoffman, *Woman's Christian Temperance*, no. 3.

99. *Anti-Saloon Campaign*, no. 29; Hoffman, *Local Option*, no. 29; Hoffman, *Woman's Christian Temperance*, no. 29.

100. Gordon, *Popular Campaign*, 31.

The Battle Cry of Prohibition
(A. C. Bane)

1. We will rally round the standard
    Of temperance and reform,
Shouting the cry of Prohibition.
    We will rally from the city
And we'll rally from the farm,
    Shouting the cry of Prohibition.

Chorus
Temperance forever, hurrah, men, hurrah!
    Down with the liquor and down with the
        bar!
We will close the rum saloons
    And protect Ohio's homes,
    Shouting the cry of Prohibition.

2. We've responded to the call
    Of our leaders in the fray,
Shouting the cry of Prohibition.
    With united temperance forces
We are abound to win the day,
    Shouting the cry of Prohibition.
        To Chorus

3. We've enlisted in our army many
    Mighty men of note,
Shouting the cry of Prohibition.
    Thousands more are volunteers,
Humble men with voice and vote,
    Shouting the cry of Prohibition. *To Chorus*

4. We are bearing as our battle flags
    Old Glory and the Cross,
Shouting the cry of Prohibition.
    Christ is our valiant leader
And we can not suffer loss,
    Shouting the cry of Prohibition.
        To Chorus 101

Tramp! Tramp! Tramp!

Rise! Oh, Rise
1. At our table, here we sit, hour by hour and
    night by night,

And the song and jest, and wit and wine
    go round.
But beneath the starry skies, or sweet home's
    beloved eyes,
    Have you never heard a voice of warning
        sound?

Chorus
Rise! oh rise to nobler manhood!
    Dash the tempting cup away!
And with purpose firm and sure,
    Let your vows for aye endure,
    As you take the onward, upward,
        Temp'rance way.

2. There are gay and merry hours, when the
    mirth is wild and high,
    And the wine has reached the fevered
        heart and brain,
But above the glee and shout, and the
    laughter ringing out,
    Have you never heard the warning voice
        again? *To Chorus*

3. Brothers, life had glorious heights for our
    youthful feet to climb;
    There are shining crowns that we may
        work and win;
Like excelsior, a cry, ringing down from
    summits high
    Sings to us through all the revel's wildest
        din. *To Chorus*

4. We will loose no friendly grasp, we will
    never turn aside,
    From the youthful friendships, formed
        and nourished here,
But with manly purpose strong, let us sing a
    grander song,
    As we pledge anew in accents strong and
        clear. *To Chorus* 102

Temperance Rallying Song
(Mrs. Van Alstyne)

1. Friends of Temperance quick to arms, we
    must struggle for the right;

---

101. *Ohio State Prohibition*, 14.

102. Hull, *Hull's Temperance*, 123, Bradbury and Stearns, *Temperance Chimes* (1867 and 1878), 113, Philip Phillips, *Day-School Singer*, 148–49, and Macy, *Temperance Song-Herald*, 95, use verses 3 and 4 only. Root, *Musical Fountain*, 30–31, includes all the verses.

And our noble cause with vigor we'll
defend,
See the foe is gaining ground, we must meet
him in the fight,
And be faithful and courageous to the end.

Chorus
Marching onward, ever onward,
Sounding still the battle cry;
Soon the tyrant shall be slave,
To our army bold and brave!
We shall gain a glorious victory by and by.

2. Like the fatal wind that sweeps o'er the
desert's burning plain;
Is the deep and deadly poison of his
breath,
While the aged and the young he is binding
with a chain,
That will lead them on by thousands
down to death. *To Chorus*

3. Throw our banner to the breeze, let the
wings that claim redress,
Be our signal and our watchword as we go.
Like the veterans of the past, we will never,
never, rest,
Till our weapons deal destruction to the
foe. *To Chorus*103

Work! Work! Work!
(Robert Merry)

1. Here and there throughout the land many
Sons of Temperance stand,
They are working for the good of fallen
man;
They've a noble work to do, and they never
will retreat
Till they have accomplished all the good
they can.

Chorus
Work! work! work! Ye Sons of Temperance,
Cheer up, for your cause is right,
And beneath the Temperance flag
We will drive Intemperance back,

And we never will be vanquished in the
fight.

2. We not only give the Pledge, but give help
to keep it, too.
Each Division-room's a home for every one
Who forsakes the drunkard's ranks to begin
his life anew;
All are welcome, and we close our doors
on none. *To Chorus*

3. Here the old and young are safe, and are
longing for the day
When our Order shall extend to all
mankind,
And the motto, Purity, with Fidelity and
Love,
Shall give freedom to the body and the
mind. *To Chorus*104

Bright and Sparkling Water
(Emma Woodville)

1. From the mountain's rugged brow, from
the valley green and low,
From the dew that sparkles on each
laughing flower,
Comes the bright, the bubbling spring, and
its praises we will sing
In the spring-time of life's precious
evening hour.

Chorus
Water! bright and sparkling water!
Now we offer praise to thee;
And we pledge our heart and hand
A united temperance band
This Eureka Band of Hope shall ever be.

2. Hope's our motto, faith and trust; By the
temperance cause we must
Hope to raise the fallen from the deadly
snare;
From the crooked path of sin we will bring
the wanderers in
To our temperance circle and its kindly
care. *To Chorus*

103. Bradbury and Stearns, *Temperance Chimes* (1867 and 1878), 28; Leslie, *Good Templar* (1886 and
1888), 25. Perkins, *Crystal Fountain*, 105, omits verse 2.
104. Bradbury and Stearns, *Temperance Chimes* (1867 and 1878), 29; Leslie, *Good Templar* (1886 and
1888), 25.

3. While our hearts are young and warm,
    while our pulse beats high and strong,
  Let us walk in wisdom's safe and pleasant
    ways;
Shunning carefully the path that will lead us
    down to wrath,
  Satan's victims through intemperance'
    glowing maze. *To Chorus*105

Gallant Leaders

1. In the early morning light, in the thickest
    of the fight,
  See our gallant leaders moving down the
    line,
To encounter in the fray every foe that blocks
    the way,
  Every foe to human progress and the
    right.

Chorus
Tramp, tramp, tramp, the boys are coming,
  Cheer up comrades as we may,
Up with freedom's temperance flag,
  Down with Rum's polluted rag,
  For the Temperance men are joining in
    the fray.

2. In the early mists of dawn, shall our
    bloodless sword be drawn.
  Till the whiskey men are driven to the
    rear,
In the shadows of the even, still there's work
    to do for Heaven.
  And the reapers are the Angels hovering
    near. *To Chorus*

3. With our righteous conflict gained,
    heavenly good shall be attained,
  And the world be carried nearer to the
    sun,
For in every triumph won, light celestial
    shines upon
  The eternal harvest, in the world to come!
    *To Chorus*106

Boys in Blue for Prohibition
(Wm. B. Marsh)

1. Now the Union fight is over, North and
    South shake hands once more,
  And the boys in blue rejoicing homeward
    come,
But our Union volunteers form again with
    lusty cheers,
  All equipped to fight the hated tyrant
    rum,

Chorus
Hark! hark! hark! the bells are ringing,
  Prohibition is their cry,
Wrongs inflicted in the past wake our people
    up at last,
  And they march determined now to win
    or die.

2. Let this gladsome 'natal strain ring o'er
    valley, hill and plain,
  In the North and South, as well as East
    and West,
Let them know this is no play, but we mean
    just what we say,
  And we're going to put their boasting to
    the test. *To Chorus*

3. Sailors, soldiers, all unite, in the common
    cause to fight,
  Once again to muster at our Union's call,
Quarter they don't ask or give, won't permit
    this curse to live,
  But will purge our land from hated
    alcohol. *To Chorus*107

Rum, Rum, Rum!

1. There's a slavery that binds captive
    thousands in our land,
  And it fetters both the body and the soul;
'Tis the slavery of drink, and its unrelenting
    hand,
  Slays the tortured victims under its
    control.

Chorus
Rum, Rum, Rum! the home is wailing–
　Not a home escapes its woe!
Death and ruin widely flow from the party
　licensed still–
　　Men and women, up! This monster
　　overthrow!

2. From the White House to the cot, rum is
　tyrant everywhere,
　Boasting loudly of its crime-cursed revenue:
That it fills the land with woe, what does
　party care?
　　Only rum-made, blood-stained gold it has
　　in view. *To Chorus*

3. Liquor men in Congress, still are demanding
　special aid,
　　Which no honest trade or business could
　　expect;
They would be relieved of tax, 'till more
　drunkards shall be made,
　　To consume their surplus rum! Let all
　　reflect. *To Chorus*

4. Rum in Congress, rum in Courts, rum in
　Legislature reigns;
　Rum o'er pulpit and o'er press is holding
　sway:
Shall it bind both church and state in its
　party license chains,
　　And its hundred thousand victims yearly
　　slay? *To Chorus*

5. Down, down, down! Behold them there!
　What a mighty stricken host!
　Full six hundred thousand yearly marching
　down–
Down to death, enslaved by rum, while of
　liberty we boast!
　　Freedom's banner droops, the vengeful
　　Heavens frown! *To Chorus*[108]

To the Front!

1. To the front, on to the front, little women,
　little men;
　　There is much of useful labor you may do

In the battle-field of life where man's enemy
　is rife,
　　Put your armor on, and wage the warfare,
　　too.

Chorus
Come, oh come, and join our army,
　Come with us, be ever true;
In the battle-field of life where man's enemy
　is rife,
　　Put your armor on, and wage the warfare,
　　too.

2. You may think because you're young, that
　you are not overstrong,
　　And that others will not heed you if you
　　try;
But, my little friends, be sure, your success
　must be secure,
　　If you ask the Lord to grant you victory.
　　To Chorus

3. Then on bravely to the front, little women,
　little men,
　　Like brave David, in the grand old
　　story-book;
Such a little lad was he, yet he slew the
　enemy,
　　And with only little pebbles from the
　　brook. *To Chorus*[109]

Vote, Vote, Vote, the Boys Are Marching

1. There's a movement strong and grand
　spreading over all the land,
　　Giving hope of peace and gladness to the
　　world;
'Tis a battle for the right, and our boys are in
　the fight,
　　And our flag of prohibition is unfurled.

Chorus
Vote, vote, vote, the boys are marching,
　Cheer up comrades, never yield;
We are ready for the fray,
　And we'll surely win the day,
　　And we'll drive the League of Liquor from
　　the field.

108. Durant, *Prohibition Home*, 44–45.
109. Stearns, *Band of Hope*, 59.

2. Shall our birthright be denied? Shall we
    see our laws defied
    By a league of liquor dealers, who
    demand,
In a tone of bitter hate, that within our own
    loved State
    No law that checks their hellish trade
    must stand? *To Chorus*

3. No! the edict has gone forth from the
    South, the East, the North,
    From the valleys to the highest mountain
    domes;
With our fortunes and our lives, we'll protect
    our sons and wives,
    And defend the sacred altars of our
    homes. *To Chorus*110

The Prohibition March
(Minnie Willis Baines)

1. In their prison cells they sit, fettered by the
    curse of drink,
    Through the length and breadth of this
    our beauteous land,
And polluted by the crimes it inspires upon
    the brink
    Of the gallows' trap, its wretched victims
    stand.
Tramp, tramp, tramp, the boys are marching,
    Carrying the Prohibition vote,
Which shall wipe this direful curse
    From the earth it bathes in blood,
    God's glory and the good of man
    promote.

2. In their beggared homes they sit, wan and
    pale and hollow-eyed,
    Wives and mothers broken hearted, in
    despair;
And they hear the children's cries with a grief
    they cannot hide,
    For the sorrows they are powerless to
    repair.

Tramp, tramp, tramp, our boys are marching,
    Cheer up, mothers, they will come;
With a ballot, pure and white,
    They will conquer in the fight,
    And will subjugate the foe that ruins
    home.

3. Lo, the blessed work of Christ in his
    conquest of men's souls
    Is obstructed by this traffic born of hell.
But when once 'tis overthrown by our
    victories at the polls,
    Peace and happiness and blessing will
    prevail.
Tramp, tramp, tramp, the boys are marching,
    Heading the column, comes St. John;
Noble Leonard, grand and true,
    In the vanguard marches, too,
    While a multitude, applauding, follow
    on.111

The Grand Rally

1. Oh! the sadness of our homes, when the
    rule of liquor comes,
    With so many thousand falling 'neath its
    power;
And we sought to stem the tide, and the evil
    set aside,
    But we seemed to have no refuge in the
    hour.

Chorus
Hark! Hark! Hark! our God is speaking,
    Telling of his power and love;
And the people in His might, are springing
    to the fight;
    And we'll shout aloud the vict'ry from
    above.

2. We have seen the angry nod of the
    enemies of God,
    And our Sabbath they have sworn they'll
    set aside,

110. *Prohibition Campaign Song Book*, 15–16; Stearns, *Prohibition Songster*, no. 52. Miller, *Patriotic No-License*, no. 1, entitles this selection "The Great Movement." Dungan et al., *Acorn Temperance*, no. 33, and Biederwolf and Lawson, *Best Temperance Songs*, no. 5, entitle this selection "There's a Movement" and make other changes.
111. *Prohibition Campaign Song Book*, 2.

And they made a great parade, with their
    brazen front displayed;
  And they thought we'd just be taken in
    the tide. *To Chorus*

3. Yes, our Sabbaths we'll defend—Homes
    with love and joy shall blend;
  And we'll sweep old Alcohol into the sea;
And in God we'll make our boast, and his
    glorious promise trust;
  And we'll sing the blessed anthem of the
    free. *To Chorus*[112]

The Coming Day

1. In the wretched haunts of vice, where the
    shadows of despair
  Hide the sunlight that would gladly enter
    in,
Where the widow droops her head, where
    the orphans cry for bread,
  Oh, 'tis there the work of love we must
    begin!

Chorus
Shout! oh, shout! the day is dawning;
  Soon the clouds will break away,
And the rock and hills shall ring
  With hosannas that we'll sing,
  For the promise of that great and glorious
    day.

2. With an earnest love of truth, with a
    hatred of the wrong,
  Brother, sister, friend, and neighbor shall
    unite;
Oh! that happy time will be all creation's
    jubilee!
  And the angels, too, will bless the
    wondrous sight. *To Chorus*

3. Bid the slumb'ring souls awake, and the
    fainting heart restore,
  There is mercy, there is hope, for everyone;
See the Temp'rance flag unfurled o'er the
    re-awakening world!

'Tis the signal of the conflict we've begun.
  To Chorus

4. Lift your eyes unto the hills, and the
    brilliant rays behold,
  Like a crown of glory on the brow of day;
'Tis the herald of a time when the
    Temp'rance bells shall chime,
  And to righteousness shall everything give
    way.

Final Chorus
Shout! oh, shout! the day is dawning, etc.
  On the morning of that resurrection
    day.[113]

Tramp, Tramp
(James Yeames)

1. 'Neath the Templar flag enrolled, firm our
    principles we hold,
  Casting far from us the wine cup away;
For we hate the drunkard's drink,
  And from his sad fate would shrink,
While we try to usher in a sober day.
  Tramp, tramp, tramp, we're onward
    marching;
Cheer up, comrades, let's be gay;
  See, our banners forward go,
Soon the foe our power shall know,
  And his dark and fouled dominions pass
    away.

2. Every bosom beats with joy, happy every
    girl and boy,
  For from drink's enslaving chain we are
    free;
Undismayed the foe we fight, soon his hosts
    we'll put to flight,
  And his hapless captives set at liberty.
Strike, then, strike for home and freedom,
  Drink, with its tyranny o'erthrow,
The ensnaring habit break, the deceiving cup
    forsake,
  Lest at last all its fatal curse you know.

112. Stearns, *National Temperance*, 40; *Prohibition Campaign Song Book*, 8; Hudson, *Temperance Songster*, no. 34. Miller, *Patriotic No-License*, no. 10, entitles this selection "We'll Defend Our Homes" and makes slight modifications at the end of each verse.

113. Stearns, *National Temperance*, 42; Leslie, *Good Templar* (1886 and 1888), 25.

3. Loud our tuneful notes we raise in our
   great Deliverer's praise,
   By His gracious help, alone, do we stand;
Praise the Lord for past success, pray Him
   still our cause to bless,
   And the curse of drink to banish from
   our land.
Sing, then, sing unto Jehovah,
   Worship the Lord at His throne,
At His feet cast every crown, lay your laurels
   humbly down,
   All the glory shall be thine, O Lord,
   alone.[114]

[From the Homes That Rum
Hath Cursed]

(J. T. Wright)

1. From the homes that rum hath cursed,
   from the hearts that rum hath
   crushed,
   Prayers ascend to heav'n for loved ones—
   God doth hear;
Stricken souls do not despair, for the Lord
   doth answer prayer,
   And the day of your deliv'rance draweth
   near.

Chorus
Tramp, tramp, tramp, the boys are marching:
   Victory! victory! hear them shout—
Onward! sound the bugle notes, charge the
   enemy with votes,
   From his stronghold we will drive the
   demon out.

2. Christian men, 'gainst rum, we pray, while
   ye vote the other way,
   For "protection" of the devil's chiefest aid,
Or for license—high or low, and thus legal
   rights bestow
   On the blight of rum, this cursed, foul
   "free trade"? *To Chorus*

3. Will ye temp'rance men proclaim
   temp'rance only in the name,
   And defend the liquor traffic at the polls?

With the "rummies" now ye stand—they'll be
   swept from off the land,
   As the wave of Prohibition onward rolls.
   To Chorus

4. Come, ye men of every name, never mind
   your party's claim—
   Join the party with an issue true and grand,
Prohibition leads the way—dawns the bright
   and glorious day
   When you'll vote for "God, and Home,
   and Native Land." *To Chorus*[115]

Come and Join Our Army

1. Old King Alcohol has long been a tyrant
   bold and strong
   And he holds a bloody scepter in this
   town.
Will you join our Temp'rance cause? Will you
   say to him now, pause!
   Will you come and help us crush this
   monster down?

Chorus
Come! Come! Come! and join our army!
   Help us put the traffic down;
Stand up boldly for the right, then the foe
   we'll put to flight,
   And we'll drive the cruel tyrant from the
   town.

2. O now voters, will not you come and join
   this army true?
   For your ballot at the polls will help
   restrain
This great enemy of truth and protect our
   boys and youth,
   And 'twill help the cause of Temp'rance
   to maintain. *To Chorus*

3. Shall this bloated tyrant come with this
   whisky, beer and rum,
   And our country fair with ruin cover o'er?
Friends of God and man arise! Fight till all
   beneath the skies
   Bear the curse of Old King Alcohol no
   more. *To Chorus*[116]

---

114. Leslie, *Good Templar* (1888), 63.
115. Mead and Chambers, *Clarion Call*, 101.
116. Miller, *Patriotic No-License*, no. 8.

W.C.T.U. Marching Song

1. We are Christian women strong, marching
forth 'gainst sin and wrong,
  With our Woman's Temp'rance Union
  true and brave;
L.T.L's. with us shall stand, with their true
and loyal band,
  And the home and nation from saloons,
  we'll save.

Chorus
Tramp! Tramp! Tramp! we all are marching,
  For God, native land and home;
Waving high our banner bright, emblem of
love, truth and right;
  We will free our nation from the curse of
  rum.

2. Frances Willard's beloved name, we will to
the world proclaim,
  As we follow in the party of purity,
For the work which she begun, ne'er shall
cease till vict'ry's won,
  And our God will give the promised
  liberty. *To Chorus*

3. All our earthly work will cease, crowned
with life and joy and peace,
  When the Savior reigns supreme from
  shore to shore,
Then by His redeeming grace, we shall see
His blessed face,
  In that land of light and glory evermore.
  To Chorus[117]

L.T.L. Marching Song

1. We're the youth of this great land, working
at the Lord's command,
  With our Loyal Temp'rance Legion brave
  and strong;
All our life is in His care, we have strength to
do and dare,
  As we march against the hosts of sin and
  wrong.

Chorus
Tramp! Tramp! Tramp! we all are marching,
  On to victory so grand,

And beneath these colors true, Starry flag,
Red, White and Blue,
  We will drive the liquor traffic from the
  land.

2. Prohibition is our cry, as we wave our
banner high,
  Pressing onward in the glorious
  temp'rance fight;
All saloons will have to go, with their poverty
and woe,
  For we're growing stronger in the cause of
  right. *To Chorus*

3. Heaven's glory will appear, and we'll raise a
mighty cheer,
  When the world is filled with justice,
  truth and love,
Then our work on earth will end, with the
angels we'll ascend,
  There to dwell with Christ in glory land
  above. *To Chorus*[118]

The Temperance Army

1. We are soldiers true and brave, marching
forth our land to save,
  From the liquor traffic with its crime and
  woe;
We'll press onward in the fight, for the cause
of truth and right,
  Till all nations go to war against the foe.

Chorus
Tramp! Tramp! Tramp! we all are marching;
  Sounding loud the battle-cry,
And beneath our banner bright, gleaming in
the temp'rance light,
  We will win a glorious vict'ry by-and-by.

2. God will help us win the day, if we work
and vote and pray,
  For all Christians should in solid phalanx
  stand:
We'll drive out the demon, rum, saving
church and school and home,
  Then the earth will be like heaven's
  border land. *To Chorus*

117. Roush, *Temperance Rally*, 20.
118. Ibid., 26.

3. How our shouts of praise will sound, all
    the whole wide world around,
  When the reign of great King Alcohol is
    o'er;
That will be a day of peace, crime and
  poverty shall cease,
  And we'll march on till we reach the
    golden shore. *To Chorus*[119]

Save the Flag

1. Save the banner of the true, Starry flag,
    Red, White and Blue,
  Blessed ensign of love, truth and purity;
May her stripes and bright stars wave, o'er the
  free and o'er the brave,
  Till the nation from intemp'rance shall be
    free.

Chorus
Save the stars and stripes forever!
  Glorious emblem of the true;
May she float o'er hill and plain, free from
  rum's polluted stain;
  Save the colors of our grand Red, White
  and Blue.

2. Let us teach our girls and boys, greatest of
    all earthly joys,
  To be loyal to the flag of liberty,
With her colors shining bright, they will wage
  the temp'rance fight,
  And their God will give them glorious
    victory. *To Chorus*

3. We'll defeat the powers of wrong, by the
    right that makes us strong,
  And we'll save Old Glory's folds from
    ev'ry foe;
Stainless shall our ensign be, emblem of that
  liberty,
  Foretaste of the home in heaven here
    below. *To Chorus*[120]

Vote for Prohibition
(E. A. Hoffman)

1. O the days of old are past, we are waking
    up at last,
  To the perils that assailed the homes so
    long!
Things were growing worse and worse,
    through this bitter, bitter, curse,
  Till we vowed to stay this cruel, cruel wrong.

Chorus
Vote, vote, vote, for prohibition,
  Vote to banish the saloon,
Let us stay this awful curse growing ev'ry year
  the worse,
  For we have no further use for the saloon.

2. The saloon men stand aghast while our
    ranks are filling fast,
  And they see the dread handwriting on
    the wall;
Let us push the work along, fight with steady
  heart and strong,
  And the evil traffic very soon must fall.
    To Chorus

3. Float your banners in the breeze over lands
    and over seas,
  And let "Home and Native Land" your
    motto be;
Sing to God a triumph song and the battle
  push along,
  And the fight will issue soon in victory.
    To Chorus[121]

Prohibition Land
(Frances B. Damon)

1. There's a pleasant land I know, where the
    children safely go,
  Passing nevermore saloons upon the street;
There's no crimson hand of greed, stealing
  bread the children need,
  Sending home the father with unsteady
    feet.

119. Ibid., 5.
120. Ibid., 8.
   121. *Anti-Saloon Campaign*, no. 3; Hoffman, *Woman's Christian Temperance*, no. 3. Hoffman, *Local Option*, no. 3, entitles this selection "Vote for Local Option" and replaces "prohibition" in the chorus with "local option."

Chorus
Prohibition, land of promise!
    That's the land I long to see;
Never nation taketh toll, from the tempter of
    the soul,
    In the land of prohibition that shall be.

2. There for all the years to come every man
    may have a home;
    There temptations evermore are on the
    wane;
Greed and drink together bind, and you'll
    surely, surely find
    Peace and plenty, health and gladness on
    the gain. *To Chorus*122

Rally for Victory
(H. H. Barstow)

1. From the land of palm and cane to the
    wooded hills of Maine,
    And from Plymouth Rock unto the
    Golden Gate,
Rings the Nation's war with rum, not with
    cannon, flag nor drum,
    But with ballots, and the battles of debate.

Chorus
Tramp, tramp, tramp, the states are marching,
    One by one to victory;
But we cannot win the fight, till the state we
    love is white,
    So we'll wage it till the victory we see.

2. Towns that long have lain appalled,
    thronging cities rum-enthralled,
    Now re-echo with the struggle to be free;
'Tis a fight for God above, and for all on
    earth we love,
    Rally then for God, our state and victory!
    To Chorus

3. Never say it can't be done, God will end
    what He's begun,
    While a town is unredeemed we dare not
    stay;

Hoary, proud, imperial state, great in wrong,
    in good more great,
    Arm us, Lord, to cleanse her greatest
    wrong away! *To Chorus*123

On the Boys Come Marching

1. Oh! the day has come at last,
    When the glorious tramp is heard,
And the boys come marching fifty thousand
    strong,
    And we grasp each other's hands,
While our hearts are full of joy,
    As the glorious song of temperance rolls
    along.

Chorus
On, on, on, the boys come marching,
    Like a grand, majestic sea,
And we'll dash away the rum
    From the homes we loved so well,
    And we'll stand beneath the temperance
    banner, free.

2. Oh! the feeblest heart grows strong,
    And the most despondent sure,
And we hear the thrilling songs on every
    hand,
    For we know that want and woe,
We no longer shall endure,
    When the curse of rum is driven from
    our land. *To Chorus*

3. Oh! the war has just begun,
    And we never mean to rest,
Till the demon rum is driven from our shore;
    But we'll fight with all our might,
And we'll win the day at last,
    And we'll shout the cry of victory o'er and
    o'er. *To Chorus*124

From Niagara to the Sea

1. From the land of palm and cane,
    To the wooded hills of Maine,

---

122. *Prohibition Campaign Song Book*, 21.
123. Ibid., 24. *Ohio State Prohibition*, 13, entitles this selection "The Anti-Saloon War Song," changes the last two lines of the chorus to "But we cannot win the fight until thirty-six are white, / So we'll press the battle on from sea to sea," and modifies verse 3.
124. In Gordon, *Popular Campaign*, n.p., "Yes, yes, yes" replaces "on, on, on" in the final chorus.

And from the Plymouth Rock unto the
Golden Gate,
Rings the Nation's war with rum,
Not with cannon, not with drum,
But with ballots and the battles of debate.

Chorus
Tramp, tramp, tramp, the States are
marching,
One by one to victory;
"1920" is the year,
Sound the slogan loud and clear,
Ringing, ringing from Niagara to the Sea.

2. Now we say IT CAN BE DONE—
Soon we'll have them on the run,
With each State in Prohibition ranks to stay.
Then we'll march to Washington
With our banners free from rum—
Hallelujah, hallelujah, what a day!
To Chorus[125]

We're Tenting Tonight

Coming with the Temp'rance Pledge

(J. C. Macy)

1. We're coming tonight with the Temp'rance
pledge—
Brother! we come to you!
So give us your name and pledge your word—
You'll find us comrades true!

Chorus
Many are the hearts that are weary tonight,
Weary of the days of sin;
Many are the hearts waiting for the time
When Temp'rance laws shall win!
So we're coming tonight, coming tonight,
Coming with the Temp'rance pledge!

2. We're coming tonight with the Temp'rance
pledge—
Coming, as oft before!
Be true to yourself—to manhood's pride,
And be a slave no more! *To Chorus*

3. Then rally, with cheers for the Temp'rance
pledge!
Rally and win the day!
For never again must drink prevail,
To drive all joy away! *To Chorus*[126]

The New Camp Ground

(J. B. Townsend)

1. We are tenting today on a new camp
ground,
O comrades so true and so brave;
'Tis the breaking of dawn and we hear the
sound
Of reveille, our country to save.
Many are the hearts that are praying today—
Praying that we may be strong;
Many are the soldiers preparing for the fray
To fight against the wrong.
Tenting today, tenting today,
Tenting on the new camp ground.

2. The shadows of night fast are fading away,
The mem'ries of years that are gone;
And the colors of morning, the "Blue" and
the "Gray,"
Are blending to herald the dawn.
Many who have fought in the "gray" and the
"blue"
Are tenting on the new camp ground.
The foes of the past now are comrades true,
For a common foe is found.
Tenting today, *etc.*

3. Yes, tenting today on a new camp ground,
The bugle is calling to arms,
And thousands of patriots arise at the sound
To guard home and country from harm.
Many of our comrades may fall in this fight,
Our loved ones may weep o'er the slain,
Our voices be silent at role-call tonight,
But the battle will not be in vain.
Tenting today, *etc.*[127]

125. Dailey and Mead, *Prohibition Chimes*, no. 77.
126. Macy, *Temperance Song-Herald*, 21–22.
127. *Prohibition Campaign Songster*, 1.

Praying Tonight
(E. A. Hoffman)

1. There are hearts bowed in sorrow and tears
tonight,
Pleading for heaven's peace,
And petitions are offered at the throne
For Jehovah to send release.

Chorus
Many are the hearts that are weary tonight,
Weary with the woe and grief,
Longing for a brighter, a better day,
And praying for relief;
Praying tonight, praying tonight,
Praying for the scourge to cease.

2. Many firesides are shaded with grief
tonight,
Many their tears and sighs,
And each heart-breaking moan and sob of woe
Unto heaven for mercy cries. *To Chorus*

3. There are hearts touched with anguish and
pain tonight,
Sorrow is ev'rywhere;
Tears of children and wives plead heaven's aid;
Tender Father, hear their prayer.

Final Chorus
Many are the hearts that are weary tonight, etc.
Praying God to send release.[128]

Happy Tonight
(E. A. Hoffman)

1. Many happy hearts are rejoicing tonight,
Right has gained a victory;
Many hearts are glad o'er the triumph won,
To God the glory be.

Chorus
Happy tonight, happy tonight,
Happy o'er the victory;
Happy tonight, happy tonight
To the Lord the glory be.

2. Long the bitter curse of intemperance,
Filled the land with misery;
Wrong has been assailed and we have
prevailed,
To God the glory be. *To Chorus*

3. O ye freemen, true, who have won the
fight,
Ye have made the people free;
Lay aside the sword, you have your reward,
To God the glory be. *To Chorus*[129]

Working for the Rum-God's Doom
(John R. Clements)

1. We are working away for the Rum-god's
doom;
Lend us a hand to aid:
The battle's fierce; the foe is strong;
But we are undismayed.

Chorus
Happy are the hearts full of gladness tonight;
Happy at the Rum-god's doom;
Happy are the hearts fighting for the right,
To chase away the gloom.
Happy tonight, happy tonight,
Happy in the Rum-god's doom.

2. We are working away for the Rum-god's
doom;
This blackest fiend of hell,
Who ruins homes, who blights and kills
And binds men with his spell. *To Chorus*

3. We are working away for the Rum-god's
doom,
Nor need we battle long;
The morning breaks, the sky shows blue;
Soon, soon the Victor song. *To Chorus*[130]

128. *Anti-Saloon Campaign*, no. 22; Hoffman, *Local Option*, no. 22; Hoffman, *Woman's Christian Temperance*, no. 21.

129. *Anti-Saloon Campaign*, no. 37; Hoffman, *Local Option*, no. 37; Hoffman, *Woman's Christian Temperance*, no. 37; Biederwolf and Lawson, *Best Temperance Songs*, no. 40.

130. Clements, *Shaw's Campaign*, 5.

Marching through Georgia

Song of the Blue Ribbon Brigade
(Frank C. Filley)

1. Come rally to our standard; our colors are
    true blue,
    Come rally round its glorious folds; t'will
    comfort bring to you,
Come rally, every drinking man, your life it
    will renew,
    And bring you a grand and glorious
    victory.

Chorus
Hurrah! Hurrah! the Badge of Blue for me,
    Hurrah! Hurrah! from Drink t'will set you
    free,
Remember that our motto is—Gospel
    Temperance for me,
    We're marching on to glory and to
    victory.

2. Come every trembling drunkard; we'll take
    you by the hand,
    We'll set you firm upon your feet;
    a freeman you shall stand,
Help us to drive King Alcohol forever out our
    land,
    And gain a grand and glorious victory.
        To Chorus

3. God bless the noble ladies, whose hearts
    are in the cause,
    God help them in their pious work;
    they're worthy of applause,
They are doing more for Temperance than all
    our country's laws,
    They'll gain a grand and glorious victory.
        To Chorus

4. Come everyone, and sign our pledge, t'will
    blessings bring to you,
    And pin our symbol on your breast, our
    glorious badge of blue,
T'will bring you health and happiness, and
    every blessing too,
    You'll gain a grand and glorious victory.
        To Chorus[131]

Ring the Knell of Bacchus

1. Ring the knell of Bacchus, boys, we'll
    sound it loud and long,
    And ring it with a spirit that will wake
    and stir the throng!
And ring it like teetotalers a thousand
    thousand strong,
    For we are marching to victory.

Chorus
Hurrah! hurrah! we hail the jubilee!
    Hurrah! hurrah! the law shall make us free!
Freemen, rally round us from the center to
    the sea,
    For we are marching to victory.

2. Rouse we then, the people, boys, enlist
    them one and all,
    And let us each be faithful now, and true
    to duty's call;
Before our ranks King Alcohol and his
    strongholds shall fall,
    For we are marching to victory. *To Chorus*

3. Lo! the star is gleaming, boys, the glorious
    Temp'rance Star,
    And from its brightest beaming, see the
    lustre spreads afar;
And total prohibition soon shall close each
    tavern bar,
    For we are marching to victory. *To Chorus*

4. Let union be our motto, boys, as we go
    hand in hand,
    To drive the demon-drink from this and
    every land;
And God above, the God of love, His blessing
    will command,
    For we are marching to victory. *To Chorus*[132]

We've Buckled on Our Armor

1. They tell us that the woods are full, they're
    coming right along;
    Wake the chorus up to-night, we'll have
    another song.
Sing it as we mean to sing it, half a million
    strong,
    While we go marching for temperance.

---

131. Filley, *Red, White, and Blue*, 14–15.
132. Stearns, *National Temperance*, 57.

Chorus
Hurrah! hurrah! we'll shout the jubilee,
 Hurrah! hurrah! from rum we will be
  free;
So we'll sing the chorus from the center to
  the sea,
 While we go marching for temperance.

2. We have buckled on the armor, we are
  marching for the right,
 There's no such word as fail for us, for
  God is in the fight.
We'll win the day, for now we see the
  dawning of the light,
 While we go marching for temperance.
  To Chorus

3. These mad reformers soon will fail, that's
  what the rummies said;
 'Tis nothing but excitement, of such
  things we have read;
But while they're causing tears to fall, and
  children cry for bread,
 We'll go marching for temperance.
  To Chorus

4. Thus we'll form a thoroughfare for
  temperance and her train;
 No limits to its latitude, on ocean or on
  main;
Rum shall fall before us, for resistance is in
  vain,
 While we go marching for temperance.
  To Chorus

5. There's many a saddened heart to-night,
  that's bled for weary years;
 Eyes that long have looked to God
  through many scalding tears;
Soon our joyful songs shall fall upon their
  listening ears,
 While we go marching for temperance.
  To Chorus

6. Come sign the pledge as we have done and
  soon we'll win the day;
 The army now is rallying, the foe will
  soon give way;

The drunkard's home shall thrive again
  'neath temperance' peaceful sway,
 While we go marching for temperance.
  To Chorus[133]

We Hail the All-Auspicious Day

1. We hail the all-auspicious day, prohibits
  alcohol,
 Within our land to have it say we answer
  to its call,
Treat it as we mean to treat it, for the time to
  come,
 To a dose of Prohibition.

Chorus
Hurrah! hurrah! we'll carry on this war,
 Hurrah! hurrah! as it never was before,
'Till every one redeemed shall come in
  armour for the fight,
 Shouting aloud for Prohibition.

2. All praise to him directs the fight, we
  muster one and all,
 To the battle in the cause of right, to see
  the tyrant fall;
Bury in oblivion, for all the years to come,
 Rum, in the wave of Prohibition.
  To Chorus

3. God sent it as a precious boon, from his
  unsparing hand,
 It reached the people none too soon, to
  save our noble land;
We'll take it, and we mean to keep it for all
  time to come,
 Shouting the cry for Prohibition.
  To Chorus[134]

Our Next Campaign, Boys

1. We have stood in battle, boys, when bullets
  fell like hail;
 Now we meet another foe, our courage
  shall not fail;
Forward! then we'll conquer rum; the liquor
  lines assail!
 Down with the rum-curse forever!

---

133. Ibid., 34–35. *Prohibition Campaign Song Book*, 11, and Hudson, *Temperance Songster*, no. 64, omit verses 3, 4, and 6.

134. Perine and Mash, *National Prohibition Hymnal*, 43.

Chorus

Hurrah! Hurrah! We march to victory;
  Hurrah! Hurrah! From rum we shall be free;
From hill, plain and vale, from the mountain to the sea;
  Down with the rum-curse forever!

2. Life we'll spend in conflict, boys, this is our last campaign;
  We've enlisted for the war, 'till this rum-foe is slain;
This shall be our battle-cry from East to Western main—
  Down with the rum-curse forever!
    To Chorus

3. Ballots now, not bullets, boys, not bayonet and gun;
  Not the roar of deadly strife, from rise to set of sun;
Yet, the vic'try shall be greater, when the field is won;
  Down with the rum-curse forever!
    To Chorus

4. We have met one slav'ry, boys, in blood we put it down;
  Now the liquor slav'ry next, our bloodless arms shall crown;
We shall meet it face to face, despite its demon frown;
  Down with the rum-curse forever!
    To Chorus

5. Make no compromises, boys, for license party's sake;
  That will aid the liquor-foe, its fetters stronger make;
If we would be truly free, its bondage we must break;
  Down with the rum-curse forever!
    To Chorus

6. Rally to our standard, boys, that stainless greets the light;
  Prohibition Home Protection leads us in the fight;

God and home and native land, inspire our souls with might;
  Down with the rum-curse forever.
    *To Chorus*135

Victory's in Sight

1. The battle now has opened and we'll rally to the fight,
  We're gaining troops from everywhere to struggle for the right,
And we see before us a future grand and bright
  For the Prohibition Party.

Chorus

Hurrah! hurrah! we're fighting for the right,
  Hurrah! hurrah! for victory's in sight,
And the people everywhere are rising in their might,
  For the Prohibition Party.

2. Republicans have told us that our wool we must protect,
  But boys are more than sheep to us, and them we can't neglect;
The votes of those who love their boys we certainly expect
  For the Prohibition Party. *To Chorus*

3. The Democrats refused to heed petitions long and loud;
  Before their whisky master they've in submission bowed;
Then leave their ranks and come and join the still increasing crowd,
  For the Prohibition Party. *To Chorus*136

Our Battle Song
(Ella Alexander Boole)

1. Bring the good old bugle, boys! we'll sing another song,
  Sing it with the spirit that will move the world along,
Sing it as we used to sing it, fifty thousand strong,
  While we are marching for Temperance.

135. Durant, *Prohibition Home*, 13.
136. *Prohibition Campaign Song Book*, 1

Chorus
Hurrah! hurrah! we'll bring the jubilee,
  Hurrah! hurrah! the vote shall make us
    free!
So we'll sing the chorus from the mountain
    to the sea,
  While we are marching for Temperance.

2. How the dear old friends will shout when
    they hear the joyful sound,
  How our foes will "right about" when it's
    noised the world around,
That we've routed them and left them slain
    upon the ground,
  While we are marching for Temperance.
    To Chorus

3. Yes, and there are Temperance men who
    are standing on this floor,
  They love this honored cause as they
    never loved before,
Hardly can they be restrained from cheering
    as of yore,
  While we are marching for Temperance.
    To Chorus

4. "Prohibition hast'ning on will never gain
    its cause,"
  So the politicians tell us, but 'tis vain we
    pause,
For they do not know, alas; that we'll bind
    them by the laws,
  While we are marching for Temperance.
    To Chorus

5. So we'll make a thoroughfare for
    Temperance and her train,
  Clear through the constitution, the
    amendment will be plain;
Treason flees before us for resistance is in vain,
  While we are marching for Temperance.
    *To Chorus*137

Our Banner, Prohibition

(George E. Thrall)

1. From New England's granite hills to
    Dixie's grassy plains,

Freedom's sons join hands again, a loving
    spirit reigns,
Shadowed o'er by new device, all free of
    bloody stains,
  With our banner, Prohibition.

Chorus
Hurrah, hurrah, the cruel work is done,
  Hurrah, hurrah, Columbia is one.
Now on old Gambrinus we turn every man
    his gun,
  With our banner, Prohibition.

2. Quarrels of the past have been out for all
    they're worth,
  Solid in the South no more, no more the
    solid North;
But a solid country is what we will be
    henceforth,
  With our banner, Prohibition. *To Chorus*

3. When the Blue and Gray were matched,
    we fought with awful might.
  Now with force united, and with weapons
    keen and bright.
We'll attack saloonists till they vanish out of
    sight,
  With our banner, Prohibition. *To Chorus*

4. When at last from liquor lords we've set
    the people free,
  From our homes delivered, what
    hosannas there will be
Welcoming our triumph from the Rockies to
    the sea,
  With our banner, Prohibition.
    *To Chorus*138

Voting Song

(Herbert Whitney)

1. Come and gather round, my friend! we'll
    sing a temperance song,
  Sing it with a spirit that will start our
    cause along,
Sing it as we soon shall sing it—fifty thousand
    strong,
  While we are voting for temperance.

137. Leslie, *Good Templar* (1886), 43.
138. Ibid.

Chorus
Hurrah! hurrah! 'twill bring the Jubilee!
  Hurrah! hurrah! the vote will make us
  free!
Soon we'll sing the chorus from the
  mountains to the sea,
  While we are voting for temperance.

2. We shouted for old parties till we almost
  split our throat;
  We've carried our petitions in, enough to
  sink a boat;
We've preached and prayed and pleaded, and
  done everything but vote,
  But *now* we are voting for temperance.
  To Chorus

3. We'll fight it out upon this line if't takes a
  hundred years;
  We've burnt the bridge behind us, and
  we've flung away our fears;
We'll gain the battle inch by inch, you'll
  know it by our cheers,
  While we are voting for temperance.
  To Chorus[139]

Under the Star Spangled Banner
(Antoinette Arnold Hawley)

1. All the air is ringing with a nation's
  peaceful joy;
  Stately music chiming glad with every
  whizzing toy;
Yet the licensed dram-shop yawns for every
  mother's boy
  Under the Star Spangled Banner.

Chorus
Hurrah! Hurrah! We hail the land to be;
  Hurrah! Hurrah! When truly, grandly
  free;
Licensed wrong shall never find a shield from
  sea to sea
  Under the Star Spangled Banner.

2. Women! where our pennons float on every
  wind that blows;
  Women! 'mid the roses and the far
  Alaskan snows;

Let your mighty protest rise from every
  hearth that glows
  Under the Star Spangled Banner.
  To Chorus

3. Hark! above the tumult swells a clear
  triumphant song
  From the great white-ribbon host, three
  hundred thousand strong;
God and Home and Country, bid us right
  this giant wrong
  Under the Star Spangled Banner.
  To Chorus

4. Christ, the King, commanding, every
  weapon burnished bright;
  Peaceful war we're waging; "Brothers, help
  us win the fight";
Christian votes must conquer in this battle
  for the right,
  Under the Star Spangled Banner.
  To Chorus[140]

Contest Song
(Minnie B. Horning)

1. Raise your voices, children, let's sing
  another song;
  Sing about the contest work, and sing it
  loud and long;
Tell it to the boys and girls, the young folks
  brave and strong,
  How we are speaking for temperance.

Chorus
Hurrah! hurrah! we'll raise the standard high;
  Hurrah! hurrah! 'Tis ours to do or die;
We're the coming people and we'll sound the
  battle-cry,
  Marching from contest to conquest.

2. Silver, gold, and jewels are the medals that
  we earn;
  Many thousand earnest hearts have won
  them each in turn;
But better than the medals are the lessons
  that we learn,
  While we are speaking for temperance.
  To Chorus

139. Silver Lake Quartette, *Prohibition Bells*, 87.
140. Gordon, *Temperance Songster*, no. 132; Law, *Temperance Bells*, no. 50.

3. Striving for the honors is a joy that never
tires;
Learning words of burning hope from
wisdom's holy fires;
"Preferring one another," is the spirit it inspires,
While we are speaking of temperance.
To Chorus[141]

When We Vote the Saloons Out

1. Come and gather 'round, my friends; we'll
sing a temp'rance song;
Sing it with a spirit that will start our
cause along;
Sing it as we soon shall sing it—many
thousand strong,
When we shall vote the saloons out.

Chorus
Hurrah! hurrah! 'twill bring the jubilee!
Hurrah! hurrah! the vote will make us
free!
Soon we'll sing the chorus from the
mountain to the sea,
While we go marching to vict'ry.

2. How the mothers and the wives will shout
to hear the sound,
How the hearts of children too with
happiness will bound;
How the blessed news will spread the whole
wide world around
When we shall vote the saloons out.
To Chorus

3. Many homes will then be bright that now
are full of woe;
Business then will be quite brisk, which
now is very slow;
Churches will be crowded full, where now
few people go,
When we shall vote the saloons out.
To Chorus

4. Come, then, all ye loyal men and join us
in the fight;
Come and join the army that you know is
in the right;

Come and help us win the day, 'twill fill the
foe with fright,
When we shall vote the saloons out.
To Chorus[142]

No License Shall Triumph

1. Wake ye people, everywhere, and strike a
mighty blow,
Strike the enemy of home, of native land
the foe;
Sound the order through the town that each
saloon must go,
And then No license shall triumph.

Chorus
Hurrah! hurrah! lift high the banner white!
Hurrah! hurrah! we've 'listed for the fight.
Alcohol and all his kin we'll bury out of
sight,
Whene'er No license shall triumph.

2. License, low, or even high, are sins we'll
not endure,
No license only is our plan, we have no
other cure.
Fight it out upon this line, and victory is
sure,
And then No license shall triumph.
To Chorus

3. License, friends, is but a trick to let the
demon in.
Never yet was vict'ry won by compromise
with sin.
Vote then straight against it, boys, and you
are sure to win,
And then No license shall triumph.
To Chorus

4. Long our town has waited for the work
that we must do,
Laurels are in waiting for the noble
temp'rance crew,
Great the vict'ry we shall win, if we are brave
and true,
Whene'er No license shall triumph.

141. Gordon, *Temperance Songster*, no. 67.
142. Miller, *Patriotic No-License*, no. 2. Note that verse 1 and the refrain are the same as "Voting Song."

Final Chorus
Hurrah! hurrah! we'll drive the traffic out!
    Hurrah! hurrah! the foe we'll put to
      route;
When at last our town is free, we'll raise a
    mighty shout,
    That No License has triumphed.[143]

Voting for Freedom

1. Hurrah for prohibition, boys! We'll vote
    the ticket straight;
    Vote it with a willing hand, a heart that's
      free from hate;
Vote it while the angels on the heights of
    glory wait,
    While we are voting for freedom.

Chorus
Hurrah! hurrah! we'll sound the jubilee;
    Hurrah! hurrah! for votes that make us
      free;
So we'll drive the liquor from the land into
    the sea,
    While we are voting for freedom.

2. How the hills will echo when we civilize
    the land;
    How the stars will twinkle when we
      mobilize our band;
Come, then Christian soldiers and unite
    both heart and hand
    While we are voting for freedom.
      To Chorus

3. So we'll drive the liquor curse from over
    hill and plain;
    Saloons and license system will forever
      cease to reign;
The Woman's Temp'rance Union shall the
    right of suffrage gain,
    While we are voting for freedom.
      To Chorus

4. Christians will be victors if they vote just as
    they pray;
    God will grant us freedom if we drive
      saloons away;

Oh! how we'll sing his praises on that
    prohibition day,
    When we're through voting for freedom.
    To Chorus[144]

Working for Temperance #1

1. Come, ye Christian women, there is work
    for us to do.
    Come, and join our righteous band, the
      W.C.T.U.
God will help us win the day if we are brave
    and true,
    For we are working for temperance.

Chorus
Hurrah! Hurrah! we'll sound the jubilee;
    Hurrah! Hurrah! we're bound for liberty;
So we'll fight the traffic till we gain the
    victory,
    For we are working for temp'rance.

2. How the birds will sing their songs when
    prohibition comes;
    How the bells of church and school will
      peal with silv'ry tones;
How old glory's folds will wave in triumph
    o'er our homes;
    When we're through working for
    temp'rance. *To Chorus*

3. From the cross of Jesus radiates the
    heav'nly light,
    Showing us so plain the paths of justice,
      truth and right;
In its glorious brightness we will wear our
    bows of white,
    While we are working for temp'rance.
      To Chorus

4. At last when all our work is o'er and vict'ry
    is complete;
    In glory land so bright and fair we'll fall at
      Jesus' feet,
And in that golden city, angels will each
    victor greet,
    For we've been working for temp'rance.
      To Chorus[145]

143. Ibid., no. 3.
144. Roush, *Temperance Rally*, 14.
145. Ibid., 17.

Working for Temperance #2

1. We are temp'rance soldiers marching in
     the heav'nly light;
   Jesus, mighty Victor, is our Captain in the
     fight;
With His cross we'll triumph in the cause of
     truth and right,
   For we are working for temp'rance.

Chorus
Hurrah! Hurrah! we'll sound the jubilee;
   Hurrah! Hurrah! we're sure of victory;
So we'll keep on marching in the path of
     purity,
   For we are working for temp'rance.

2. How the heavens echo when our voices
     join in song;
   How old Satan grumbles at our
     temp'rance army strong;
How all earth rejoices as our forces march
     along,
   For we are working for temp'rance.
     To Chorus

3. "King Alcohol must tremble," is the motto
     of our band;
   Entire prohibition o'er the wide world we
     demand;
Saloons with all their vices shall be driven
     from the land,
   While we are working for temp'rance.
     To Chorus

4. When Christ descends on judgment day
     with music in the air;
   He'll take us home to glory land—that city
     bright and fair,
And with the angels 'round His throne, we'll
     greet each other there,
   For we've been working for temp'rance.
     To Chorus[146]

Marching to Victory #1

1. Rally, Christian soldiers in a mighty
     temp'rance band;
   March against the pow'r of rum in solid
     phalanx grand;

Jesus Christ, our Leader bids us save our
     native land,
   As we press onward to vict'ry.

Chorus
Hurrah! Hurrah! we'll sound the battle-cry;
   Hurrah! Hurrah! King Alcohol must die;
Yes, we'll free our nation from the traffic
     by-and-by,
   For we are marching to vict'ry.

2. How the mother's heart will thrill with joy
     as ne'er before;
   How the sunlight of God's love will shine
     from shore to shore;
How the banner of the cross will wave
     forevermore,
   When we have won glorious vic'try.
     To Chorus

3. At the dawn of golden day o'er valley, hill
     and plain,
   Celestial glory will appear and peace and
     justice reign,
All the wide world will be free from poverty
     and pain,
   For we'll have gained final vict'ry.
     To Chorus

4. "Glory in the highest," guardian angel
     bands will sing,
   When the bells of triumph o'er the land
     begin to ring,
Then all earth will praise the Lord, her great
     eternal King,
   And we shall be crowned with vict'ry.
     To Chorus[147]

The March to Victory
(G. W. Dungan)

1. Going forth to victory we see a gallant
     band,
   North, and South, and East, and West,
     o'er all this glorious land;
Springing forth with courage true to meet the
     hostile clan;
   On! on! on! then, to vict'ry!

146. Ibid., 23.
147. Ibid., 3.

Chorus
Hurrah! hurrah! we'll join the glorious band;
   Hurrah! hurrah! together we will stand,
Till the woes of drunkenness are driven from
   our land;
    On! on! on! then, to vict'ry!

2. From the home, the shop, the field, the
   cry is going forth;
   Naught can stop the march of votes that
    comes from South to North.
Shop and office swell the cry, from men of
   brawn and worth;
    On! on! on! then, to vict'ry! *To Chorus*

3. Hear the God of hosts proclaim from out
   His sacred word;
   Hear it as our Lord proclaims it, as we all
    have heard,
"Drunkards cannot enter heaven," save them
   now, O Lord!
    On! on! on! then, to vict'ry! *To Chorus*

4. Break their shackles, free the men who by
   this curse are bound!
   Make the welkin ring with shouts
    wherever man is found,
Till we hear the joyous news, our land is free,
   Hurrah!
    On! on! on! then, to vict'ry! *To Chorus*[148]

Down with the Rum-Shop Forever
("Bob" Atchison)

1. Don't you hear the bugle, boys? It's ringing
   through the land,
   Coming up from Georgia, where a
    Prohibition band
Met together at the polls, and took a noble
   stand,
    Driving the Rum-shop from Georgia.

Chorus
Hurrah! Hurrah! Our nation must be free!
   Hurrah! Hurrah! We hail the jubilee!
Join this mighty chorus, ring it out o'er land
   and sea,
    "Down with the Rum-shop forever!"

2. Other states are going "dry," our cause is
   gaining ground;
   Through the South they've taken hold;
    The North is coming 'round;
Everywhere from East to West there comes
   this stirring sound,
    "Down with the Rum-shop forever!"
    To Chorus

3. Now's the time for this good state, we must
   not be left out;
   Volunteers are coming forth to put the
    foe to route;
Stand together for the fight and let them hear
   us shout;
    "Down with the Rum-shop forever!"
    To Chorus[149]

L.T.L. Rally Song
(H. W. Palmer)

1. Come and join our Legion, give us now a
   helping hand.
   Help us free the nation from the evil in
    our land.
Help us save the children; they are safe
   within our band,
    So we shall march on to Victory.

Chorus
Hurrah! hurrah! we'll sing the jubilee.
   Hurrah! hurrah! our country shall be free.
With a chain of Legions from the mountains
   to the sea,
    So we shall march on to Victory.

2. This shall be our motto, "Lifting others as
   we climb,"
   Under such a banner, we shall climb to
    heights sublime.
Onward, ever onward—we shall win the world
   in time,
    So we shall march on to Victory.
    To Chorus

3. Hear the children pleading—shall they call
   to us in vain?
   Bearing heavy burdens, living lives of toil
    and pain.

---

148. Dungan et al., *Acorn Temperance*, no. 29.
149. Ibid., no. 31.

Ours it is to rescue—fill their lives with joy
again,
   So we shall march on to Victory.
      To Chorus

4. "Total prohibition" be our watchword
evermore.
   "Total prohibition" sends the word from
   shore to shore.
Save our loved Nation from the evil at the door,
   So we shall march on to Victory.
      *To Chorus*150

Cheer Up, Prohibition Men

1. Cheer up, Prohibition men, we'll surely
win the fight,
   Never had we such a chance the nation's
   foe to smite,
Never were so many men resolved to vote for
Right,
   This year is good for Prohibition.

Chorus
Hurrah! hurrah! we wage a winning war,
   Hurrah! hurrah! each day we're winning
   more;
We will fight until we sweep the land from
   shore to shore,
   And sweep it clean for Prohibition.

2. Vote for Prohibition and saloons will have
to go,
   Educate the people, and they'll strike a
   mighty blow;
We will free the nation from the curse of
   rum and woe,
   And sweep it clean for Prohibition.
      To Chorus

3. We shall be the victors when men vote as
now they pray,
   God will grant us freedom if we vote the
   curse away,
Then we'll sing His praises on that Jubilation
day,
   When we have carried Prohibition.
      *To Chorus*151

Vote for Me
(E. A. Hoffman)

1. When you cast your ballot, father, won't
you think of me?
   Won't you vote to make the town from
   liquor-selling free?
Save me from the drink-curse, father, heed
my fervent plea
   When you are casting your ballot.

Chorus
Vote no! vote no! no license for our town;
   Vote no! vote no! and put the traffic
   down;
Will you think of me, my father, will you vote
for me
   When you are casting your ballot?

2. O how very sad and grieved your loving
heart would be
   If the traffic in our town a drunkard
   made of me!
You can save me from a life of shame and
misery
   When you are casting your ballot.
      To Chorus

3. Do not vote for the saloon and tempt your
boy to wrong;
   Save me from the danger, the enticements
   are so strong;
Vote for prohibition and so help your boy
along
   When you are casting your ballot.
      *To Chorus*152

Voting for Prohibition

1. Come and gather one and all! we'll sing a
temp'rance song,
   Sing it with a spirit that will start our
   cause along,
Sing it till our army numbers many millions
strong,
   Casting votes for Prohibition.

150. Law, *Temperance Bells*, no. 29.
151. *Anti-Saloon Campaign*, no. 4; Hoffman, *Woman's Christian Temperance*, no. 4.
152. *Anti-Saloon Campaign*, no. 41; Hoffman, *Woman's Christian Temperance*, no. 41.

Chorus
Hurrah! hurrah! bring in the Jubilee!
  Hurrah! hurrah! the vote will make us
    free!
Then we'll sing the chorus from the
    mountain to the sea,
  When we have carried Prohibition.

2. Weeping mothers, hapless wives will hear
    the blessed sound,
  Hearts of children, too, with joy and
    happiness will bound,
And the glorious tidings will be borne the
    land around,
  When we've carried Prohibition.
    To Chorus

3. Hearts that now are full of woe, will then
    be fair and bright,
  Hearts that know but deep distress will be
    made gay and light,
This will come to pass when friends of
    temperance unite,
  Casting votes for Prohibition. *To Chorus*

4. We will fight along this line till comes the
    conq'ring year,
  Never from the battle turn because the
    foe we fear;
This will nerve us to push on, the
    triumph-day is near,
  When we'll carry Prohibition. *To Chorus*

5. Wake ye people, everywhere, unite to strike
    the blow,
  In behalf of every home, against this evil
    foe;
Let it be well understood that the saloons
    must go,
  And we'll carry Prohibition. *To Chorus*153

Hurrah, the Victory Is Won
(E. A. Hoffman)

1. Let us join together in the singing of a
    song,
  And go forth in solid rank to stay a cruel
    wrong,

Which has desolated homes of millions very
    long,
  Chanting glory, hallelujah!

Chorus
Hurrah! hurrah! the victory is won!
  Hurrah! hurrah! the glory is begun!
We need but cast our ballots and the
    splendid work is done.
  Praise God! Glory, hallelujah!

2. Sing your hallelujah for the triumph of the
    right,
  Lift your hearts to God whose arm has
    helped us in the fight;
Hearts with hope and throbbing and the
    skies are growing bright,
  Sing a happy hallelujah! *To Chorus*

3. Victory is dawning and the people may
    rejoice,
  Praise is very seemly for each human heart
    and voice;
Let our hearts be lifted up in strains exalted,
    choice,
  And sing glory, hallelujah! *To Chorus*154

Just a Little Ballot
(E. A. Hoffman)

1. Just a little ballot, boys, that any hand can
    hold,
  Just a little paper that you overlap and
    fold,
Put it in the ballot box as you have done of
    old,
  And we shall win a glorious vict'ry.

Chorus
Hurrah! hurrah! the battle now is on;
  Hurrah! hurrah! the work will soon be
    done;
Put your ballots in the box, my comrades,
    one by one,
  And it will mean a glorious vict'ry.

2. Just a little ballot, boys, a piece of paper
    white,

153. *Anti-Saloon Campaign*, no. 51; Hoffman, *Woman's Christian Temperance*, no. 51.
154. Hoffman, *Local Option*, no. 30.

But it has a wondrous pow'r because it
stands for Right;
If we cast enough of them, the prospect will
be bright,
For we shall win a glorious vict'ry.
To Chorus

3. Just a little ballot, boys! You take it in your
hand,
And remember that it counts for home
and native land;
Then you put it in the box in manhood brave
and grand,
And we shall win a glorious vict'ry.
*To Chorus*155

The New "Marching through Georgia"

1. Bring the good old bugle, boys! We'll have
a grand new song;
Sing it as we mean to sing it, soon three
million strong;
Sing it as we love to sing it, while they march
along;
Rum shops are marching from
Michigan!

Chorus
Hurrah! Hurrah! let Michigan be free—
Hurrah! Hurrah! We'll hail the jubilee.
When the voters reach the polls in April you
will see
Rum shops go marching from Michigan.

2. Maine and Kansas long have stood for
prohibition straight,
North Dakota, too, is free—no license in
that state.
Both North and South are waking up; they'll
know the victory great,
When rum shops go marching from
Michigan. *To Chorus*

3. Nine whole States have now declared that
their saloons must go,
Brewers find their stock don't sell, from
par it's far below,

Twenty-six saloons a day receive the
knock-out blow,
And rum shops are marching from
Michigan. *To Chorus*156

Our Battle Song
(J. G. Dailey)

1. Ev'rywhere the woods are full, they're
coming right along.
Wake the chorus up to-night to sing
another song;
Sing it as we mean to sing it, twenty millions
strong.
So we are marching to vict'ry.

Chorus
Hurra! Hurra! My COUNTRY shall be free.
Hurra! Hurra! The STATE will follow
thee;
Then in 1920 Comes the NATION'S
JUBILEE.
So we are marching to vict'ry.

2. Onward into battle, we are marching for
the right;
No such word as fail for us, as GOD is in
the fight;
Sure to win for now we see the dawning of
the light.
So we are marching to vict'ry. *To Chorus*

3. Thus we build a thoroughfare for
Prohibition's train.
Limitless its latitude on ocean or the main,
Rum shall fall before us, for resistance is in
vain.
So we are marching to vict'ry.
*To Chorus*157

Marching to Victory #2
(Ethel M. Van Vliet)

1. Bring the good old bugle, boys, and sound
the call to war,
We're out for prohibition, now—that's
what the call is for;

155. Ibid., no. 4.
156. Ibid., back cover.
157. Dailey and Mead, *Prohibition Chimes*, no. 76.

Rally to our standard for the latest holy war,
While we are marching to victory.

Chorus
Hurrah! Hurrah! we'll bring the jubilee;
Hurrah! Hurrah! our land shall yet be free;
Shout aloud the chorus till it rings from sea
to sea,
While we are marching to victory.

2. Hear the tramp of soldiers, temperance
legions for the fray;
Hear the children shouting as they view
the glad array;
Hear the mothers singing where our
temperance laws hold sway,
While we are marching to victory.
To Chorus

3. Let us make a thoroughfare for Freedom
and her train,
To sweep across our continent and reach
from main to main;
God of Hosts is with us and resistance is in
vain,
While we are marching to victory.
*To Chorus*158

We Must Vote for Prohibition
(Frank D. Reno)

1. Jump into the wagon, boys, and ev'rybody
sing,
Sing for prohibition till the hills and
valleys ring,
Talk and toil and pray and push, the victory
to bring,
We must vote for prohibition!

Chorus
Hurrah! hurrah! we're in the fight to win;
Hurrah! hurrah! let all the world come in;
We will free our people from the
license-curse and sin,
We must vote for prohibition!

2. Blow your biggest bugle, boys, and
ev'rybody come;

Sound the fife and mandolin, and don't
forget the drum;
Play the harp and violin, and make the music
hum,
We must vote for prohibition! *To Chorus*

3. Now's the hour with courage strong to face
the cruel foe,
To heed our Leader's great command, and
strike the fatal blow;
Onward, comrades, charge the front, and lay
"the traffic" low,
We must vote for prohibition!
*To Chorus*159

They Vote for Prohibition

1. Do you see the women of the golden
sunset west,
Women who are strong and brave, the
nation's very best,
Marching to the ballot box? For with the vote
they're blest,
And they vote for prohibition.

Chorus
Hurrah! hurrah! we hail the coming day;
Hurrah! hurrah! prohibition soon will sway
From Pacific Ocean to Old Massachusetts Bay,
Women will vote for prohibition!

2. Do you hear them calling, "help us make
our country free,
From the curse of licensed drink and all
its tyranny"?
Women of the Northland and the Southland
need to be
Casting their votes for prohibition.
To Chorus

3. We will answer to their call, "We're
coming, comrades brave,
To help you from the drink-curse our
beloved land to save;
We'll give our strength, we'll give our might,
as loyal comrades gave,
To help bring the day of prohibition."
*To Chorus*160

---

158. Gordon, *Popular Campaign*, 27.
159. Ibid., 17.
160. Ibid., 27.

We Must Win Prohibition
(Anna A. Gordon)

1. Now's the day, and now's the hour, that
      calls for service new,
     Patriot service for the home, for all that's
         pure and true;
   Service for the state we love, the best we all
      can do—
      We must win prohibition.

Chorus
Must win, must win, the victory we must win;
     Must win, must win, the victory we must
         win;
Talk and work, and sing and pray, from dawn
      till close of day—
      We must win prohibition.

2. Hero men and women, all are sending out
      the light,
     Light of truth which comes from God,
         and glorious in its might;
   Truth revealing alcohol, our country's deadly
      blight,
      We must win prohibition. *To Chorus*

3. Lift aloft our country's flag, the fairest in
      the world;
     Flag of stars, against thee now the liquor
         power is hurled;
   Young Campaigners here declare, this flag
      shall not be furled,
      We must win prohibition.

Final Chorus
Old Glory! yes! the victory we must win—
     Old Glory! yes! for license is a sin—
Here we pledge ourselves to thee, thy folds
      shall stainless be,
      We must win prohibition.[161]

March of the Legions
(adapted from *The Union Signal*)

1. Bring the good old temperance pledge, and
      then we'll sing a song,
     Sing it with a spirit that will start the
         world along;

Sing it, brave young soldiers, Oh! what a
      mighty throng!
     While we go marching to victory.

Chorus
Hurrah! Hurrah! we bring the jubilee,
     Hurrah! Hurrah! the pledge will make
         you free,
So we'll join in chorus with the nations o'er
      the sea,
     While we go marching to victory.

2. License high or license low is everywhere a
      sin;
     War against King Alcohol we all may now
         begin;
   "God and Home and Native Land," the
      watchwords that will win,
      While we go marching to victory.
      To Chorus

3. We're young in years but strong in faith,
      we'll fight him with a will,
     Drive him right and drive him left from
         every vale and hill;
   Where sorrow reigns in many homes, the
      heart with joy shall thrill,
      As we go marching to victory.
      To Chorus[162]

Marching to Victory #3
(Katharine Lente Stevenson)

1. We're a gallant band, and true, enlisted for
      the fight.
     We are pledged, both heart and hand, for
         God and Home and right.
   We will stand for truth always, for purity and
      light
      As we go marching to vict'ry.

Chorus
Hurrah, Hurrah, we'll bring the jubilee;
     Hurrah, Hurrah, our Nation shall be free;
Thus we swell the chorus, on the land and on
      the sea,
     As we go marching to vict'ry.

161. Ibid., 28.
162. *Red White and Blue Songster*, 21.

2. Far too long have Rum's proud hosts
     encamped in our fair land;
   Far too long has manhood stooped to do
     his dread command;
Now we rise in God's own might and take
   our final stand
   As we go marching to vict'ry. *To Chorus*

3. How our Mothers praise the Lord to see us
     at the fore!
   How our wives and children shout that
     home is safe once more!
God and angels, too, rejoice in all this holy
   war
   As we go marching to vict'ry. *To Chorus*

4. Hear our vows, O God above, and help us
     to be true!
   This, our land, shall be redeemed from
     sin to life anew;
For this end we've listed in the W.C.T.U.
   And we go marching to vict'ry.

Final Chorus
Hurrah, Hurrah, we'll bring the jubilee;
   Hurrah, Hurrah, our Nation shall be free;
And our final chorus shall with all the
   ransomed be
   As we go marching to vict'ry.[163]

White Ribbon Song

1. Shoulder arms! The fight is on. The men
     are in the fray;
   Sounds the bugle at the dawn to come
     without delay.
Ev'ry one is ready now, white ribbons to the
   breeze,
   As we go fighting for Temp'rance.

Chorus
Hurrah! Hurrah! We'll sound the jubilee.
   Hurrah! Hurrah! From drinking we are
     free!

Ev'ry one is ready now, white ribbons to the
   breeze,
   As we go fighting for Temp'rance.

2. Down the line the Captain goes
     a-shouting, "Onward boys!"
   Ev'rybody's wide awake, the field is rife
     with noise.
All the soldiers in the world shall never
   conquer us,
   As we go fighting for Temp'rance.
     To Chorus

3. Over hill and over dale, with trouble
     ev'rywhere,
   Goes the army of the Lord our freedom
     to declare!
Nothing daunts their courage now, the
   battle's nearly o'er,
   While we go fighting for Temp'rance.
     To Chorus

4. Blue with smoke, the field is ours, the
     Sword is in our hand.
   Ev'rywhere the white flag floats, and Jesus
     has command.
Come and celebrate the day, the victory is
   won,
   That we have fought here for Temp'rance!

Final Chorus
Hurrah! Hurrah! We'll sound the jubilee.
   Hurrah! Hurrah! From drinking we are
     free!
Ev'ryone is ready now, white ribbons to the
   breeze,
   Waving the victory of Temp'rance![164]

163. Ibid., 27–28.
164. Ibid., 28–29.

7. Conclusion

Temperance writers churned out an astounding number of new lyrics for familiar tunes. While some of the temperance songbooks, such as *The Glorious Cause* (1888) and *Silver Tones* (1892), consisted mainly of music originally composed for the temperance movement, far more included a large number of preexisting melodies. George Ewing reports that there are only ten original melodies in Anna A. Gordon's *Popular Campaign Songs* (1915). *Francis Murphy's Gospel Temperance Hymnal* (1878), *The Temperance Songster* (1882), *The Gospel and Maine Law Temperance Hymnbook* (1884), and many other songbooks featured only lyrics along with the names of the tunes to which they should be sung. Robert Branham and Stephen Hartnett have pointed out that the use of familiar tunes enabled reformers to "quickly turn out songs adapted to specific occasions and purposes. More important, such topical songs based on familiar melodies enabled large groups to sing them on first reading."[1]

When considering this collection as a whole, a number of important issues emerge. First, there's the relationship between the text and the music. In a few cases, the choice of a particular tune for the temperance poetry may have been arbitrary, but almost all of the texts reflect the character of their borrowed melodies. A. G. Nichols explicitly states in the preface to *The Iron Door* that "the sentiments of these songs are better expressed, I think, in the tunes mentioned with each piece, than can be in any other; for they were blended in the mind at the inception and originated with the melody."[2] This tendency to reflect the character of the tune in the lyrics is particularly obvious when writers borrow not only the tunes, but also some of the original lyrics for inclusion in their versions. For example, five of the temperance songs set to "The Star-

1. Root, *Glorious Cause*; C. H. Mead, G. E. Chambers, and W. A. Williams, *Silver Tones: A New Temperance and Prohibition Song Book*; Ewing, *Well-Tempered Lyre*, 201; J. E. Rankin and E. S. Lorenz, *Francis Murphy's Gospel Temperance Hymnal*; Daniels, *Temperance Songster*; Munson, *Gospel and Maine*; Branham and Hartnett, *Sweet Freedom's Song*, 164.
2. Nichols, *Iron Door*, iii.

Spangled Banner" begin with Francis Scott Key's opening phrase, "O say, can you see," and others begin with similar phrases such as "Oh say, can you tell" and "Oh say, did you see."

A second issue concerns attribution of the lyrics. Names of lyricists were seldom given, particularly in the early songsters. John Pierpont, best known as the composer of "Jingle Bells," discusses this issue in the preface to his early temperance collection:

> In gathering the materials for [*Cold Water Melodies*], I have taken a tolerably wide range, and—as many of the authors of the pieces may think—no small liberties. This is true; but I hope they will excuse the liberties that I have taken, for I intended to do none of them wrong. Of many of the pieces, I could not ascertain who the authors were; on others of which the authors were named, I had good reason—judging from the fact that the same piece would often appear in different forms in different collections, as well as from the mutilations and metamorphoses that some of my own temperance canticles have undergone—to believe that the hand of "improvement" had been laid, by strangers, and I knew not therefore, except in a few instances, what I might rightfully attribute to any writer.[3]

Some of the liberties referred to by Pierpont may have been due, in part, to the passage of songs through the oral tradition. The oral conveyance of songs may also account for the slight, or sometimes significant, changes in lyrics from source to source. For example, "Virtues of Cold Water," set to the tune "Auld Lang Syne," appeared in at least nine songbooks, but six of the nine omit verses or make other changes in the lyrics.

Compared to today's standards, the copyright laws before the Civil War were relaxed, and this may also be a factor. Ewing found that "the earlier temperance editors seem to have been little interested in giving the names of authors, and though the later ones were more careful, perhaps because of tightening copyright laws, many of the works remain anonymous." Even in the early twentieth century, when copyright laws were well established, there were songbook compilers who admitted to taking liberties with texts. In 1906, O. R. Miller wrote, "I decided to take a number of the best Temperance songs and change the wording of them just here and there, adapting them especially for No-license rallies and Temperance meetings of all kinds."[4]

A third issue, one that is controversial among modern temperance scholars, deals with the use of moral suasion and coercion by temperance reformers. From the late 1700s to the years of national Prohibition (1920–1933), the efforts of

---

3. Pierpont, *Cold Water Melodies*, iii.
4. Ewing, *Well-Tempered Lyre*, 179; Miller, *Patriotic No-License*, n.p.

temperance organizations were dominated by the contrasting strategies of either appealing to the emotions and intellect, or using legal means or other enforcement. Joseph Gusfield argues that the temperance movement became increasingly coercive as the nineteenth century progressed, culminating in the work of the Anti-Saloon League and ultimately with national Prohibition. Jack Blocker agrees that early temperance reform was more suasive than coercive, but he maintains that "history reveals no simple progression toward coercion," citing the suasionist tactics employed by the Anti-Saloon League even after the passage of the Eighteenth Amendment.[5]

The temperance lyrics in this collection seem to support Blocker's view. For any given tune, we are more likely to find coercive lyrics among the songs written later in the temperance movement, but suasive lyrics continued to appear as the movement evolved. Since the temperance lyrics often reflected the character of their borrowed tune, sentimental tunes, such as "Home, Sweet Home" and "Long, Long Ago," lent themselves more to moral suasion while martial tunes, such as "Battle Cry of Freedom" and "Marching through Georgia," were better suited to inspire the "temperance army" to take the alcohol problem to the voting booth regardless of when the lyrics were published.

A fourth issue, and perhaps the most important, is the awareness of temperance writers that music was a powerful force that could be used to sway the masses. Although the songs of the temperance movement reflect their time and society, music (and the other arts) also have the power to influence society, and temperance lyricists harnessed music's power to bring about social reform.

Not all temperance lyrics are of the highest quality; Ewing compares temperance lyrics to the "second- and third-rate popular verse" of the day, and James A. Mowatt acknowledges the tendency of temperance organizations to use "popular airs of the day, sung to any wretched doggerel, [and] wholly unsuited to the object and spirit of the meetings," but temperance reformers understood music's influence and used it to their advantage. Mary Dana, writing in 1842, exclaims: "how wonderfully great is the influence of music! Set the people singing and you warm their hearts and nerve their hands to generous and noble acts. There is scarcely anyone so dead to every pleasing influence, that he cannot be roused to enthusiasm by the spirit-stirring sound of popular music. . . . Use this weapon freely, my brothers and sisters; tune your cheerful voices till you charm away the evil *spirits* which have so long troubled this beautiful world."[6]

Later, J. N. Stearns notes, "one of the most potent agencies in helping along the cause is ringing music in all departments of our work." John Clements and

5. Gusfield, *Symbolic Crusade*, 6–7; Blocker, *American Temperance*, xiv–xv.
6. Ewing, *Well-Tempered Lyre*, 234; Mowatt, *Mowatt's Temperance Glee*, iii; Dana, *Temperance Lyre*, iii.

other temperance authors saw music as a panacea: "Once the nation gets to singing the message of temperance, the greatest single stride has been taken toward the birth of the new day that sees whisky banished forever from our land. There are familiar airs and tunes that have become a part of our American heritage. To make them the vehicles for carrying the challenge and confidence of temperance and prohibition, is to endow them with a new commission and a larger usefulness."[7]

The "new day" would come only five years after the publication of Clements's songbook, but the victory was short-lived. The repeal of the Eighteenth Amendment in 1933 demonstrated that the ultimate coercive reform, total Prohibition, wasn't the final solution to the alcohol problem.

Despite the end of national Prohibition and even though the role of music has faded, the temperance movement's influence continues today. The Woman's Christian Temperance Union, established in 1874, still fights alcoholism through various activities and publications. Alcoholics Anonymous (AA), which has been compared to the nineteenth-century Washingtonians by some writers, was founded in 1935, and by 2004 it had an estimated membership of over two million worldwide. Mothers Against Drunk Driving (MADD) has focused considerable effort on enforcement of laws against drunk driving since its founding in 1980, and other organizations have joined the fight against alcoholism through contemporary forms of suasion and coercion. The sentimental tunes and naive lyrics of the temperance movement have value as curious artifacts of a bygone era, but in the broader view they also stand as important ancestors in the ongoing fight against alcoholism.[8]

7. Stearns, *Band of Hope*, ii; Clements, *Shaw's Campaign*, ii.

8. Mark Edward Lender and James Kirby Martin, *Drinking in America: A History*, 171, 182–85; Milton A. Maxwell, "The Washingtonian Movement"; Blocker, *American Temperance*, 130–33, 139–44, 158.

"HE HAD SPENT THE DAY AT THE LABORING MAN'S EXCHANGE — SALOON —"

THE RESULT OF A DAYS DRUNK.

Bibliography

Temperance Songbooks

Anti-Saloon Campaign Songs. Lebanon, Ohio: March Brothers, 1909.

Auld, Alexander. *Farmers' and Mechanics' Minstrel of Sacred Music.* Deersville, Ohio: Alexander Auld, 1866.

——. *The Ohio Harmonist.* Columbus: J. H. Riley, 1860.

Bensel, A. *The Temperance Harp.* New York: Burnett and Allen, 1842.

Biederwolf, W. E., and J. Gilchrist Lawson. *Best Temperance Songs.* Chicago: Glad Tidings Publishing, 1913.

Bigelow, G., and A. B. Grosh. *Washingtonian Pocket Companion.* Utica, N.Y.: R. W. Roberts, 1842.

Bonner, T. D. *The Mountain Minstrel.* Concord, N.H.: George S. Bonner, 1847.

Bradbury, W. B., and C. W. Sanders. *The Young Choir.* New York: Dayton and Newman, 1842.

Bradbury, Wm. B., and J. N. Stearns. *Temperance Chimes.* New York: National Temperance Society and Publication House, 1867.

——. *Temperance Chimes.* New York: National Temperance Society and Publication House, 1878.

Cake, L. B. *Popular Campaign Songs.* Clarinda, Iowa: L. B. Cake, ca. 1868.

Cassel, Flora Hamilton. *White Ribbon Vibrations.* 3d ed. Chicago: WCTU Song Book Publishing Association, 1890.

Clements, John R. *Shaw's Campaign Songs.* Boston: United Society of Christian Endeavor Publication Department, 1915.

Collection of Hymns and Songs for Temperance Meetings and Festivals. Harrisonburg, Pa.: J. H. Wartmann, 1843.

Collection of Temperance Songs. Boston, 1830–1850. Collection of broadsides at the Library of Congress, M2198.C7373.

Cornelius, R. H. *Cornelius' Prohibition Songs.* Midlothian, Tex.: R. H. Cornelius, 1911.

The Crusaders' Temperance Songster. New York: Beadle and Adams, 1874.

Dailey, J. G., and C. H. Mead. *Prohibition Chimes and What's the News?* Philadelphia: J. G. Dailey Music, 1915.

Dana, Mary S. B. *The Temperance Lyre.* New York: Dayton and Newman, 1842.

Daniels, Ione G. *Temperance Songster.* Washington, D.C.: Anvil Office, 1882.

Dungan, George W., Ernest A. Boom, and H. L. Gilmour, eds. *Acorn Temperance Songs.* Philadelphia: Praise Publishing, 1908.

Dunn, Hugh S. *Temperance Hymns.* New York: Hugh S. Dunn, 1852.

Durant, Horace B. *Prohibition Home Protection Army Campaign Songs.* Claysville, Pa.: Mrs. H. Abraham Durant, 1884.

Excell, E. O. *Inspiring Hymns.* Chicago: E. O. Excell, 1914.

———. *Joy to the World.* Chicago: Hope Publishing, 1915.

Filley, Frank C. *Red, White, and Blue Ribbon Gospel Temperance Songster.* San Francisco: B. F. Sterett, 1878.

Fillmore, A. D. *Temperance Musician.* Cincinnati: Applegate, 1854.

Fillmore, Charles M., and J. H. Fillmore. *Fillmores' Prohibition Songs.* Cincinnati: Fillmore Brothers, 1900.

Fobes, Walter K. *Temperance Songs and Hymns.* Boston: Walter K. Fobes, 1889.

Gordon, Anna A. *Jubilee Songs.* 7th ed. Evanston, Ill.: National Woman's Christian Temperance Union Publishing House, 1923.

———. *Marching Songs for Young Crusaders.* Chicago: Ruby I. Gilbert, 1885.

———. *Popular Campaign Songs.* Evanston, Ill.: National WCTU Publishing House, 1915.

———. *Songs of the Young Woman's Christian Temperance Union.* Chicago: Woman's Temperance Publishing Association, 1889.

———. *The Temperance Songster.* Cincinnati: Fillmore Music House, 1904.

———. *The White Ribbon Hymnal.* Chicago: Woman's Temperance Publishing Association, 1892.

Gould, W. F., and A. B. Grosh. *Washingtonian Pocket Companion.* 3d ed. Utica, N.Y.: B. S. Merrell, 1843.

Guthrie, James M. *The Manual for the Teetotal Army.* Delaware, Ohio: Teetotal Publication House, 1867.

Hart, Lucius, ed. *The Juvenile Temperance Harp.* New York: James B. Dunn, 1857.

Herbert, Sidney. *Young Volunteer Campaign Melodist.* Boston: James M. Usher, 1864.

Hoffman, Elisha A. *Local Option Campaign Songs.* Benton Harbor, Mich.: Elisha A. Hoffman, 1909.

———. *Woman's Christian Temperance Union Campaign Songs.* Chicago: Emily M. Hill, 1910.

Hudson, R. E. *Temperance Songster.* Alliance, Ohio: R. E. Hudson, 1886.

Hull, Asa. *Hull's Temperance Glee Book.* Enlarged ed. Boston: Oliver Ditson, 1877.

Jarden, Samuel. *The Prohibition Banner.* Baltimore: William A. Zimmerman, 1883.

Law, E. Norine. *Temperance Bells, No. 1.* Indianapolis: Publishing House of Pentecost Bands, 1908.

Leslie, J. H. *Good Templar Songster.* Harry White, 1886.

———. *Good Templar Songster.* 2d ed. Harry White, 1888.

Lorenz, E. S. *New Anti-Saloon Songs.* New York: Lorenz Publishing, 1905.

Macy, J. C. *Temperance Song-Herald.* Boston: Oliver Ditson, 1885.

McCauley, W. F. *Anti-Saloon Songs.* Dayton: Lorenz, 1899.

McCreery, J. L. *A Collection of Temperance Songs for Common Tunes.* Dubuque: C. B. Dorr, 1878.

Mead, C. H., and G. E. Chambers. *The Clarion Call.* New York: Funk and Wagnalls, 1889.

Mead, C. H., G. E. Chambers, and W. A. Williams. *Silver Tones: A New Temperance and Prohibition Song Book.* Warnock, Ohio: W. A. Williams, 1892.

Merryman, T. J. *Amendment Songs Set to Familiar Tunes.* Nebraska City, Nebr.: A. L. Holmes, 1889.

Miller, O. R., ed. *Patriotic No-License Songster.* New York: National Temperance Society, 1906.

M'Kechnie, John. *The Lyre of Temperance.* New York: J. M'Kechnie, 1860.

Moffitt, W. O. *The National Temperance Songster.* Dubuque, Iowa: Gay and Schermerhorn, 1878.

Mowatt, James Alexander, ed. *Mowatt's Temperance Glee Book, No. 1.* New York: Hebbeard and Munro, 1874.

Munson, H. C. *The Gospel and Maine Law Temperance Hymn Book.* South Berwick, Me.: J. D. Blaisdell, 1884.

Nichols, A. G. *The Iron Door and Other Temperance Songs.* Kingston, N.Y.: Daily Freeman Steam Printing House, 1878.

Ohio State Prohibition Campaign Songs. Westerville, Ohio: American Issue Publishing, 1916.

Perine, Oscar A., and William E. Mash [Marsh]. *The National Prohibition Hymnal and Gospel Temperance Songster.* Brooklyn: Oscar A. Perine and William E. Mash, 1883.

Perkins, William Oscar. *The Crystal Fountain.* Boston: G. D. Russell, 1878.

Phillips, Philip. *Day-School Singer.* Cincinnati: Wilson, Hinkle, 1870.

Pierpont, John. *Cold Water Melodies and Washingtonian Songster.* Boston: Theodore Abbot, 1842.

Plimpton, Job. *The Washingtonian Choir.* Boston: J. Plimpton, 1843.

Potter, R. K. *The Boston Temperance Songster.* Vols. 1 and 2. Boston: White and Potter, 1847.

Prohibition Campaign Song Book. Springfield, Ohio: New Era, 1885.

Prohibition Campaign Songster. Cincinnati: John Church, 1888.

Rankin, J. E., and E. S. Lorenz. *Francis Murphy's Gospel Temperance Hymnal.* New York: A. S. Barnes, 1878.

The Red White and Blue Songster. Florence, N.J.: National Woman's Christian Temperance Union, 1915.

Root, G. F. *The Glorious Cause.* Chicago: Woman's Temperance Publishing Association, 1888.

——. *The Musical Fountain.* Enlarged ed. Chicago: Root and Cady, 1867.

Roush, Frank E. *Temperance Rally and Campaign Songs.* 2d ed. Lynchburg, Ohio: Frank E. Roush, 1907.

Saunders, Nathaniel. *The Temperance Songster.* Providence, R.I.: Handy and Higgins, 1867.

Sherwin, W. F., and J. N. Stearns, eds. *Bugle Notes for the Temperance Army.* New York: National Temperance Society and Publication House, 1871.

Silver Lake Quartette. *Prohibition Bells and Songs of the New Crusade.* New York: Funk and Wagnalls, 1888.

Songs of the Temperance Reform. New York: Lorenz Publishing, 1905.

Sons of Temperance. *Music and Odes of the Order.* Philadelphia: S. Douglas Wyeth, 1848.

Stearns, J. N., comp. *Band of Hope Songster.* New York: National Temperance Society and Publication House, 1885.

———. *National Temperance Hymn and Song Book.* New York: National Temperance Society and Publication House, 1880.

———. *Prohibition Songster.* New York: National Temperance Society and Publication House, 1887.

Stearns, J. N., and H. P. Main. *Trumpet Notes for the Temperance Battle-Field.* New York: National Temperance Society and Publication House, 1888.

Thompson, Edwin, comp. *Thompson's Band of Hope Melodies.* Boston: Wright and Potter, 1864.

Towne, T. M. *Temperance Anthems.* Chicago: David C. Cook, 1881.

Trowbridge, Asa R. *The Temperance Melodeon.* Boston: Theodore Abbot, 1844.

The Union Temperance Song Book. Boston: Isaac Tompkins, 1844.

The Washingtonian Tee-Totalers' Minstrel. New York: J. Slater, ca. 1845.

Washington Temperance Songbook. Harrisburg, Pa.: Hickok and Cantine, 1842.

The Women's Temperance Songster. New York: A. J. Fisher, 1874.

Other Sources

Aitch, N. H. *The Golden Book of Favorite Songs: With Words and Music for All Occasions, Also Song Histories.* 10th ed. Chicago: Hall and McCreary, 1915.

Arthur, T. S. *Ten Nights in a Bar-Room and What I Saw There.* Chicago: David C. Cook, 1900.

Bartlett, M. L. *Bartlett's Music Reader for Day Schools.* Chicago: Echo Music, 1907.

Bliss, P. P. "Hold the Fort!" (sheet music). Chicago: Root and Cady, 1870. From "Music for the Nation: American Sheet Music," Library of Congress, http://memory.loc.gov/cgi-bin/ampage (accessed June 2, 2003).

Blocker, Jack S., Jr. *American Temperance Movements: Cycles of Reform.* Boston: Twayne Publishers, 1989.

Blumberg, Leonard U. "The Institutional Phase of the Washingtonian Total Abstinence Movement." *Journal of Studies on Alcohol* 39 (1978): 1591–1606.

Branham, Robert James, and Stephen J. Hartnett. *Sweet Freedom's Song: "My Country 'Tis of Thee" and Democracy in America.* Oxford: Oxford University Press, 2002.

Brown, Eli F. *Youth's Temperance Manual: An Elementary Physiology.* Cincinnati: Van Antwerp, Bragg, 1888.

Burkholder, J. Peter. "Borrowing." *Grove Music Online*. Ed. L. Macy, http://www .grovemusic.com.proxy.lib.ohio-state.edu (accessed July 15, 2005).

Cartledge, T. M., W. L. Reed, Martin Shaw, and Henry Coleman. *National Anthems of the World*. New York: Arco Publishing, 1978.

Chase, Gilbert. *America's Music: From the Pilgrims to the Present*. 3d ed. Urbana: University of Illinois Press, 1987.

Cherrington, Ernest H. *The Evolution of Prohibition in the United States of America*. Westerville, Ohio: American Issue Press, 1920.

Collinson, Francis. *Traditional and National Music of Scotland*. London: Routledge and Kegan Paul, 1966.

Crawford, Richard, ed. *The Civil War Songbook*. New York: Dover, 1977.

Cunningham, Peter. *The Songs of England and Scotland*. Vol. 2. London: James Cochrane, 1835.

Dallin, Leon, and Lynn Dallin. *Heritage Songster: 332 Folk and Familiar Songs*. 2d ed. Dubuque, Iowa: Wm. C. Brown, 1980.

Dannenbaum, Jed. *Drink and Disorder: Temperance Reform in Cincinnati from the Washingtonian Revival to the WCTU*. Urbana: University of Illinois Press, 1984.

Dichter, Harry, and Elliott Shapiro. *Early American Sheet Music: Its Lure and Its Lore, 1768–1889*. New York: R. R. Bowker, 1941.

Dickens, Charles. *American Notes; and The Uncommerical Traveler*. Philadelphia: T. B. Peterson, 1850.

Dohn, Norman Harding. "The History of the Anti-Saloon League." Ph.D. diss., Ohio State University, 1959.

Epstein, Dena J. *Music Publishing in Chicago before 1871: The Firm of Root and Cady, 1858–1871*. Detroit: Information Coordinators, 1969.

Ewen, David. *All the Years of American Popular Music*. Englewood Cliffs, N.J.: Prentice-Hall, 1977.

Ewing, George W. *The Well-Tempered Lyre: Songs and Verse of the Temperance Movement*. Dallas: Southern Methodist University Press, 1977.

55 Songs and Choruses for Community Singing. Boston: C. C. Birchard, 1917.

Foote, Henry Wilder. *Three Centuries of American Hymnody*. Cambridge: Harvard University Press, 1940.

Frost, Maurice, ed. *Historical Companion to Hymns Ancient and Modern*. London: William Clowes and Sons, 1962.

Furnas, J. C. *The Life and Times of the Late Demon Rum*. New York: G. P. Putnam's Sons, 1965.

Gleadhill, T. S., ed. *Songs of the British Isles*. London: Swan and Pentland, n.d.

Gusfield, Joseph R. *Symbolic Crusade: Status Politics and the American Temperance Movement*. Urbana: University of Illinois Press, 1963.

Hamm, Charles. *Putting Popular Music in Its Place*. New York: Cambridge University Press, 1995.

———. *Yesterdays: Popular Song in America*. New York: W. W. Norton, 1979.

Heaps, Willard A., and Porter W. Heaps. *The Singing Sixties*. Norman: University of Oklahoma Press, 1960.

Heart Songs Dear to the American People. Boston: Chapple Publishing, 1909.

Hitchcock, H. Wiley. *Music in the United States: A Historical Introduction.* 4th ed. Upper Saddle River, N.J.: Prentice-Hall, 2000.

Jones, J. Ithel, E. A. Payne, A. Ewart Rusbudge, and E. P. Sharpe. *The Baptist Hymn Book Companion.* London: Psalms and Hymns Trust, 1962.

Klieforth, Alexander Leslie, and Robert John Munro. *The Scottish Invention of America, Democracy, and Human Rights.* Lanham, Md.: University Press of America, 2004.

Lehmann, William C. *Scottish and Scotch-Irish Contributions to Early American Life and Culture.* Port Washington, N.Y.: Kennikat Press, 1978.

Lender, Mark Edward, and James Kirby Martin. *Drinking in America: A History.* New York: Free Press, 1982.

Mattingly, Carol. *Well-Tempered Women: Nineteenth-Century Temperance Rhetoric.* Carbondale: Southern Illinois University Press, 1998.

Maxwell, Milton A. "The Washingtonian Movement." *Quarterly Journal of Studies on Alcohol* 11 (1950): 410–52.

McConathy, Osborne, ed. *The School Song Book.* Boston: C. C. Birchard, 1909.

Metcalf, Frank J. *American Writers and Compilers of Sacred Music.* New York: Abingdon Press, 1925.

Nathan, Hans. *Dan Emmett and the Rise of Early Negro Minstrelsy.* Norman: University of Oklahoma Press, 1977.

"Old Dan Tucker: A Celebrated Ethiopian Ballad" (sheet music). New York: Atwill, 1843. From "Music for the Nation: American Sheet Music," Library of Congress, http://memory.loc.gov/cgi-bin/ampage (accessed June 2, 2003).

One Hundred and One Best Songs. Chicago: Cable, 1915.

Paskman, Dailey, and Sigmund Spaeth. *"Gentlemen, Be Seated!" A Parade of the Old-Time Minstrels.* Garden City, N.Y.: Doubleday, Dorian, 1928.

Peterson, Jane Anne. "Rum, Ruin, and Revival: Protestant Hymns and the Temperance Movement." Master's thesis, Southern Illinois University at Edwardsville, 1998.

Rodeheaver, Homer A. *Hymnal Handbook for Standard Hymns and Gospel Hymns.* Chicago: Rodeheaver, 1931.

Rohrer, James Russell. "Battling the Master Vice: The Evangelical War against Intemperance in Ohio, 1800–1832." Ph.D. diss., Ohio State University, 1985.

Root, George F. *The Story of a Musical Life.* Cincinnati: John Church, 1891.

Rorabaugh, W. J. *The Alcohol Republic: An American Tradition.* New York: Oxford University Press, 1979.

Rumberger, John J. "Social Origins and Function of the Political Temperance Movement in the Reconstruction of American Society, 1825–1917." Ph.D. diss., University of Pennsylvania, 1968.

Sacks, Howard L., and Judith Rose Sacks. *Way Up North in Dixie: A Black Family's Claim to the Confederate Anthem.* Urbana: University of Illinois Press, 2003.

Sankey, Ira D. *My Life and the Story of the Gospel Hymns.* Philadelphia: Sunday School Times, 1907.

Sankey, Ira D., James McGranahan, and George C. Stebbins. *Gospel Hymns No. 5.* New York: Biglow and Main, 1887.

Silber, Irwin. *Songs of the Civil War.* New York: Columbia University Press, 1960.

Spaeth, Sigmund G. *A History of Popular Music in America.* New York: Random House, 1948.

Stecker, Michelle J. "A Respectable Revolution: The Dynamics of Religion and Gender in the Ohio Woman's Temperance Crusade, 1873–74." Ph.D. diss., University of Toledo, 2000.

Wiswell, John. *Fifty Cartoons Taken from "If the Devil Should Come to Kansas."* Columbus: Richart and Cavaness, 1901.

Zug, John. *The Foundation, Progress, and Principles of the Washington Temperance Society of Baltimore.* Baltimore: John D. Troy, 1842.

Index